The Christian's Daily Challenge

The Christian's Daily Challenge

Compiled by
E.F. and L. Harvey

BRITISH ADDRESS
Harvey Christian Publishers
P.O. Box 510
Cheadle
Stoke-on-Trent
ST10 2NQ
Tele 01538 756391
E-mail: jjcook@mac.com

UNITED STATES ADDRESS
Harvey Christian Publishers, Inc.
3107 Hwy. 321, Hampton, TN 37658
Tel./Fax (423) 768-2297
E-mail: books@harveycp.com
http://www.harveycp.com

Sixth Edition 2001
Seventh Edition 2006

Printed in USA

Cover design and photography by Malcolm Farrar

ISBN-10   1-932774-01-7
ISBN-13   978-1-932774-01-6

Printed by
Old Paths Tract Society Inc.
Shoals, Indiana 47581

AUTHORS' PREFACE

A title such as that used for this volume should not be lightly chosen. Nor has it been in this case. For some years, it has seemed to us that one of the greatest present needs of Christianity was a challenge to Christians themselves. We live in the shadow, as it were, of periods of Church History that have produced many men and women of deepest piety who have witnessed widespread and lasting revivals. In our own era we sense an unrest about spiritual things resulting in much organized effort to bring the careless back to the Church. But what will be the result if our religious centers are not true nurseries for the spiritual infants?

The first great need of the hour is, we believe, an awakening among Christians. "Judgment must begin at the house of God." They must be aroused to lay hold of their purchased privileges. They must be challenged once again to become men and women of prayer, zeal, compassion, faith, joy and holy living. They will then warn the sinner by living as though they really believed in eternal realities. They will attract the worldling by proving they have something better than he has. And once he is won they will surround him by a loving, undivided, expectant atmosphere in which the new convert can develop and learn to win others to Christ.

In our bimonthly, *The Message of Victory*, we have labored for years to send forth such a challenge. To strengthen and support the message of our workers and missionaries, we have combed every biography, sermon book, anthology or old periodical we could lay hold of. In many a city we have spent hours in secondhand book shops, delving out precious nuggets now out of print.

We have packed our files with copy from these books and clippings from magazines. As space would allow, this material has filled the pages of *The Message of Victory,* and letters from all parts have poured in telling of help and inspiration received. Many have enquired for books containing similar helpful material. We have acted as agents for books now in print that pass on the same message, but it did seem a great pity that a large proportion of the best writings was unavailable, in many cases because the books were out of print, and in others because few people had the money to purchase or the time to sort out the priceless bits from those works on the market today.

As a companion effort to our bimonthly *The Message of Victory,* we sought then to prepare a tear-off calendar with further challenges to Christians. But after some work and prayer on the quotations, we realized that these exceptional poems and extracts should have a more permanent form than that of a yearly tear-off calendar. Other pressing claims made it impossible to prepare such a calendar yearly. Puzzled and perplexed we went to prayer, where the idea of a daily reading book was presented to us. Further guidance was sought that we might know of a certainty that this book would have God's blessing upon it. We were inspired and encouraged to the venture by the words of Nehemiah 8:10, "Then he said unto them, Go your way, eat the fat, and drink the sweet, and send portions to them for whom nothing is prepared." Various parts of this wonderful verse were applied to our undertaking. We had the fat and sweet of some of the godliest biographies. We were to send—not in this case take—portions to those for whom nothing was prepared: the fat—that which would give protection and nourishment; the sweet—that which would give quick energy and inspiration for the day's action and battles.

"Feeding the sheep" is rather a routine job—much less spectacular and much less applauded than the "finding of the sheep." Our Savior three times impressed upon Peter that his commission was to feed His lambs and sheep. Peter, then, later exhorts his elders to feed the flock, and promises them that when the Chief Shepherd appears they will receive a crown of glory that fadeth not away. Today many appeals are made to the unconverted, but much less time is given to "feeding" those that have been found with that which will help them to grow in grace and knowledge.

As is the case when a project is of God, we were given enthusiastic helpers. Typists, filing clerks, and proof readers who had a "mind to work" considered it a privilege to labor with us. In fact, we had offers for more help than we could use at the time. We wish to show our appreciation to those who assisted in editorial and typing work. Others in practical ways undertook tasks that set us free to concentrate on this effort.

We have purposely selected from as large a range of authors as possible. Although these have had varying religious backgrounds, anything of a controversial nature has been avoided. Each writer has been quoted only as his writing has supported the challenge in question. The use of extracts from any given author should not be taken as an approval of all of his works.

We have found the task a great one, but one of peculiar personal blessing. We now send it forth with simple faith that these challenges will indeed bless, feed, and inspire many of the Lord's true children scattered everywhere.

Edwin & Lillian Harvey
Glasgow,
25th August, 1954.

PUBLISHERS' FOREWORD

I stared at the three hundred and sixty-five manuscripts my parents had prepared for the printer. They were stacked in neat piles and divided into various subjects. Why, I puzzled, when they were meticulously typed and proofed, did they lie there day after day? "Aren't you sending your book to the printers?" I finally asked my parents. "It's ready, isn't it?"

They smiled at me and answered patiently, "Yes, it's ready. But we want each reading to be bathed in prayer. In the coming years, it will be read by people in crisis, people facing bereavement, discouraged and lonely people. We want to be sure we have God's mind on the order in which we put all these readings."

It sounded reasonable and I was satisfied. But I could not realize then, being only nine years of age, how vitally crucial that period of waiting on God would prove to be. I could not foresee the many letters we would receive from all around the world, telling us how some particular reading, on some particular day, saved some young person from making a wrong decision, encouraged a pastor or missionary to keep faithful to the cross, or gave hope in the moment of despair.

Fifty-two years have passed since those manuscripts lay on our living-room table. My husband and I felt it was now time to reset the text as it had been recopied for years until it was becoming less and less legible with each printing. We have kept a page for each reading, and where there was extra space, have added appropriate quotations from my parents' files. We are deeply grateful to Margaret Smith for putting the complete book on disc and to Beulah Freeman and Jean Ward for their invaluable help in proofreading.

It is 2006 and times are changing fast. But we truly believe that a book that has been bathed in prayer at the outset, will continue to bless the lives of us moderns and bring us closer to God.

Trudy and Barry Tait
Hampton, TN. 2006

ACKNOWLEDGMENTS

In seeking to obtain permission to use copyright material, we have met with a most courteous and kindly response from both publishers and authors. We take this occasion to express our thanks in the following instances: J. W. Arrowsmith, Ltd. for quotations by Josephine Butler; The Algiers Mission Band for extracts from the writings of I. Lilias Trotter; A. & C. Black, Ltd. for the poems by Ella Wheeler Wilcox; Simpkin, Marshall, Ltd. and Oswald Chambers Publications for extracts by Oswald Chambers from "If Ye Shall Ask" and "The Graciousness of Uncertainty"; The Christian Literature Crusade for extracts by George Ingram from "Life and Life Abundant," and an extract by Norman Grubb from their periodical, "The Floodtide"; James Clarke & Co., Ltd. for selections by J. H. Jowett from "The School of Calvary," and an extract from "Illustrations From Art" by James Burns, M.A.; Thomas Y. Crowell & Co. for the poem by Sarah Knowles Bolton; Dodd, Mead & Co. for the poems by Angela Morgan; The Epworth Press for extracts by Thomas Cook from "New Testament Holiness"; The Evangelical Publishers for their copyrighted poems by Annie Johnson Flint, and for poems from "The Evangelical Christian" by William Luff, Grace Noll Crowell and Martha Snell Nicholson; Hodder & Stoughton, Ltd. for selections by Sister Eva from "The True Meaning of Life," and from "The Life of Sister Eva," by Sister Annie Whisler; also extracts by Alexander Maclaren from his sermons in "Triumphant Certainties"; Houghton, Mifflin Co. for the poem "Thy Will," by John Hay; The Japan Evangelistic Band for extracts by Barclay F. Buxton from "Life's Possibilities," as well as selections by A. Paget Wilkes from "Dynamic of Service"; Lillenas Publishing Co. for the poems by Mrs. F. W. Suffield and F. M. Lehman; The Lutterworth Press for extracts by C. T. Studd and John Harrison from "C. T. Studd" and "Successor to C. T. Studd," as well as extracts by Hudson Taylor from "Hudson Taylor's Legacy," granted jointly with the China Inland Mission; The China Inland Mission for the poem "Afraid," by Rev. E. H. Hamilton from "The Triumph of John and Betty Stam," and for extracts from "Hudson Taylor's Legacy"; Marshall, Morgan & Scott, Ltd. for extracts by Andrew Murray from "Absolute Surrender"; James Nisbet & Co. for extracts by R. A. Torrey and G. Matheson from "Revival Addresses" and "Times of Retirement"; Messrs. Thomas Nelson & Sons, Ltd. and The National Sunday School Union for extracts by J. R. Miller from "Come Ye Apart"; Miss Beveridge for the hymn, "Not One Step More," from Celestial Songs, compiled by her father; Mrs. Howard Hooker for quotations by her father, the late Reader Harris, K.C.; Fleming H. Revell Co. for extracts by S. D. Gordon from "Quiet Talks on Prayer"; The Salvationist Publishing & Supplies Ltd. for selections by General

Wm. Booth, Mrs. Booth, Samuel Logan Brengle, Mrs. Elizabeth S. Brengle and Kate Lee; The Stirling Tract Enterprise for quotations by Ronald Davies from "Lal Sahib"; The Wesleyan Methodist for the poems "The Builder" by Esther Pritchard Moore, and "Has My Brother Aught Against Me?"; Miss Wells for the use of two poems by her father, Amos R. Wells; The Metropolitan Church Association for the poems of T. Harris and L. F. Mitchell and the quotation from H. B. Bitzer.

Many of the poems, quotations and extracts used in the book have been accumulated over a period of years from such varied sources that in numbers of cases it has been impossible after considerable effort to trace either the publisher or the author. Where omissions have been made and due credit has not been given, we beg indulgence.

COMPENSATION

The easy path in the lowland hath little of grand or new,
But a toilsome ascent leads on to a wide and glorious view;
Peopled and warm is the valley, lonely and chill the height,
But the peak that is nearer the storm-cloud is nearer the stars of light.

Launch on the foaming stream that bears you along like a dart, –
There is danger of rapid and rock, there is tension of muscle and heart;
Glide on the easy current, monotonous, calm, and slow,
You are spared the quiver and strain in the safe and quiet flow.

For rapture of love is linked with the pain or fear of loss,
And the hand that takes the crown must ache with many a cross;
Yet he who hath never a conflict hath never a victor's palm,
And only the toilers know the sweetness of rest and calm.

—*Frances Ridley Havergal.*

January 1
Keep challenging yourself!

"And God is able to make all grace abound toward you; that ye, always having all sufficiency in all things, may abound to every good work" (2 Cor. 9:8). "Stir up the gift of God, which is in thee" (2 Tim. 1:6).

Since God is able to make all grace abound always in all things why should there be so many dwarfed, impotent Christians? The lack cannot be with the Source of Supply. It must, therefore, lie in the failure of Christians to draw from this abundance. Throughout the coming year let everyone challenge himself concerning these wonderful possibilities contained in the promises of God.

Keep challenging yourself! The moment that you become satisfied with yourself or with your work, that moment you begin to slip backwards. Challenge your thoughts, your actions, and everything that you achieve.

The development of this inner life of ours is the most important task that we have to achieve. Not the mere making of money. Not the attainment of fame or station, nor of that fleeting thing called acclaim. We must become content within ourselves. We must satisfy that hunger of the heart. By challenging the adverse forces that strive to push us from our line of purpose, we build a character!

Desire is the cornerstone of achievement. But, without will or purpose, even desire remains dormant. Keep challenging yourself! You can rout every pygmy of your nature if you will but decide to do so!

> Thou broadenest out with every year,
>   Each breadth of life to meet;
> I scarce can think Thou art the same,
>   Thou art so much more sweet.
>
> With gentle swiftness lead me on,
>   Dear God, to see Thy face;
> And meanwhile in my narrow heart
>   O make Thyself more space!
>   —*F. W. Faber.*

To be discontented with the divine discontent and to be ashamed with the noble shame, is the very germ and first upgrowth of all virtue.—*Charles Kingsley.*

A year of prayer

"My soul, wait thou only upon God; for my expectation is from him"
                                            (Psa. 62:5).
"Therefore I will look unto the Lord: I will wait for the God of my salvation"
                                            (Micah 7:7).
"But it is good for me to draw near to God" (Psa. 73:28).

Lord, at the threshold standing,
  I ask this gift from Thee,
That all this year Thy grace is giving,
  A year of prayer may be.
Give me a Golden Censer
  Burning with incense rare,
And make my life a holy priesthood
  Of ceaseless praise and prayer.

Help me to pray for sinners,
  With travail pangs of love,
Till souls are born and sins forgiven
  By power from above.
Help me to take from Jesus
  My healing, breath by breath,
And lift by prayer, the lives that languish
  In sickness, sin and death.

And from my glowing Censer
  Shall holy incense rise
Before the golden altar yonder,
  The altar of the skies;
And Jesus shall present it
  With His own incense rare,
While the heavens are hushed in silence
  To hear a sinner's prayer.

Then back to earth, the Master
  The answering fire shall send,
And earth and heaven begin to witness
  The Advent and the end.
Lord, for that Consummation
  Our hearts and lives prepare,
And that its coming we may hasten,
  Give us a Year of Prayer.
                    —*A. B. Simpson.*

It will never be altogether well with us till we convert the universe into a prayer-room, and continue in the Spirit as we go from place to place.—*George Bowen.*

Faithfulness in small things

"He that is faithful in that which is least is faithful also in much"
(Luke 16:10).
"Who then is a faithful and wise servant, whom his lord hath made ruler over his household?" (Matt. 24:45).

Do not wait for some great work to be dropped down in your lap. Do some little thing for God. If David had never tackled the bear and the lion he would not have been so successful with Goliath of Gath. Nothing is small that is done for God. You do not know what it may lead to.—*Reader Harris.*

> No service in itself is small;
> None great, though earth it fill;
> But that is small that seeks its own,
> And great that seeks God's will.
> —*Unknown.*

I think that the folks who are faithful in that which is least will wear very radiant crowns. They are the people who are great in little tasks. They are scrupulous in the rutty roads of drudgery. They are the folks, who when they are trudging "through the Valley of Baca, make it a well." They win the triumphs amid small irritations. They are as loyal when they are wearing aprons in the kitchen as if they wore purple and fine linen in the visible presence of the King. They finish the obscurest bit of work as though it were to be displayed before an assembled Heaven by Him Who is Lord of light and glory. Great souls are these who are faithful in that which is least!

Our Lord lived for thirty years amid the little happenings of the little town of Nazareth. Little villages spell out their stories in small events. And He, the young Priest of glory, was in the carpenter's shop. He moved amid humdrum tasks, and petty cares, and village gossip, and trifling trade, and He was faithful in that which is least. He wore His crown on other than state occasions, it was never off His brow.—*J. H. Jowett.*

January 4
Make men see

"Make all men see what is the fellowship" (Eph. 3:9).
"Lord, I pray thee, open his eyes that he may see. And the Lord opened the eyes of the young man and he saw" (2 Kings 6:17).

Lorado Taft, the noted sculptor, related an incident of summer camp life on the banks of a lake where sunsets were exceptionally beautiful. One evening, a little nursemaid asked if she might run to her home nearby and "show the sunset" to her people.

"Certainly," answered Mr. Taft; "but they will see it, won't they?"

"No. I never saw the sunset until you came."

It is a great privilege to make the beauty of the Christian life compellingly attractive to others.

> As we meet and touch each day
> The many travelers on our way,
> Let every such brief contact be
> A glorious, helpful ministry.
> —*S. Coleridge.*

Many a groping soul has seen the Gospel long before he has ever heard the grand old story with his ears. Such an one was the Chinaman who applied to a missionary for baptism. When asked where he had heard the Gospel, the reply was, "Nowhere, but I have seen it." He then told of the remarkable transformation he had witnessed in a depraved opium smoker, noted for his violent temper. But he had met Christ, and the change wrought had broadcast the Gospel message more effectively than any sermon. "Oh," said the candidate for baptism, "I have not heard the Gospel, but I have seen it."

The story is told of Gordon Maxwell, missionary to India, that he went to a Hindu Pundit and asked him if he would teach him the language. The Hindu replied: "No, Sahib, I will not teach you my language. You would make me a Christian."

Gordon Maxwell replied: "You misunderstand me. I am simply asking you to teach me your language."

The Hindu replied again: "No, Sahib, I will not teach you. No man can live with you and not become a Christian."

What is your load?

"And hast borne, and hast patience" (Rev. 2:3).
"Bear ye one another's burdens" (Gal. 6:2).

Many things in common use these days have markings to indicate the load they can support. The great cranes on our quay sides display on their large boards: "Load 20 tons." The bridges by which we cross rivers and railways are marked in the same way, forbidding vehicles of more than a certain weight to pass over them. Steamers have their plimsoll-line for the same purpose and can be loaded only to that limit. Even the very humble fuse from my electric amplifier—a thin, silvery strand of wire, so frail that it must be protected in a glass tube—proudly boasts its capabilities with "Load 1 ampere" marked on it.

Now that which counts in God's higher order of things is known in the same way—by its load or burden. What do you carry? What is your load? "For the Kingdom of God is not in word but in power," that is to say, not in empty profession and lip-service, but in power-carrying power—ability to get under the load and move something. We can all talk, but can we lift one another's burdens, and so fulfill the law of Christ?

Of the greatest of all burden-bearers, even the Lord Jesus Himself, it is said: "He bare our sins in his own body on the tree." Amazing burden! "He beareth away the sin of the world" with agony and bloody sweat. Was there ever such a load? All the blasphemies and disobediences, the envyings, jealousies and strifes of men, and every sin imaginable to the fallen sons of Adam, borne right away, as far as the East is from the West, to be remembered against us no more for ever.

Now where do you come in all this? Are you carrying anything? What is your load? Can the Lord say of you as He did of the Church at Ephesus (Rev. 2:3), "Thou hast borne and hast patience"? How much can the Lord put upon you? What is your crumpling-up point? Will you squeal and grumble and grouse, or will you take it all and more besides, and still say like Paul, "this light affliction"?—*John Harrison.*

> Now the two kinds of people on earth I mean
> Are the people who lift and the people who lean.
> Wherever you go, you will find the earth's masses
> Are always divided in just these two classes.
> And, oddly enough, you will find, too, I ween,
> There is only one lifter to twenty who lean.
> In which class are you? Are you easing the load
> Of overtaxed lifters who toil down the road?
> Or are you a leaner and let others bear
> Your portion of labor, and problems, and care?
> —*Ella Wheeler Wilcox.*

Make God's promises yours

"Who through faith . . . obtained promises" (Heb. 11:33).
"More to be desired are they than gold, yea, than much fine gold: sweeter also than honey and the honeycomb" (Psa. 19:10).

When I am asked for my favorite promises, I smile. It is not one text more than another, but a whole Bible blesses me, assures me, warns and corrects and comforts me. A hundred promises whisper to me. I never know when one of the promises—perhaps one that I have not met for days or even months—may suddenly stand before me, beckon me, speak to me tenderly, comfortingly, authoritatively, austerely; speak to me as though God were speaking to me face to face.

The ancient heroes of the Cross obtained promises by faith. You can buy a Bible for a few pence. And the Bible teems with promises. They are on almost every page. But you will not see them, your mind will not grasp them, your heart will receive no strength and consolation from them—if you have not faith. The man who goes through the Bible without faith is like the Boers and natives who walked over the diamond fields of Africa all unconscious of the immeasurable wealth beneath their feet.

When I reply that it is the whole Bible which blesses me, I do not mean that there is no one promise that looms large to me, but rather that there are so many which bless me and meet my daily needs that I am like a man with a home full of sweet children, every one of whom is so dear to him that he cannot tell which he loves most and which is most needful for his happiness.

My spiritual needs are manifold, and there seems to be a promise just suited to my every need, that matches my need as a Yale key matches a Yale lock, as a glove fits a hand, as light answers to my eye and music to my ear, as the flavor of delicious food matches my sense of taste, and as the attar of roses answers my sense of smell; as the love of one's beloved and the faithfulness of one's friend answer the hunger of the heart.—*Samuel Logan Brengle.*

Fulfilling God's plan

"I am the Lord thy God which . . . leadeth thee by the way that thou shouldest go" (Isa. 48:17).
"I have raised him up in righteousness, and I will direct all his ways"
(Isa. 45:13).

Every human soul has a complete and perfect plan, cherished for it in the heart of God—a divine biography marked out which it enters into life to live.

No room for a discouraged or depressed feeling, therefore, is left you. Enough that you exist for a purpose high enough to give meaning to life, and to support a genuine inspiration. If your sphere is outwardly humble, if it even appears to be quite insignificant, God understands it better than you do, and it is a part of His wisdom to bring out great sentiments in humble conditions, great principles in works that are outwardly trivial, great characters under great adversities and heavy loads of incumbrance. The tallest saints of God will often be those who walk in the deepest obscurity and are even despised or quite overlooked by man. Let it be enough that God is in your history and that the plan of your biography is His, the issue He has set for it is the highest and the best.—*Horace Bushnell.*

> God grant me these: the strength to do
> Some needed service here;
> The wisdom to be brave and true;
> The gift of vision clear,
> That in each task that comes to me
> Some purpose I may plainly see.
>
> God teach me to believe that I
> Am stationed at a post,
> Although the humblest 'neath the sky,
> Where I am needed most;
> And that at last, if I do well,
> My humblest services will tell.
>
> God grant me faith to stand on guard,
> Uncheered and oft alone,
> And see behind each duty hard
> My service to the Throne.
> Whate'er my task, be this my creed:
> I am on earth to fill a need.
> —*Unknown.*

Does the heavenly Guest abide?

"I in them, and thou in me, that they may be made perfect in one"
(John 17:23).
"What? know ye not that your body is the temple of the Holy Ghost which is in you, which ye have of God, and ye are not your own?" (1 Cor. 6:19).

If you had knocked at the door of my heart any time before my conversion, and had asked, who dwells in here, I would have answered that no one dwells here but Martin Luther! And if I had opened the door, and you had come in, you would have seen a raw-headed monk, with a shaven crown and a hair shirt, with two tables of stone under his pillow and a knotted scourge hanging beside his bed. But if you were to knock at the door of my heart tonight, I would answer that Martin Luther no longer lives here; Jesus Christ alone lives here!
—*Martin Luther.*

A friend of mine said recently, "I like the term, 'Holy Ghost,' for the word Ghost in the old Saxon was the same as the word for Guest." Whether that be so or not, it may certainly be said that the Holy Ghost is the Holy Guest. He has come into the world and visits every heart seeking admittance as a guest. He may come to the soul unbidden, but He will not come in unbidden. He may be refused admission and turned away. But He comes. He is in the world like Noah's dove, looking for an abiding place. He comes as a Guest, but as an abiding one, if received. He forces Himself upon no one. He waits for the open door and the invitation.

He comes gently. He comes in love. He comes on a mission of infinite goodwill, of mercy and peace and helpfulness and joy. He is the Advocate of the Father and of the Son to us men. He represents and executes the redemptive plans and purposes of the Triune God. As my old teacher, Daniel Steele, wrote, "He is the Executive of the Godhead."—*Samuel Logan Brengle.*

When Ignatius was on his trial at Rome, he was asked by the Emperor, "What is the meaning of your name, Theophorus?" (God-bearer). He promptly replied, "He who has Christ in his breast." And all Christians are God-bearers, whether they realize it or not. The unspeakably glorious mystery of an indwelling Holy Ghost is the possession of even the weakest and most failing child of God.

(From *New Testament Holiness* by Thomas Cook. Used by permission of the Epworth Press.)

Sacrificial message bearing

"He came . . . to minister, and to give his life" (Matt. 20:28).
"Greater love hath no man than this, that a man lay down his life for his friends" (John 15:13).

The late King George the Fifth was about to begin his speech opening the Naval Conference in London. It was to be broadcast all over North America through fifty-nine radio stations. The current was to flow through one set of wires energized by one generator.

At the last moment, someone in the Columbia broadcasting rooms tripped over the wires and broke them. Instantly the chief control operator grasped the broken ends. For twenty minutes he literally spliced them through his body, until the break could be repaired. Spasms shook his arms, but he heroically held on, and the operation was a success, thanks to his grit. A greater than any earthly king has a message for lost and dying men. Sinners have broken the wires. Splice them, Christian preachers, missionaries, parents, friends! Let the message of redeeming love pass through you!

True, it may cost you something. Why shouldn't it? Jesus Christ was commissioned to carry His Father's emancipation proclamation to a world of sin-bound slaves. The message passed through His own precious body and left it hanging limply on a cross, broken and bleeding and breathless. But it came through! The message came through!

Can we ever pay our debt to Christ? In a small measure—yes, by letting the glad tidings pass through us to others who have never heard.

—Gospel Echoes.

When shall God be able to say to the devil, "Hast thou seen My Christians of today? No longer do they seek for gold or pleasure, for honors or ease; from henceforth My Christians will spill their blood for the love and cause of My beloved Son, and the salvation of the neediest of men."—*C. T. Studd.*

January 10
Joyful Christians

"And they worshipped him, and returned to Jerusalem with great joy: And were continually in the temple, praising and blessing God" (Luke 24:52-53). "Rejoice in the Lord alway: and again I say, rejoice" (Phil. 4:4).

Evidently God means His people to be enthusiastic, buoyant, glad. A joyless Christian is a stumblingblock to the world and an offence to his brethren and to God. One of the chief secrets of the success of the early Christians was that they were filled with gladness which was all-satisfying. Men judge of religion by those who are considered to possess it, and they will embrace or reject it according to the manner in which it is exhibited before them. They are attracted more by radiant faces than by eloquence or argument or any other human power. When we show them something better than they have and carry about the advertisement of a gladness which rises superior to all circumstances, we shall win men for Christ.

The joy of the Lord is our strength. The average type of Christian life will have to be raised before there can be any great advance of the Kingdom of Christ. Many of God's people have just as much gloom and depression and as many cares and anxieties as the people of the world. "How is it," said a godly minister to the writer recently, "that we so very seldom meet with a really joyful Christian?" It is certain we do not find in our churches so much of the exultant, exuberant joy which our fathers had.

(From *New Testament Holiness* by Thomas Cook. Used by permission of the Epworth Press.)

> Not sadly, Lord, I take Thy choice,
> Not fearfully I take my way;
> My trustful hand in Thine I lay,
> And walk beside Thee and rejoice.
> —*Lord Alfred Tennyson.*

Remember your life is to be a singing life. It has to be one of perpetual joy bubbling up from the wells of salvation.

This world is God's grand cathedral for you. You are to be one of God's choristers, and there is to be a continual sacrifice of praise and thanksgiving going up from your heart, with which God shall be continually well pleased.

And there should be not only the offering of the lips, but the surrender of the life with joy. Yes, with joy and thankfulness, and not with hesitancy and constraint. Every faculty of our nature should be presented to Him in gladsome service, for the Lord Jehovah is our song and delight, as well as our salvation and strength.—*W. Hay Aitken.*

Prevailing prayer

"And he said, I will not let thee go, except thou bless me" (Gen. 32:26).

Miss Winkworth's translation of Dessler's hymn expresses the energy of a soul determined to find not only blessing, but the One Who gives the blessing:

> "I will not let Thee go, Thou help in time of need!
> Heap ill on ill,
> I trust Thee still;
> Even when it seems that Thou wouldst slay indeed!
> Do as Thou wilt with me,
> I yet will cling to Thee;
> Hide Thou Thy face; yet help in time of need;
> I will not let Thee go!"

It requires much courage to be alone with God, to elect to retire for a time, and even for long times and to listen to His voice only. It requires more courage than is needed to meet human opposition or to battle with an outward enemy, and is altogether different from worship in the congregation with others around us. Let everyone who doubts this make the trial, in humble determination, "I will not let thee go, except thou bless me," until Thou admittest me to the inner sanctuary of Thy presence, and speakest to me. For it is then that the keen searchlight of His presence reveals the innermost recesses of the soul, so that the creature who has been bold enough to seek such a solitary interview with the Creator, shall fall on his face, as Daniel did, in self-abasement: "I, Daniel, fainted, and was sick certain days." It is then that all which is self, all subtle egotism—the egotism which takes such a multitude of forms—is searched and hunted out of the soul. It cannot live in His presence. The praise of men becomes as dust beneath the feet, and the soul trembles even to receive any honor of men, or to be recognized in this world as of any worth.

—*Josephine Butler.*

> When one that holds communion with the skies
> Has filled his urn where these pure waters rise,
> And, once more mingles with us meaner things,
> It is as though an angel shook his wings;
> Celestial fragrance fills the circuit wide,
> That tells us whence these odors are supplied.

—*Unknown.*

"And truly our fellowship is with the Father, and with his Son Jesus Christ"
(1 John 1:3).

January 12
Too big for God to use

"God resisteth the proud, but giveth grace unto the humble" (James 4:6).
"For thus saith the high and lofty One that inhabiteth eternity, whose name is Holy; I dwell in the high and holy place, with him also that is of a contrite and humble spirit, to revive the spirit of the humble, and to revive the heart of the contrite ones" (Isa. 57:15).

One of the last messages of G. Fred Bergin, Director of the Ashley Down Orphan Homes, Bristol, was: "Tell my younger brethren that they may be too big for God to use them, but they cannot be too small."

> "Too big for God to use me!"
>   This is the reason why
> Poor longing souls are famished
>   Who come, and go, and die!
> O God, my Savior, help me
>   In deep humility
> To make a full surrender
>   Henceforth to own but Thee.
>
> "Too big for God to use me!"
>   But if I am possessed
> With unction through His Spirit,
>   Then shall my work be blessed;
> I'll count myself as nothing,
>   Seek Christ to magnify,
> And use my gifts in service
>   My Lord to glorify.
>   *—Unknown.*

There is a story told of a very brilliant preacher who, wherever he went, moved crowds to enthusiasm by his splendid eloquence, culture and genius. He possessed every attractive gift of mind and body, and he was accompanied by a poor, blind brother who had no gifts at all but simply lived a holy life, and knelt in prayer while the man of power and intellect preached. One day, when an assembly had been stirred and lifted up to an unusual ecstasy of fervor and devotion, the preacher had a vision. He saw Heaven opened and the glory of the great throne streamed down; but he saw, to his surprise, that it shone not upon his head, but upon the face of the lowly brother kneeling at his feet, and from that face it was reflected upon the faces of the crowd. Then he knew that the power came not through his genius and eloquence, but through the pure life and fervent prayers of the brother at his side.

The world notes inconsistencies

"Cleanse thou me from secret faults" (Psa. 19:12).
"Be diligent that ye may be found of him without spot, and blameless"
(2 Peter 3:14).

The world's only estimate of religion is holiness. The world wants men who are saved from secret faults. A little crack will spoil the ring of the coin. The world expects that a Christian man shall be free from little tricks of gain and all crooked ways of business, even though they of the world made light of them. They expect, and rightly, that the Christian should be more gentle and patient and generous than he who does not profess to be a disciple of the Lord Jesus. For the sake of those who take their notion of religion from our lives we need put up this prayer earnestly, "Cleanse thou me from secret faults."

Doubts are born not so much of bad books as of un-Christlike Christians. Prejudices against religion find much of their strength in the keen and hard (business) ways of religious people; or else in their easygoing indifference about the little things of daily life. No amount of "heavenly-mindedness" can make up for the lack of the exactness in our words, or of straightforwardness in our dealings.—*Mark Guy Pearse.*

Let your lives preach.—*George Fox.*

If you want your neighbor to know what the Christ spirit will do for him, let him see what it has done for you.—*Henry Ward Beecher.*

> To be sincere. To look life in the eyes
>   With calm, undrooping gaze. Always to mean
>   The high and truthful thing. Never to screen
> Behind the unmeant word the sharp surprise
> Of cunning; never tell the little lies
>   Of look or thought. Always to choose between
>   The true and small, the true and large, serene
> And high above Life's cheap dishonesties.
> —*Maurice Smiley.*

The men God wants

"Seest thou a man diligent in his business? he shall stand before kings; he shall not stand before mean men" (Prov. 22:29).
"And straightway he called them: and they left their father Zebedee in the ship with the hired servants, and went after him" (Mark 1:20).

God never goes to the lazy or the idle when He needs men for His service. When God wants a worker He calls a worker. . . . Scripture and history attest this truth.

Moses was busy with the flock at Horeb. Gideon was busy threshing wheat by the wine-press. Saul was busy searching for his father's lost beasts. David was busy caring for his father's sheep. Elisha was busy plowing with twelve yoke of oxen. Nehemiah was busy bearing the King's wine cup. Amos was busy following the herds. Peter and Andrew were busy casting a net into the sea. Matthew was busy collecting customs. Saul was busy persecuting the friends of Jesus. William Carey was busy making shoes. John Milton was busy mastering classics. Martin Luther was busy performing penance. John Bunyan was busy tinkering pots and pans. Roger Williams was busy as a stenographer. Adoniram Judson was busy investigating religious truth. Charles Spurgeon was busy as a teacher.

God never called an idler into His service. The busy workers are the men God wants.

> This is the gospel of labor;
> Ring it, ye bells of the kirk—
> The Lord of Love came down from above
> To live with the men who work.
> —*Henry Van Dyke.*

When God made the oyster, He guaranteed his absolute economic and social security. He built the oyster a house, his shell, to shelter and protect him from his enemies. When hungry, the oyster simply opens his shell and food rushes in for him. He has freedom from want.

But when God made the eagle He declared: "The blue sky is the limit— build your own house!" So the eagle built on the highest mountain. Storms threaten him every day. For food he flies through miles of rain and snow and wind. But think of it, the eagle, not the oyster, is the emblem of America.
—*Morris Mandel.*

Proving our love

"Hereby perceive we the love of God, because he laid down his life for us: and we ought to lay down our lives for the brethren. But whoso hath this world's goods, and seeth his brother have need, and shutteth up his bowels of compassion from him, how dwelleth the love of God in him?" (1 John 3:16-17).

We cannot walk with Christ and have small hearts, for His heart embraced the world and broke for its redemption. We cannot walk with Christ and have cold, hard hearts, for His love constrains us and fills us with tender sympathy and pity.—*Unknown.*

The anointed soul has full sympathy with David Brainerd, the missionary: "I long to be a flame of fire, continually glowing in the divine service, preaching and building up Christ's kingdom to my latest, my dying hour." This desire springs up in the experience of pardon, but it does not become a passion inflaming all the soul like a mighty furnace, till love fills its utmost capacity.

The feet of Jesus were ever hasting towards lost men. His mighty heart was ever yearning over the spiritually blind and dead. It is natural that the fullness of love to Christ should bring us into sympathy with this dominant passion of His holy soul, and that our footsteps should ever be toward the perishing. There is a grave mistake somewhere when a person imagines that he has mounted up to the plane of the "higher life" and feels no quickened impulse towards sinners dying in their sins around him. That ecstasy of delight must be spurious which inclines its possessor to sit still and selfishly enjoy the raptures of divine love, instead of going forth to communicate and widely diffuse the joy.

—*Daniel Steele.*

Oh, for a passionate passion for souls,
　　Oh, for a pity that yearns;
Oh, for a love that loves unto death,
　　Oh, for a fire that burns.
　　　　　—*Amy Carmichael.*

Let me never fancy I have zeal till my heart overflows with love for every man living.—*Henry Martyn.*

Adoniram Judson went as a missionary to Burma. He so burned with the desire to preach the Gospel before he learned the language that he walked up to a Burman and embraced him. The man went home and reported that he had seen an angel. The living Christ was so radiant in Judson's countenance that men called him "Mr. Glory-face." When Christian workers really come to know the love God has given unto them, the Gospel will become irresistible.

January 16
Courageous in our witness

"Deal courageously, and the Lord shall be with the good" (2 Chron. 19:11).
"Whosoever therefore shall be ashamed of me and of my words in this adulterous and sinful generation; of him also shall the Son of man be ashamed, when he cometh in the glory of his Father with the holy angels" (Mark 8:38).

Two men came into a moderately filled railway carriage and sat down in front of a Christian named John Smith, and soon began to drink, sing, swear, and blaspheme. After a while Mr. Smith held the following soliloquy with himself:

"John, those men belong to the devil. There is no doubt about it, and they are not a bit ashamed of it. To whom do you belong? Why, to the Lord Jesus of course. Are you glad or sorry? Glad of course. Who knows that those men belong to the devil? Everybody who hears them. Who knows that you belong to the Lord Jesus Christ? Why, no one, I'm afraid. Are you willing that those men and others should know it? Of course I am. Will you let them know it? I will. When? Now."

Then John Smith sang, "All hail the power of Jesus' Name." The other passengers became interested; the swearers became abusive, and presently asked, "What are you making that row for?"

"I'm singing for my Master," replied John Smith. "For the last half hour you have been singing and standing by your master; for the rest of the journey I am going to stand by mine. Christ is my Master. I am as proud of Him as you are of your master. Now, if the other passengers do not object, I am going to have my turn."

"Sing on," cried a chorus of voices. And sing he did. The blasphemers soon changed into another carriage.

Then an old gray-headed man grasped John Smith's hand and said, "I am eighty years old. I have preached the Gospel for many years. I wanted to rebuke those blasphemers, but I had not the courage. I have not much longer to live, but, God helping me, I will never again refuse to show my colors."

> What have I said for Jesus today?
> Though I have talked of numberless things,
> (Words that were commonplace, grave, or gay,
> I have sent forth on invisible wings).
> Have I spoken one word for my Lord—
> Dropped one seed by the way
> As the moments have sped,
> And the chances have fled—
> Today?
> —*Jean H. Watson.*

26

The divine likeness

"If we have been planted together in the likeness of his death, we shall be also in the likeness of his resurrection" (Rom. 6:5).
"Renewed . . . after the image of him that created him" (Col. 3:10).

"Unaccountable this!" said the Wax, as from the flame it dropped melting upon the Paper beneath.

"Do not grieve," said the Paper, "I am sure it is all right."

"I was never in such agony!" exclaimed the Wax, still dropping.

"It is not without a good design, and will end well," replied the Paper. The Wax was unable to reply at once, owing to a strong pressure; and when it again looked up it bore a beautiful impression, the counterpart of the seal which had been applied to it.

"Ah! I comprehend now," said the Wax, no longer in suffering. "I was softened in order to receive this lovely durable impress. Yes; I see now it was all right, because it has given to me the beautiful likeness which I could not otherwise have obtained."

Are you walking with the Master through the rugged way of life,
  Glorifying Him in all you say and do?
Are you ready for the conflict, fearing not the deadly strife,
  Is the image of the Savior stamped on you?

Is the glory of His grace shining thro' your radiant face,
  Are you sealed to Him, the royal One and true?
Can the world see in your face Heaven's touch of saving grace?
  Is the image of the Savior stamped on you?
                                        —*Thoro Harris.*

January 18

The Bible stored in the heart

"Thy word have I hid in mine heart, that I might not sin against thee"
(Psa. 119:11).
"Holding fast the faithful word" (Titus 1:9).

If you want to be strong Christian people, hide the Bible in your heart. When I was a boy the practice of good Christian folk was to read a daily chapter. I wonder if that is kept up. I gravely suspect it is not. There are, no doubt, a great many causes contributing to the comparative decay amongst professing Christians of Bible reading and Bible study.

And no religious literature, sermons, treatises, still less magazines and periodicals, will do for Christian men what the Bible will do for them. You make a tremendous mistake, for your own soul's sake, if your religious reading consists of what people have said and thought about Scripture, more than in the Scripture itself. Why should you dip your cans into the reservoir when you can take them up to where the spring comes gushing out of the hillside, pure and limpid and living?

Then there is the drive of our modern life which crowds out the Word. Get up a quarter of an hour earlier and you will have time to read your Bibles. It will be well worth the sacrifice, if it is a sacrifice. I do not mean by reading the Bible what, I am afraid, is far too common, reading a scrap of Scripture as if it were a kind of charm. But I would most earnestly press upon you that muscle and fiber will distinctly atrophy and become enfeebled, if Christian people neglect the first plain way of hiding the Word in their heart, which is to make the utterances of Scripture as if incorporated with their very being, and part of their very selves. —*Alexander Maclaren.*

The Rev. Charles Garret tells us that the early Methodists so loved their Bible that they were called "Bible bigots" and "Bible moths." He goes on to say:

"They hid God's Word in their hearts. They were mighty in the Scriptures. It was spirit and life to them. Hence, with hearts full of love to God and man, and to God's Word, they went to the work to which they were called. When I hear any class of men spoken of as 'being like the first Methodists,' I always ask, are they diligent Bible students? If not, they cannot be like them, for they were men of one Book."

God's gold mines

"The Almighty shall be thy gold" (Job 22:25—R.V.).
"Oh how great is thy goodness, which thou hast laid up for them that fear thee; which thou hast wrought for them that trust in thee before the sons of men!" (Psa. 31:19).

Searching through the papers of a young man who had died on one of the earth's rich gold fields, the following poem was found. He had been lured on by the quest of "gold," and went out to make his fortune in the gold digging. But the hardships brought on severe illness, which resulted in his death. It was at this time that Christ revealed Himself to him as the "true gold."

> I once thought contentment was bought with gold,
> So I went to the land where the rich tide rolled,
> And I eagerly sought, midst disease and death,
> To grasp it, nor feared I the withering breath
> > Of the damp chilling mine,
> > When I saw it shine.
> Nay, I laughed when I thought of what wealth was mine.
>
> But it fled—and it left me diseased and worn,
> And I grieved 'mid a night which might know no morn.
> But into my darkness the Savior came
> From Satan His blood-bought one to claim,
> > And He opened the mine
> > Of His love Divine,
> And His Word bid its gems round my heart to shine.
>
> Oh how softly He whispered, "'Tis mine to roll
> The mountain of sin off thy laboring soul!"
> How full was my freedom, relieved of its load,
> And He gave me a name, 'twas "a son of God."
> > And He said, "In the mine
> > Leave earth's gold to shine,
> The riches of grace are eternally thine."

Most of us have turned to the tinsel of this world, the bauble of fame, or some other illusive vain object before making the discovery of the gold of the Christian's inheritance that surpasses all else.

January 20
Prayer solves life's problems

"Men ought always to pray, and not to faint" (Luke 18:1).
"He shall call upon me, and I will answer him; I will be with him in trouble:
I will deliver him, and honour him" (Psa. 91:15).

I see more than ever that those who are given up to God in continual prayer, are men of business, both for earth and Heaven; they go through the world with composure, are resigned to every cross, and make the greatest glory of the greatest cross. On the other hand, if not given up to God in prayer, every cross brings the greatest perplexity and robs them of the little love and patience they enjoy. To be all alive to God is, as it were, two heavens; to be unstable and not a whole Christian, is two hells.—*William Bramwell.*

Not one step more, Heavenly Father,
Would I take without Thy call;
Prone to race and rush—oh, rather
At Thy feet now would I fall!
Eyes, be blind, for God to view it;
Feet, be stopp'd, leave Him the road;
Hands can only touch to rue it;
Soul, be still, know He is God!
—*J. Robertson and R. F. Beveridge.*

I suspect I have been allotting habitually too little time to religious exercises as private devotion, religious meditation, Scripture reading, etc. Hence I am lean, cold, and hard. God would perhaps prosper me more in spiritual things if I were to be more diligent in using the means of grace. I had better allot more time, say two hours or an hour and a half, to religious exercises daily, and try whether by so doing I cannot preserve a frame of spirit more habitually devotional, a more lively sense of unseen things, a warmer love to God, and a greater degree of hunger and thirst after righteousness, a heart less prone to be soiled with worldly cares, designs, passions, and apprehension, and a real undissembled longing for Heaven, its pleasures and its purity.
—*William Wilberforce.*

30

Sermons in shoes

"But be ye doers of the word, and not hearers only, deceiving your own selves"
(James 1:22).
"Do not ye after their works: for they say, and do not" (Matt. 23:3).

As every one of you is a preacher, and every life is a sermon, let me inquire of you: what sort of a sermon are you preaching? Do you find your texts in the shop or in the stock market, and preach that the chief end of life is to make money? Then you are making more converts to Mammon than to Christ. Do some of you preach that self-indulgence is the "one thing needful"? Then you will draw more to the pleasure party and the playhouse than you will to the prayer-meeting. It boots but little that the Eighth Commandment is taught from this pulpit if any of you are guilty of sharp practices in your business, or refuse to give every man his due. What is done by God's professing people outside of the sanctuary carries more weight than anything said within the sanctuary—even though Paul himself stood in the pulpit.

Today this world's sorest need is for more Christlike men and women. The sermons it needs are sermons in shoes.—*Theodore Cuyler.*

I'd rather see a sermon than hear one any day;
I'd rather one would walk with me than merely show the way;
The eye's a better pupil, and more willing than the ear;
Fine counsel is confusing, but example's always clear.

The best of all the preachers are the men who live their creeds,
To put some good in action is what everybody needs.
I soon can learn to do it, if you let me see it done,
I can watch your hands in action, while your tongue too fast may run.

The lectures you deliver may be very wise and true,
But I'd rather get my lessons by observing what you do;
I may not often understand the high advice you give,
But there's no misunderstanding how you act and how you live.
—*Unknown.*

January 22
Blameless but not unblamed

*"That ye may be blameless and harmless . . . without rebuke, in the midst of
a crooked and perverse nation" (Phil. 2:15).*
"To the end he may stablish your hearts unblameable in holiness before God"
(1 Thess. 3:13).

The word "blameless" means free from every form of willful wrong or
intentional misdoing against our fellowmen; the word "harmless" means sincere,
simple, without admixture of sin and vileness in the sight of God. To be the
first is far, far the easier. It would not be so if the word "blameless" meant
"unblamed," for no man, however blameless, can escape being blamed. The
experience of ages has shown that the shield of innocence, which a good man
carries with him through the world, cannot be so white that none will throw
dust at it. Some of the holiest and noblest men that ever lived have been—and
sometimes all through their lives—very targets for the arrows of abuse. So
long as Envy has restless eyes, and Calumny a fertile imagination, and Malice
a myriad of voices which bellow in the shade—so long will there be enemies,
persecutors, and slanderers of the very saints of God.

The stainless purity of Joseph saved him not from infamous accusations,
nor the noble meekness of Moses from bitter criticisms, nor the splendid services
of Samuel from open ingratitude. Of the stern self-denial of John the Baptist
they could only say, "He hath a devil"; of the boundless sympathy of the Savior
of mankind, they dared to mutter, "Behold a gluttonous man and a winebibber,
a friend of publicans and sinners." If ever we feel discouraged at the thought
that there are natures which guilelessness fails to disarm, or unselfishness to
win, let the Cross reveal to us the high lesson that we may still be utterly
blameless, though it may be that we live no day unblamed.—*Dean Farrar.*

You have no enemies, you say?
Alas, my friend, the boast is poor;
He who has mingled in the fray
Of duty, that the brave endure,
Must have made foes! If you have none,
Small is the work that you have done:
You've hit no traitor on the hip;
You've dashed no cup from perjured lip;
You've never turned the wrong to right;
You've been a coward in the fight!
—*Charles Mackay.*

The God of the impossible

"For my strength is made perfect in weakness" (2 Cor. 12:9).
"The things which are impossible with men are possible with God"
(Luke 18:27).

"The things which are impossible with men are possible with God!" I said a little while ago that there is many a man who has learned the lesson: It is impossible with men. Then he gives up in helpless despair, and lives a wretched Christian life, without joy, or strength, or victory. And why? Because he does not humble himself to learn that other lesson: With God all things are possible.

Your religious life is every day to be a proof that God works impossibilities; your religious life is to be a series of impossibilities made possible and actual by God's almighty power. That is what the Christian needs. He has an almighty God that he worships, and he must learn to understand: I do not want a little of God's power, but I want—with reverence be it said—the whole of God's omnipotence to keep me right, and to live like a Christian.—*Andrew Murray.*

Yes, face it out to the end: cast away every shadow of hope on the human side as a positive hindrance to the Divine. Heap the difficulties together recklessly, and pile on as many more as you can find: you cannot get beyond the blessed climax of impossibility. Let faith swing out to Him. He is the God of the impossible.

Exhaust the human possibilities of a situation and then trust God to do what is humanly impossible.—*I. Lilias Trotter.*

> Two glad services are ours,
> Both the Master loves to bless:
> First to serve with all our powers,
> Then with all our helplessness.
> —*Charles Fox.*

Be listening

"Incline your ears to the words of my mouth" (Psa. 78:1).
"Their ears are dull of hearing" (Acts 28:27).
"Let these sayings sink down into your ears" (Luke 9:44).

I have a phonograph into whose sensitive gelatine cylinders I dictate my literary work. One busy day, I dictated a large amount of matter, filling up every cylinder. I spent nearly two days getting through a great amount of literary labor, and felt very much relieved that it was off my hands.

But when my typist proceeded to copy the messages which I had spoken into these cylinders, she could not understand the words, they were all jargon and confusion. The reason was very simple. I had neglected to shave off the former dictation before giving the new message. I had really dictated a lot of matter into the ears that were already filled and, therefore, it had made no impression. My work was lost, my labor was in vain. But I learned a lesson that was worth all it cost, and that is, that we must be empty before we can be filled. God cannot speak His messages into full ears. The Holy Ghost cannot pour His fullness into those who are already full.—*A. B. Simpson.*

> Among the things that this day brings
> Will come to you a call,
> The which, unless you're listening,
> You may not hear at all:
> Lest it be very soft and low,
> Whate'er you do, where'er you go,
> Be listening.
>
> Then whatsoe'er the call may be,
> To service small or great,
> To cross the seas and speak God's love,
> To smile, to rule a state—
> When God shall come and say to you,
> "Here is the thing that you must do,"
> Be listening.
>
> —*Unknown.*

Nothing in life should be dreaded so much as that the soul should ever lose its sensitiveness to God; that God should ever speak and find the ear just dull enough to miss what He has said; that God should have some active will for some human will to perform, and our heart be not the first in the world to be ready to obey.—*Henry Drummond.*

Guidance through hindrance

"So he shall open, and none shall shut: and he shall shut, and none shall open" (Isa 22:22).

"He that openeth, and no man shutteth; and shutteth, and no man openeth" (Rev. 3:7).

"I always thought that if we prayed for guidance we would get it, but here I have prayed earnestly for the way to be opened up, and it seems as if every door so far has been closed," said the girl petulantly.

"Perhaps the closed doors are the very guidance you are seeking for," answered her mother.

"What do you mean?" was the surprised question.

"Just this, when the way is blocked, it may mean that at present that is not the door God wishes you to enter; if you still continue praying and doing His will, you may rest assured that the right door will open in due time. Do you not remember how Paul, when he was starting on his second missionary journey, found barriers set up by the Holy Spirit, which prevented him from going where he had intended, and how it was a clear leading of Providence, though at the time neither he nor his companions may have recognized it as such? Many a door is closed in order to force one out along the line of God's wise choice. If the doors Paul wanted to enter had not been closed, the Gospel would not have had a chance to enter Europe, and who knows but we should have been the heathen today instead of the foreign nations to whom we are sending missionaries?"

> I wondered why God closed the door,
> On what I fondly planned;
> I tried in vain to open it,
> And could not understand;
> Was it through error of my own,
> This disappointment sore,
> Or something I had failed to do?
> —But God had shut the door
> Because He'd planned some better thing,
> Some blessing on before,
> Far richer than I ever dreamed,
> That's why God shut the door.
> —Clara Simpson.

"The steps of a good man are ordered by the Lord" (Psa. 37:23).

Cross-bearing—our calling

"Whosoever doth not bear his cross, and come after me, cannot be my disciple" (Luke 14:27).
"If any man will come after me, let him . . . take up his cross daily"
(Luke 9:23).

The Christian's proper work is to bear the cross. This is his calling, his trade or profession. It is the business of a watchmaker to make watches; it is the business of every Christian to bear the cross, at home, abroad, in the shop, in the store, in the market place, or in the field. He has many discouragements, many solicitations to lay it aside. It sometimes presses heavily upon him, but the sight of the crown inspires him with fresh vigor; he glows, and bounds along the heavenly road. By the cross, i.e., by his conduct, the Christian is distinguished from the lover of the world. While he bears the cross, the cross will bear him. It will guide him through labyrinths of darkness. As a shield, it will protect him in dangerous conflicts.

Among the Romans, criminals about to be crucified were compelled to bear their own cross to the place of execution, but the Christian bears his to the place of triumph. If it should prove at any time so heavy as to crush him down to death, as did Stephen's, like him he beholds the heavens opened, the King in His beauty, and the crown of celestial glory. He comes off more than a conqueror.

> Who suffer with our Master here
> We shall before His face appear,
> And by His side sit down;
> To patient faith the prize is sure;
> And all that to the end endure
> The cross, shall wear the crown.
> In hope of that ecstatic pause,
> Jesus, we now sustain the cross,
> And at Thy footstool fall;
> Till Thou our ravish'd spirits fill,
> And God is All in All.
> —*Religious Emblems.*

If God plants a cross in your pathway, you cannot escape it and get to Heaven.

The cross of Christ is the sweetest burden that ever I bore; it is such a burden as wings are to a bird, or as sails to a ship, to carry me forward to my desired haven. Those who by faith see the invisible God and the fair city, make no account of present losses and crosses.—*Samuel Rutherford.*

Missionary to my neighbors

"Inasmuch as ye have done it unto one of the least of these my brethren, ye have done it unto me" (Matt. 25:40).

"Is not this the fast that I have chosen? . . . Is it not to deal thy bread to the hungry, and that thou bring the poor that are cast out to thy house? when thou seest the naked, that thou cover him: and that thou hide not thyself from thine own flesh?" (Isa. 58:6-7).

Sophie was a New York scrubwoman who used to say that she had been called to preach, but being poor she learned instead to scrub. She longed to be a foreign missionary, but when she told of this desire to her heavenly Father, she received His answer in this dialogue:

The Lord asked her, "Where were you born?"

"In Germany, Father."

"Where are you now?"

"In America."

"Well, aren't you a foreign missionary already?" When she understood that, the Father said to her, "Who lives on the floor above you?"

"A family of Swedes."

"And on the floor above them?"

"Why, some Swiss."

"And in the rear house are Italians, and a block away are some Chinese. Now you have never said a word to these people about My Son. Do you think that I will send you thousands of miles away to foreigners and heathen when you have them all around, and you never care enough about them to speak with them about their souls?"

So to her neighbors and others Sophie became a witness for Jesus. And by denying herself in every possible way she saved enough money from scrubbing to educate a missionary in Japan and send a teacher to work down South. God has His opportunities for service waiting for every willing Christian.

> When we stand before the Master
> Will it matter very much,
> Which of us owned the office,
> And which the scrubbing brush?
> —*Unknown.*

A MISSIONARY IS: God's man, in God's place, doing God's work, in God's way, for God's glory.

January 28
Right use of time

"Behold, thou hast made my days as an handbreadth; and mine age is as nothing before thee" (Psa. 39:5).
"Pass the time of your sojourning here in fear" (1 Peter 1:17).

He who knows the value of time, and will redeem it from useless chitchat and trifling visits, will find enough for all the purposes of his own salvation, the cultivation of his mind, and the work of the ministry. He to whom time is not precious, who lives not by rule, never finds time sufficient for anything, is always in a hurry, and never capable of bringing one good purpose to proper effect.—*Adam Clarke.*

People complain because their days are few, then act as though there could be no end to them.—*Addison.*

> When as a child I laughed and wept, time crept.
> When as a youth I dreamed and talked, time walked.
> When I became a full grown man, time ran.
> And later as I older grew, time flew.
> Soon I shall find while traveling on, time gone.
> Then in the great eternity, what then?
> —*Unknown.*

Spend your time in nothing which you know must be repented of. Spend it on nothing on which you might not pray for the blessing of God. Spend it on nothing which you could not review with a quiet conscience on your dying bed. Spend it on nothing which you might not safely and properly be doing if death should surprise you in the act.—*Richard Baxter.*

> 'Tis not for man to trifle! Life is brief.
>   And sin is here.
> Our age is but the falling of a leaf,
>   A dropping tear.
> We have no time to sport away the hours;
> All must be earnest in a world like ours.
>   —*Horatius Bonar.*

The orderly arrangement of time is like a ray of light which darts itself through all our occupations.—*Unknown.*

Prayer in the morning

"I pray thee, send me good speed this day" (Gen. 24:12).
"I love them that love me; and those that seek me early shall find me"
(Prov. 8:17).

No pressure of business or household duties should crowd out prayer. An eminent Christian merchant told me that it was his rule to secure a good quiet half-hour in his chamber on his knees and over his Bible before he met his family; and then he went into his business—as Moses came down from the mount—with his face shining. Doctor Arnold, of Rugby, had a favorite morning hymn, which opens with these stirring lines:

> "Come, my soul, thou must be waking;
> Now is breaking
>   O'er the earth another day.
> Come to Him Who made this splendor;
> See thou render
>   All thy feeble powers can pay."
> *—Theodore Cuyler.*

The devil is aware that one hour of close fellowship, hearty converse with God in prayer, is able to pull down what he hath been contriving and building many a year.—*Flavel.*

He that saveth his time from prayer shall lose it, and he that loseth his time for communion with God shall find it again in added blessing and power and fruitfulness.—*J. H. Stumpf.*

A good day begins with God. A wise merchant would no more think of going to the store without communion with Christ, than without coat or hat or shoes. I used to have a very poor watch, and I had to set it every morning in order that I might make from it a guess about the time of day. Our souls are poor timepieces, utterly disordered and every morning we need to set them by the Sun of Righteousness.—*De Witt Talmage.*

Unclasped possessions

"But what things were gain to me, those I counted loss for Christ. Yea doubtless, and I count all things but loss for the excellency of the knowledge of Christ Jesus my Lord: for whom I have suffered the loss of all things, and do count them but dung, that I may win Christ" (Phil. 3:7-8).

It was on one of his birthdays that David Livingstone said: "I will place no value on anything that I have or may possess, except in relation to the kingdom of Christ. If anything that I have will advance the interest of that kingdom it shall be given or kept as by giving or keeping it I shall most promote the glory of Him to Whom I owe all my hopes, both for time and eternity. May grace be given me to adhere to this."

> I could not choose a larger bliss
>   Than to be wholly Thine; and mine
> A will whose highest joy is this,
>   To ceaselessly unclasp in Thine.
>
> Beneath the splendor of Thy choice,
>   Thy perfect choice for me, I rest;
> Outside it now I dare not live,
>   Within it I must needs be blest.
>
> Then may Thy perfect glorious will
>   Be evermore fulfilled in me,
> And make my life an answering chord
>   Of glad, responsive harmony.
>
> Oh! it is life indeed to live
>   Within this kingdom strangely sweet;
> And yet we fear to enter in,
>   And linger with unwilling feet.
>
> We fear this wondrous will of Thine
>   Because we have not reached Thy heart.
> Not venturing our all on Thee
>   We may not know how good Thou art.
>   —*Jean Sophia Pigott.*

God never gave this gift of His Holy Spirit to any human soul who had not come to the point that he would sell all he had to get it. While there is a spark of insubordination or rebellion or dictation, one will never get it. Truly submissive and obedient souls only enter this kingdom. Anywhere He tells you to go, anything He tells you to sacrifice or fly from, you will have to do. The Spirit is one of His choice gifts that He has reserved for His choice servants—those who serve Him with all their hearts.—*Catherine Booth.*

The fruitfulness of affliction

"The more they afflicted them, the more they multiplied and grew"
(Exod. 1:12).
"So the Lord blessed the latter end of Job more than his beginning"
(Job 42:12).

The reason why we are led into trouble and out again is not merely that we may value happiness the more from having lost it once and found it again, but that we may bear upon our nature some impress which could not have been stamped except on natures just so softened to receive it. There stands your man who has been through some terrible experience and found relief. Perhaps it was a terrible sickness in which he was drawn back from the very gates of death. Perhaps it was some mighty task which the world seemed to single him out to do, to fail in which would have been ruin, and in which it seemed at one time certain that he must fail. Perhaps it was a midnight darkness that settled down over all truth, so that it seemed hopeless ever again to know anything truly of God or man.

Whatever it was, the experience has come and passed. There stands your man, relieved, released, out in the sunlight on the other side of it. What do you ask of him as he stands there? Is your sense of fitness satisfied if he is only relieved, released; if he is only like a man who, after a hard fight with the waves, has got his footing once more just where he was when he was swept away? Certainly not. The human sense of fitness asks more than that. He must have seen something in the dark, or in the transition from the dark back to the light again, which pure, unclouded light could not have shown him. Into this kneaded and tortured life there must have been pressed some knowledge which the life in its best health was too hard and insensitive to take, some knowledge which the life, restored to health, shall carry as the secret of inexhaustible happiness forth into eternity. Without these revelations the midnight and the torture would be inexplicable and hideous. But these revelations depend upon the way the soul's eyes look for help.—*Phillips Brooks.*

> He who for love has undergone
> The worst that can befall,
> Is happier thousandfold than one
> Who never loved at all.
> A grace within his soul has reigned,
> Which nothing else can bring—
> Thank God for all that I have gained
> By that high suffering!
> —*Houghton.*

February 1
Hearts aflame

"The God that answereth by fire, let him be God" (2 Kings 18:24).
"He shall baptize you with the Holy Ghost, and with fire" (Matt. 3:11).

Fire makes warm; it makes to glow. You stand before a furnace door, behind which is a glowing fire. You have in your hand a bar of iron; it is cold, and black, and forbidding, and there is no beauty in it. But you take that cold, dark, forbidding bar of iron, and you open the furnace door and thrust it into the glowing fire. Soon it is warm, then it becomes red hot and glows with marvelous beauty, and you have the cold bar of iron glowing with fire. You and I are cold—oh, how cold we are! And the Lord Jesus takes us and He plunges us into the fire of the Holy Spirit. We begin to grow warm, and soon we glow, glow with love to God, glow with love for perishing souls.

Men and women, the great need of the day is men and women on fire. Brethren, that is what we need in the pulpit, ministers on fire. What cold men most of us preachers are! Orthodox enough, it may be, and we present the most solemn truth with great force of reason and great beauty of rhetoric and most convincing eloquence, and our audiences sit there and admire our strong preaching, but they do not repent of their sins. Why not? Because we are not on fire. We convince the intellect, but we do not melt the heart. But put a minister who is on fire in the pulpit, and the audience will melt.

But we need that kind of people in the choir as well. What beautiful choirs we have nowadays! Why, they sing almost like angels, and the people sit there admiring them, but nobody is converted by their singing. But when we get a man on fire to sing, or a woman on fire to sing, something is brought to pass.

That is what we need in our Sunday School classes. We set a young man or a young woman to teach a Sunday School class, and they know the lesson capitally and study all the latest "helps," and make the lesson tremendously interesting, but the boys and girls and men and women in their classes are not converted, because the teachers are not on fire.—*R. A. Torrey.*

Holiness is both the secret and source of spiritual passion. Apart from a burning passion, both Christian living and spiritual ministry are ineffective.

How basic is spiritual passion in personal living! When it is absent, the individual is frustrated by burdensome dissatisfaction and haunted by an inescapable sense of divine disappointment.—*Dr. Frank Bateman Stanger.*

Our only care, to please God

"For they loved the praise of men more than the praise of God" (John 12:43).
"Do I seek to please men? for if I yet pleased men, I should not be the servant of Christ" (Gal. 1:10).

It is a light thing to be judged of man's judgment, and all the lighter since they are so prone to judge by a false standard. What is it to me that men condemn me if God only approve? The longer I live, the less I think of human opinions on the great questions of right and wrong as God sees them. They will judge both themselves and others falsely. Even the Church sometimes condemns and excommunicates her best men. I have known cases, and could name them, in which I am confident they have done this very thing. They have cut men off from their communion, and now everybody sees that the men excommunicated were the best men of the Church.

It is a blessed thought that the only thing we need to care for is to please God. The only inquiry we need make is—What will God think of it? We have only one mind to please, and that the Great Mind of the universe. Let this be our single aim, and we shall not fail to please Him. But if we do not aim at this all we can do is only an abomination in His sight.—*Charles G. Finney.*

May I have grace to live above every human motive; simply with God and to God, and not swayed, especially in missionary work, by the opinions of people not acquainted with the state of things, whose judgment may be contrary to my own.—*Henry Martyn.*

> Make not a man your measuring-rod
> If you would span the way to God;
> Heed not our petty "worse" or "less,"
> But fix your eyes on perfectness.
> Make for the loftiest point in view,
> And draw your friends along with you.
> —*Amos R. Wells.*

Heaven's bank

"For all the promises of God in him are yea, and in him Amen" (2 Cor. 1:20). "Who through faith . . . obtained promises" (Heb. 11:33).

The precious promises of our great God are expressly intended to be taken to Him, and exchanged for the blessing which they guarantee. Prayer takes the promise to the Bank of Faith, and obtains the golden blessing. Mind how you pray. Make real business of it. Let it never be a dead formality. Some people pray a long time, but do not get what they are supposed to ask for, because they do not plead the promise in a truthful, businesslike way. If you were to go into a bank, and stand an hour talking to the clerk, and then come out again without your cash, what would be the good of it? If I go to a bank, I pass a check across the counter, take up my money, and go about my business: that is the best way of praying. Ask for what you want, because the Lord has promised it. Believe that you have the blessing, and go forth to your work in full assurance of it. Go from your knees singing, because the promise is fulfilled: thus will your prayer be answered. It is not the length of your prayer, but the strength of your prayer which wins with God; and the strength of prayer lies in your faith in the promise which you have pleaded before the Lord.—*C. H. Spurgeon.*

> I have a never-failing bank,
> A more than golden store,
> No earthly bank is half so rich,
> How can I then be poor?
>
> Sometimes my Banker smiling says:
> "Why don't you often come?
> And when you draw a little note,
> Why not a larger sum?
>
> "Why live so niggardly and poor?
> Your bank contains a-plenty;
> Why come and take a one-pound note
> When you might have a twenty?"
>
> Because my Banker is so rich,
> I have no cause to borrow;
> I'll live upon my cash today,
> And draw again tomorrow.
> —*Unknown.*

Excelling the world in zeal

"Who gave himself for us, that he might . . . purify unto himself a peculiar people, zealous of good works" (Titus 2:14).
"Your zeal hath provoked very many" (2 Cor. 9:2).

Have you ever listened to the enthusiastic roar of football spectators over a ball kicked to a goal? Have you seen men crowd and push in their zeal to get a standing-place in the stadium? Such zeal and enthusiasm is considered legitimate! But where is the zeal for Christ? Bushnell has said: "If your pulse ordinarily beats sixty times a minute when you think of other themes and talk about other themes, and if your pulse does not go up to seventy-five or eighty when you come to talk about Christ and Heaven, it is because you do not know the one, and have a poor chance of getting to the other."

A clergyman once asked David Garrick why it was that the acted word of the theatre was more powerful than the spoken word from the pulpit. In reply, the actor said: "Ah, my dear sir, you of the pulpit speak truth as if it were fiction; we in the theatre speak fiction as if it were truth."

On this subject Spurgeon said: "I feel right glad to meet with a zealous man nowadays, for zeal for God has become a rare quality in the land. Fashion and art and society and literature, each one evokes zeal of a certain kind; but we are not overdone with those who are zealous in the matter of religion."

Any man that wishes to act on the mind of another must believe something, and believe it in his very soul. Sincerity and earnestness, in fact a certain degree of enthusiasm, are essential to give effect to spoken thought. A man must brood over his own thoughts till his mind takes fire, and then he may hope to fire other minds.—*T. T. Lynch.*

His earnest love, His infinite desires,
His living, endless, and devouring fires,
Do rage in thirst, and fervently require
A love 'tis strange it should desire.

We cold and careless are, and scarcely think
Upon the glorious spring whereat we drink,
Did He not love us we could be content:
We wretches are indifferent.

'Tis death, my soul, to be indifferent;
Set forth thyself unto thy whole extent,
And all the glory of His passion prize,
Who for thee lives, Who for thee dies.
—*Thomas Traherne.*

45

The father heart of God

"For the eyes of the Lord run to and fro throughout the whole earth, to shew himself strong in the behalf of them whose heart is perfect toward him"
(2 Chron. 16:9).
"Thou God seest me" (Gen. 16:13).

God is not blind, or deaf, or indifferent, or indigent. He is not "the silent God" that some people in their self-conceit and wayward unbelief suppose. He knows how to be silent, and how to hide Himself from the proud in heart. But He cannot hide Himself anywhere in His big universe from childlike faith and pure, obedient, longsuffering, patient love.—*Samuel Logan Brengle.*

> O Father-Eye, that hath so truly watched;
> O Father-Hand that hath so gently led;
> O Father-Heart, that by my prayer is touched—
> That loved me first, when I was cold and dead.
>
> Still do Thou lead me on, with faithful care,
> The narrow path to Heaven, where I would go;
> And train me for the life that waits me there,
> Alike through love and loss, through weal and woe.
> —*From the German Hymn.*

Mr. John Rollo tells a story of a customer who one day went into a draper's shop and saw a small boy with outstretched arms standing while the proprietor of the shop placed package after package from the shelves into his waiting arms. As the pile grew higher and the weight heavier the customer turned to the boy saying: "My lad, you'll never be able to carry all that."

But the boy turned round and said with a smile: "My father knows how much I can carry."

Have you been burdened? Have you known trouble, or sorrow, or even bereavement? Your Father knows how much you can carry, and will with the testing make a way of escape by your being able to bear it. Your merciful Father will always grant a sufficient grace and a proportionate strength.
—*Arnold Pickering.*

The power of association

"We saw certainly that the Lord was with thee" (Gen. 26:28).
"And the master saw that the Lord was with him, and that the Lord made all that he did to prosper in his hand. And Joseph found grace in his sight"
(Gen. 39:3-4).
"It hath fully been shewed me, all that thou hast done" (Ruth 2:11).

When Lord Peterborough once visited the godly Archbishop Fénelon, he remarked: "If I stay here any longer, I shall become a Christian in spite of myself."

A friend of Bernard of Clairvaux remarked that as soon as he had entered Clairvaux, he felt that God was in the place. "Whichever way I turned, my eyes marveled and I thought I saw a new heaven and a new earth."

A peasant once told Erskine, "There is always a sense of God where you are."

And a doctor coming away from the dying bed of Horace Bushnell wrote, "Felt as I left the house a mighty conviction of spiritual realities and a desire to live in them."

The godly McCheyne once said, "How few believers carry much of the odor of Heaven along with them!"

A Persian fable says: One day
A wanderer found a lump of clay
So redolent of sweet perfume,
Its odor scented all the room.

"Who art thou?" was his quick demand,
"Art thou some gem from Samarkand,
Or Spikenard in this rude disguise,
Or other costly merchandise?"

"Nay! I am but a lump of clay."
"Then whence this wondrous sweetness—say?"
"Friend, this the secret I disclose:
I have been dwelling with the rose."
                                        —Unknown.

Secret prayer

"I have prayed for thee" (Luke 22:32).
"Daniel . . . prayed" (Dan. 6:10).
"Elisha . . . prayed" (2 Kings 4:32-33).

The great people of the earth today are the people who pray. I do not mean those who talk about prayer, or those who say they believe in prayer, or yet those who can explain about prayer; but I mean these people who *take* time and *pray.* They have not time. It must be taken from something else. This something else is important, very important, and pressing, but still less important and less pressing than prayer. There are people that put prayer first, and group the other items in life's schedule around and after prayer.

These are the people today who are doing the most for God: in winning souls; in solving problems; in awakening churches; in supplying both men and money for mission posts; in keeping fresh and strong these lives far off in sacrificial service on the foreign field where the thickest fighting is going on; in keeping the old earth sweet a while longer.

It is wholly a secret service. We do not know who these people are, though sometimes shrewd guesses may be made. I often think that sometimes we pass some plain-looking woman quietly slipping out of church—gown been turned two or three times; bonnet fixed over more than once; hands that have not known much of the softening of gloves; and we hardly give her a passing thought, and do not know, nor guess, that perhaps *she* is the one who is doing far more for her church and for the world, and for God than a hundred who would claim more attention and thought, *because she prays*, truly prays as the Spirit of God inspires and guides.

Let me put it this way: God will do as a result of the praying of the humblest one here what otherwise He would not do.—*S. D. Gordon.*

Salvation and joy

"Thou hast put gladness in my heart, more than in the time that their corn and their wine increased" (Psa. 4:7).
"But the fruit of the Spirit is love, joy, peace, longsuffering, gentleness, goodness, faith" (Gal. 5:22).

Happiness is to be a feature of religion to the last. That odious caricature of Christianity which offers to the view of the world a man with all the doctrines of the Gospel on his lips, but gloom on his brow, disquiet in his eye, and sourness in his bearing, has done infinite injustice to our benign religion, and infinite harm to those who never knew its worth. Now, as in the days of Solomon, "her ways are ways of pleasantness, and all her paths are peace." Now, as in the days of David, she "put gladness in my heart, more than in the time that their corn and their wine increased." Now, as in the days of Paul, she gives "joy and peace in believing."

Happiness is not a separable appendage of true piety: it is part of it, and an essential part: "The joy of the Lord is your strength." Some would regard happiness as if it were to religion what a fine complexion is to a human countenance—a great addition to its beauties, if present, but if not, no feature is wanting. In the sacred writings, from first to last, it is regarded as a feature which we cannot remove without both wounding and defacing. The kingdom of God is not only "righteousness," but "righteousness and peace, and joy in the Holy Ghost."—*William Arthur.*

> In the sunshine of His presence
> I cannot silent keep;
> Let those who are in darkness
> Sit down to sigh and weep.
>
> He has promised to be with me,
> So surely I must sing;
> Let those be dumb and cheerless,
> Who cannot praises bring.
>
> "In Christ," this is my watchword,
> Wellspring of joy and peace;
> For as I travel homeward,
> My praises still increase.
> —*E. S. M.*

God takes our hand

"Even there shall thy hand lead me, and thy right hand shall hold me"
(Psa. 139:10).
"I took them by the hand to lead them out" (Heb. 8:9).

The way is dark, my child! But leads to light.
I would not always have thee walk by sight.
My dealings now thou canst not understand.
I meant it so; but I will take thy hand,
> And through the gloom
> Lead safely home
> My child!

The day goes fast, my child! But is the night
Darker to Me than day? In Me is light!
Keep close to Me, and every spectral band
Of fears shall vanish. I will take thy hand,
> And through the night
> Lead up to light
> My child!

The path is rough, my child! But oh! how sweet
Will be the rest, for weary pilgrims meet,
When thou shalt reach the borders of that land
To which I lead thee, as I take thy hand;
> And safe and blest
> With Me shall rest
> My child!

The throng is great, my child! But at thy side
Thy Father walks: then be not terrified;
For I am with thee; will thy foes command
To let thee freely pass; will take thy hand,
> And through the throng
> Lead safe along
> My child!

Thy cross is heavy, child! Yet there was One
Who bore a heavier for thee: My Son,
My well-beloved. For Him bear thine; and stand
With Him at last; and, from thy Father's hand,
> Thy cross laid down,
> Receive a crown,
> My child!

—*Unknown.*

Life and life abundant

"Then said Jesus . . . I am come that they might have life, and that they might have it more abundantly" (John 10: 7, 10).
"For whosoever hath, to him shall be given, and he shall have more abundance" (Matt. 13:12).

In imagination I want you to come with me to a ward in one of our big hospitals, and here before us we see a man. He has been seriously ill for months; in fact, as we approach his bed we are hardly sure whether he is alive or dead. But, as we watch him closely, we see that his chest moves slightly, and, on feeling his pulse, we find that it still beats feebly. True, he is alive, but should the ward catch fire he is too weak to save himself, and it is quite certain that he is not strong enough to rescue anybody else. But he is alive. He has Life.

Now come with me again in imagination to Putney Bridge. Today is the Oxford and Cambridge Boat Race, and as we look over the bridge, there, almost at our feet, we see the two boats with their eight oarsmen in each. These men have been training for weeks, some for months, and today they are to go through one of the greatest ordeals that any athlete is ever asked to undergo—a race of four-and-a-quarter miles, from Putney to Mortlake, and as we watch them start we realize that their bodies are just tingling with Life. They have Life abundant.

There is a vast difference between the sick man in the hospital ward and these training athletes. The one has Life, the others Life in Abundance. There is all the difference also in the spiritual world. Some Christians have life, i.e., they are really converted people, but they know nothing of the Abundant Life which Jesus Christ came to give His people. "I am come that they might have life, and that they might have it more abundantly."—*George S. Ingram.*

> There is always something over
>   When we trust our gracious Lord;
> Every cup He fills o'erfloweth—
>   His great rivers all are broad.
> Nothing narrow, nothing stinted,
>   Ever issues from His store,
> To His own He gives full measure,
>   Running over, evermore.
>   —*Margaret E. Barber.*

Christianity on the "go"

"Go out quickly into the streets and lanes" (Luke 14:21).
"Go into the highways" (Matt. 22:9).
"Go into the village" (Matt. 21:2).
"Go into the city" (Matt. 26:18).
"Go ye and teach all nations" (Matt. 28:19).
"Go ye into all the world" (Mark 16:15).

Florence Nightingale went from her beautiful home to the bedside of dying soldiers.

Billy Bray, the miner, went into the villages around about and taught Christ and witnessed for "his Father."

Elizabeth Fry, although a mother, went into the prisons.

Robert Raikes went through the streets and gathered up the ragged children.

Whenever Christianity has flourished ordinary people have "gone" across the backyard to a neighbor; the factory worker has witnessed at the bench of a work-mate; the office girl has crossed the room to speak at another desk; and the student has taken the message to the classroom and campus.

Christianity at its best, is religion on the march. It is a mobile thing, an adventure, an experience that thrives best on the highway, not in the closet. Wesley felt his heart warmed at Aldersgate. He left that prayer-meeting to leap into the saddle. Thus the Methodist Church was born. He found his faith more virile on the highway than in the cloister.

Christianity is a "saddlebags" religion. Its genus is its ability to meet life on the run; to lead a mobile attack on the great issues men have to face. It was born on the highway in the heart of the One Who called twelve others to follow Him up and down the trails and caravan routes of Palestine.

It has been a world factor whenever it has been true to its genesis. It has failed whenever it has settled down. It is always at its best when marching into new frontiers. If the Church is to meet the challenge of today, it can do so only as it recaptures the ability to adjust itself to the extremely complex issues raised by our civilization.

Growing or standing still

*"The Lord make you to increase and abound in love one toward another"
(1 Thess. 3:12).
"Ye did run well; who did hinder you that ye should not obey the truth"
(Gal. 5:7).
"The righteous shall flourish like the palm tree; he shall grow like a cedar in
Lebanon" (Psa. 92:12).*

A flower that is arrested in its development, a tree that never reaches its full
height, a human soul that might have glorified God and have become a blessing
to men and that is inwardly crippled, that has come to a standstill because of
some inbred singularity or deformity—how painful such sights are!

Souls at a standstill—one so often meets them. There was a good beginning
once, when an hour of blessing or a longer period of special grace brought new
life-power which ought to have developed. Aspirations were born, and one
saw with joy the initial stages of inward transformation, the hopeful beginnings
of new life. Years later one meets that man again. What has happened? He
has not fallen away, or turned aside from the accepted paths. He has not gone
back to serve the world and sin, but he is stuck; his growth is at a standstill; he
is inwardly crippled and is a pathetic sight. The first zeal has died down. The
first love has grown cold. Little sins don't matter quite so much now—the
little foxes that spoil the grapes. He is content with an average spiritual life
and gives up aspiring after obviously unattainable holiness and perfection.
Instead of looking at Christ the perfect example, and letting the contemplation
of His beauty and glory transform him "from glory to glory" into His image, he
measures himself by the standard of everyday Christians, and consoles himself
over his failures with the thought of other people's faults and imperfections.

No wonder the fragrance and bloom of the divine life gradually disappear,
that the shining eyes grow dull, and that the joy in the Lord and the power of
His might dwindles away until there is nothing left but a poor human being
who is a bitter disillusionment to himself and others.—*Sister Eva.*

Let me then be always growing,
Never, never standing still,
Listening, learning, better knowing
Thee, and Thy most blessed will;
That the Master's eye may trace,
Day by day, my growth in grace.
—*John Bate.*

53

The peace of God our barometer

"Let the peace of God RULE in your hearts" (Col. 3:15).
"Now the Lord of peace himself give you peace always" (2 Thess. 3:16).

What we cannot do quietly we cannot do safely. Whatever mars our tranquility or interferes with our inward repose, is detrimental to spiritual life. If we find that a given course of action tends to break our peace, we may be certain that there is poison in the draught, which, as in the old stories, has been detected by the shivered cup, and we should not drink any more. Conscience may discern no evil, but the peace of God is a more delicate instrument, dealing with questions too subtle for conscience to answer, and operating in a higher sphere.

The peace of God will approve of nothing into which Christ cannot be introduced and assigned the seat of honor. It should be to us what the barometer is to the sailor, and if it sinks, let us take the warning. Whenever we find it in peril, we must retrace our steps. In all matters of doubt, when contending impulses and reasons distract, and seem to pull in the opposite directions, our safety is to "let the peace of God" decide which is to prevail. Under His watchful rule the soul settles down into resolute and calm obedience to the law of Christ. The hearts and lives of men are made troubled, not by circumstances, but by themselves. We are restless because our wills are not in harmony with the will of God. (From *New Testament Holiness* by Thomas Cook. Used by permission of the Epworth Press.)

With that deep hush subduing all
    Our words and works that drown
The tender whisper of Thy call,
As noiseless let Thy blessing fall
    As fell Thy manna down.

Drop Thy still dews of quietness,
    Till all our strivings cease;
Take from our souls the strain and stress
And let our ordered lives confess
    The beauty of Thy peace.

Breathe through the heats of our desire
    Thy coolness and Thy balm;
Let sense be dumb, let flesh retire;
Speak through the earthquake, wind, and fire,
    O still, small voice of calm.
                                        —*J. G. Whittier.*

The price of precious things

"That the trial of your faith, being much more precious than of gold that perisheth, though it be tried with fire, might be found unto praise and honour and glory at the appearing of Jesus Christ" (1 Peter 1:7).

There are sometimes rare and beautiful wares brought into the market that are invoiced at almost fabulous rates. Ignorant people wonder why they are priced so high. The simple reason is that they cost so much to procure. That luxurious article labeled £75 was procured by the adventurous hunter, who, at the hazard of his neck, brought down the mountain-goat, out of whose glossy hair the fabric was wrought. Yonder pearl that flashes on the brow of the bride is precious, because it was rescued from the great deep at the risk of the pearl-fisher's life, as he was lifted into the boat half-dead, with the blood gushing from his nostrils. Yonder ermine, flung so carelessly over the proud beauty's shoulder, cost terrible battles with Polar ice and hurricane. All choicest things are reckoned the dearest.

And so it is that the best part of a Christian is that which was procured at the sorest cost. Patience is a beautiful trait, but is not worn oftenest by those who walk on life's sunny side in silver slippers. It is the product of dark nights of tempest, and of those days of adversity whose high noon is but a midnight. For "the trying of your faith worketh patience." Purity of soul is like purity in gold, where the hottest fires turn out the most refined and precious metals from the crucible.—*Theodore Cuyler.*

> When other things are broken, they are nothing worth,
> Unless it be to some old Jew or some repairer;
> But hearts, the more they're bruised and broken here on earth
> In Heaven are so much the costlier and the fairer.
> —*W. R. Alger.*

Those who are broken in wealth, and broken in self-will, and broken in worldly reputation, and broken in their affections, and broken oft-times in health; those who are despised and seem utterly forlorn and helpless, the Holy Ghost is seizing upon, and using for God's glory. "The lame take the prey," Isaiah tells us. God must have broken things.

"By reason of breakings they purify themselves" (Job 41:25).

Practical Christian living

"And the very God of peace sanctify you wholly; and I pray God your whole spirit and soul and body be preserved blameless unto the coming of our Lord Jesus Christ" (1 Thess. 5:23).

Entire sanctification means the sanctification of everything. The sanctification, for example, of the daily work; that is, doing it to the Lord, and therefore doing it as well as we can. If a plowman be entirely sanctified, he will plow a straight furrow—or at least try his best to do so. If he be a mason, he will put no bad work into his walls; if a doctor, he will care more about curing his patients than about getting larger fees; if he be a minister of religion, he will strive to serve the people of his charge to the utmost of his ability. I do not believe in the entire sanctification of any man who does his daily work in a slovenly way, who keeps his books so badly that he contracts debts without knowing whether he will ever be able to pay them, and spends other people's money rather than his own. Entire sanctification means that a man will be perfectly upright in all his business transactions, even in buying and selling horses, and in paying income tax.—*Benjamin Hellier.*

Are we not princes, we who stand
As heirs beside the Throne?
We who can call the Promised Land
Our heritage, our own,
And answer to no less command
Than God's, and His alone?

Shall we upon such titles leave
The taint of sin and shame?
Shall we the children of a King
Who hold so grand a claim,
Tarnish by any meaner thing,
The glory of our name?
—*Unknown.*

You may safely trust those who make conscience of the meanest work; who, in kindling a fire or sweeping a floor, have an eye uplifted to the glory of God; who ennoble life's humblest employment by aiming at a noble end; and who address themselves to their business in the high and holy belief that when duty—however humble it may be—is well done, God is glorified.—*Dr. Guthrie.*

The privilege of prayer

"The Lord will hear when I call unto him" (Psa. 4:3).
"Then shalt thou call, and the Lord shall answer" (Isa. 58:9).

The privilege of prayer to me is one of my most cherished possessions, because faith and experience alike convince me that God Himself sees and answers, and His answers I never venture to criticize. It is only my part to ask. It is entirely His to give or withhold as He knows best. If it were otherwise, I would not dare to pray at all. In the quiet of home, in the heart of life and strife, in the face of death, the privilege of speech with God is inestimable.

I value it more because it calls for nothing that "the wayfaring man, though a fool" cannot give—that is, the simplest expression to his simplest desire. When I can neither see, nor hear, nor speak, still I can pray so that God can hear. When I finally pass through the valley of the shadow of death, I expect to pass through it in conversation with Him.—*Sir Wilfred Grenfell.*

> Who hath God within his call,
> Naught can fail him, naught appall,
> God's enough, for God is all.
> —*St. Theresa.*

When we depend upon organizations, we get what organizations can do; when we depend upon education, we get what education can do; when we depend upon man, we get what man can do; but when we depend upon prayer, we get what God can do.—*Dr. A. C. Dixon.*

> What wond'rous grace! Who knows its full extent?
> A creature, dust and ashes, speaks with God—
> Tells all his woes, enumerates his wants,
> Yea, pleads with Deity, and gains relief.
> 'Tis prayer, yes, 'tis 'effectual, fervent prayer,'
> Puts dignity on worms, proves life divine,
> Makes demons tremble, breaks the darkest cloud,
> And with a princely power prevails with God!
> And shall this privilege become a task?
> My God, forbid! Pour out Thy Spirit's grace,
> Draw me by love, and teach me how to pray.
> Yea, let Thy holy unction from above
> Beget, extend, maintain my intercourse
> With Father, Son, and Spirit, Israel's God,
> Until petitions are exchanged for praise.
> —*Irons.*

The happiness of being nothing

"Let us not be desirous of vain glory, provoking one another, envying one another" (Gal. 5:26).

"Let nothing be done through strife or vainglory; but in lowliness of mind let each esteem other better than themselves" (Phil. 2:3).

> "The beginning of greatness is to be little;
> The increase of greatness is to be less;
> And the perfection of greatness is to be nothing."
> —*Quoted by D. L. Moody.*

Some time since I took up a little book in which various persons related their own experiences. Two of them agreed in remarking that they were never happy until they ceased striving to be great men.

This remark struck me, as you know the most simple remark will strike us when Heaven pleases. It occurred to me at once that most of my sins and sufferings were occasioned by an unwillingness to be nothing which I am, and by consequent struggling to be something. I saw that if I could but cease struggling and consent to be anything or nothing, just as God pleases, I might be happy.

You will think it strange that I mention this as a new discovery. In one sense it was not new; I had known it for years. But I now saw it in a new light. My heart saw it and consented to it. And I am comparatively happy.

My dear brother, if you can give up all desire to be great and feel heartily willing to be nothing, you will be happy, too. . . . If you can stand aside from the race which too many other ministers are running and say, from your heart, "Let those who choose to engage in such a race divide the prize; let one minister run away with the money, and another with the esteem, and a third with the applause; I have something else to do, a different race to run; be God's approbation the only prize for which I run; let me obtain that, and it is enough"; I say if you can, from your heart, adopt this language, you will find most of your difficulties and sufferings vanish.—*Edward Payson.*

What anxiety and misery result from this yielding to the desire to be somebody! There is the vying among the young in the Christian Endeavor; jealousy in the Women's Guild; a race for honors among the elders or deacons. It spreads to those about us and often upsets and sometimes even tears to pieces a whole church or community. What a blessed experience shall be ours if we apply Mr. Payson's simple recipe for happiness!

The greatest day in our lives

"For ye are dead, and your life is hid with Christ in God" (Col. 3:3).
"I am crucified with Christ: nevertheless I live: yet not I, but Christ liveth in me" (Gal. 2:20).

George Müller, who built five great orphanages and maintained them by simple faith in God, when asked the secret of his service, replied: "There was a day when I died," and as he spoke he bent lower, until he almost reached the floor. Continuing, he added, "Died to George Müller, his opinions, preferences, tastes, and will; died to the world, its approval or censure; died to the approval or blame even of my brethren or friends; and since then I have studied only to show myself approved unto God."

In later life he said: "I was converted in November, 1825, and I only came into full surrender of the heart four years later, in July, 1830. The love of money was gone, the love of place was gone. God, God, God, God alone became my portion. I found my all in Him. I wanted nothing else.

"I ask affectionately, my beloved brethren, have you fully surrendered your heart to God? Or is there this thing or that with which you are taken up irrespective of God?"

If we refuse to be corns of wheat falling into the ground and dying; if we will neither sacrifice prospect nor risk character and property and health, or when we are called, relinquish home and break family ties for Christ's sake and His Gospel, then we shall abide alone.

"Buried with Christ," and raised with Him too;
What is there left for me to do?
Simply to cease from struggling and strife,
Simply to "walk in newness of life."

"Risen with Christ," my glorious Head,
Holiness now the pathway I tread;
Beautiful thought, while walking therein:
"He that is dead is freed from sin."

"Living with Christ," Who "dieth no more,"
Following Christ, Who goeth before;
I am from bondage utterly freed,
Reckoning self as "dead indeed."

—*T. Ryder.*

February 19
When love must wound love

"Let the righteous smite me; it shall be a kindness" (Psa. 141:5).
"Faithful are the wounds of a friend" (Prov. 27:6).

We must never take a one-sided idea of love. Its modes of expression are as many and varied as the needs which call it forth. We loudly acclaim the love that will forget self, pouring out its very blood in deeds of mercy to the stricken and destitute. That love, too, enthralls us, that will rise to a single act of sacrificial devotion in the hour of need. But where can we place that love that faces misunderstanding and malice, when with the knife of truth, as St. Paul aptly expresses it—"speaking the truth in love"—it wounds to heal?

The greatest evidence that our motive was only of love is that if we must wound love for its highest need, we suffer equally with the wounded. Also, that it is not an impetuous outburst of a moment, but a task to which we have given much prayer, Bible study, and reflection.

It takes great love to stir the human heart
To live beyond the others and apart.
A love that is not shallow, is not small,
Is not for one or two, but for them all.
Love that can wound love for its higher need;
Love that can leave love, though the heart may bleed;
Love that can lose love, family and friend,
Yet steadfastly live, loving, to the end.
A love that asks no answer, that can live
Moved by one burning, deathless force—to give.
Love, strength, and courage; courage, strength, and love:
The heroes of all time are built thereof.
—Charlotte Perkins Stetson.

Holy love is a consuming fire for evil. It strikes with sorrow, and what it strikes it breaks, but breaks to save. The anathemas against the Pharisee proceed from the same heart as the Beatitudes.—*Dr. Pressensé.*

There is often severity in kindness, often kindness in severity.—*H. S. Brown.*

Meditation on the word

"Meditate on these things" (1 Tim. 4:15).

"This book of the law shall not depart out of thy mouth; but thou shalt meditate therein day and night, that thou mayest observe to do according to all that is written therein: for then thou shalt make thy way prosperous, and then thou shalt have good success" (Joshua 1:8).

We must read the Book *thoughtfully.* Thoughtfulness is in danger of being a lost art. Newspapers are so numerous and literature so abundant, that we are becoming a bright but not a *thoughtful* people. Often the stream is very wide, but has no depth. Fight shallowness. Insist on reading thoughtfully. A very suggestive word in the Bible for this is "meditate." Run through and pick out this word with its variations. The word underneath that English word means to mutter, as though a man were repeating something over and over again, as he turned it over in his mind. We have another word, with the same meaning, not much used now—ruminate. We call a cow a ruminant because she chews the cud. She will spend hours chewing the cud, and then give us the rich milk and cream and butter which she has extracted from her food. That is the word here—ruminate. Chew the cud, if you would get the richest cream and butter here.

And it is remarkable how much chewing this Book of God will stand in comparison with other books.—*S. D. Gordon.*

When quiet in my house I sit,
    Thy Book be my companion still;
My joy Thy sayings to repeat,
    Talk o'er the records of Thy will,
And search the oracles divine,
Till ev'ry heartfelt word be mine.

O may the gracious words divine,
    Subject of all my converse be;
So will the Lord His follower join,
    And walk and talk Himself with me:
So shall my heart His presence prove,
And burn with everlasting love.
           —Charles Wesley.

Holy courage

"Grant unto thy servants, that with all boldness they may speak thy word"
(Acts 4:29).
"They spake the word of God with boldness" (Acts 4:31).

Holy courage is not the sort of courage that men are most acquainted with. It is what the world most needs, and yet it is what the world and worldly churchmen most criticize and hate.

Holy courage is a perpetual burning condemnation of all manner of ungodliness. It is not earth-born or brain-born; it is a celestial species of experience and character. Holy courage blooms only on the stem of an utterly pure conscience; it blossoms only under the noonday of spiritual light in the soul. He who has the consciousness of an unfettered holy courage in his inmost soul knows, to a good degree, what are the emotions of an angel. But holy courage is enthroned in the heart, and will be enthroned there only when self has been utterly crucified. Only when the love of fame and power and place and ease, only when mental pride and ecclesiastical pride, and all physical and spiritual impurity are washed away—only then does holy courage wrap the soul with unflinching bravery.

People always praise this holy courage when it does not come too close to them. Those who have yet the remains of the carnal mind admire this courage as they do a volcano—at a handsome distance.

There is as deep a need for unflinching holy boldness today as ever. Holy courage is as much needed in the pulpit as ever. It is not the gift of the Church; it does not fall from ordaining hands. It does not spring from strong nerves. It is not the product of culture, politics or military life. This holy courage comes of conscious purity and the filling baptism of the Holy Ghost.—*G. D. Watson.*

> Fearless Spirit, dwell with me,
> I myself would fearless be;
> Calm and strong amid alarms,
> Leaning on almighty arms.
> Taught in God's own school to be
> Dead to self, and one with Thee.
> —*Unknown.*

One influencing a community

"Hast thou considered my servant Job, that there is none like him in the earth, a perfect and an upright man, one that feareth God, and escheweth evil?" (Job 1:8).

Wherever a godly person enters, he is a greater blessing than if the greatest monarch were entering. So let it be with you.—*Jonathan Edwards.*

I would give more for one poor woman, whose poverty only makes her laugh and sing; who is contented with her humble lot; who bears her burdens with cheerfulness; who is patient when trouble comes upon her; who loves everyone, and who with a kind and genial spirit goes about doing good, than for all the dissertations on the doctrines of Christianity that could be written, as a means of preventing infidelity.

I have seen one such woman, who was worth more than the whole church to which she belonged and its minister put together; and I was the minister, and my church was the church.

She lived over a cooper shop. The floor of her apartment was so rude and open that you could sit there and see what the men were doing below. She had a sort of a fiend for a husband—a rough, brutal shipmaster.

She was universally called "Mother." She literally, night and day, went about doing good. I do not suppose all the ministers in the town where she lived carried consolation to so many hearts as she did. If a person was sick or dying, the people in the neighborhood did not think of sending for anyone else half so soon as for her.

I tell you, there was not much chance for an infidel to make headway there. If I wanted to convince a man of the reality of Christianity, I said nothing about historic evidence; I said, "Don't you believe Mother — is a Christian?" and that would silence him.

Where there is a whole church made up of such Christians as she was, infidelity cannot thrive. You need not be afraid of it making its way into such a church. The Word of God stands sure under such circumstances, so that nothing can successfully rise against it.—*Henry Ward Beecher.*

Rations for the day's march

"My voice shalt thou hear in the morning, O Lord: in the morning will I direct my prayer unto thee, and will look up" (Psa. 5:3).

Every day should be commenced with God and upon the knees. He begins the day unwisely who leaves his chamber without a secret conference with his heavenly Father. The true Christian goes to his closet both for his panoply and his "rations" for the day's march and its inevitable conflicts. As the Oriental traveler sets out for the sultry journey by loading up his camel under the palm tree's shade, and by filling his flagons from the cool fountains that sparkle at its roots, so doth God's wayfarer draw his fresh supply from the unexhausted spring. Morning is the golden time for devotion. The mercies of the night provoke to thankfulness. The buoyant heart that is in love with God makes his earlier flight like the lark towards the gates of Heaven. Gratitude, faith, dependent trust, all prompt to early interviews with Him Who, never slumbering Himself, waits on His throne for our morning orisons. No pressure of business nor household duties should crowd out prayer.—*Theodore Cuyler.*

Do not have your concert first, and then tune your instrument afterwards. Begin the day with the Word of God and prayer, and get first of all into harmony with Him.—*James Hudson Taylor.*

Most of us would do more for God if we would do less and spend more time in getting ready. When Luther had a specially busy and exciting day, he always allowed himself longer time than usual for his private devotions. A wise man once said he was too busy to be in a hurry; he meant that if he allowed himself to become hurried he could not do what he had to do. It is possible to have so much to do that we get nothing done. A workman would soon faint if he did not stop for meals. The mower must stop occasionally to sharpen his scythe, and it is just as necessary that busy workers should have quiet periods to renew their wasted strength and seek preparation for further usefulness and service.

(From *New Testament Holiness* by Thomas Cook. Used by permission of the Epworth Press).

"Continue in prayer, and watch in the same with thanksgiving" (Col. 4:2).

Action

"Wist ye not that I must be about my Father's business?" (Luke 2:49).
"Not slothful in business; fervent in spirit; serving the Lord" (Rom. 12:11).

Christian life is action; not a speculating, or a debating, but a *doing.* One thing, and only one, in this world has eternity stamped on it. Feelings pass; resolves and thoughts pass; opinions change. What you have done lasts—lasts in you. Through ages, through eternity, what you have done for Christ, that, and only that, you are.—*F. W. Robertson.*

> Make haste, O man, to do
> Whatever must be done;
> Thou hast no time to lose in sloth,
> Thy day will soon be gone.
>
> Up then with speed, and work;
> Fling ease and self away;
> This is no time for thee to sleep,
> Up, watch, and work and pray!
>
> The useful, not the great,
> The thing that never dies;
> The silent toil that is not lost—
> Set these before thine eyes,
> —*Horatius Bonar.*

The world will steal upon us if we do not watch continually. No man, as a Christian, should be found on the same spot two days together.

What are you waiting for? Is it some unseen event which is to lift you out of your deathly state and stranded position—that indefinite, undefined "something," which "somehow" is to put things all right? Ah, don't be deceived; tidal waves don't sweep across stagnant pools.

Depend on Christ's presence

"And, behold, I am with thee, and will keep thee in all places whither thou goest, and will bring thee again into this land; for I will not leave thee, until I have done that which I have spoken to thee of" (Gen. 28:15).
"He hath said, I will never leave thee, nor forsake thee" (Heb. 13:5).

An old writer comments upon the above passage thus: "The Greek has five negatives, and may thus be rendered: 'I will not, not leave thee, neither will I not, not forsake thee.' The precious promise, you will perceive is renewed five times, that we might have strong consolation and vigorous confidence."

It is impossible to conceive how words could be better arranged to express the unchangeable friendship of God toward those who put their trust in Him. Dr. Doddridge renders it: "I will not, I will not leave thee; I will never, never, never forsake thee."—*James Caughey.*

"With you"; not merely looking down out of the sky at you struggling in your work, but by your very side, closer than the nearest colleague, holding you by the hand, whispering words of strange power for you to use, and words of still stranger power for your own heart only, calming, and strengthening, and gladdening it; so that if you are "men wondered at" by others, you are a great deal more wondered at by yourself. You are so "marvelously helped," that you "never would have thought it!" No, of course not; but, you see, His thoughts towards you in your work were much better than yours, and you can say:

> And now I find Thy promise true,
> Of perfect peace and rest;
> I cannot sigh—I can but sing
> While leaning on Thy breast,
> And leaving everything to Thee
> Whose ways are always best.
> —*Frances Ridley Havergal.*

Industrious waiting

"The Lord is good unto them that wait for him" (Lam. 3:25).
"Neither hath the eye seen, O God, beside thee, what he hath prepared for him that waiteth for him" (Isa. 64:4).

Perhaps the greatest lesson which the lives of literary men teach us, is told in a single word—WAIT! Every man must patiently bide his time. He must wait.

We seem to live in the midst of a battle—there is such a din, such a hurrying to and fro. In the streets of a crowded city it is difficult to walk slowly. You feel the rushing of the crowd, and rush with it onward. In the press of our life it is difficult to be calm. In this stress of wind and tide, all professions seem to drag their anchors, and are swept out into the main. The voices of the present say—Come! But the voices of the past say—Wait! With calm and solemn footsteps the rising tide bears against the rushing torrent up stream, and pushes back the hurrying waters. With no less calm and solemn footsteps, nor less certainty, does a great mind bear up against public opinion, and push back its hurrying stream. Therefore, should every man wait—should bide his time. Not in listless idleness, not in useless pastime, not in querulous dejection, but in constant, steady endeavors, always willing and fulfilling, and accomplishing his task, that when the occasion comes he may be equal to the occasion. And if it never comes, what matters it to the world whether I or you, or another man, did such a deed, or wrote such a book, so be it the deed and book were well done.—*H. W. Longfellow.*

There is an old spiritual that runs:

> Slow me down, Lawd. I'se agoin' too fast,
> I can't see my brother when he's walking past.
> I miss a lot o' good things day by day,
> I don't know a blessin' when it comes my way.
> —*Unknown.*

The price of truth

"If thou criest after knowledge, and liftest up thy voice for understanding; If thou seekest her as silver, and searchest for her as for hid treasures; Then shalt thou understand the fear of the Lord, and find the knowledge of God"
(Prov. 2:3-5).

Getting saved is not like taking a holiday outing. The men and women who are full of the truth—who are walking embodiments of the truth—have not become so without effort. They have digged for truth; they have loved it; they have longed for it more than for their necessary food; they have sacrificed all for it. When they have fallen they have risen again, and when defeated they have not yielded to discouragement, but with more care and watchfulness, and greater earnestness, they have renewed their efforts for it. They have counted not their lives dear unto themselves that they might know the truth. Wealth, ease, a name among men, reputation, pleasure, everything the world holds, has been counted as dung and dross in their pursuit of truth, and just at that point where truth took precedence over all creation they found it—the truth that saves the soul, that satisfies the heart, that answers the questions of life, that brings fellowship with God, and joy unutterable, and perfect peace.

—Samuel Logan Brengle.

"Buy the truth, and sell it not" (Prov. 23:23).

> Great truths are dearly bought. The common truth,
> Such as men give and take from day to day,
> Comes in the common walk of easy life,
> Blown by the careless wind across our way.
>
> Great truths are greatly won, not found by chance,
> Nor wafted on the breath of summer dream;
> But grasped in the great struggle of the soul,
> Hard buffeting with adverse wind and stream.
>
> *—Horatius Bonar.*

Wounded to be fruitful

"Every branch that beareth fruit, he purgeth it, that it may bring forth more fruit" (John 15:2).

"Now no chastening for the present seemeth to be joyous but grievous: nevertheless afterward it yieldeth the peaceable fruit of righteousness"
(Heb. 12:11).

It is said that when Mr. Cecil was once walking, in deep dejection of spirit, in the Botanical Gardens at Oxford, his attention was arrested by a fine pomegranate cut almost through the stem. On asking the gardener the reason, he got an answer which explained the wounds of his own bleeding spirit. "Sir," he said, "this tree used to shoot so strong that it bore nothing but leaves. I was, therefore, obliged to cut it in this manner, and when it was almost cut through then it began to bear plenty of fruit."—*Denton.*

> Oh, let me suffer, till I know
> The good that cometh from the pain,
> Like seeds beneath the wintry snow,
> That wake in flowers and golden grain.

> Oh, let me suffer, till I find
> What plants of sorrow can impart;
> Some gift, some triumph of the mind,
> Some flower, some fruitage of the heart.

> The hour of anguish passes by;
> But in the spirit there remains
> The outgrowth of its agony,
> The compensation of its pains.

> In meekness, which suspects no wrong,
> In patience, which endures control,
> In faith, which makes the spirit strong,
> In peace and purity of soul.
> —*Thomas C. Upham.*

Overcoming the world

"For whatsoever is born of God overcometh the world: and this is the victory that overcometh the world, even our faith" (1 John 5:4).
"Be not overcome of evil, but overcome evil with good" (Rom. 12:21).
"He that overcometh shall inherit all things; and I will be his God, and he shall be my son" (Rev. 21:7).

Now the first thing in overcoming the world is that the spirit of covetousness in respect to worldly things and objects be overcome. The man who does not overcome this spirit of bustling and scrambling after the good which this world proffers has by no means overcome it. Overcoming the world implies rising above its engrossments. When a man has overcome the world, his thoughts are no longer engrossed and swallowed up with worldly things. A man certainly does not overcome the world unless he gets above being engrossed and absorbed with its concerns.

What is a religion good for that does not overcome the world? What is the benefit of being born into such a religion if it leave the world still swaying its dominion over our hearts? What avails a new birth which after all fails to bring us into a likeness to God, into the sympathies of His family and of His kingdom; which leaves us still in bondage to the world and to Satan? What can there be of such a religion more than the name? With what reason can any man suppose that such a religion fits his heart for Heaven, supposing it leaves him earthly-minded, sensual, and selfish?

Do the great mass of professed Christians really overcome the world? It is a fact beyond question that with them the things of this world are the realities, and the things of God are mere theories. Who does not know that this is the real state of great multitudes in the nominal church?

What are those things that set your soul on fire—that stir up your warmest emotions and deeply agitate your nervous system? Are these the things of earth, or the things of Heaven, the things of time, or the things of eternity, the things of self, or the things of God?

How is it when you go into your closet? Do you go there to seek and find God? Do you in fact find there a present God, and do you hold communion there as friend with Friend? How is this?—*Charles G. Finney.*

> Turn your eyes upon Jesus,
>   Look full in His wonderful face;
> And the things of earth will grow strangely dim
>   In the light of His glory and grace.
>   —*Helen H. Lemmel.*

March 1
Ministering circumstances

"I am among you as he that serveth" (Luke 22:27).
"Yea, every pot in Jerusalem . . . shall be holiness unto the Lord of hosts"
(Zech. 14:21).

Through whatever I am to live, I live Christ; I set upon everything the imprint of my Lord! Nothing is allowed to become an alien minister. No circumstance is allowed to raise the flag of revolt. Bengel made every circumstance in his life pay tribute to Christ. Let me quote a little extract from an exquisite little book of Thomas Boston's, whose life was abounding in labors: "Learn that heavenly chemistry of extracting some spiritual thing out of earthly things. To this end endeavor after a heavenly frame, which will, as is recorded of the philosopher's stone, turn every metal into gold. When the soul is heavenly, it will even scrape jewels out of a dunghill." All of which means that a man in Christ can make his adverse environment ideal. He can make his disappointments his ministers. He can make his adversities the King's witnesses.¯ *J. H. Jowett.*

Lord, of all pots and pans and things,
    Since I've no time to be
A saint by doing lovely things
    Or watching late with Thee,
Or dreaming in the twilight,
    Or storming Heaven's gates,
Make me a saint by getting meals,
    Or washing up the plates.

Although I must have Martha's hands
    I have a Mary mind;
And when I black the boots and shoes,
    Thy sandals, Lord, I find.
Thou Who didst love to give men food,
    In room or by the sea,
Accept this service that I do¯
    I do it unto Thee.
        —An English Servant Girl.

March 2
Faith's bright outlook

"Rejoicing in hope" (Rom. 12:12).
"We through patience and comfort of the scriptures might have hope"
(Rom. 15:4).

Unbelief paints all God's beautiful pictures of Christian hope and promise in the darkest hues. Faith grasps them and appropriates them for the individual in the darkest hours. The story is told of a little girl who had an infidel father. Anxious to instill his principles into his little daughter's mind, he hung a motto in her bedroom which read, "God is Nowhere." Faith in the heart of the little girl, however, interpreted these dark words differently. They read, "God is Now Here." Have we such a childlike faith that can read present help into the darkest suggestions of unbelieving friends and even Satan himself?

Henry Ward Beecher brings out the same thought in a little story. "A cold cinder and a burning lamp started out one day, to see what they could find. The cinder came back and wrote in its journal that the whole world was dark. It did not find a place wherever it went, in which there was light. Everywhere was darkness. The lamp when it came back, wrote in its journal, 'Wherever I went it was light. I did not find any darkness in my journey. The whole world was light.' What was the difference? The lamp carried light with it, and illumined everything about it. The dead cinder carried no light, and found none."

How incomprehensible is the love of God! His ways are indeed past finding out. How many of His providences are like the cloud between the Israelites and the Egyptians—if looked on by unbelievers, or without faith, it is a cloud of darkness; but if viewed according to the privilege of the Lord's people, it is no longer darkness, but light and safety. May this be your experience; may you feel that the Hand which inflicts the wound supplies the balm, and that He Who has emptied your heart has filled the void with Himself.—*Hudson Taylor.*

> You cannot put one little star in motion,
> You cannot shape one single forest leaf,
> Nor fling a mountain up, nor sink an ocean,
> Presumptuous pygmy, large with unbelief.
> You cannot bring one dawn of regal splendor,
> Nor bid the day to shadowy twilight fall,
> Nor send the pale moon forth with radiance tender,
> And dare you doubt the One Who has done all?
> —*Ella Wheeler Wilcox.*

Bible study necessary to prayer

"And it shall be with him, and he shall read therein all the days of his life: that he may learn to fear the Lord his God, to keep all the words of this law and these statutes, to do them" (Deut. 17:19).
"Jesus saith unto them, Did ye never read in the scriptures?" (Matt. 21:42).

There is a tendency to leave the Bible out of the closet. We hear a great deal of earnest counsel concerning secret prayer. We are urged both to open and close the day at God's feet. We are taught that prayer is the Christian's vital breath. And not a word too much can be said on this subject. If we would live strong, noble, beautiful, radiant, and useful Christian lives, we must get seasons of secret prayer into all our busy days. But we must take our Bibles with us into the closet. While we talk to God, we must also let God talk to us. God feeds us through His Word. It is *into all truth* that the Holy Spirit leads Christ's disciples. Seasons of prayer without meditation on some word of God cannot yield the full blessing that we need.—*J. R. Miller.*

Little of the Word with little Prayer is death to the spiritual life. Much of the Word with little Prayer gives a sickly life. Much Prayer with little of the Word gives emotional life. But a full measure of the Word and Prayer each day gives a healthy and powerful life.—*Andrew Murray.*

While now Thine oracles we read
    With earnest prayer and strong desire,
Oh, let Thy Spirit from Thee proceed,
    Our souls to awaken and inspire,
Our weakness help, our darkness chase,
And guide us by the light of grace.
            —*Charles Wesley.*

The "Burman Missionary" tells the story of an old man who years ago, when a heathen, came into possession of a copy of the Psalms in his native language, which had been left behind by a traveler stopping at his house. He began to read and before he had finished the book he had resolved to cast his idols away. For twenty years he worshiped the eternal God revealed to him in the Psalms, using the fifty-first (which he had committed to memory) as a daily prayer. Then having occasion to go to R—, he fell in with a white missionary, who gave him a New Testament. With joy unspeakable he read for the first time the story of salvation. "Twenty years I have walked by starlight," he said; "now I see the sun."

Losing ourselves to save others

"He saved others; himself he cannot save" (Matt. 27:42).
"And that he died for all, that they which live should not henceforth live unto themselves" (2 Cor. 5:15).

To save others, He must sacrifice Himself; to deliver others, He must surrender Himself. It must be the one or the other. He could not do both—save others and save Himself also.

God has not called us to a life of ease and enjoyment, but to a life of self-renunciation, self-crucifixion, and entire devotion to His will and redemptive purposes. Let us beware of the false enthusiasm which professes to burn for God, but is indifferent to the claims of our brother-man. Let us seek to be filled with the Christ-in-us enthusiasm which burned in the heart of the great apostle of the Gentiles—the enthusiasm which compelled him to look upon himself as a debtor to all men, and which made him the mighty spiritual force that he was in his own day, that he is in our day, and that he will be to the end of time.

The great need of the age is men, not rich men, not wise men, not learned men—we have them in abundance—but men of deep convictions, men who are conscious of the all-consuming power of the love of God, men with whom it is a passion to save men, men who are prepared to dare all things and endure all things in order to finish the work which they feel in their inmost soul that God has given them to do.

May God make us men and women of this stamp, and may we live so that those who know us best may be able to say of each one of us when we have passed away, "He saved others; himself he could not save. She saved others; herself she could not save."—*Griffith John.*

Earth's truest heroes hold their lives but lightly,
Ready to peril all for others' gain,
Thinking but little of the joy hereafter,
Only absorbed in soothing this world's pain.

Labor as Christ, with nought of self behind you,
He had no 'vantage from His death to win.
Ruler of Heaven and earth through countless ages,
Why came He, poor, unto a world of sin?

Deep in each nature lies a note heroic;
Though in the soul its music ne'er may wake,
Longing to burst self's trammels wide asunder,
Hardship enduring for its own stern sake.
—*G. F. Browning.*

Unanswered prayers

"For this thing I besought the Lord thrice, that it might depart from me. And he said unto me, My grace is sufficient for thee; for my strength is made perfect in weakness" (2 Cor. 12: 8-9).

"O my Father, if it be possible, let this cup pass from me: nevertheless not as I will, but as thou wilt" (Matt 26:39).

He was a Christian, and he prayed. He asked for strength that he might do greater things, but he was given infirmity that he might do better things. He asked for riches that he might be happy; he was given poverty that he might be wise. He asked for power that he might have the praise of men; he was given weakness that he might feel the need of God. He asked for all things that he might enjoy life; he was given life that he might enjoy all things. He received nothing that he had asked for, yet all that he had hoped for. . . . His prayer is answered; he is indeed the most blessed of men.

> I thank Thee, Lord, for my unanswered prayers,
> Unanswered save Thy quiet, kindly "Nay";
> Yet it seemed hard among my heavy cares—
> That bitter day.

> I wanted joy; but Thou didst know for me
> That sorrow was the gift I needed most,
> And in its mystic depths I learned to see
> The Holy Ghost.

> I wanted health; but Thou didst bid me sound
> The secret treasuries of pain,
> And in the moans and groans my heart oft found
> Thy Christ again.

> I wanted wealth; 'twas not the better part;
> There is a wealth with poverty oft given.
> And Thou didst teach me of the gold of heart—
> Best gift of Heaven.

> I thank Thee, Lord, for these unanswered prayers,
> And for Thy word, the quiet, kindly "Nay,"
> 'Twas Thy withholding lightened all my cares
> That blessed day.
>
> —*Dr. Oliver Huckel.*

True service lives for ever

"Thine alms are had in remembrance in the sight of God" (Acts 10:31).
"This also that she hath done shall be spoken of for a memorial of her"
(Mark 14:9).

No work done for Christ perishes. No action that helps to mold the deathless mind of a saint of God is ever lost. Live for Christ in the world and you carry with you into eternity all the results of the world's business that are worth the keeping. The river of life sweeps on, but the gold grains it held in solution are left behind deposited in the holy heart. "The world passeth away, and the lust thereof; but he that doeth the will of God abideth forever."

Worldly sharpness, acuteness, versatility, are not the qualities in request in the world to come. The honor, fame, respect, obsequious homage that attend worldly greatness up to the grave's brink will not follow it one step beyond. If this be all that we have gained by the toil of our hand or the sweat of our brow, the hour is fast coming when we shall discover that we have labored in vain and spent our strength for naught.

But while these pass, there are other things that remain. Not one unselfish thought, not one kind and gentle word, not one act of self-sacrificing love done for Jesus' sake in the midst of a man's common work, but will have left an indelible impress on the soul when he passes out to his eternal destiny.

So live, then, that this may be the result of your labors. So live that your work may become a discipline for that glorious state in which work shall be worship, and labor shall be rest; where the worker shall never quit the temple, nor the worshiper the place of work, because there is "no temple therein; for the Lord God Almighty and the Lamb are the temple of it."—*John Caird.*

Consecration is not wrapping one's self in a holy web in the sanctuary, and then coming forth after prayer and twilight meditation, and saying, "There, I am consecrated." Consecration is going out into the world where God Almighty is, and using every power for His glory. It is taking all advantages as trust funds—as confidential debts owed to God. It is simply dedicating one's life, in its whole flow, to God's service.—*Henry Ward Beecher.*

My all under God's control

"Yield yourselves unto God . . . and your members as instruments of righteousness unto God" (Rom. 6:13).
"Yield yourselves unto the Lord" (2 Chron. 30:8).

Consecration of ourselves to God is another of the duties we owe to ourselves. Every member of our body, every faculty of our mind, every moment of our time, every action of our life, appears full of importance and interest. This hand is the hand of a rational being, and ought therefore never to be used in a way unbecoming such a character. This tongue is the tongue of an accountable being, and ought therefore never to speak at random. This understanding belongs to an immortal being, and ought therefore to be used particularly in reference to subjects connected with eternity, and not to be exclusively, or principally employed about things of momentary importance. This heart is the heart of a sinner redeemed by the mercy of God. This body, this mind, this heart, have been solemnly consecrated to Christ, and I have therefore no right to use them for my own purposes, except when my interest is also the interest of the Savior.

—*John Hunt.*

Lord, what have I that I may offer Thee?
Look, Lord, I pray Thee, and see.

What is it thou hast got?
Nay, child, what is it thou hast not?
Thou hast all gifts that I have given to thee:
Offer them all to Me,
The great ones and the small,
I will accept them one and all.

I have a will, good Lord, but it is marred;
A heart both crushed and hard:
Not such as these the gift
Clean-handed lovely saints uplift.

Nay, child, but wilt thou judge for Me?
I crave not thine, but thee.

Ah, Lord, Who lovest me!
Such as I have now give I Thee.

—*Christina Rossetti.*

Clear up misunderstandings now

"Thou shalt not avenge, nor bear any grudge against the children of thy people, but thou shalt love thy neighbour as thyself: I am the Lord"
(Lev. 19:18).
"For if ye forgive men their trespasses, your heavenly Father will also forgive you" (Matt. 6:14).
"Say not thou, I will recompense evil: but wait on the Lord, and he shall save thee" (Prov. 20:22).

Oh, my dear friends, you who are letting miserable misunderstandings run on from year to year, meaning to clear them up some day; you who are keeping wretched quarrels alive because you cannot quite make up your mind that now is the day to sacrifice your pride and kill them; you who are passing men sullenly upon the street, not speaking to them out of some silly spite, and yet knowing that it would fill you with shame and remorse if you heard that one of those men were dead tomorrow morning; you who are letting your neighbor starve, till you hear that he is dying of starvation, or letting your friend's heart ache for a word of appreciation or sympathy, which you mean to give him some day, if you only could know and see and feel, all of a sudden, that "time is short," how it would break the spell! How you would go instantly and do the thing which you might never have another chance to do.—*Phillips Brooks.*

> Has my brother aught against me?
>   Have I wronged him in the past?
> Have I harbored unkind memories?
>   Have I false aspersions cast?
>
> Have I aught against my brother?
>   False? Imaginary? True?
> Have I thought him cold and distant,
>   Helped by Satan thus to view?
>
> Has some fancied hurt or slander
>   Raised some form of injured pride?
> Then forgive me, O my brother,
>   I'll not stem revival's tide.
>   —*Wesleyan Methodist.*

Praise brings victory

"By him therefore let us offer the sacrifice of praise to God continually, that is, the fruit of our lips giving thanks to his name" (Heb. 13:15).
"Thou shalt rejoice in every good thing which the Lord thy God hath given unto thee, and unto thine house" (Deut. 26:11).

No one needs to be told that the surest method to obtain new favors from an earthly benefactor is to be thankful for those which he has already bestowed.

I have somewhere met with an account of a Christian who was shipwrecked upon a desolate island while all his companions perished in the waves. In this situation he spent many days in fasting and prayer that God would open a way for his deliverance, but his prayers received no answer.

At length, musing on the goodness of God in preserving him from the dangers of the sea, he resolved to spend a day in thanksgiving and praise for this and other favors. Before the conclusion of the day a vessel arrived, and it restored him in safety to his country and friends.

Another instance equally in point we find in the history of Solomon. At the dedication of the Temple many prayers were made and many sacrifices offered without any token of the divine acceptance. But when singers and players on instruments began to thank the Lord, saying, "He is good: for his mercy endureth for ever"—then the glory of the Lord descended and filled the Temple.

The reason why praise and thanksgiving thus prevail with God is that they, above all other duties, glorify Him. "Whoso offereth praise," says He, "glorifieth me." And those who thus honor Him will be honored by Him in return.—*Edward Payson.*

> At the Name of Jesus
>   Satan's host doth flee;
> On then, Christian soldiers,
>   On to victory!
> Hell's foundations quiver
>   At the shout of praise:
> Brothers, lift your voices,
>   Loud your anthems raise!
>   —*S. Baring-Gould.*

March 10

Do something about it

"As there was a readiness to will, so there may be a performance also out of that which ye have" (2 Cor. 8:11).
"Be strong, and do it" (1 Chron. 28:10).
"Whatsoever he saith unto you, do it" (John 2:5).

In the beginning God looked out over the universal waste. Hopeless outlook! The Spirit of God moved over the face of the waters—order evolved out of chaos. He did something about it.

All was darkness—the deep, silent, echoless darkness of the eternities. God said, "Let there be light," and there was light. He did something about it.

Every mile of human progress—whether in the realm of education, of science and invention, of the alleviation of suffering, of morals or of grace—has been hewn out, inch by inch, by people who set themselves to do something about it.

Circumstances hedge you in. You feel yourself doomed to the life of defeat. It is not true. It is not true. Rise and call upon your God. The Name of Jesus Christ still casts its sacred spell.

In His Name and for His sake, *do something about it.—Arrows.*

> We shall do so much in the years to come,
>   But what have we done today?
> We shall give our gold in a princely sum,
>   But what did we give today?
>
> We shall lift the heart and dry the tear,
>   We shall plant a hope in the place of fear,
> We shall speak the words of love and cheer,
>   But what did we speak today?
>   *—Unknown.*

Piety cannot consist of specific acts only, such as prayer or ritual observances, but is bound up with all actions, concomitant with all doings, accompanying and shaping all life's business. Man's responsibility to God is the scaffold on which he stands as daily he goes on building life. His every deed, every incident of mind, takes place on this scaffold, so that unremittingly man is at work either building up or tearing down his life, his home, his hope of God.
                    —Abraham Heschel.

How to read the Bible

"How readest thou?" (Luke 10:26).
"Blessed is he that readeth" (Rev. 1:3).

Each must judge for himself what best meets his need. Many holy men of God have found blessing and food for their souls, and power for life and service, as they have read right through the Scriptures within a short period. Others again have stilled their hunger by giving themselves to prolonged, deep meditation of shorter passages in the Word. From personal experience I am convinced that thorough reading and assimilation of the Word of God is of infinitely greater value than a superficial picking here and there, or a haphazard turning up of single verses. Genuine hard work at conquering difficult passages always brings its reward in fruit and blessing. The one great essential is always that we should, whenever possible, find some practical expression in our lives for that which we have read, so that we become doers of the Word, and not hearers (or speakers) only. The Scripture revelation of the will of God must be the plumb-line of our actions, and the guiding star of our lives. Every question, great or small, must be settled in the light of the Word of God, and every circumstance of our lives find its interpretation there.—*Sister Eva.*

I supposed I knew my Bible,
  Reading piecemeal, hit and miss,
Now a bit of John, or Matthew,
  Now a snatch of Genesis. . . .
But I found that thorough reading
  Was a different thing to do,
And the way was unfamiliar
  When I read the Bible through.

We who like to scan the Bible,
  Dip and dabble here and there,
Just before we kneel a-weary,
  And yawn through a hurried prayer. . .
Try a worthier procedure,
  Try a broad and steady view;
We will kneel in very rapture,
  When we read the Bible through!
      —*Amos R. Wells.*

Christ's letter to the world

"Ye are our epistle . . . known and read of all men" (2 Cor. 3:2).
"Ye are manifestly declared to be the epistle of Christ" (2 Cor. 3:3).

The great object for which Jesus Christ came into this world, and for which His Gospel is preached, is to form godly character. Christlieb was right when he said that the "living Christian is the world's Bible," and there are millions in our land who seldom look at any other. We whose business it is to preach Christianity, must also remember that people look at us when outside of our pulpits to discover exactly what we mean when we are in our pulpits. If our conduct before the community contradicts the utterances on God's day in God's house, then the most eloquent tongue becomes a tinkling cymbal.

A certain parishioner once remarked, "My pastor's discourses are not brilliant, but his daily life is a sermon all the week." Paul stood behind all his inspired writings; the "living epistle" moves us as deeply as any words he ever sent to Rome or to Corinth.—*Theodore Cuyler.*

I am my neighbor's Bible;
    He reads me when we meet;
Today he reads me in my home;
    Tomorrow in the street.
He may be relative or friend,
    Or slight acquaintance be;
He may not even know my name;
    Yet he is reading me.

Dear Christian friends and brothers,
    If you could only know
How faithfully the world records just
    What we say and do,
Oh, we would make our record plain,
    And labor hard to see
Our worldly neighbors won to Christ,
    While reading you and me.
                              —Unknown.

The meek assured of God's guidance

"The meek will he guide in judgment: and the meek will he teach his way"
(Psa. 25:9).
"So the Lord alone did lead him, and there was no strange god with him"
(Deut. 32:12).

"How shall I know the voice of God?" comes to us as an almost complaining question. "I think that I am led of God sometimes, but the thing I undertake ends in disaster; my own soul is not satisfied, and others are not helped. I am bound to believe that I was mistaken and that it was some other voice than His which called me in that direction." Get where God wants you to be in your own soul, then your ears will be unstopped to distinguish His voice from others.—*Elizabeth S. Brengle.*

He who has a rectified musical ear knows whether the sound he hears be true harmony; he does not need first to be at the trouble of the reasonings of a mathematician about the proportion of the notes. He that has a rectified palate knows what is good food as soon as he tastes it, without the reasoning of a physician. When a holy action is suggested to a holy soul, that soul at once sees a beauty in it and closes with it. On the contrary, if an unholy action be suggested to it, its sanctified taste nauseates it. Thus a holy person is led by the Spirit.—*Jonathan Edwards.*

I never remember, in all my Christian course, a period now of sixty-nine years and four months, that I ever sincerely and patiently sought to know the will of God by the teaching of the Holy Ghost, through the instrumentality of the Word of God, but I have ALWAYS been directed rightly. But if honesty of heart and uprightness before God were lacking, or if I did not patiently wait upon God for instruction, or if I preferred the counsel of my fellowmen to the declarations of the Word of the living God, I made great mistakes.

—George Müller.

Choice gifts in plain coverings

"Judge not according to the appearance" (John 7:24).
"Do ye look on things after the outward appearance?" (2 Cor. 10:7).

> But all God's angels come to us disguised;
> Sorrow and sickness, poverty and death,
> One after other lift their frowning masks,
> And we behold the seraph's face beneath,
> All radiant with the glory and the calm,
> Of having looked upon the front of God.
> —*J. R. Lowell.*

Life is so generous a giver, but we, judging its gifts by their coverings, cast them away as ugly or heavy or hard. Remove the covering and you will find beneath it a living splendor, woven of love, by wisdom, with power. Welcome it! Grasp it, and you touch the angel's hand that brings it to you!

Everything we call a trial, a sorrow, or a duty, believe me, that angel's hand is there, the gift is there, and the wonder of an overshadowing presence. Our joys too: be not content with them as joys. They, too, conceal diviner gifts. Life is so full of meaning and purpose, so full of beauty beneath its covering that you will find earth but cloaks your heaven. Courage then to claim it: that is all! But courage you have, and the knowledge that we are pilgrims together, wending through an unknown country our way home.—*Fra Giovanni.*

> *Joy* dwells not in external things,
> It hath an inner birth;
> The sweetest bird in darkness sings,
> And fairest flowers oft nurture stings—
> Such is our life on earth.
>
> Then measure not by outward show
> The depth of real *joy;*
> The heart can o'er the darkest woe
> A stream of sunlight softly throw,
> Or purest bliss destroy.
> —*W. J. Brock.*

Radiance through prayer

"And when Aaron and all the children of Israel saw Moses, behold, the skin of his face shone" (Exod. 34:30).

"And they said one to another, Did not our heart burn within us, while he talked with us by the way, and while he opened to us the Scriptures?"
(Luke 24:32).

"My heart was hot within me, while I was musing the fire burned: then spake I with my tongue" (Psa. 39:3).

Observe but the man who is much in Heaven, and you observe he is not like others; there is something of that which he hath seen above appeareth in all his duty and conversation. Nay, take but the same man, immediately when he is returned from these views of bliss, and you perceive he excels himself. If you would set on this employment, even so would it be with you. Men would see your face shine, and say, "Surely he hath been with God."—*Richard Baxter.*

John G. Paton, the well-known missionary, had sacred childhood memories of a father who really prayed. He describes it thus:

"Our home consisted of a 'but' and a 'ben,' and a mid-room, or chamber, called the 'closet'. . . . The closet was a very small apartment betwixt the other two, having room only for a bed, a little table, and a chair, with a diminutive window shedding a diminutive light on the scene. This was the sanctuary of that cottage home. Thither daily, and oftentimes a day, generally after each meal, we saw our father retire, and 'shut to the door'; and we children got to understand, by a sort of spiritual instinct (for the thing was too sacred to be talked about), that prayers were being poured out there for us, as of old by the High Priest within the veil in the Most Holy Place. We occasionally heard the pathetic echoes of a trembling voice, pleading as for life, and we learned to slip out and in past that door on tiptoe, not to disturb the holy colloquy.

"The outside world might not know, but we knew, whence came that happy light, as of a newborn smile, that always was dawning on my father's face. It was a reflection from the Divine Presence, in the consciousness of which he lived. Never, in temple or cathedral, in mountain or in glen, can I hope to feel that the Lord God is more near, more visibly walking and talking with men, than under that humble cottage roof of thatch and oaken wattles."

Independent of circumstances

"I have learned, in whatsoever state I am, therewith to be content. I know both how to be abased, and I know how to abound: every where and in all things I am instructed both to be full and to be hungry, both to abound and to suffer need" (Phil. 4:11-12).

The other word is in Way's translation of Phil. 4:11, where he says, "I have learned in all things to be independent of circumstances." The last clause struck me forcibly. God can bring us on and on to that place where we are independent of circumstances—they will neither change us nor cause us to fret, nor will we be unduly elated when they are good, nor downcast when they are bad—these are the very days to try this thing out. Let us ask Him to make us just that— "independent of circumstances," because so dependent on Him.

—John Harrison.

When winds are raging o'er the upper ocean,
　　And billows wild contend with angry roar,
'Tis said, far down beneath the wild commotion,
　　That peaceful stillness reigneth evermore.

Far, far beneath, the noise of tempest dieth,
　　And silver waves chime ever peacefully;
And no rude storm, how fierce soe'er he flieth,
　　Disturbs the Sabbath of that deeper sea.

So, to the soul that knows Thy love, O Purest,
　　There is a temple peaceful evermore,
And all the babble of life's angry voices
　　Dies hushed in stillness at its sacred door.

—Harriet Beecher Stowe.

Peace does not dwell in outward things, but within the soul. We may preserve it in the midst of the bitterest pain, if our will remains firm and submissive. Peace in this life springs from acquiescence even in disagreeable things, not in an exemption from bearing them.—*Fénelon.*

Choose the best

"Mary hath chosen that good part" (Luke 10:42).
"Covet earnestly the best gifts: and yet shew I unto you a more excellent way" (1 Cor. 12:31).

It is not always a defect to mind one thing at a time. And an aptness so to do, to employ the whole vigor of the mind on the thing in hand, may answer excellent purposes. Only you have need to be exceeding wary, lest the thing you pursue be wrong. First, be well assured not only that it is good, but that it is the best thing for you at that time, and then, whatsoever your hand findeth to do, do it with your might.—*John Wesley.*

> God has His best things for the few
> That dare to stand the test;
> God has His second choice for those
> Who will not have His best.
>
> It is not always open ill
> That risks the Promised Rest;
> The better, often, is the foe
> That keeps us from the best. . . .
>
> Give me, O Lord, Thy highest choice;
> Let others take the rest;
> Their good things have no charm for me,
> For I have got THY best.
> —*A. B. Simpson.*

Life is so short and time so fleeting that much which one would wish to do must fain be omitted. He is fortunate who perceives at a glance what it will do, and what it will not do, to omit. This invaluable faculty, if not possessed in a remarkable degree naturally, is susceptible of cultivation to a considerable extent. Let any one adopt the practice of reflecting, every morning, what must necessarily be done during the day, and then begin by doing the most important things first, leaving the others to take their chance of being done or left undone. In this way attention first to the things of first importance soon acquires the almost irresistible force of habit, and becomes a rule of life. There is no rule more indispensable to success.—*Character and Conduct.*

Watch against temptation

"Blessed are those servants, whom the lord when he cometh shall find watching" (Luke 12:37).
"Watch and pray, that ye enter not into temptation" (Matt. 26:41).

Temptations, however, owe much of their peril and of their power to the fact that they commonly spring upon us unawares. Satan is no more likely to advertise the time and method of his assaults in advance than a burglar is to send us word that he will be trying the bolts of our front door at one o'clock tomorrow morning. "I say unto you all, Watch," is the command of our Master.—*Theodore Cuyler.*

Opportunity knocks but once only, but temptation bangs on the door repeatedly.

Kate Lee was one of the Salvation Army's best jewels. She gave up everything to become a soul-winner and earned by her sacrificing, loving care for others the name of Angel Adjutant. She says this about her severe temptations:

"I have found the need of great watchfulness, and have needed much prayer to keep my soul in touch with God and on fire for precious souls. Although I was sanctified and no longer under the power of sin, yet in his subtlety the devil has come again and again and striven to bring me down. Sometimes he has come as an angel of light, so that I have been led to the very verge of sin, tempted to indulge in what seemed at the moment harmless, perhaps because others who professed as much as I did, indulged in it too. Tempted to shrink from the sacrifice that a separated life must mean, tempted to give way to the flesh, one's natural desires and inclinations, I have even allowed the devil to take me to the edge of a great spiritual precipice, but God, in His mercy, has flashed His wonderful light upon my pathway in time to show me where I was, and what would be the outcome if I yielded to the temptation. Oh, how it caused me to pray and seek strength which enabled me to overcome!"

Life blood for lasting results

"How am I straitened (pained) till it be accomplished" (Luke 12:50).
"He shall see of the travail of his soul and shall be satisfied" (Isa. 53:11).

Service without sacrifice secures no results, no achievement, no victory that is worth the name. If we would keep our life we shall lose it, but if we empty it out in loving service we shall make it a lasting blessing to the world. No high thing can be done easily or without cost. To be consumed in God's work as "a living sacrifice" means burning up and burning out; the candle will grow shorter and the battery weaker. That is a true symbol of the consecrated life, which is inscribed on the tomb of Dr. Adam Clarke—a burning candle, with the superscription, "I give light by being myself consumed." We give light by giving up our lives to Him Who loved us. We are consumed by the zeal of His house while we carry light and salvation to those for whom He died.

(From *New Testament Holiness* by Thomas Cook. Used by permission of the Epworth Press).

A woman leaving church heavily burdened over the condition of slavery, put up a silent prayer to God to help her in a humble but effective way to smite a blow for the freedom of the slaves. Her answer came through an inspiration to write the book, *Uncle Tom's Cabin*, and being a wife and mother, she set out to write it under great difficulties. This is what it cost her: "I suffered exquisitely in writing *Uncle Tom's Cabin*," she tells us. "It may be truly said that I wrote it with my heart's blood. Many times in writing I thought my health would fail utterly, but I prayed earnestly that God would help me through." Is it any wonder that her book is still widely read?

Again, how many of us have not been greatly helped through the reading of Hudson Taylor's life by Mrs. Howard Taylor? Her writings are still blessing many although the author has gone on. Why? She tells us the secret: "How well I understand your feeling about the difference it makes HOW a life is written. This one, good as it is (a biography we had just read), seems to me to stop short of the mark, short of really reproducing in some degree the spiritual power of the life itself. It is one thing to tell about it, is it not, and another to make it, in some sense, live again? That is what I long for so much in your dear father's life: that it may live again! But that is what it costs. It counts, it is the one thing that counts. But no one knows, except the Lord Himself, all that it costs. And that is what takes TIME, as well as lifeblood. It cannot be done to order. One has to live—not merely think and write. I live in this book and for it in a way no words can tell."

March 20
Christ our environment

"The Lord is round about his people" (Psa. 125:2).
"For in him we live, and move, and have our being" (Acts 17:28).

That is the same thing as to say, "The Lord is the environment of His people"; to "be round about" is just to environ. Now the environment is a very important thing. There is nothing so sad as to be unsuited to one's environment. When you take a fish out of water it dies. Why? Because the water is its environment. When you keep a bird from the open air, it pines. Why? Because the open air is its environment. When you debar man from God, he both pines and dies. Why? Because God is his environment. Man is the only creature in this world that does not know what is good for him—does not know his own environment. The fish darts from the hook that would draw it out of the water. The bird tries to escape from the snare of the fowler. But man is very easily led away from his water of life, from his native air. He quits the real water for a painted imitation of it, the real air for a bit of colored space. Therefore he is of all creatures the most miserable.—*George Matheson.*

> As the bridegroom to his chosen,
> As the king unto his realm,
> As the keep unto the castle,
> As the pilot to the helm,
> So, Lord, art Thou to me.
>
> As the fountain in the garden,
> As the candle in the dark,
> As the treasure in the coffer,
> As the manna in the ark,
> So, Lord, art Thou to me. . . .
>
> As the ruby in the setting,
> As the honey in the comb,
> As the light within the lantern,
> As the father in the home,
> So, Lord, art Thou to me.
>
> As the sunshine to the heavens,
> As the image to the glass,
> As the fruit unto the fig-tree,
> As the dew unto the grass,
> So, Lord, art Thou to me.
> —*J. Tauler.*

Christ's love expels evil

"Perfect love casteth out fear" (1 John 4:18).

"If a man love me, he will keep my words: and my Father will love him, and we will come unto him, and make our abode with him" (John 14:23).

It is quite idle, by force of will, to seek to empty the angry passions out of our life. Who has not made a thousand resolutions in this direction, only and with unutterable mortification to behold them dashed to pieces with the first temptation? The soul is to be made sweet not by taking the acidulous fluids out, but the putting something in—a great love, God's great love. This is to work a chemical change in them, to renovate and regenerate them, to dissolve them in its own rich fragrant substance. If a man let this into his life, his cure is complete; if not, it is hopeless.—*Henry Drummond.*

R. L. Stevenson tells a story of a young man traveling in Spain, and in a lonely part, finding lodgment in an old castle. In the room he occupied there hung on the wall the picture of a beautiful but sensuous woman. Gradually the woman's face inflamed his imagination, it became an obsession which he could not shake off. Even in sleep the face haunted him, awaking within him evil thoughts and poisoning his heart and mind. Vainly he struggled against it, but without success; the image pursued him wherever he went. In this castle in which he lived he had only met the senor and his wife, both of noble origin but poor. One day, passing up the staircase, he met face to face their daughter, of whose existence even he was ignorant. Young and beautiful, their eyes met, and in that momentary glance, love, fresh and pure, awoke in his heart. Filled with its strange glow and amazement, he entered his room and looked up at the picture. Then he found its spell was gone. Instead of holding him he felt hatred and shame. The pure affection had done what no mental struggle could do.

Such is the expulsive power of a pure affection. Victory over sin is not gained by self-effort, but by opening the heart to the love of Christ. His love rushing in sweeps all foul affections out, and raises the whole being into the heights of peace and victory.—*James Burns.*

March 22

All for Christ

"I would to God, that not only thou, but also all that hear me this day, were both almost, and altogether such as I am" (Acts 26:29).
"That God may be all in all" (1 Cor. 15:28).

All our teaching about consecration will be in vain, unless it come to that—God must be *all*. What is the meaning of our talk about giving ourselves as a living sacrifice? It cannot be, unless it is actually true that in our life God is *all*. What is the reason of so much complaint of feebleness, of failure, of lost blessing, of walking in the dark? It is nothing but this: God does not get His place amongst us.—*Andrew Murray.*

The most of the difficulties of trying to live the Christian life arise from attempting to half live it.—*Henry Drummond.*

> My whole though broken heart, O Lord,
>   From henceforth shall be Thine;
> And here I do my vow record—
>   This hand, these words, are mine;
> All that I have, without reserve,
>   I offer here to Thee;
> Thy will and honor all shall serve
>   That Thou bestow'st on me.
>
> All that exceptions save I lose;
>   All that I lose I save;
> The treasures of Thy love I choose,
>   And Thou art all I crave.
> My God, Thou hast my heart and hand;
>   I all to Thee resign;
> I'll ever to this covenant stand,
>   Though flesh hereat repine.
>   —*Richard Baxter.*

I gave up all for Christ, and what have I found? I have found everything in Christ!—*John Calvin.*

To action in life's eventide

"For Zion's sake will I not hold my peace, and for Jerusalem's sake I will not rest" (Isa. 62:1).
"We his servants will arise and build" (Neh. 2:20).

C. T. Studd was a man of action and not of words. At fifty years of age, already having served in China and India as a missionary, he went out to an unevangelized part of Africa. Doctors predicted an early death, and loved ones opposed his going, but a divine purpose burned within him. God kept him going in Africa for twenty years, though his body was called a museum of tropical diseases. He died in action. Studd says:

"Too long have we been waiting for one another to begin! The time for waiting is past! The hour of God has struck! War is declared! In God's Holy Name let us arise and build! 'The God of Heaven, He will fight for us,' as we for Him. We will not build on the sand, but on the bedrock of the sayings of Christ, and the gates and minions of hell shall not prevail against us. Should such men as we fear? Before the whole world, aye, before the sleepy, lukewarm, faithless, namby-pamby Christian world, we will dare to trust our God. We will venture our all for Him, we will live, and we will die for Him, and we will do it with His joy unspeakable singing aloud in our hearts. We will a thousand times sooner die trusting only in our God, than live trusting in man. And when we come to this position the battle is already won, and the end of the glorious campaign in sight. We will have the real Holiness of God, not the sickly stuff of talk and dainty words and pretty thoughts; we will have a masculine Holiness, one of daring faith and works for Jesus Christ."

> The sunset burns across the sky
> Upon the air its warning cry;
> The curfew tolls from tower to tower,
> "Our children, 'tis the last, last hour."
> The works that past years might have done
> Must crowd the hours of setting sun;
> And through all lands Christ's saving Name
> We must in fervent haste proclaim!
> —*Unknown.*

Ministry of meditation

"O how I love thy law! It is my meditation all the day" (Psa. 119:97).
"Meditate upon these things; give thyself wholly to them; that thy profiting may appear to all" (1 Tim. 4:15).

We are to employ the ministry of meditation. I care not how unpractical the counsel may seem in this busy, hurrying, breathless day. If we men and women are ever to attain unto life and make progress in its way we have got to find time to go to school and learn. I think one of the cant phrases of our day is the familiar one by which we express our permanent want of time. We repeat it so often that by the very repetition we have deceived ourselves into believing it. It is never the supremely busy men who have got no time. So compact and systematic is the regulation of their day, that, whenever you make a demand upon them, they seem to be able to find additional corners to offer for unselfish service.

I find that when I have comparatively little to pack into my traveling-bag it seems as full as when I have much. The less we have to pack the more carelessly we pack it, and the traveling-bag appears to be full. There is many a man who says he has no time, who proclaims his day to be full, but the fullness is the result of careless packing. I confess, as a minister, that the men to whom I most hopefully look for additional service are the busiest men. They are always willing to squeeze another item into their bulging traveling-bag.

But even though our plea were legitimate, if our time were crowded, if the traveling-bag were packed, if we cannot find a corner of the day for meditation in the school of Christ, then we must take something out and make room for it.

I think if we search our bags we shall find many and many a rag which takes up space, but which is of very little worth, and which might very safely be banished. But if even all the contents were valuables, even assuming that they were pearls, the Master has declared that the secret of progressive living is to sacrifice the pearl of inferior value for the pearl of transcendent worth. Even assuming that the newspaper is not a rag, but a jewel, I do not think it wise to cram so many into one bag that there is no room for the book of Revelation, the title-deeds of "the house not made with hands, eternal in the heavens." No, if we mean truly to "live," we have got to find time for the highest of all exercises, meditation upon the eternal things of God.—*J. H. Jowett.*

The duty of plain speaking

"Seeing then that we have such hope, we use great plainness of speech"
(2 Cor. 3:12).
"The prophet that hath a dream, let him tell a dream; and he that hath my
word, let him speak my word faithfully. What is the chaff to the wheat? saith
the Lord" (Jer. 23:28).
"Great is my boldness of speech" (2 Cor. 7:4).

Luther and Knox and Wesley and Fletcher, and many others who have arrested the attention of their fellows, have been charged with bitterness of spirit and harshness of utterance. Had they contented themselves with honeyed words lisped in monotone, or an occasional refrain about the sweet by and by in a minor key, they would have not succeeded. Their hearts were on fire, and the words which flowed from their lips and pens were red hot also. Why, the things that Luther said were far stronger than anything you will hear or read today.

Shall we who live in these last days speak less plainly? Shall we whom God has called to so glorious a work be less explicit? God forbid. If the love of God is shed abroad in our hearts it will be pure and tender; it will also be true and terrible. Love utters strong words and strikes strong blows to save souls, to rescue the perishing, to glorify God. So let us one and all be kind and loving, but desperately earnest in carrying out the life-work God has given us. Time is short. Eternity will be long. We have no time to lose.—*Reader Harris.*

> Heirs of the truth they held of old,
>   The truth for which men were martyrs;
> We lack the love that made them bold,
>   Stronger than fires and waters.
>
> Brave hearts we lack, that yearn and long,
>   Touched with diviner feeling;
> The simple faith that made weak men strong,
>   True to their work and willing.
> —*Henry Hogg.*

Certainly it is possible to reconcile meekness, yea, and kindness, with the utmost plainness of speech. But this will infallibly be termed bitterness by those who do not receive it in love. Their returning us hatred for goodwill is the cross we are called to bear.—*John Wesley.*

March 26
Christis able

"Thou shalt call his name JESUS: for he shall save his people from their sins" (Matt. 1: 21).
"He brought me up also out of an horrible pit, out of the miry clay, and set my feet upon a rock, and established my goings" (Psa. 40:2).

A converted Chinaman once said, "I was down in a deep pit, half sunk in the mire, crying for someone to help me out. As I looked up I saw a venerable gray-haired man looking down at me.

"'My son,' he said, 'this is a dreadful place.'

"'Yes,' I answered, 'I fell into it; can't you help me out?'

"'My son,' was his reply, 'I am Confucius. If you had read my books and followed what they taught, you never would have been here.'

"'Yes, Father,' I said, 'but can't you help me out?'

"As I looked he was gone.

"Soon I saw another form approaching, and another man bent over me, this time with closed eyes and folded arms. He seemed to be looking to some far-off place.

"'My son,' Buddha said, 'just close your eyes and fold your arms, and forget all about yourself. Get into a state of rest. Don't think about anything that can disturb. Get so still that nothing can move you. Then, my child, you will be in such a delicious rest as I am.'

"'Yes, Father,' I answered, 'I will when I am above ground. Can't you help me out?' But Buddha, too, was gone.

"I was just beginning to sink into despair when I saw another Figure above me, different from the others. There were marks of suffering on His face. I cried out to Him, 'O Father, can You help me?'

"'My child,' He said, 'what is the matter?'

"Before I could answer Him, He was down in the mire by my side. He folded His arms about me and lifted me up; then He fed me and rested me. When I was well He did not say, 'Now, don't do that again,' but He said, 'We will walk on together now.' And we have been walking together until this day."

This was a poor Chinaman's way of telling of the compassionate love and help of the Lord Jesus.—*D. L. Moody.*

One day at a time

"The day is thine" (Psa. 74:16).

One secret of a sweet and happy Christian life is learning to live by the day. It is the long stretches that tire us. We think of life as a whole, running on for us. We cannot carry this load until we are threescore and ten. We cannot fight this battle continually for half a century. But really there are no long stretches. Life does not come to us all at one time; it comes only a day at a time. Even tomorrow is not ours till it becomes today, and we have nothing whatever to do with it but pass down to it as a fair and good inheritance today's work well done and today's life well lived.

It is a blessed secret, this of living by the day. Anyone can carry his burden, however heavy, till nightfall. Anyone can do his work, however hard, for one day. Anyone can live sweetly, patiently, lovingly, and purely till the sun goes down. And this is all that life means to us—just one little day. "Do today's duty; fight today's temptation, and do not weaken and distract yourself by looking forward to things you cannot see and could not understand if you saw them." God gives us nights to shut down the curtain of darkness on our little days. We cannot see beyond. Short horizons make life easier and give us one of the blessed secrets of brave, true and holy living.

I saw that I could no more believe for the future than I could breathe for the future, and perceived that I must be contented to live by the moment and rely upon God to sustain me in spiritual existence just as confidently as for sustainment in natural existence.—*Phoebe Palmer.*

"The just shall live by faith" (Heb. 10:38).

> One day at a time, with its failures and fears,
> With its hurts and mistakes, with its weakness and tears,
> With its portion of pain and its burden of care;
> One day at a time we must meet and must bear.
>
> One day at a time, and the day is *His* day;
> He hath numbered its hours, though they haste or delay.
> His grace is sufficient . . . we walk not alone!
> As the day, so the strength that He giveth His own.
> —*Annie Johnson Flint.*

March 28
Pain reveals our nothingness

"It is good for me that I have been afflicted" (Psa. 119:71).
"I have chosen thee in the furnace of affliction" (Isa. 48:10).

In casting up the incidental blessings of the year, I found none to compare to my illness; it gave such a life, such a reality and nearness, to my prospect of futurity; it told me in language so conclusive and intelligible, that here is no abiding city.—*Sir Thomas F. Buxton.*

Pain teaches us our nothingness. Health permits us to swell in self-esteem and gather much which is unreal; sickness makes our feebleness conspicuous, and at the same time breaks up many of our shams. We need solid grace when we are thrown into the furnace of affliction; gilt and tinsel shrivel up in the fire. The patience in which we somewhat pride ourselves, where is it when sharp pangs succeed each other like poisoned arrows setting the blood on flame? The joyful faith which could do all things, and bear all sufferings, is it always at hand when the time of trial has arrived? The peace which stood aloft on the mountain's summit and serenely smiled on storms beneath, does it hold its ground quite so easily as we thought it would when at our ease we prophesied our behavior in the day of battle?

How I have felt dwarfed and diminished by pain and depression! The preacher to thousands could creep into a nutshell, and feel himself smaller than the worm which bored the tiny round hole by which he entered. I have admired and envied the least of my Lord's servants, and desired their prayers for me, though I felt unworthy of the kind thoughts of the weakest of them.

We are most of us by far too great. A soap bubble has a scant measure of material in it for its size, and most of us are after the same order. It is greatly for our good to be reduced to our true dimensions. It is comfortable to be small; one has more room and needs less, and is better able to hide away. When storms are out a low bush or narrow eaves may shelter a sparrow, while a larger bird must bear the beat of the rain and the wind. To be nothing, and to feel less than nothing, is most sweet, for then we cower down under the great wings of God, as the little chick beneath the brooding hen, and in utter helplessness we find our strength and solace. Nothing goes but that which ought to go; the flower falls, but the seed ripens; the froth is blown away, but the wines on the lees are perfected. When nought remains but the clinging of a weeping child who grasps his Father's hand, nought but the smiting on the breast of the publican who cries, "God be merciful to me, a sinner," nought but the last resolve, "Though he slay me, yet will I trust in Him," no real loss has been sustained, say rather, a great gain has come to the humbled heart.
—*C. H. Spurgeon.*

Consult your guide book

"For whatsoever things were written aforetime were written for our learning; that we through patience and comfort of the scriptures might have hope"
(Rom. 15:4).
"For the commandment is a lamp; and the law is light" (Prov. 6:23).

If you want to hold the truth fast, and not let it slip, you must read, and read, and reread the Bible. You must constantly refresh your mind with its truths, just as the diligent student constantly refreshes his mind by reviewing his textbooks, just as the lawyer who wishes to succeed constantly studies his law books, or the doctor his medical works.

John Wesley, in his old age, after having read, and read, and reread the Bible all his life, said of himself: *"I am homo unius libri"*—a man of one book. The truth will surely slip, if you do not refresh your mind by constantly reading and meditating on the Bible.

The Bible is God's recipe book for making holy people. You must follow the recipe exactly, if you want to be a holy, Christlike person.

The Bible is God's guidebook to show men and women the way to Heaven. You must pay strict attention to its directions, and follow them accurately, if you are ever to get there.

The Bible is God's doctor's book, to show people how to get rid of soul-sickness. You must diligently consider its diagnosis of soul-diseases, and its methods of cure, if you want soul-health.—*Samuel Logan Brengle.*

When the Word of God is neglected, the inevitable consequence is—confusion in the Church, collapse in the home and chaos in the land.

> Is there a guide to show that path?
> The Bible:—he alone who hath
> The Bible, need not stray;
> Yet he who hath, and will not give
> That heavenly Guide to all that live,
> Himself shall lose the way.
> —*James Montgomery.*

Living above men's opinions

"Only be thou strong and very courageous" (Josh. 1:7).
"Be of good courage, and he shall strengthen thine heart" (Psa. 27:14).
"And he spake boldly in the name of the Lord Jesus, and disputed against the Grecians: but they went about to slay him" (Acts 9:29).

Why will you keep caring for what the world says? Try, oh! try, to be no longer a slave to it. You can have little idea of the comfort of freedom from it—it is bliss! All this caring for what people will say is from pride. Hoist your flag and abide by it. In an infinitely short space of time all secrets will be divulged. Therefore, if you are misjudged, why trouble to put yourself right? You have no idea what a great deal of trouble it will save you.

—General Gordon.

> Speak Out! and banish all thy fear;
> Speak Out! and let thy words be clear;
> Speak Out! for God shall see and hear—
> Speak Out!
> *—Unknown.*

If there be one thing upon earth that mankind loves and admires better than another, it is a brave man—a man who dares look the devil in the face and tell him he is the devil.—*James A. Garfield.*

A courageous man is one who fears God thoroughly, and fears neither man nor devil beside.—*Dr. Arnold.*

To sin by silence when they should protest makes cowards out of men.
—Abraham Lincoln.

O God, my Father, give me the even courage of Jesus, Who went quietly on, unruffled and unafraid, even though the end of the road meant disaster. I do not have to succeed. I must be true at any price, whether I succeed or fail. Give me the courage to fail, if necessary, doing the highest I know. Amen.
—S. Jones.

Blessing others

"I have received commandment to bless" (Num. 23:20).
"Then David returned to bless his household" (2 Sam. 6:20).

Every man has left behind him influences for good or for evil that will never exhaust themselves. The sphere in which he acts may be small, or it may be great. It may be his fireside, or it may be a kingdom, a village or a great nation. But act he does, ceaselessly and forever. . . .
Whatever sphere you fill, carry into it a holy heart, and you will radiate around you life and power, and leave behind you holy and beneficent influences.

—The Royal Path of Life.

He was not always singing;
Yet everywhere he went,
His quiet smile was bringing
A savor of content.

He was not always talking
Of Heaven or of God;
But those who kenned his walking,
Found flowers where he trod.

He was not always shouting
That he alone was right;
Had patience with the doubting,
Until they reached the light.

He was not always praying
Aloud, for men to hear;
His life was just displaying
The fact that God is near.

Today our lips are praising
A good man passing by;
Don't let it end with gazing:
Be like him—you and I.

—Howard T. N. Ussher.

April 1
Through weakness to strength

"Jesus saith unto them, Fill the waterpots with water" (John 2:7).

The miracle of Cana has been shining out these days. "Fill the waterpots with water," has been the watchword, undiluted weakness transmuted into undiluted strength. It seemed to me as if the first thing we expect of God is that He will tinge our water with the wine of His power. Then when we learn a little better we look for His wine, but feel it must still have an admixture of our water. It is but slowly that we come to see that the mingling is not His way with us. It is all weakness up to the brim, exchanged for His "All Power."

—*I. Lilias Trotter.*

Some people are too strong for God to do much with them. If they were weaker in themselves, they might become stronger in God.

> I am so weak, dear Lord, I cannot stand
> One moment without Thee!
> But oh! the tenderness of Thine enfolding,
> And oh! the faithfulness of Thine upholding,
> And oh! the strength of Thy right hand!
> That strength is enough for me.
> —*Frances Ridley Havergal.*

Have you learned to deal so closely with an almighty God that you know Omnipotence is working in you? In outward appearance there is often so little sign of it. The Apostle Paul said, "I was with you in weakness, and in fear, and in much trembling, and . . . my preaching was . . . in demonstration of the Spirit and of power." From the human side there was feebleness; from the divine side there was divine Omnipotence. And that is true of every godly life; and if we would only learn that lesson better, and give a wholehearted, undivided surrender to it, we should learn what blessedness there is in dwelling every morning and every hour and every moment with an almighty God.—*Andrew Murray.*

"Most gladly therefore will I rather glory in my infirmities, that the power of Christ may rest upon me" (2 Cor. 12:9).

Joy in prayer

"I thank my God upon every remembrance of you, Always in every prayer of mine for you all making request with joy" (Phil. 1:3-4).
"And at midnight Paul and Silas prayed, and sang praises unto God"
(Acts 16:25).
"Rejoice evermore. Pray without ceasing. In everything give thanks"
(1 Thess. 5:16-18).

There is no drudgery in true prayer. He to whom communion with God the Father is a task has not advanced far in grace. . . . There cannot be a more sad departure from the true spirit of prayer than to treat it as a punishment. We often feel like weeping over the millions of benighted souls to whom the gladness of prayer is perverted into sadness through sacerdotal despotism. All who through faith in Christ have boldness and access or introduction to God "make requests with joy."—*Daniel Steele.*

Go to your closet as if you were going to meet your dearest friend; cast yourself at His feet, bemoan your coldness, extol His love to you, and let your heart break with a desire to love Him. Get recollection—a dwelling within ourselves—a being abstracted from the creature and turned towards God. For want of such a frame, our times of prayer are frequently dry and useless; imagination prevails, and the heart wanders, whereas we pass easily from recollection to delightful prayer.—*John Fletcher.*

He that loveth little, prayeth little; but he that loveth much, prayeth much.
—*St. Augustine.*

From ev'ry stormy wind that blows,
From ev'ry swelling tide of woes,
There is a calm, a sure retreat;
'Tis found beneath the mercy-seat.

There is a place where Jesus sheds
The oil of gladness on our heads—
A place than all beside more sweet;
It is the bloodstained mercy-seat. . . .

There, there on eagle wing we soar,
And time and sense seem all no more;
And Heaven comes down our souls to greet,
And glory crowns the mercy-seat.
—*Hugh Stowell.*

April 3
Every Christian a soul-winner

"And as ye go, preach, saying, The kingdom of heaven is at hand" (Matt. 10:7).
"And go quickly, and tell his disciples that he is risen from the dead; and,
behold, he goeth before you into Galilee; there shall ye see him" (Matt. 28:7).

When the Master gave His great commission, "as ye go, preach," He meant
by it—as ye go, shine; as ye go, testify of Me; as ye go, heal the sick body and
the sick soul; as ye go, bear fruit, and live out the Gospel entrusted to you! It
was the sermons of heroic and holy living that shook the world and have come
down ringing and resounding through the centuries. And the preaching which
this sinning and sobbing old world of ours needs today is of the same character.
The only way in which we can hope to reproduce, in any good degree, the glory
of that apostolic era is by the same living manifestation of Jesus Christ. The
best sermon that you and I can furnish is: Christ liveth in me.

To you in these pews comes the command as directly as to me in this pulpit,
"Go ye and preach!" It comes to every child of converting grace with the gift
of that grace. No sooner does our Lord, by His Spirit, make you Christians
than He bids you become soul-winners also. "Let him that heareth say, Come."
—Theodore Cuyler.

I confess that I do not see how Christianity is ever to carry the day unless
the great bulk of our church membership becomes also a ministry. Is it possible
for any man to be a true Christian himself, and yet to be doing nothing to make
other men Christians too? Who, if he could, would like to be plodding
heavenward in a path only wide enough for one?—*Hitchcock.*

> In His furrowed fields around us,
>   God has work for all who will;
> Those who may not scatter broadcast,
>   Yet may plant it hill by hill.
>
> Yearning hearts are often near us,
>   Conscious of their Spirit-need;
> These are hills prepared by Heaven
>   To receive the precious seed.
>
> Shall we find these hills, and plant them?
>   Shall we scatter when we may?
> Or with idle hands stand waiting
>   Till the seed-time pass away?
>
> Glory waits the faithful workmen
>   Who perform their Master's will;
> Then, O Christians! will ye weary
>   Of this planting hill by hill?
>   *—A. T. Allis.*

Walking with God

"Walk humbly with thy God" (Micah 6:8).
"Noah was a just man . . . and walked with God" (Gen. 6:9).

God never goes back, and if we walk with Him, we never shall. Walking is a regular uniform motion, step by step, each one in advance of the last. It is not a rush, a leap, a spurt, but a steady progress from one point to another. Those who walk with God are not always speaking of balmy days and bright hours of fellowship that are gone. It is better with them now than ever in the past. They do not now and then climb to ecstatic heights and then descend into the valley of lukewarmness. The Christian life with them means steady progress. They go from point to point, from strength to strength, enjoying more, loving more, understanding more, receiving more, and giving more—in all respects they go forward. Such Christians are never satisfied with present experience, "the goal of yesterday is always the starting-point of today."

Napoleon believed that still further conquests were necessary to the existence of his empire, that only by pushing its bounds farther and farther could he retain the territory he had conquered. In the Christian life this is certainly true. Going forward is the only security against going back. It is much to be born of the Spirit, and still more to be filled with the Spirit, but these experiences do not exempt us from the necessity of daily progress in Divine things. By slow degrees the likeness of Christ is perfected, as day by day we sensibly dwell in the secret of His presence.

Walking with God means step by step in the will of God. A man who carries a lantern at night does not see the whole path home. The lantern lights only a single step in advance, but when that step is taken another is lighted, and so on until the end of the journey. In like manner God lights our way. He makes one step plain, and when we take that, another, and then another. We have nothing to do with life in the aggregate. Each moment brings its duties, responsibilities, burdens, and needs. Our business is to live a moment at a time, and that moment for God. Dr. Kitto's advice is, "Think not on a holy life, but on a holy moment as it flies. The first overwhelms by its immensity, the other sweetens and refreshes by its lightness and present stimulus; and yet a succession of holy moments constitutes a holy life."

(From *New Testament Holiness* by Thomas Cook. Used by permission of the Epworth Press).

So may'st thou walk! from hour to hour
　　Of every brightening year;
　　Keeping so very near
To Him, Whose power is love, Whose love is power.

So may'st thou walk! in His clear light,
　　Leaning on Him alone,
　　Thy life His very own,
Until He takes thee up to walk with Him in white.
　　　　　　　　—*Frances Ridley Havergal.*

Contentment in any sphere

"I have learned, in whatsoever state I am, therewith to be content"
(Phil. 4:11).
"I will praise thee for ever, because thou hast done it: and I will wait on thy name; for it is good before thy saints" (Psa. 52:9).

Nothing in this world can equal the religion of the Lord Jesus Christ, especially when the love of God becomes the ruling principle of the soul. To struggle with outward sin is hard work, to fight with the risings of evil nature is hard work; but when the soul receives that all-cleansing blood, when the mind enjoys this indwelling God, when He reigns alone, then we find the benefit of this great salvation. All is quiet, all is calm. You stand unmoved. Water, fire, devils, men—all cannot disturb your rest.—*William Bramwell.*

Madame Guyon, persecuted and imprisoned for her love for God and souls, could say in her imprisonment: "I passed my time in great peace, content to pass the rest of my life there if such was the will of God. I sang songs of joy, which the maid who served me learned by heart as fast as I made them, and we together sang Thy praises, O my God! The stones of my prison looked, in my eyes, like rubies. I esteemed them more than all the gaudy brilliancies of the world. My heart was full of that joy Thou givest to them that love Thee in the midst of their greatest crosses."

I sought earth's gold, and gained more greed;
I sought earth's fame, and found more need;
I sought earth's pleasures, and found more pain.
Who follows earth's phantoms follows in vain.
I heeded God's call, took up my cross;
Forsook the world—its tinseled dross;
I gave myself to God and man,
Fell in with God's unselfish plan,
And found the gold of undug mines
For fadeless crowns whence life's light shines;
And fame, beyond the hurt of years;
And joy that jewels all my tears.
Who follows Christ follows not in vain,
For life or death, with Christ, is gain.
—*Unknown.*

Use or lose

"He . . . hid his lord's money" (Matt. 25:18).
"Take therefore the talent from him" (Matt. 25:28).

God's law in the spiritual life is "use or lose." The unused faculty dies out. The capacities we have for loving and serving God are taken from us. That which was once possible becomes forever impossible. The future once open to us is closed. We are permanently crippled, limited, paralyzed, deadened.

Had we followed the openings given to us, had we used the talent committed to us, endless expansion and fullness of joy would have been ours, but now our chances are past. We have had our opportunity, we have for years been on probation, but now it is over for us. How gladly would a man renounce all that sin has brought him, if only he could stand again with his talent in hand, and all life's opportunities before him.

If there is one truth more than another on which the young may begin to build their life, it is this: that each time you decline a duty to which your better self prompts you, you become less capable of doing it; and, on the other hand, that each humble and painful effort after what is good is real growth in character.—*Marcus Dods.*

Paganini, the world-famous violinist, left his greatest treasure, his violin, to his native city of Genoa. For reasons of his own he made the single condition, that the instrument should never be played again. Today we see what a mistake this was for like all other things made of wood it deteriorated more rapidly with disuse than with the constant handling.

And now as it lies worm-eaten in its lovely case it is only valuable as a relic. What a striking reminder of a law that governs our lives. When we cease to serve others we become useless to God and to man. We must use or lose.

> It was only one talent the servant received,
> And its value of so little worth;
> But the lord of that servant was painfully grieved,
> Because it was hid in the earth. . . .
>
> The talents God gave you indeed may be few,
> It may be He gave you but one;
> But trade on the one He has given to you,
> If you hope to receive His "well-done."
> —*Unknown.*

The Bible our inheritance

"Seek ye out of the book of the Lord, and read" (Isa. 34:16).
"Heaven and earth shall pass away, but my words shall not pass away"
(Matt. 24:35).

I wonder if some of us realize what a legacy and inheritance the Bible really is—God's Word to us. It is yellow with age, and travel-stained. It has come through many ages, many hands, and many lands. It has come out of the world of Noah and his Ark, of Abraham and his flock, into a world their shepherd races could not dream of, but it has come inspired with such a power as our world can hardly understand. It comes to us, in the stress and strain of our life today, like music from a far country. It is like cooling waters in a hot and thirsty land. It is like a still small voice that speaks to a troubled soul in the night and says, "Be strong and of a good courage."

> The Book of God! And is there then a book
>   Which on its front that awful title bears?
>   Who hold it, what high duty must be theirs,
> And what high privilege, therein to look,
> To read, mark, learn, digest! But in this nook
>   Of earth, pent up and blinded by earth's cares,
>   Its hopes and joys, if man the treasure dares
> To scorn, such scorn shall the great Author brook!
>
> How longed the holy men and prophets old
>   God's truth to see! How blest, whom He hath willed
> To see His truth in His own Book enrolled!
>   Pure is the Book of God, with sweetness filled;
> More pure than massive, unadulterate gold,
>   More sweet than honey from the rock distilled.
>   *—Bishop Mant.*

If asked the remedy for the heart's deepest sorrow, I must point to "the old, old story," told in an old, old Book, and taught with an old, old teaching, which is the greatest and best gift ever given to mankind.—*William Gladstone.*

The men who have been studying the Bible for fifty years have never got down to the depths of the ever-living stream.—*D. L. Moody.*

Strength for God-given burdens

"Every man shall bear his own burden" (Gal. 6:5).
"Bear ye one another's burdens" (Gal. 6:2).
"Cast thy burden upon the Lord" (Psa. 55:22).

The Hebrew word translated "burden" really signifies that which is given to us, or that which is appointed to every man to bear. We must, therefore, understand the Psalmist to say—whatever thy God lays upon thee, thou must lay it upon the Lord. He has cast thy lot upon Him. But can this text be reconciled with the two others? Yes, quite easily. We are commanded to bear our own burdens, and this requires the resolute performance of our own duties. God will not release us from duty, but He will sustain us in the doing of it. The load which is laid upon us will not crush us, for He will give us strength equal to our day. If other people wonder why and how we march along under the load without breaking down, our only answer is, "We put this load upon the strength which God puts into us. His grace was sufficient to enable us to bear the burden."

God's wonderful and gracious offer is to lighten our loads by putting Himself, as it were, into our souls, and underneath the loads. This is a supernatural process, and the whole walk of faith through life is the simple but sublime reliance upon an almighty arm that is never seen but always felt. This accounts for the fact that the word "trust" is the keyword of Old Testament theology, and the word "believe" is the keywords in the New Testament. They both mean substantially the same thing. And when our heavenly Father saith, "Cast thy burden upon Me," and our loving Redeemer saith, "Cast the load of thy sins upon Me," They expect us to take Them at Their word.—*Theodore Cuyler.*

There is strength for the load He gives us,
And balm for the thorn He sends,
But none for the needless burdens
And none for our selfish ends.

For His yoke is easy to carry,
And His burden is light in weight;
He will do His share of the labor,
For He is a true yoke-mate.

Are we weary and heavy-laden?
Are we anxious and full of care?
That is not the cross of His giving,
But the one that we make and bear.
—*Annie Johnson Flint.*

109

God's servants are joyful

"My servants shall sing for joy of heart" (Isa. 65:14).
"Shewing the glad tidings of the kingdom of God" (Luke 8:1).

Comes there to me an embassy from a royal house in sackcloth, and smeared with dust, to represent a great king? He must account for it that he fell among robbers, and that he had a hard fight, and then show his vouchers, and I will believe that he is an ambassador. Ordinarily a king's servants represent a king by their demeanor, by their beauty of apparel, and by the abundance of the treasures they bring. What do you represent? What do people think of Christ's care of His family when they see you, querulous, anxious, sleepless, nerveless? You, without the quiver of a song; you, without one sparkle of effervescence; you, with the smoke of a wick just as it is expiring and extinguished, but not with the brightness of it—what is to be the thought of Christianity when men see you?—*Henry Ward Beecher.*

> Yes, they had been with Him, and others knew,
>   Some inner radiance made their faces shine;
> The glory of the sacred Upper Room
>   Illumined them with holy light divine.
>
> I wonder if the people know today
>   That we, too, have sweet fellowship with Him!
> Do we reflect the brightness of His love?
>   Or has that glory, with the years, grown dim?
>   —*Alice E. Sherwood.*

One of the first things the devil touches is a man's song. Test this! Why does the devil touch the song? Why does he hate praise? Because he is fallen from the heavenly choir himself. See Ezek. 28:12-19. "Thy tabrets . . . thy pipes" speak of the excellent position he held as Choirmaster of Heaven! So having lost his position, he now hates praise and song.

Singing brings the spirit up into liberty. We are no good for the fighting till we know something of this freedom inside. Therefore, get back the song.
                     —*John Harrison.*

Look up

"I will lift up mine eyes unto the hills, from whence cometh my help. My help cometh from the Lord, which made heaven and earth. . . . He that keepeth thee will not slumber" (Psa. 121:1-3).

In these first words of one of the greatest psalms of David, the nobleness which we immediately feel seems to lie in this, that David will seek help only from the highest source. "I will lift up mine eyes unto the hills, from whence cometh my help." Nothing less than God's help can really meet his needs. He will not peer into the valleys. He will not turn to fellowmen, to nature, to work, to pleasure, as if they had the relief he needed. "I will lift up mine eyes unto the hills, from whence cometh my help. My help cometh from the Lord, which made heaven and earth."

There are no times in life when opportunity, the chance to be and do, gathers so richly about the soul as when it has to suffer. Then everything depends on whether the man turns to the lower or the higher helps. If he resorts to mere expedients and tricks, the opportunity is lost. He comes out not richer nor greater; nay, he comes out harder, poorer, smaller for his pain. But if he turns to God, the hour of suffering is the turning hour of his life. Opportunity opens before him as the ocean opens before one who sails out of a river. Men have done the best and worst, the noblest and the basest things the world has seen, under the pressure of excessive pain. Everything depended on whether they looked to the depths or to the hills for help.—*Phillips Brooks.*

When the sky is black and lowering, when thy path in life is drear,
Upward lift thy steadfast glances, 'mid the maze of sorrow here.
From the beaming Fount of gladness shall descend a radiance bright;
And the grave shall be a garden, and the hours of darkness light.

For the Lord will hear and answer when in faith His people pray;
Whatso'er He hath appointed shall but work thee good alway.
E'en thy very hairs are numbered, God commands when one shall fall;
And the Lord is with His people, helping each and blessing all.

—*Unknown.*

April 11

Intercession for others

"So we fasted and besought our God for this: and he was entreated of us"
(Ezra 8:23).
"For this child I prayed; and the Lord hath given me my petition which I
asked of him" (1 Sam. 1:27).

In the records of Mrs. Beecher Stowe's life we are told that in her later years her consecration took high forms and she especially devoted herself to intercession. There came a time in her history when one who was very dear to her seemed about to sink away from the faith in which she trusted, and she set herself resolutely to avert this calamity. She put the full force of her intellect to work upon this conflict. Letter after letter found its way from her pen to the foreign town in which skepticism was doing its worst for the soul she loved. She wrote, she reasoned, she argued, she pleaded, in vain. Then she turned to her great faith. She secluded herself from all but God, and set her whole faith to labor for her soul's desire. A few weeks after a letter reached her saying, "At Christmas-time a light came to me. I see things differently now."

—*W. Robertson Nicol.*

> The weary ones had rest, the sad had joy
>   That day, and wondered "how."
> A plowman, singing at his work, had prayed,
>   "Lord, help them now."
> Away in foreign lands they wondered "how"
>   Their simple word had power.
> At home, the Christians, two or three, had met
>   To pray an hour.
> Yes, we are always wondering, wondering "how,"
>   Because we do not see
> Someone, unknown, perhaps, and far away,
>   On bended knee!
>   —*The Cleric.*

Make me sensible of real answers to actual requests, as evidence of an interchange between myself on earth and my Savior in Heaven.

—*Thomas Chalmers.*

The might of little things

"The little foxes, that spoil the vines" (Cant. 2:15).

"Dead flies cause the ointment of the apothecary to send forth a stinking savour: so doth a little folly him that is in reputation for wisdom and honour" (Eccl. 10:1).

The sum of life is made up of little things. They determine character and often decide our destiny. As the peasant's coarse frock and the monarch's robe are both made up of many small threads woven together, so is the garment of character woven together, out of the innumerable thoughts and words and deeds of each person's daily existence. It is in the little things that Bible piety makes itself most winsome, and the mischief wrought by inconsistent Christians arises from the indulgence of petty sins that are as destructive as moths upon the garment.

Dr. Maclaren pithily says that "white ants pick a carcass clean sooner than a lion will." The little meannesses of word and look, the irritations of temper, the small duplicities of speech, the "white lies" that are only whitewashed, the small affronts and petty spites, the thoughtless neglect of other people's welfare, and the paltry excuses by which we strive to excuse ourselves from painful duty—all these make up an aggregate of sin. A snowflake is a tiny thing that might melt in an infant's hand. But enough of these may be heaped up by a blizzard on a railway track to stall the most powerful engine and its train. So is it the aggregate amount of inconsistent acts and neglects of duty that impair the influence of the individual Christian; they may accumulate into snowbanks that block up revivals and bring a whole church to a standstill. No sin is a trifle; no sin can be safely allowed to get headway.

"Let that worm alone, and it will kill your tree," was said once to a gardener in a nobleman's park. The gardener neglected the little borer, and the next year's yellow leaves showed the slow assassination of the tree.

—*Theodore Cuyler.*

But what is life? Drops make the sea;
　And petty cares and small events,
　Small causes and small consequents,
Make up the sum for you and me;
　Then, oh, for strength to meet the stings
　That arm the points of little things.
—*Unknown.*

April 13
Share your blessings

"Not seeking mine own profit, but the profit of many" (1 Cor. 10:33).
"I was an hungred, and ye gave me meat: I was thirsty, and ye gave me drink: I was a stranger, and ye took me in: Naked, and ye clothed me: I was sick, and ye visited me: I was in prison, and ye came unto me" (Matt. 25:35-36).

Nothing is more pitiful than a life spent in thinking of nothing but self, yes, even in thinking of nothing but one's own soul.—*Canon Farrar.*

Nearly all of our controversies and combats arise from the fact that we are trying to get something from each other. There will be peace when our aim is to do something for each other. Society will take an immeasurable step toward peace when it estimates a citizen by his output rather than by his income.

—*W. J. Bryan.*

I had a little tea-party
    This afternoon at three;
'Twas very small, three guests in all—
    Just I, Myself, and Me.
Myself ate up the sandwiches,
    While I drank up the tea,
'Twas also I who ate the pie,
    And passed the cake to Me.
—*Unknown.*

The way to get is to scatter that you have. Give, and you shall gain. If you ask me how I shall get riches I make thee this answer—scatter that thou hast, for giving is gaining. But you must take heed and scatter it according unto God's will and pleasure: that is, to relieve the poor withal, to scatter it amongst the flock of Christ; whosoever giveth so shall surely gain, for Christ saith, "Give, and it shall be given unto you." It shall be given unto you—this is a sweet word, we can not well away with that; but how shall we come by it?— Give.—*Bishop Latimer.*

In care for the sick and poor, Christianity stands almost alone. You see but little of this anywhere but among true Christians. It is, however, an essential requisite in their character. "Pure religion and undefiled before God and the Father is this, To visit the fatherless and widows in their affliction, and to keep himself unspotted from the world."—*John Hunt.*

Those who give have all things; they who withhold, nothing.
—*Hindu Proverb.*

Keeping time with God

"My times are in thy hand" (Psa. 31:15).
"To every thing there is a season, and a time to every purpose under the heaven" (Eccl. 3:1).

Traversing one night a city street, I was startled by a sharp clanging above my head. On looking up, I found myself directly beneath the tower wherein a huge clock was striking the midnight hour. I took my watch from my pocket, and lo, the slender, overlying hands were pointing exactly to the hour of twelve. It scarcely seemed possible that that tiny piece of mechanism in my hand could keep time with the huge machinery that filled the whole room of the tower, but the proof was before me, and as I gazed at the two pairs of hands of such diverse proportions, I understood as never before that the most insignificant being needed only to be clean, in running order, and divinely regulated, to keep time with Divinity itself.—*Christian Observer.*

No matter by what routes God may see fit to lead His children, the train of deliverance and needed help will always move on schedule time. Behold Job, apparently deserted by both God and man, sitting in the ashes, a spectacle both to angels and men, a mystery to Satan; yet not forgotten by Him Whose ways are perfect. The train arrives. His latter glory is greater than the former; for a small moment he was forsaken, but with great mercies did God gather him.

Elijah goes from his retreat to find the widow who is commanded to feed him. At the gate of Zarephath a widow comes out to gather sticks to kindle her last fire, and to cook her last meal; just then the "train arrives." As he reaches the city, the widow is there. Not "a widow," but *the* widow God has spoken of. To both, this is a deliverance. Elijah finds a home; the widow, a supply to her needs until God sends plenty to all around.

To send a minister to board with a widow whose "woodpile" consisted of two sticks, and whose pantry was supplied with just enough for two meals with two to feed, may seem strange to man; but God's way is perfect.

—*The Earnest Christian.*

April 15
The Lord will provide

"Therefore take no thought, saying, What shall we eat? or, What shall we drink? or, Wherewithal shall we be clothed? (For after all these things do the Gentiles seek:) for your heavenly Father knoweth that ye have need of all these things" (Matt. 6:31-32).

Observe here particularly that we, the children of God, should be different from the nations of the earth, from those who have no Father in Heaven, and who therefore make it their great business, their first anxious concern, what they shall eat, and what they shall drink, and wherewithal they shall be clothed. We, the children of God, should, as in every other respect, so in this particular also, be different from the world, and prove to the world that we believe that we have a Father in Heaven, Who knoweth that we have need of all these things.—*George Müller.*

> Oh, this life of faith is certainly worth living,
> And there's not a moment dull throughout the year;
> For the cruse of oil is never, never failing,
> And the meal tub's always got a handful more.
> —*John Harrison.*

The Committee I work under is a conveniently small Committee, a very wealthy Committee, a wonderfully generous Committee, and is always sitting in session—the Committee of the Father, the Son and the Holy Ghost.

We have a multimillionaire to back us up, out and away the wealthiest person in the world. I had an interview with Him. He gave me a checkbook free and urged me to draw upon Him. He assured me His Firm clothes the grass of the field, preserves the sparrows, counts the hairs of the children's heads. He said the Head of the Firm promised to supply all our need, and, to make sure, One of the Partners, or rather Two, were to go along with each member of our parties, and would never leave us or fail us.

He even showed me some testimonials from former clients. A tough old chap with a long beard and hard-bitten face said that on one occasion supplies had arrived and been delivered by black ravens, and on another, by a white-winged angel. Another little old man who seemed scarred and marked all over like a walnut shell said he had been saved from death times untold, for he had determined to put to proof the assurance that he who would lose his life for the Firm's sake should find it. He told stories more wonderful than novels and Arabian Nights, of escapes and hardships, travels and dungeons, and with such a fire in his eye and laugh in his voice, added, "But out of all of them the Partner delivered me."—*C. T. Studd.*

Influencing our neighbors

"Let everyone of us please his neighbour for his good to edification"
(Rom. 15:2).
"For from you sounded out the word of the Lord . . . your faith to God-ward is spread abroad; so that we need not to speak any thing" (1 Thess. 1:8).

We do not realize the importance of the unconscious part of our life ministry. It goes on continually. In every greeting we give to another on the street, in every moment's conversation, in every letter we write, in every contact with other lives, there is a subtle influence that goes from us that often reaches further and leaves a deeper impression than the things themselves that we are doing at the time. It is not so much what we do in this world as what we are, that tells in spiritual results and impressions.—*J. R. Miller.*

We scatter seeds with careless hand,
And dream we ne'er shall see them more;
But for a thousand years
Their fruit appears,
In weeds that mar the land,
Or healthful store.

The deeds we do, the words we say—
Into still air they seem to fleet,
We count them ever past;
But they shall last—
In the dread Judgment they
And we shall meet.
—*John Keble.*

Every man is a missionary, now and forever, for good or for evil, whether he intends or designs it or not.—*Thomas Chalmers.*

If only ten of us were to apply ourselves diligently to good things, the ten would become twenty, the twenty fifty, the fifty a hundred, the hundred a thousand, and the thousand would influence the whole town.—*Chrysostom.*

George Fox, the leader of the Quakers, once said that every Quaker ought to light up the country for ten miles around. What is your influence?

Consider Him

"His name shall be called Wonderful, Counsellor, The mighty God, The everlasting Father, The Prince of Peace" (Isa. 9:6).
"The counsel of the Lord standeth for ever, the thoughts of his heart to all generations" (Psa. 33:11).

We are filled with perplexity. Life is a labyrinth, the universe is a riddle, we walk in a maze. We are at our wit's end. Wise men and philosophers cannot answer our anxious questions about the mystery of life; none can solve the problems of triumphant evil and thwarted goodness, of pain and sorrow and loss and death. And again we look, and lo! we discover that in Him "are hid all the treasures of wisdom and knowledge" (Col. 2:3). He answers our questions. He solves our riddles. We rest in Him as our *"Counselor."*

Again, we are oppressed with our utter littleness and weakness. We feel as helpless as an insect in the presence of the giant forces of the material universe. We are powerless to resist the vast world movements of men, the strikes, the conspiracies, the huge combinations, the wars, the political and social upheavals. And in our horror and despair we look again, and lo! we see Him in the earthquake and tempest, "towering o'er the wrecks of time," stilling the storm, raising the dead, calming the fierce, wild passions of men, and slowly but surely enlightening and molding the nations; and we cry out, *"The mighty God!"*

Again, we are bereft and lonely and heart-sore. We cry like an orphaned child in the night, and there is none to help, and no one understands. Then He draws nigh with infinite comprehension of our heartache and weariness and pain and with fathomless consolations He folds us in the embrace of His love; and we pillow our heads and our hearts on His bosom, and nestle close and whisper, *"The everlasting Father! The Prince of Peace!"*

—*Samuel Logan Brengle.*

He calms the strife of the warring will,
    He softens the hardest breast;
He speaketh peace to the troubled soul,
    And giveth the weary rest.
He feeds the hungry with bread from Heaven,
    And then in the thirsty strife,
He cleaves the rock in the desert way,
    And sends the water of life.
                    —*Unknown.*

Many voices have offered me a home for my quiet hours. Thou alone hast promised me a covert in my storm.—*George Matheson.*

True faith produces results

"Work out your own salvation with fear and trembling. For it is God which worketh in you both to will and to do of his good pleasure" (Phil 2:12-13). "For as the body without the spirit is dead, so faith without works is dead also" (James 2:26).

God worketh in you, therefore you can work; otherwise it would be impossible. God worketh in you, therefore you must work; otherwise He will cease from working.—*John Wesley.*

True faith should result in God's work in us, and be quickly followed by God's work through us. Devils believe, but they do no good works; they only tremble. That is about all some believers do, they tremble. Let us beware of a workless faith.—*Reader Harris.*

Don't wait for something to turn up, but turn it up yourself. The common apology for indolence, which clothes itself with the sanctity of a resignation to the Divine will has been too long employed. . . . To wait God's time in this matter (revival) is not to wait at all, and that sitting still or standing still is not the submission of piety, but an expression of the sloth and recklessness of unbelief.

It is an unhappy division that has been made between faith and works. Though in my intellect I may divide them, just as in the candle I know there is both light and heat; but yet, put out that candle, and they are both gone! One remains not without the other; so it is with faith and works.—*Selden.*

It is almost as presumptuous to think you can do nothing as to think you can do everything.—*Phillips Brooks.*

> So he died for his faith. That is fine—
>   More than most of us do.
> But stay, can you add to that line
>   That he lived for it, too? . . .
>
> But to live: every day to live out
>   All the truth that he dreamt,
> While his friends met his conduct with doubt,
>   And the world with contempt—
>
> Was it thus that he plodded ahead,
>   Never turning aside?
> Then we'll talk of the life that he led—
>   Never mind how he died.
>   —*Ernest H. Crosby.*

April 19
Godlikeness through prayer

"They looked unto him, and were radiant: and their faces were not ashamed" (Psa. 34:5—N.K.J.V.).
"And all that sat in the council, looking stedfastly on him, saw his face as it had been the face of an angel" (Acts 6:15).

He who wrestles most earnestly with God in his closet is most likely to go forth to his converse with men anointed for his mission. His garments smell of the spices of Paradise. His face shines as the face of an angel, and he unavoidably becomes in his sphere "the light of the world."—*Stephen Olin.*

The more familiar acquaintance we have with God the more do we partake of Him. He that passes by the fire may have some gleams of heat, but he that stands by it hath his color changed. It is not possible that a man should have any long conference with God and be no whit affected. If we are strangers to God it is no wonder our faces become earthly, but he that sets himself apart to God shall find a majesty and awful respect put upon him in the mind of others.
—*Bishop Hall.*

How lovely are the faces of
    The men who talk with God,
Lit with an inner sureness of
    The path their feet have trod.

How gentle is the manner of
    A man who walks with Him,
No strength can overcome him,
    And no cloud his courage dim.

Such lives are free from doubt and fear,
    While others merely plod.
But lovely faces mark the men
    Who walk and talk with God.
        —*Prosser Thomson.*

We are often surprised at the outward calmness of men who are called upon to do unpleasant and most trying deeds, but could we have seen them in secret, we should have known the moral preparation which they underwent before coming out to be seen by men. Be right in the sanctuary. Be steadfast in prayer if you would be calm in affliction. Start your race from the throne of God itself if you would run well and win the prize.—*Joseph Parker.*

Time, the stuff of life

"For what is your life? It is even a vapour, that appeareth for a little time, and then vanisheth away" (James 4:14).

"We are . . . sojourners, as were all our fathers: our days on the earth are as a shadow, and there is none abiding" (1 Chron. 29:15).

God hath given to man a short time here upon earth, and yet upon this short time eternity depends.—*Jeremy Taylor.*

> "Time is the stuff of life"—
> Then spend not thy days while they last
> In dreams of an idle future,
> Regrets for a vanished past.
> —*W. E. H. Lecky.*

Feel your pulse—it beats—what does it declare? That your time is going; for at every stroke it has one less to give. Look, therefore, on time as ever coming nearer to its end, and spend its golden moments as in your dying day you will wish to have spent them.

As a follower of Jesus, shun as much as possible such upbraiding reflections as these upon a dying bed or in the eternal world: My Savior never spent one idle moment. But, oh, how much of my time that should have honored Him was idled away! What far brighter holiness might I have reached! How much better might I have served my Lord! How much more might I have done for Him Who did so much for me, had I but well improved that time I trifled uselessly away.—*J. G. Pike.*

> Lose the day loitering, 'twill be the same story
> Tomorrow, and the next more dilatory,
> For indecision brings its own delays,
> And days are lost lamenting o'er lost days.
> Are you in earnest? Seize this very minute!
> What you can do, or think you can, begin it!
> Only engage, and then the mind grows heated;
> Begin it, and the work will be completed.
> —*Johann Wolfgang von Goethe.*

The way to life narrow

"Enter ye in at the strait gate: for wide is the gate, and broad is the way, that leadeth to destruction, and many there be which go in thereat: Because strait is the gate, and narrow is the way, which leadeth unto life, and few there be that find it" (Matt. 7:13-14).

Narrow is the road. Yes, if you are to be a Christian you must have your whole life concentrated on, and consecrated to, one thing; and, just as the vagrant rays of sunshine have to be collected into a focus before they burn, so the wandering manifoldnesses of our aims and purposes have all to be brought to a point, "This one thing I do," and whatsoever we do we have to do it as in God, and for God, and by God, and with God. Therefore, the road is narrow because, being directed to one aim, it has to exclude great tracts on either side, in which people that have a less absorbing and lofty purpose wander and expatiate at will. As on some narrow path in Eastern lands, with high, prickly-pear hedges on either side, and vineyards stretching beyond them, with luscious grapes in abundance, a traveler has to keep on the road, within the prickly fences, dusty though it may be, and though his thirsty lips may be cracking.

I remember once going to that strange island-fortress off the Normandy coast, which stands on an isolated rock in the midst of a wide sandy bay. One narrow causeway leads across the sands. Does a man complain of having to keep it? It is safety and life, for on either side stretches the tremulous sand, on which, if a foot is planted, the pedestrian is engulfed. So the narrow way which we have to travel is a highway cast up, on which no evil will befall us, while on either side stretch away out to the horizon the treacherous quicksands. Narrowness is sometimes safety. If the road is narrow it is the better guide, and they who travel along it travel safely. Restrictions and limitations are the essence of all nobleness and virtue. "So did not I because of the fear of the Lord."—*Alexander Maclaren.*

"For I determined not to know any thing among you, save Jesus Christ, and him crucified" (1 Cor. 2:2).

He chooses wisely

"He shall choose our inheritance for us" (Psa. 47:4).
"It is the Lord: let him do what seemeth him good" (1 Sam. 3:18).

In the morning of life I chose for myself—I chose the beautiful and good things set before me, and now in the evening, when the shadows are closing round, He chooses for me. If I have worn a crown of roses, shall I not gladly change it for one of thorns, if it brings me nearer? When my earthly paradise faded, and its best human companionship was withdrawn, and I was left alone, then my Lord remembered my first request—for companionship with Him. And how could He choose better than He had chosen—to share His solitude, to know the sweet and awful companionship of suffering, of darkness, of the vision of the whole world's sin, for which He was wounded to death, and of the slow hours counted in silent pain? I thank thee, O God!—*Josephine Butler.*

> Sometime, when all life's lessons have been learned,
>   And sun and stars forevermore have set,
> The things which our weak judgment here has spurned—
>   The things o'er which we grieved with lashes wet—
> Will flash before us out of life's dark night,
>   As stars shine most in deeper tints of blue;
> And we shall see how all God's plans were right,
>   And how what seemed unkind was love most true.
>
> And we shall see, that while we weep and sigh,
>   God's plans go on as best for you and me;
> How, when we called, He heeded not our cry,
>   Because His wisdom to the end could see;
> And e'en as prudent parents disallow
>   Too much of sweet to craving babyhood,
> So God, perhaps, is keeping from us now
>   Life's sweetest things, because it seemeth good. . . .
>
> If not today, be thou content, poor heart!
>   God's plans, like lilies pure and white, unfold;
> We must not tear the close-shut leaves apart;
>   Time will reveal the calyxes of gold.
> And if, through patient toil, we reach the land
>   Where tired feet, with sandals loosed, may rest,
> When we shall clearly know and understand,
>   I think that we shall say that God knew best.
>   —*Mrs. M. R. Smith.*

April 23

Work—a blessing

"Your work shall be rewarded" (2 Chron. 15:7).
"In all labour there is profit" (Prov. 14:23).

Thank God every morning when you get up that you have something to do that day, which must be done whether you like it or not. Being forced to work, and forced to do your best, will breed in you temperance and self-control, diligence and strength of will, cheerfulness and content, and a hundred virtues that the idle never know.—*Charles Kingsley.*

Work is given men only, not so much perhaps, because the world needs it. Men make work, but work makes men. An office is not the place for making money, it is a place for making men. A workshop is not a place for making machinery, for fitting engines and turning cylinders; it is a place for making souls; for fitting in the virtues to one's life; for turning out honest, modest, whole-natured men. So it is with the work of the State or the Church. This is why it never hurries—because it is as much for the worker as the work.

For one man to do too much for the world is in one sense the whole world's loss. So, it may be, God withdraws His workers, even when their hands are fullest and their souls most ripe: to fill the vacancies with still growing men, and enrich with many for the loss of one.—*Henry Drummond.*

Happy we live, when God doth fill
Our hands with work, our hearts with zeal;
For every toil if He enjoin,
Becomes a sacrifice divine,
And like the blessed spirits above,
The more we serve, the more we love.
—*Charles Wesley.*

When God comforts a man, it is very often by giving him work. The calmness of God comes to the obedient child of God.

Floods on dry ground

"Jesus stood and cried, saying, If any man thirst, let him come unto me, and drink" (John 7:37).
"I will pour water upon him that is thirsty, and floods upon the dry ground"
(Isa. 44:3).

Here is a promise to those who are thirsty! How generous God is! How He loves to open the riches of His grace! God is not content with just a shower of grace; He loves to give so that all are filled, and so He uses the word "floods." Lay hold on that word "floods," because it is the promise and the measure of God—"floods upon the dry ground."

Now this is what God offers to do for us here: in the wilderness of this world to give the water that really satisfies, that meets your need, that saves you from sin, and fills you with joy and peace in believing, that water of life that brings spiritual power and blessing.

He gives this promise to those who have failed, to those who have hindered His grace, to those who have not been true to Him, to those who have hardened their hearts. Oh, wonderful grace! Oh, wonderful love! Oh, wonderful patience and longsuffering of God! He sends this promise to failures such as we are.

Listen to what He says in Isa. 43:22: "But thou hast not called upon me." They have failed in prayer; prayer has been restrained. Friends, let us search our own hearts. Is that true of you? You might have drawn near to the Father, and come to the Throne of Grace, but you restrained prayer. You have hurried over your morning prayer; you have been too tired in the evening to pray. You have gone after other things, and not given time to prayer.

Secondly, He says, "I will pour floods upon the dry ground" (Isa. 44:3). That is revival blessing. Floods, where you do not expect it, floods where till now there has been little or nothing of the working of God's Holy Spirit, nothing but dryness and desert and wilderness.—*Barclay Buxton.*

April 25
Love much

"Ye yourselves are taught of God to love one another" (1 Thess. 4:9).
"Owe no man any thing, but to love one another" (Rom. 13:8).

To love is better, nobler, more elevating, and more sure, than to be loved. To love is to have found that which lifts us above ourselves; which makes us capable of sacrifice; which unseals the forces of another world. He who is loved has gained the highest tribute of earth; he who loves has entered into the spirit of Heaven. The love which comes to us must always be alloyed with the sad sense of our own unworthiness. The love which goes out from us is kept bright by the ideal to which it is directed.—*Bishop Westcott.*

Every year I am more convinced that the waste of life lies in the love we have not given, the powers we have not used, the selfish prudence which will risk nothing, and which, shirking pain, misses happiness as well.
—*Mary Cholmondeley.*

Love much. Earth has enough bitter in it.
    Cast sweets into its cup whene'er you can.
No heart so hard, but love at last will win it;
    Love is the grand primeval cause of man.
    All hate is foreign to the first great plan.

Love much. Your heart will be led out to slaughter
    On altars built on envy and deceit.
Love on, love on! 'Tis bread upon the water;
    It will be cast in loaves yet at your feet.
    Unleavened manna, most divinely sweet.

Love much. Your faith will be dethroned and shaken,
    Your trust betrayed by many a fair, false lure.
Remount your faith, and let new trusts awaken,
    Though clouds obscure them, yet the stars are pure;
    Love is a vital force and must endure.
—*Ella Wheeler Wilcox.*

The Bible—the light of the home

"Thy word is a lamp unto my feet, and a light unto my path" (Psa. 119:105).
"And there was a thick darkness in all the land of Egypt three days . . . but all the children of Israel had light in their dwellings" (Exod. 10:22-23).

In parlors all aflash with gaslight, and gleaming mirror, and blazing chandelier, and candelabra, there may be Egyptian darkness, while in some plain room, which a frugal hand has spread with hospitality and refinement, this one Lamp may cast a glow that makes it a fit place for heavenly coronations. We invoke no shadows to fall upon the hilarities of life. We would not have every song a dirge, and every picture a martyrdom, and every step a funeral pace. God's lamp hung in the parlor would chill no joy, would rend no harmony, would check no innocent laughter. On the contrary, it would bring out brighter colors in the picture. It would expose new gracefulness in the curtains. It would unroll new wreaths from the carpet. It would strike new music from the harp. It would throw new polish into the manners. It would kindle with light borrowed from the very throne of God all the refinements of society.

O, that the Christ Who was born in a barn would come to our parlor! We need His hand to sift the parlor music. We need His taste to assort the parlor literature. We need His voice to conduct the parlor conversation. We are apt to think of religion as being a rude, blundering thing, not fit to put its foot upon Axminster, or its clownish hands on beautiful adornments, or lift its voice amid the artistic and refined; so, while we have Jesus in the nursery when we teach our children to pray, and Jesus in the dining-hall when we ask His blessing upon our food, and Jesus in the sitting-room when we have family prayers, it is a simple fact that from ten thousand Christian homes in this country Christ is from one end of the year to the other shut out of the parlor.—*De Witt Talmage.*

"So far as I can remember, my mother never sat down and delivered to me a lecture on the subject of the Bible," writes a minister. "She did not need to. She inspired in me a feeling of reverence for the Book by the way she handled it, in turning to it in the hours of crisis, and by enthroning it in solitary splendor on the little center table." If your child never sees you read or reverence it, you may be sure that he is not likely to do differently, or to think it very important. What place does the Bible occupy in your home?

April 27

God prepares His instruments

"God hath chosen . . . the weak things of the world to confound the things which are mighty" (1 Cor. 1:27).
". . . Out of weakness were made strong" (Heb. 11:34).

Dec. 20, 1912. Somehow God tells me all my life has been a preparation for this coming ten years or more. It has been a rough discipline. Oh, the agony of it! The asthma, what has not that meant, a daily and nightly dying! The bodily weakness! The being looked down upon by the world folk! The poverty! And have I not been tempted? Tempted to stop working for Christ! Doctors! Relatives! Family! Christians! Who has not declared I tempted God by rising up, and "going at it" again? It has not been I, it has been Christ Who has carried me through. . . . Only this is a poor weak worm of a creature that God has chosen to put into the fiery furnace and walk with Him, and bring him out again. And now! Ah, yes, He seems to be pouring health and strength into me, and a burning, consuming desire to live, to live for Christ and men. Glory! Glory! It is Jesus, supreme. He is my chief love and my Chief.—*C. T. Studd.*

When Nature wants to take a man
And shake a man
And wake a man;
When Nature wants to make a man
To do the Future's will;
When she tries with all her skill
And she yearns with all her soul
To create him large and whole . . .
With what cunning she prepares him!
How she goads and never spares him,
How she whets him and she frets him,
And in poverty begets him . . .
How she often disappoints
Whom she sacredly anoints,
With what wisdom she will hide him,
Never minding what betide him
Though his genius sob with slighting
And his pride may not forget!
Bids him struggle harder yet.
Makes him lonely
So that only
God's high messages shall reach him
So that she may surely teach him
What the Hierarchy planned.
—*Angela Morgan.*

Harmony in the will of God

"Thy kingdom come. Thy will be done in earth, as it is in heaven"
(Matt. 6:10).

Suppose the members of our bodies, instead of being controlled by the will of the head, had each a separate, independent will of its own. Would they not, in this case, become useless, and even mischievous?

Something like this, you are sensible, occasionally takes place. In certain diseases the members seem to escape from the control of the will and act as if they were governed by a separate will of their own.

When this is the case, terrible consequences often ensue. The teeth shut suddenly and violently and lacerate the tongue; the elevated hands beat the face and other parts of the body; the feet refuse to support it, and it rolls in the dust, a melancholy and frightful spectacle. Such effects we call convulsions.

There are convulsions in the moral as well as in the natural world, and they take place when the will of man refuses to be controlled by the will of God. Did all men submit cordially to His will, they would live together in love and harmony and, like members of a healthy body, would all promote each other's welfare and that of the whole system. But they have refused to obey His will and have set up their own wills in opposition to it; and what has been the consequence?

Convulsions, most terrible convulsions, which have, in ten thousand thousand instances, led one member of this great body to injure another, and not only disturbed but almost destroyed the peace of society. What are wars, insurrections, revolutions? What are robberies, piracies, murders, but convulsions in the moral world—convulsions which never would have occurred had not the will of man refused to submit to the will of God.

And never will these convulsions cease, never will universal love and peace and happiness prevail, until the rebellious will of man shall again submit to the controlling will of God, and His will shall be done in earth as it is in Heaven.
—*Edward Payson.*

The best will is our Father's will,
And we may rest there calm and still;
O make it hour by hour thine own,
And wish for naught but that alone
Which pleases God.
—*Paul Gerhardt.*

"And whether one member suffer, all the members suffer with it; or one member be honoured, all the members rejoice with it" (1 Cor. 12:26).

April 29
Take time to be holy

"What, could ye not watch with me one hour?" (Matt. 26:40).
"Therefore let us not sleep, as do others; but let us watch and be sober"
(1 Thess. 5:6).

"No time to pray!"
Oh, who so fraught with earthly care
As not to give to humble prayer
Some part of day?

"No time to pray!"
'Mid each day's danger, what retreat
More needful than the mercy seat?
Who need not pray?

"No time to pray!"
Must care or business, urgent call
So press us as to take it all
Each passing day.

What thought more drear
Than that our God His face should hide,
And say, through all life's swelling tide,
"No time to hear!"

My soul, if thou wouldst muse more, the fire would burn more. Why dost thou not retire oftener with thyself? Thou wouldst be better fitted for the world if thou wert less worldly. If thou hadst more heavenly fire thou wouldst have more earthly power. Is there no secret pavilion into which thou canst go and warm thyself? Is there no holy of holies where thou canst catch a glow of impulse that will make thee strong? Is it not written of the Son of man that "as he prayed the fashion of his countenance was altered"? Yes; it was from His prayer that His transfigured glory came. It was from the glow of His heart that there issued the glow of His countenance. It was when He was musing that the fire kindled.

O my soul, wouldst thou have thy life glorified, beautified, transfigured to the eyes of men? Get thee up into the secret place of God's pavilion, where the fires of love are burning. . . . Thy prayers shall be luminous; they shall light thy face like the face of Moses when he wist not that it shone. Thy words shall be burning; they will kindle many a heart journeying on the road to Emmaus. Thy path shall be lambent; when thou hast prayed in Elijah's solitude thou shalt have Elijah's chariot of fire.—*George Matheson.*

An exalted calling

"Ye have not chosen me, but I have chosen you, and ordained you, that ye should go and bring forth fruit, and that your fruit should remain"
(John 15:16).
"He is a chosen vessel unto me, to bear my name before the Gentiles"
(Acts 9:15).

It is something to be a missionary! The morning stars sang together and all the sons of God shouted for joy when they saw the field which the first missionary was to fill. The great and terrible God, before Whom angels veil their faces, had an only Son, and He was sent to earth as a Missionary Physician.

It is something to be a follower, however feeble, in the wake of the Great Teacher and only Model Missionary that ever appeared among men. And now that He is head over all things, King of kings and Lord of lords, what commission is equal to the one the missionary holds from Him?

May I venture to invite young men of education, when laying down the plan of their lives, to take a glance at that of a missionary? For my part, I never cease to rejoice that God has appointed me to such an office.

—*David Livingstone.*

Hold high the torch; you did not light its glow—
'Twas given you by other hands, you know.
'Tis yours to keep it ever burning bright,
Yours to pass on when you no more need light.

For there are other feet that we must guide,
And other forms go marching by our side;
Their eyes are watching every smile and tear,
And efforts which may often cost us dear
Are sometimes just the very helps they need,
Actions to which their souls would give most heed;
So that in turn they'll hold the torch and say,
"I watched a friend who carried it this way. . . ."

Hold high the torch! You did not light its glow—
'Twas given you by other hands, you know.
I think it started down its pathway bright
The day the Maker said, "Let there be light."

—*Unknown.*

May 1
Man molds man

"He that walketh with wise men shall be wise: but a companion of fools shall be destroyed" (Prov. 13:20).
"Take heed to thyself, lest thou make a covenant with the inhabitants of the land whither thou goest, lest it be for a snare in the midst of thee" (Ex. 34:12).

Forces which invisibly mold our destiny are continually at work around us and within us. "All things by a law divine in another's being mingle," and there is no influence so mighty as that of spirit on spirit. We are shaped into baseness or nobleness by our companionships. They not only declare what we are, but they also make us what we are. Each man is not only forming his own character for eternity but also that of others.

When we come in contact with men we do not know what impress they leave upon us. When spiders spin their webs in bushes they leave none that you can see at midday. But the next day the dew that has lodged upon them reveals them, and then you can see that the bushes were covered with them. And the influences which men exert upon you, you often cannot see when you receive them. It is only when they are subsequently revealed in your life that you become aware of them.—*Sel.*

As diamonds are ground best with their own powder, so men are best molded by men.—*Henry Ward Beecher.*

If you are not warming the world, the world is chilling you. If you take a red-hot ball out of a furnace and lay it down upon a frosty moor, two processes will go on—the ball will lose its heat and the surrounding atmosphere will gain. There are two ways by which you equalize the temperature of a hotter and a colder body, the one is by the hot one getting cold, and the other is by the cold one getting hot. If you are not warming the world, the world is freezing you. Every man influences all about him, and receives influences from them, and if there be not more exports than imports, he is a poor creature at the mercy of circumstance.—*Alexander Maclaren.*

Our association with unholy people will either make them desire to be holy, or us to be unholy.—*Unknown.*

Stay near the Shepherd

"Be sober, be vigilant; because your adversary the devil, as a roaring lion, walketh about, seeking whom he may devour" (1 Peter 5:8).
"Submit yourselves therefore to God. Resist the devil, and he will flee from you. Draw nigh to God, and he will draw nigh to you" (James 4:7-8).

Think what a cruel mockery it were if the shepherd should say, "Little lamb, be sober, be vigilant, the old lion is about. Be not so eager after thy buttercups and daisies as to keep no sharp lookout; and if he comes upon thee, stand up bravely against him, and he will run away." Then the shepherd goeth away over the hills and home. The lamb scarce ventures so much as to nibble, in the eagerness of its watch, and in its fears. And lo, with the darkness there cometh the lion. What of watchfulness and brave resistance? One stroke of that paw, and the lamb is dead! Is that it? Then let him who knoweth anything of his own heart despair. Eat and drink, for tomorrow we die.

No; thou and I, my brother, are no match for the old lion. Be sober, be vigilant, be not so eager after anything that *thou dost suffer the Good Shepherd to go far from thee. Keep looking up that thou mayest see Him.* Thy safety is only in His presence; thou canst rest only in His shadow. Cast all the care of thy safety upon Him, and then let all thy thought and prayer and effort be to keep close to Him. The only peril lies where Peter found it, following Him afar off. John was too close to his Lord to be tempted to deny Him. Right in under that mighty Hand is the place of our resistance.

Thus the practical Apostle James puts it: "Submit yourselves therefore to God." "Resist the devil, and he will flee from you." "Draw nigh to God, and he will draw nigh to you." Our effort is to get near to God, and to keep there, *then* we are more than conquerors through Him that loved us. "I will say of the Lord, He is my refuge," where I run and hide from my foes. Then, "I will say of the Lord, He is . . . my fortress," where I turn and fight against them. "Surely he shall deliver thee."—*Mark Guy Pearse.*

May 3
Time for tasks God assigns

"I must work the works of him that sent me, while it is day: the night cometh, when no man can work" (John 9:4).
"I have finished the work which thou gavest me to do" (John 17:4).

Every one of us has some work assigned to us by God Himself. We are in the world on divine missions—sent from God to take some specific part in blessing the world.

To do this work we have just a "day" of time. Each one's day is his lifetime. A day is a brief time: it is not long from the rising to the setting of the sun. It is a fixed time: when the sun comes to his going down, no power in the universe can prolong his stay for one moment. When Death comes he will not wait one instant. Unfinished then, unfinished for ever.

Yet the day is long enough for God's plan. The sun never sets too soon for His purpose. Each little life is long enough for the little part of the world's work allotted to it. This is true even of the infant that lives but an hour, merely coming into this world, smiling its benediction, and flying away. It is true of the child, of the young man or young woman, of him who dies in maturity of his powers, with his hands yet full of unfinished tasks. No one can ever offer as an excuse for an unfulfilled life-work that the time given to him was too short. It is always long enough if only every moment of it be filled with simple faithfulness.

To have our work completed at the end, we must do it while the day lasts. Mr. McCheyne had on his watch-dial a picture of the setting sun, and over it the words, "The night cometh." Every time he looked at his watch to see the hour he was reminded of the shortness of life, and of the urgent necessity for earnestness in duty. We should all catch the lesson.—*J. R. Miller.*

> Father in Heaven, may I never wait
> Till the work of my life is begun too late!
> "Wait" is a fearful word!

Two kinds of peace

"But the wisdom that is from above is first pure, then peaceable, gentle, and easy to be entreated, full of mercy and good fruits" (James 3:17).
"He giveth quietness" (Job 34:29).

There is a peaceableness which comes *before* purity; and it is *not* beautiful. It is the gentleness of a shallow nature. There is all the difference in the world between the peace of an inland lake and the peace of the great sea. The one is calm because it is sheltered from the storm, the other because it has lulled the breeze to rest upon its bosom. Even so is it with the passions of the heart. There are lives among us which are only inland lakes. They roll not, they toss not; and yet we do not deem them beautiful. We feel that their peace has cost them no struggle; they are calm because they cannot help it. But there are other lives which are like the great sea. Theirs is not the peace of passionlessness, but of passion—of that purity called love.—*George Matheson.*

I have a treasure which I prize;
    The like I cannot find;
There's nothing like it in the earth:
    It is a quiet mind.

But 'tis not that I'm stupefied,
    Or senseless, dull, or blind;
'Tis God's own peace within my soul
    Which forms my quiet mind.

My Savior's death and risen life
    To give this were designed;
And that's the root and that's the branch
    Of this, my quiet mind.
                    —*Unknown.*

It was into the real world that Christ came, and He comes to us, not to snatch us away by some miracle from the conflict of life, but to give us His peace in our hearts, whereby we may be calmly steadfast while the conflict rages, and be able to bring to the torn world the healing of that peace.
                    —*William Temple.*

Champions for truth

"I sought for a man . . . that should . . . stand in the gap before me"
(Ezek. 22:30).
"Speak ye every man the truth to his neighbour" (Zech. 8:16).

Truth has been out of fashion since man changed his robe of fadeless light for a garment of faded leaves. Noah built and voyaged alone. His neighbors laughed at his strangeness, and perished in style. Abraham wandered and worshiped alone. Sodomites smiled at the shepherd, followed the fashion, and fed the flames. Daniel dined and prayed alone. Elijah sacrificed and witnessed alone. Jeremiah prophesied and wept alone. Jesus loved and died alone.

And of the lonely way His disciples should walk, He said, "Straight is the gate, and narrow is the way, which leadeth unto life, and few there be that find it."

Of their treatment by the many who walk in the broad way, He said, "If ye were of the world, the world would love his own; but because ye are not of the world . . . therefore the world hateth you."

The Church in the wilderness praised Abraham and persecuted Moses. The Church of the Kings praised Moses and persecuted the prophets. The Church of Caiaphas praised the prophets and persecuted Jesus. The Church of the Popes praised the Savior and persecuted the saints. And multitudes now, both in the Church and the world, applaud the courage and fortitude of the patriarchs and prophets, the apostles and martyrs, but condemn as stubbornness or foolishness like faithfulness to truth today.

Wanted today—men and women, young and old, who will obey their convictions of truth and duty at the cost of fortune and friends and life itself.

Then to side with Truth is noble when we share her wretched crust,
Ere her cause bring fame and profit, and 'tis prosperous to be just;
Then it is the brave man chooses, while the coward stands aside,
Doubting in his abject spirit, till his Lord is crucified,
And the multitude make virtue of the faith they had denied.

Count me o'er earth's chosen heroes—they were souls that stood alone
While the men they agonized for hurled the contumelious stone;
Stood serene, and down the future saw the golden beam incline
To the side of perfect justice, mastered by their faith divine,
By one man's plain truth to manhood, and to God's supreme design.
                                                    —*James R. Lowell.*

Filled when emptied

"What fellowship hath righteousness with unrighteousness? and what communion hath light with darkness? And what concord hath Christ with Belial? or what part hath he that believeth with an infidel? And what agreement hath the temple of God with idols? for ye are the temple of the living God; as God hath said, I will dwell in them" (2 Cor. 6:14-16).

The love of Thee flows just as much
As that of ebbing self subsides;
Our hearts (their scantiness is such)
Bear not the conflict of two rival tides.

Both cannot govern in one soul;
Then let self-love be dispossess'd;
The love of God deserves the whole,
And will not dwell with so despised a guest.
—*Madame Guyon.*

I firmly believe that the moment our hearts are emptied of pride, selfishness, ambition, self-seeking, and everything that is contrary to God's law, the Holy Ghost will come and fill every corner of our hearts. But if we are full of pride, conceit, ambition, self-seeking, pleasure, and the world, there is no room for the Spirit of God. I believe many a man is praying to God to fill him when he is full already with something else.—*D. L. Moody.*

If thou couldst empty all thyself of self,
Like to a shell dishabited,
Then might He find thee on the ocean shelf
And say, "This is not dead,"
And fill thee with Himself instead:

But thou art all replete with very thou,
And hast such shrewd activity,
That, when He comes, He says, "This is enow
Unto itself—'Twere better let it be:
It is so small and full, there is no room for Me."
—*T. E. Brown.*

"There was no room . . . in the inn" (Luke 2:7).

A test of true greatness

"Confess your faults one to another, and pray one for another, that ye may be healed" (James 5:16).
"I do remember my faults this day" (Gen. 41:9).

True greatness never shows better than in the acknowledgment of wrong.
—*Unknown.*

Be always ready to own any fault you have been in. If you have at any time thought, spoken or acted wrong, be not backward to acknowledge it. Never dream that this will hurt the cause of God; no, it will further it. Be, therefore, open and frank when you are taxed with anything; do not seek either to evade or disguise it, but let it appear just as it is, and you will thereby not hinder, but adorn the Gospel.—*John Wesley.*

Humbling ourselves is sweeter than being humiliated.—*Reader Harris.*

A man should never be ashamed to own that he has been in the wrong, which is but saying that he is wiser today than he was yesterday.
—*Alexander Pope.*

The blessedness of owning one's fault is shown by the frank and illuminating admission of St. Theresa. After stating her lack of ability as a singer, she proceeds:

"I saw that some other novices could instruct me. But I was too proud to ask any questions. I was afraid that my great ignorance should be discovered. Shortly afterwards a good example was set before me, and then, when God had once opened my eyes to my sinful pride, I was content to ask information and help even of little children. And yet, and this surprised me, I lost no credit or honor thereby. Nay, it seemed to me that my Lord after that gave me better skill and a better memory. I could sing but very ill, and I was troubled at this, not because I failed in my worship of God, but because so many heard me, and thus I was disturbed on the mere point of honor and praise. I told them that I could not do what others did, and what was expected of me. At first I had some difficulty in this, but it soon became both natural and pleasant to me to tell the truth. By these nothings—and they are really nothings and I am sufficiently nothing when such things could put me to so much pain—and by little and little, His Divine Majesty vouchsafed to supply me with strength. I was never good at the choir, and I tried to do my part for it in folding up the mantles of the singers; and, methought, in that I was serving the angels of God who so well praised Him."

Peace through prayer

"And great shall be the peace of thy children" (Isa. 54:13).
"But thou hast not called upon me, O Jacob; but thou hast been weary of me, O Israel" (Isa. 43:22).

How many professing Christians suffer from fears, trials, temptations, and irritabilities that would be needless if they had spent time with God in quiet. God gives a calm trust and other special delights to those who pray.

Many of us could trace the cause of our restlessness and worry to the same difficulty as the little girl in the following story:

One night the mother of two little girls was away at bedtime, and they were left to do as they would.

"I'm not going to pray tonight," said Lillian, when she was ready for bed.

"Why, Lillian!" exclaimed Amy, with round eyes of astonishment.

"I don't care; I'm not going to. There isn't any use."

So she tumbled into bed, while Amy knelt and prayed. The little prayer finished, and light extinguished, Amy crept into bed. There was a long silence; then Lillian began to turn restlessly, giving her pillow a vigorous thump and saying crossly: "I wonder what is the matter with this pillow?"

Then came a sweet little voice from Amy's side—"I guess it's 'cause there isn't any prayer in it."

A few minutes more of restlessness and Lillian was out of bed and knelt in prayer. Then all was quiet and peaceful, and the two little girls slept.

Dear child of God, is there a prayer in your pillow when you go to sleep at night?

Prayer is a safety-valve for the mind and the soul. If Christianity were practically applied to our everyday life, it would so purify and vitalize the race that at least one-half of our sickness and sorrow would disappear.

—*Dr. William Sadler.*

Sweet hour of prayer! sweet hour of prayer!
That calls me from a world of care,
And bids me, at my Father's throne,
Make all my wants and wishes known;
In seasons of distress and grief
My soul has often found relief,
And oft escaped the tempter's snare
By thy return, sweet hour of prayer.

—*William Walford.*

Joy where Christ reigns

"These things I speak in the world, that they might have my joy fulfilled in themselves" (John 17:13).
"In thy presence is fulness of joy" (Psa. 16:11).

The filling of the Holy Ghost will bring us joy and fullness of joy. The fullness of the Spirit must crowd out pain, doubt, fear, and sorrow, and bring the joy of Christ to fill our being. What is it makes the melody in an organ? It is not the touch of skillful fingers only on the keys, but it is the filling of the pipes by the movement of the pedals. I may try in vain to play the most skillful tune, unless the organ is filled; and so our songs of praise are dead and cold until the breath of God fills all the channels of our being. Then comes the heart-song of praise and the overflowing fountain of gladness.—*A. B. Simpson.*

> Where Jesus reigns there's joy untold;
> There's wealth that's richer far than gold;
> There's service glad and courage true;
> There's power to be, and strength to do;
> There's sacrifice and sweet content;
> There's grace divine and mercy sent;
> There's triumph over self and sin;
> And blessed peace abides within;
> There's truest faith that seldom wanes;
> There's love supreme where Jesus reigns;
> Are these all found, dear heart, in you?
> —*Unknown.*

Not to be a Christian costs the sacrifice of the highest, deepest, purest, holiest, most overflowing joy that can be known right here on earth.
—*Unknown.*

The only way to be constantly happy is to be constantly looking to and coming to a Crucified Savior; renouncing all our own worth; cleaving to Him for all; giving up everything that clashes with our fidelity to Him; receiving from His fullness "grace upon grace"; relying on His every promise, and guarding against aught that might for a moment bring distance and darkness between our souls and our Lord.—*Samuel Pearce.*

God's fearless messengers

"And I will set up shepherds over them which shall feed them: and they shall fear no more, nor be dismayed, neither shall they be lacking, saith the Lord"
(Jer. 23:4).
"For I have not shunned to declare unto you all the counsel of God"
(Acts 20:27).

Although the following advice, from the pen of G. D. Watson, may apply particularly to ministers and preachers, it can also come as an appeal to all of us, rank and file Christians. Which of us has not some portion of God's flock for which our conscience tells us we are responsible? The challenge is to every true Christian, that he may be given that holy courage that will defy all hell until precious souls are won to Christ:

"The world and the visible Church both need messengers of God so perfectly purged by the Spirit and filled with Him as not to fear rich and cultured sinners, who are not ever afraid of offending someone, who have no fear about their salaries or the votes of the conference, who are not afraid to preach very simple Bible sermons, who are not afraid of telling their experience, who are not in the least afraid of the flattery or abuse of the whole world. They need men who so bury themselves in the bosom of God that the created universe cannot scare them; men who so fix their eyes on Jesus that they are oblivious to stained glass, pipe organs, fine clothes, and the foolish whims of proud theatre-going church members; men who walk so close with God that when they preach the people feel as if a solemn section of eternity were falling on them.

"But this holy courage cannot be studied out, nor thought out, nor volitioned out, nor counterfeited. It comes only into an utterly purified heart, and is one of the fruits of perfect love."

It is easy to appear a Daniel in a country where there are no lions.
—Unknown.

Be careful that what you take for sweetness is not cowardice, and what you take to be the defense of the truth is not theological sourness.—*Reader Harris.*

God polishes His own

"But Jesus said unto them, Ye know not what ye ask: can ye drink of the cup that I drink of? and be baptized with the baptism that I am baptized with?"
(Mark 10:38).
"Thou hast enlarged me when I was in distress" (Psa. 4:1).

The Christian prays for fuller manifestations of Christ's power, and glory, and love to him; but he is often not aware that this is in truth praying to be brought into the furnace; for in the furnace only it is that Christ can walk with His friends, and display, in their preservation and deliverance, His own almighty power. Yet when brought thither, it is one of the worst parts of the trial that the Christian often thinks himself, for a time at least, abandoned.—*Cecil.*

She asked to be made like her Savior,
     And He took her at her word,
And sent her a heart-crushing burden
     Till the depths of her soul were stirred.
She asked for a faith strong, yet simple.
     He permitted the dark clouds to come;
She staggered by faith through the darkness,
     As the storms did her soul overwhelm. . . .

She asked to lean hard on her Savior;
     He took human props quite away,
Till no earthly friend could help her,
     And she could do nothing but pray.
I saw her go out to the vineyard
     To harvest the golden grain;
Her eyes were still moistened with weeping,
     Her heart was still throbbing with pain.

But many a heart that was broken,
     And many a wrecked, blighted life
Was made to thank God for her coming,
     And rejoiced in the midst of the strife.
She had prayed to be made like her Savior,
     And the burden He gave her to bear
Had been but the great Sculptor's training:
     Thus answering her earnest prayer.
                              —*Unknown.*

God's Word a never-failing well

"I have given them THY WORD" (John 17:14).
"Thy word was unto me the joy . . . of mine heart" (Jer. 15:16).

We treat our Bibles, not as old almanacs, but as books for the present—new, fresh, adapted for the hour. Abiding sweetness dwells in undiminished freshness in the ancient words upon which our fathers fed in their day. Glory be to God, we are feasting on them still; or if not, we ought to be; and can only blame ourselves if we do not!

The wells of Abraham served for Isaac, and Jacob, and a thousand generations. Come, let us let down our buckets, and with joy draw water out of the old wells of salvation, digged in the far-off days when our fathers trusted in the Lord, and He delivered them! We need not fear that we shall be superstitious or credulous. The promises of the Lord are made to all who will believe them: faith is itself a warrant for trusting. If thou *canst* trust, thou mayest trust.

After being fulfilled hundreds of times, the words of promise still stand to be yet further made good. Many a time and oft have we stooped down to the spring-head in the meadow, and quaffed a cooling draught. It is just as full and free, and we may drink today with as much confidence as if we now stooped for the first time. Men do not keep their promises over and over again; it would be unreasonable to expect it of them. They are cisterns, but Thou, O Lord, art a fountain! All my fresh springs are in Thee.—*C. H. Spurgeon.*

> This Book unfolds Jehovah's mind,
> This Voice salutes in accents kind,
> This Friend will all your need supply,
> This Fountain sends forth streams of joy,
> This Mine affords us boundless wealth,
> This Good Physician gives us health,
> This Sun renews and warms the soul,
> This Sword both wounds and makes us whole,
> This Letter shows our sins forgiven,
> This Guide conducts us safe to Heaven,
> This Charter has been sealed with blood,
> This Volume is the Word of God.
> *—Enc. of Poetical Illustrations.*

A strange, mysterious life pervades the Bible, which makes it not only an inexplicable mystery, but an indestructible Book. It is also life-giving. Its Living Waters make everything to live, wherever the river of God cometh. The living Spirit of God here speaks to the responsive spirit of man.

—Dr. A. T. Pierson.

Faith rises above difficulties

"If thou canst believe, all things are possible to him that believeth"
                                                        (Mark 9:23).
"This is the victory that overcometh the world, even our faith" (1 John 5:4).

Unbelief begins at the obstacle, and then tries to work for God, but the obstacle shuts out the sight of God. Unbelief looks at the mountain of difficulty. Faith says, "I like mountain scenery, let me get on to the top and see the view." Faith begins with God, and the obstacle becomes as a molehill.—*Reader Harris.*

It is men of faith who have saved the world, not men of knowledge.
                                                        —*Sir Wilfred Grenfell.*

Faith is the source of power, a principle of action; men of faith have always been men of action. Where there is belief there must be something to believe.
                                                        —*Graham Scroggie.*

The beginning of anxiety is the end of faith, and the beginning of true faith is the end of anxiety.—*Unknown.*

Faith is the basis of all great, active enterprises.
Faith is the source, the parent of all true feeling.
Faith constitutes the free bond of union between God and man.
Faith always has an object and always has results.
Faith, unexercised, becomes weak; faith, in frequent exercise, becomes strong.
Our faith in God will be in proportion to our consecration to God—a life of true faith is a life of entire consecration.
Faith is the one great law of the life of holy beings.
Living by faith without knowledge is living in the truest divine light.
When we are led in the way of faith, we are led by God Himself.
                                                        —*Thomas Upham.*

Be Spirit-filled

"Be filled with the Spirit" (Eph. 5:18).
"Blessed are they which do hunger and thirst after righteousness: for they shall be filled" (Matt. 5:6).

Such is God's command to each of us. To be filled with the Spirit is not left to our choice whether we will receive it or not. It is not merely a privilege which we may or may not enjoy. It is God's command which no one can neglect without being disobedient to Him. Any Christian who does not experience the fullness of the Spirit is unfaithful to his Lord, and culpably negligent of God's choicest gift of grace. He is unbelieving towards God, and is content to be lukewarm in His service when he might be a flame of fire.

There are signs everywhere that very few have received the fullness of the Spirit. What feebleness in service there is! How much labor expended with little or no fruit in the conversion of souls! How little joy in prayer, or power to pray so that answers are received! How little divine light received directly through the Word! How little mourning over sinners! How little real love to the people of God, of whatever name or race they may be! How God's holy Name is being blasphemed on earth, because His people come so short in these things!

Let the time past suffice us for this weakness and deadness. Let us arise and shake ourselves from the dust. Let us be willing to receive from God this choicest gift of His grace to us, His Holy Spirit. It is God's command, and therefore possible.—*Barclay Buxton.*

"Be filled with the Spirit." In the Greek that is, "Be being filled with the Spirit." If I am full, how am I to be "being filled"? I must give to others, and as I give, God will give me more. That is what God wants us for, to flow through us. "Ye shall receive power, after that the Holy Ghost is come upon you; and ye shall be witnesses unto me." The Greek is, "You shall be receiving power continuously after the Holy Ghost is come upon you." The continuous reception and transmission of the power of God is the privilege of the saint of God. Such a privilege carries with it an equal responsibility. The promise is unto YOU.—*Reader Harris.*

> I am so needy, Lord, and yet I know
> All fullness dwells in Thee;
> And hour by hour that never-failing treasure
> Supplies and fills, in overflowing measure,
> Thy grace is enough for me!
> —*Frances Ridley Havergal.*

Keep in touch with God

"I being in the way, the Lord led me" (Gen. 24:27).
"For as many as are led by the Spirit of God, they are the sons of God"
(Rom. 8:14).

"In the way"—God's purpose and plan for your life and mine. How important it is that we make it our business to be "in the way" so that the great purposes of God for our lives might be fulfilled. It is only as His Holy Spirit is followed that we will be prompted to little acts of usefulness and blessing; otherwise, our lives are filled up with trifles that self prompts to be done. Time taken for quiet alone with God will give us the chance to hear what He would have us to do, and thus we, "being in the way," the Lord can guide and lead us to take His messages to needy souls.

> Only a word, yes, only a word
> That the Spirit's small voice whispered "Speak,"
> But the worker passed onward, unblessed and weak,
> Whom you were meant to have stirred
> To courage, devotion and love anew,
> Because when the message came to you,
> You were out of touch with your Lord.
>
> Only a note, yes, only a note
> To a friend in a distant land.
> The Spirit said, "Write." But then you had planned
> Some different work, and you thought
> It matters little. You did not know
> 'Twould have saved a soul from sin and woe.
> You were out of touch with your Lord.
>
> Only a day, yes, only a day,
> But oh, can you guess, my friend,
> Where the influence reaches, and where it will end?
> Oh, the hours that you frittered away!
> The Master's command is "Abide in me."
> And fruitless and vain will your service be
> If out of touch with your Lord.
> —*Jean H. Watson.*

Never deny God anything

"The Holy Ghost, whom God hath given to them that obey him" (Acts 5:32).
"Hath the Lord as great delight in burnt offerings and sacrifices, as in obeying the voice of the Lord? Behold, to obey is better than sacrifice"
(1 Sam. 15:22).

The fulfillment of irksome duties is the test of sincere obedience. When pleasure and service are identical, it is easy to be diligent in heavenly business. But when flesh and blood rebel against a known duty, it is time to invoke the aid of divine grace. Every personal feeling and private affection must give way before the imperative demands of our Lord and Master. Contention for the faith is far less pleasant than communion with Christ; but the neglect of the precept may involve the withdrawal of the privilege.—*C. H. Spurgeon.*

Florence Nightingale said: "If I could give you information of my life it would be to show how a woman of very ordinary ability has been led by God in strange and unaccustomed paths to do in His service what He has done in her. And if I could tell you all, you would see how God has done all, and I nothing. I have worked hard, very hard, that is all; and I have never refused God anything."

It seems to me we need to ask more seriously than in bygone days, what is really the will and command of our blessed Lord and to set about obeying Him, not merely in attempting to obey. I do not know that we are told anywhere in the Bible to try to do anything. "We must try to do the best we can," is a very common expression; but I remember some years ago, after a remark of that kind, looking very carefully through the New Testament to see under what circumstances the disciples were told to *try* to do anything. I was surprised that I did not find any instance. Then I went through the Old Testament with the same result. There are many commands apparently impossible to obey, but they were all definite commands.

God gives His Spirit, not to those who long for Him, not to those who pray for Him, not to those who desire to be filled always; but He does give His Holy Spirit to them that obey Him.—*Hudson Taylor.*

May 17
Prayer a mighty influence

"And all things, whatsoever ye shall ask in prayer, believing, ye shall receive"
(Matt. 21:22).
"And whatsoever we ask, we receive of him, because we keep his commandments, and do those things that are pleasing in his sight"
(1 John 3:22).

If there is one thing I think the Church needs to learn, it is that God means prayer to have an answer, and that it hath not entered into the heart of man to conceive what He will do for His child who gives himself to believe that his prayer will be heard.

Many complain that they have not the power to pray in faith, to pray the effectual prayer that availeth much. The message I would fain bring them is that the blessed Jesus is waiting, is longing, to teach them this.

He teaches us to pray not only by example, by instruction, by command, by promises, but by showing us Himself, the ever-living Intercessor, as our Life. It is when we believe this, and go and abide in Him for our prayer life too, that our fears of not being able to pray aright will vanish, and we shall joyfully and triumphantly trust our Lord to teach us to pray, to be Himself the life and the power of our prayer.

May God open our eyes to see what the holy ministry of intercession is to which, as His royal priesthood, we have been set apart. May He give us a large and strong heart to believe what mighty influence our prayers can exert. And may all fear as to our being able to fulfill our vocation vanish as we see Jesus, living ever to pray, living in us to pray, and standing surety for our prayer life.—*Andrew Murray.*

Men cannot represent God who do not get answers to prayer from Him.
—*E. M. Bounds.*

Every great movement of God can be traced to a kneeling figure.
—*D. L. Moody.*

If you spend several hours in prayer daily, you will see great things.
—*John Nelson.*

A ministry for all

"Behold I send you forth" (Luke 10:3).
"Instantly serving God day and night" (Acts 26:7).

The disciples did not stop to organize themselves into Conferences or Councils, into Synods or General Assemblies. Each man spoke the word which the Holy Spirit gave to him. Peter talks to Cornelius, and his assembled kinsfolk, until the Spirit descends upon them, and they are converted and baptized. Paul preaches to the Philippian jailer and condenses the core of the Gospel into a single sentence. Philip overtakes a titled foreigner in his chariot by the roadside, and a "Bible reading" is extemporized on the spot. That was preaching—truth teaching—in its most elementary form. Aquila and Priscilla become expounders of the new Gospel, with the gifted Apollos for their pupil. Down at Joppa, industrious Dorcas takes to preaching also, but womanlike she employs her needle as her instrument. Her actions speak louder than words. And so the hive is busy. Everyone who has a message delivers it; everyone who can heal a sick man or mend a crippled limb performs the miracles of love; everyone who has a lamp lets it shine. Their Lord and Master is glorified by their "bearing much fruit."—*Theodore Cuyler.*

The Gospel commands the sinner to come and the Christian to go.
—*D. L. Moody.*

> To talk with God no breath is lost;
> Talk on.
> To walk with God no strength is lost;
> Walk on.
> To toil with God no time is lost;
> Toil on.
> Little is much, if God is in it;
> Man's busiest day not worth God's minute.
> Much is little everywhere
> If God the business doth not share.
> So work with God, then nothing's lost;
> Who works with Him does well and most.
> —*Unknown.*

Influencing our loved ones

"For what knowest thou, O wife, whether thou shalt save thy husband? or how knowest thou, O man, whether thou shalt save thy wife?" (1 Cor. 7:16). "His wives turned away his heart after other gods" (1 Kings 11:4).

There is no such thing as negative influence. We are all positive in the place we occupy, making the world better or making it worse, on the Lord's side or on the devil's, making up the reason for our blessedness or banishment; and we have already done a mighty work in peopling Heaven or hell. By the force of your evil influence you have already consumed infinite values, or you have, by the power of a right influence, won whole kingdoms for God.

—De Witt Talmage.

I know not a more serious thing than the responsibility incurred by human affection. Only think of this: whoever loves you is growing like you! Neither you nor he can hinder it save at the cost of alienation. Oh, if you are grateful for but one creature's love, rise to the height of so pure a blessing. Drag them not down by the very embrace by which they cling to you, but through their gentleness and trust secure their consecration.—*James Martineau.*

<blockquote>
The tidal wave of deeper souls
Into our inmost being rolls,
And lifts us unawares
Out of all meaner cares.
—H. W. Longfellow.
</blockquote>

A striking example of the above principle is the case of Reubens, the great painter. His works of art are distinctly influenced by the two women who shared his life at different periods. His first wife exerted a spiritual and refined effect. While she lived, his paintings showed a dignity of refinement, culminating in his greatest masterpiece, "The Descent from the Cross."

Under the baser influence of his second wife, Reubens' paintings predominantly catered to the lower instincts of coarseness and sensuality.

If we can produce such a lasting effect upon those who love us, how careful we should be of the sway we hold over a human soul.

<blockquote>
She never found fault with you, never implied
Your wrong by her right; and yet men at her side
Grew nobler, girls purer, as through the whole town
The children were gladder that pulled at her gown—
My Kate.
—Elizabeth B. Browning.
</blockquote>

Conquests in daily life

"And chose him five smooth stones out of the brook, and put them in a shepherd's bag which he had, even in a scrip; and his sling was in his hand: and he drew near to the Philistine" (1 Sam. 17:40).

Let no one despise the day of small things. The noblest Christian lives often have their origin in some faithful word spoken in love, or in the reading of a tract, or in some small occurrence, or in a single resolution to break with some besetting sin.—*Theodore Cuyler.*

I asked the Lord to let me do
　　Some mighty work for Him;
To fight amid His battle hosts,
　　Then sing the victor's hymn.
I longed my ardent love to show,
But Jesus would not have it so.

He placed me in a quiet home,
　　Whose life was calm and still,
And gave me little things to do,
　　My daily round to fill;
I could not think it good to be
Just put aside so silently.

Small duties gathered round my way,
　　They seemed of earth alone;
I, who had longed for conquests bright
　　To lay before His throne,
Had common things to do and bear,
To watch and strive with daily care.

So then I thought my prayer unheard,
　　And asked the Lord once more
That He would give me work for Him
　　And open wide the door;
Forgetting that my Master knew
Just what was best for me to do.

Then quietly the answer came,
　　"My child, I hear thy cry;
Think not that mighty deed alone
　　Will bring the victory.
The battle has been planned by Me,
Let daily life thy conquests see."
　　　　　　　　—Unknown.

Joy in suffering

"Ye took joyfully the spoiling of your goods" (Heb. 10:34).
"My brethren, count it all joy when ye fall into divers temptations"
(James 1:2).

Perhaps there is no more remarkable manifestations of the power of the Holy Ghost in the early Church, than the sweetness and grandeur with which they endured all things for Jesus' sake. Beaten with stripes and humiliated before the council, they came together, not to condole with each other or to show their bleeding wounds, but to rejoice that they were counted worthy to suffer shame for the Name of Jesus.

Hunted out of Iconium by a mob of respectable women, pelted with stones and hooted from the community, the "disciples were filled with joy, and with the Holy Ghost." Theirs was a gladness that did not recognize their sufferings, but lifted them above persecution, and counted it but part of their coronation.

And so the power of the Holy Ghost will give us the heroism of endurance and enable us, like our Master, for the joy set before us, to endure the cross, despising the shame. It will bring about a spirit of self-denial and holy sacrifice; it will make it easy for us to let go of things and give up things "and endure all things for the elect's sake," and to say with the great apostle, "Yea, and if I be offered upon the sacrifice and service of your faith, I joy, and rejoice with you all."—*A. B. Simpson.*

> We make our songs in the day of our gladness
> When life is all laughter and joy and delight,
> When never a shadow has clouded our sunshine;
> But God giveth songs in the night. . . .
>
> He giveth songs in the night of affliction,
> When earth has no sun and the heavens no star;
> Like a comforting touch in the desolate darkness
> His voice stealeth in from afar. . . .
>
> Give us Thy songs, O Thou Maker of music!
> Teach us to sing, O Thou Bringer of joy!
> Till nothing can silence the notes of our triumph
> And naught our rejoicing destroy.
> —*Annie Johnson Flint.*

The life-changing Word

"The words that I speak unto you, they are spirit, and they are life"
(John 6:63).
"Now ye are clean through the word which I have spoken unto you"
(John 15:3).

One cannot truly read the Bible without being powerfully affected by it. Spurgeon has said: "Read the Bible, and it brings you into the association of the best people that ever lived. You stand beside Moses, and learn his meekness; beside Job, and learn his patience; beside Abraham, and learn his faith; beside Daniel, and learn his courage to do right; beside Isaiah, and learn his fiery indignation against the evildoers; beside Paul, and catch something of his enthusiasm; beside Christ, and you feel His love."

An old periodical tells an interesting story of the power this Book had on a Catholic family:
"A Roman Catholic priest in Belgium rebuked a young woman and her brother for reading that 'bad book,' pointing to the Bible. 'Mr. Priest,' she replied, 'a little while ago my brother was an idler, a gambler, a drunkard and made such a noise in the house that no one could stay in it. Since he began to read the Bible, he works with industry, goes no longer to the tavern, no longer touches cards, brings home money to his poor old mother, and our life at home is quiet and delightful. How comes it, Mr. Priest, that a bad book produces such good fruits?'"

Bishop Charles Fowler says of the Bible: "Marvelous Book! Full of divine life and power! No one can touch the hem of its garment without being healed. No one can come near enough even to stone it without being blessed. It shall rise in power and beauty, so long as there remains one sinner needing salvation or one saint hoping for Heaven."

I feel most strongly that the real way to test the inspiration of the Bible, or any other book, is not by criticizing its text, but by watching its influence upon human lives. In that, after all, we have definite and distinct evidence of its miraculous and supernatural character.—*Hudson Taylor.*

The glory of sacrifice

*"They offered great sacrifices, and rejoiced: for God had made them rejoice
. . . that the joy of Jerusalem was heard even afar off" (Neh. 12:43).*
"We glory in tribulations also: knowing that tribulation worketh patience"
(Rom. 5:3).

I utterly deny that, taken in the broadest and justest sense, Christianity
demands any sacrifices. She pays all expenses, and leaves a large margin of
profit. We may count them sacrifices in our shortsightedness, but whatever
God commands you and me to do, it is to our interest to do it. We shall not be
the losers in the long run. The books that are kept up there will strike the
balance on the right side of the ledger; and when the books are opened, and you
and I stand before our God to render an account of our stewardship here on
earth, that which we counted a sacrifice will be found then to have been a most
profitable investment. That little portion of our worldly wealth which we say
we gave away for the cause of God and humanity, will then be found the only
portion that we took with us.

If an old heathen could say on his deathbed that he had lost everything he
had except what he had given away, how much more truly can an enlightened
Christian feel that all his wise investments made to promote the cause of God
and humanity is only so much placed at interest in time, the advantage of which
will be reaped in eternity.—*Edward R. Ames.*

Gladness be with thee, Helper of the world!
I think this is the authentic sign and seal
Of God-ship, that ever waxes glad,
And more glad, until gladness blossoms, bursts
Into a rage to suffer for mankind
And recommence at sorrow.
—Unknown.

Seek first the Kingdom

"But seek ye first the kingdom of God, and his righteousness; and all these things shall be added unto you" (Matt. 6:33).

Do you make it your primary business, your first great concern to seek the kingdom of God and His righteousness? Are the things of God, the honor of His Name, the welfare of His Church, the conversion of sinners, and the profit of your own soul, your chief aim? Or does your business or your family, or your own temporal concerns, in some shape or other, *primarily* occupy your attention? Remember that the world passeth away, but that the things of God endure for ever. I never knew a child of God who acted according to the above passage, in whose experience the Lord did not fulfill His word of promise, "All these things shall be added unto you."—*George Müller.*

Again we are met with an "all things": "seek ye first the kingdom of God, and His righteousness; and all these things shall be added unto you." All *these* things, food and clothing, etc. No doubt some of us could bear witness to how really *curiously* God has fulfilled this, adding to the first sought grace of His kingdom just the thing that we didn't quite see our way to, as to some needed supply of dress, change of air, or other of "these things." Why should one ever have an anxious thought in this direction, when He has downright forbidden it on the one hand, "take no thought," etc., and when He so tenderly says, "your Father knoweth," on the other!—*Frances Ridley Havergal.*

"His divine power hath given unto us all things that pertain unto life and godliness" (2 Pet. 1:3).

> Who does God's work, will get God's pay,
> However long may seem the day,
> However weary be the way;
> Though powers and Princes thunder "nay,"
> Who does God's work will get God's pay.
> He does not pay as others pay,
> In gold, or land, or raiment gay,
> In goods that vanish and decay;
> But God in wisdom knows a way,
> And that is sure, let come what may,
> Who does God's work, will get God's pay.
> —*Unknown.*

God recompenses wisely

"I count all things but loss for the excellency of the knowledge of Christ Jesus . . . I have suffered the loss of all things . . . that I may win Christ . . . That I may know him, and the power of his resurrection" (Phil. 3:8-10).

A Christian never really loses if his gains exceed his losses. So we must not look at what we give up for Christ, but what we gain by the losing.

> Straight through my heart this fact today,
>   By Truth's own hand is driven:
> God never takes one thing away,
>   But something else is given.
>
> I did not know in earlier years
>   This law of love and kindness;
> I only mourned through bitter tears
>   My loss, in sorrow's blindness.
>
> But, ever following each regret
>   O'er some departed treasure,
> My sad repining heart was met
>   With unexpected pleasure.
>
> I thought it only happened so;
>   But Time this truth has taught me—
> No least thing from my life can go,
>   But something else is brought me.
>
> It is the Law, complete, sublime;
>   And now with Faith unshaken,
> In patience I but bide my time
>   When any joy is taken.
>
> No matter if the crushing blow
>   May for the moment down me,
> Still, behind it waits Love, I know,
>   With some new gift to crown me.
>   —*Ella Wheeler Wilcox.*

The blow most dreaded often falls to break from off our limbs a chain.
                        —*Unknown.*

God deals out our comforts and our sorrows with exact, unerring hand, in number, weight and measure. Hence we have not either joy or adversity a grain too little or too much.—*A. Toplady.*

Prayer for others

"Pray ye therefore . . ." (Matt. 9:38).
"Ask, and it shall be given you; seek, and ye shall find; knock, and it shall be opened unto you" (Luke 11:9).

Prayer is usually considered to be devotional and more or less unpractical in ordinary life. Our Lord in His teaching always made prayer, not preparation for work, but *the* work. Thank God for all the marvelous organization there is in Christian work, for medical missions and finely educated missionaries, for aggressive work in every shape and form; but these are, so to speak, but wards to the lock, the key is not in any of our organizations; the key lies exactly to our hand by our Lord's instruction, "Pray ye therefore."

When we pray for others the Spirit of God works in the unconscious domain of their being that we know nothing about, and the one we are praying for knows nothing about, but after the passing of time, the conscious life of the one prayed for begins to show signs of unrest and disquiet. We may have spoken until we are worn out, but have never come anywhere near, and we have given up in despair. But if we have been praying, we find on meeting them one day that there is the beginning of a softening in an enquiry and a desire to know something. It is that kind of intercession that does most damage to Satan's kingdom. It is so slight, so feeble in its initial stages that if reason is not wedded to the light of the Holy Spirit, we will never obey it. It seems stupid to think that we can pray and all that will happen, but remember to Whom we pray, we pray to a God Who understands the unconscious depths of personality about which we know nothing, and He has told us to pray. The great Master of the human heart said, "Greater works than these shall he do . . . And whatsoever ye shall ask in my name, that will I do."—*Oswald Chambers.*

> Can I neglect to pray, while there is one
> Who needs the help my prayer can bring?
> Can I ignore the cry of hearts as death
> Draws near, when prayer can ease the sting?
>
> Can I be blameless if I plainly see
> Within the young and tender hearts
> The stark bewilderment, the need, and breathe
> No prayer against the evil darts?
>
> Can I withhold from God the rarest alms,
> And think that I have naught to give,
> While someone needs a prayer to help him find
> The way to Christ, that he might live?
> —*Pansy B. Menge.*

Christians need backbone

"What my God saith, that will I speak" (2 Chron. 18:13).
"We know that thou art true, and carest for no man: for thou regardest not the person of men, but teachest the way of God in truth" (Mark 12:14).

One is tempted to ask, "How is backbone to be formed in the rising generation of Christians, if everything about the religious life is made so pleasant and easy? If sermons must be so light or short as hardly to involve any effort of attention on the part of the hearer, and the rest of the service is to be a bright little concert? And if the other hours of the day given us to be spent at the gates of Heaven are to be merely enlivened with 'Sunday talk'?"

We are in great danger of degenerating into molluscous Christians. Christian preachers and writers ought, I think, to be continually reminding their people of the place of self-denial in the Christian life. If we let down the tone of the Church in this respect it may please God to give her a new chapter of discipline of persecution, for that has been the great means usually employed for teaching her that the Cross has to be borne in another sense than as an ornament on a lady's bosom. "If any man will come after me, let him take up his cross daily and follow me."—*Dr. W. G. Blaikie.*

The Church needs replenishing with men and women who are prepared to disregard the opinions of men, and to estimate at their true worth the persons and influence of men. Such people are bound to make their mark in both worlds, they cannot eventually fail. They must succeed with a success that the grave will not cut short, and eternity will not lessen.

Most modern Christians are afraid to:
Face the frowns of their loved ones to say grace before meals.
Be considered old-fashioned and hold family worship in the home.
Approach their unsaved fellowman and talk to him about his soul.
Be seen on their knees or reading their Bibles.
Rebuke a wrong that is committed in their presence in the spirit of Christ.

How can we then expect to be among those "who came out of great tribulation, and have washed their robes, and made them white in the blood of the Lamb"?

John Bunyan has said: "I have determined—the Almighty God being my help and my shield—yet to suffer, if frail life might continue so long, even until the moss shall grow over my eyebrows, rather than violate my faith and my principles."

Christ's bondage brings freedom

"I am thy servant, and the son of thine handmaid: thou hast loosed my bonds"
(Psa. 116:16).
"I love my master, my wife, and my children; I will not go out free"
(Exod. 21:5).

Never, until the love of God becomes the all-absorbing, all-controlling, dominating principle of life, can we understand the seeming contradiction in Psalm 116:16, "O Lord, truly I am thy servant; I am thy servant, and the son of thine handmaid: thou hast loosed my bonds." But when every faculty is energized, every capacity filled, and the whole nature pervaded with this transcendent gift, the bondage, the irksomeness, the subtle legalism which more or less characterize the service of incipient believers, are entirely removed. The yoke of Christ no longer chafes, the last trace of servile feeling is gone, and the will of God becomes our free, spontaneous, delightful choice. . . .

Filled with divine love, we love what God loves, and in this condition the will of God is no longer as a yoke upon the neck; Christ's service is perfect freedom. Faber sings:

> "He hath breathed into my heart
> A special love of Thee,
> A love to lose my will in His,
> And by the loss be free."

(From *New Testament Holiness* by Thomas Cook. Used by permission of the Epworth Press).

How sweet the constraining love of Christ, like a furnace-blast, melting the "I must" into "I will," duty into delight. This is the highest freedom possible in earth or Heaven, when my will elects God's will with unspeakable gladness.

> I love Thee so, I know not how
> My transports to control;
> Thy love is like a burning fire
> Within my very soul.
> —*Daniel Steele.*

God does not overload His own

"And unto one he gave five talents, to another two, and to another one; to every man according to his several ability; and straightway took his journey"
(Matt. 25:15).
"Thy shoes shall be iron and brass; and as thy days, so shall thy strength be"
(Deut. 33:25).

God will not give to any of His people a larger measure of duty than they can fairly overtake; He will not give to the man with one talent the task belonging to the man with two, or to the man with two the task that appertains to more richly gifted natures. He is not the "hard man" who grinds to powder those who serve Him. He knows us altogether. He tenderly loves us, and having measured out our sufficient task, He will put upon us none other burden. But some complain: "As a matter of fact, are we not over-weighted? Is not human life generally too intense, too crowded, too burdensome?" Perhaps this is so; but there are two questions we may put to ourselves. How far do we overweight ourselves? We do it in ignorance, in covetousness, in ambition, in vanity. Many would carry far lighter burdens if only they were more lowly, content, and trustful. Do we not also overweight one another? Through our want of thought, equity, and sympathy we aggravate our neighbor's burden.

Let us not live fretful lives. God will never stretch the line of our duty beyond the measure of our strength. We ought to live with the grace of the flowers, with the joy of the birds, with the freedom of the wind and wave. Without question this is God's ideal of human life. We are expected to do no more than we can do with the time granted us, with the tools, the material, and the opportunity at our disposal. We serve no Egyptian taskmaster who watches to double the tale of bricks, but a generous Lord Who waits to make our duty our delight.—*W. L. Watkinson.*

"As thy days, thy strength shall be,"
Lord, it is Thy word to me
Who dost all the need foresee. . . .

Not supplies that I can hoard,
For the future ready stored,
Daily feast I at Thy board. . . .

As my days bring varied need,
So my strength is guaranteed,
Lord, Thou art my strength indeed.
—*Adeline Braithwaite.*

Christ is all that matters

"For me to live is Christ, and to die is gain" (Phil. 1:21).
"Whether we live therefore, or die, we are the Lord's" (Rom. 14:8).
"Christ liveth in me" (Gal. 2:20).

If we can live in Christ and have His life in us, shall not the spiritual balance and proportion which were His become ours too? If He were really our Master and our Savior, could it be that we should get so eager and excited over little things? If we were His, could we possibly be wretched over the losing of a little money which we did not need, or be exalted at the sound of a little praise which we know that we only half deserve and that the praisers only half intend? A moment's disappointment, a moment's gratification, and then the ocean would be calm again and quite forgetful of the ripple which disturbed its bosom.

—Phillips Brooks.

Polycarp of Smyrna, a beloved friend of the apostle John, was brought as an old man before the Roman governor. "I will banish you," said the governor.

The old saint replied, "You cannot do that, for I am at home wherever Christ is."

"I will take away your property."

"But I have none. And if I had, and you took it away, I should still be rich; for I have Christ."

"I will take away your good name," threatened the governor.

"That is gone already," said the undisturbed saint, "for I have long since reckoned it a great joy to be counted the offscouring of all things for Christ's sake."

"Then I will put you in prison," growled the governor.

"You may do as you please. But I shall always be free; for where Christ is, there is perfect liberty."

"Then I will take away your life."

"Then I shall be in Heaven, which is the truest life."—*Gospel Gleaners.*

Where Christ brings His cross, He brings His presence; and where He is, none are desolate and there is no room for despair.—*Elizabeth B. Browning.*

When little is much

"Better is little with the fear of the Lord than great treasure and trouble therewith" (Prov. 15:16).
"Little that a righteous man hath is better than the riches of many wicked"
(Psa. 37:16).

> Give what Thou canst; without Thee we are poor;
> And with Thee rich, take what Thou wilt away.
> —*William Cowper.*

A little with the blessing of God upon it is better than a great deal with the incumbrance of His curse. His blessing can multiply a mite into a talent, but His curse will shrink a talent into a mite. By Him the arms of the wicked are broken, and by Him the righteous are upholden. So that the great question is, Whether He be with or against us? The favor of God is to them that obtain it a better and enduring substance, which, like the widow's barrel of oil, wasted not in the evil days of famine, nor will fail.—*Bishop Horne.*

> In palaces are hearts that ask,
> In discontent and pride,
> Why life is such a dreary task
> And all things good denied.
> Yet hearts in poorest huts admire
> How love has in their aid
> (Love that not ever seems to tire)
> Such rich provision made.
> —*Richard Chevenix Trench.*

The Rev. F. H. Spence writes from Point Barrow, Alaska. "We have no telegraph, telephone, wireless, automobile, overland limited, or airship; but neither do we have the saloon, the brothel, or Sabbath desecration; and the house of God is filled. Three times a week do they flock to God's house, and with them all their children, from the oldest to the youngest. Their faith is simple. If they lack food they pray to God to give to them. If any are sick, they ask Him to restore them to health. Gentle are they, kind and generous to one another. It may be at times we look with longing eyes at the privileges you enjoy, and then the peace and faith and quiet of these people steal over us, and we are content."

June 1
Only one life

"Thou hast granted me life" (Job 10:12).
"For it is not a vain thing for you; because it is your life" (Deut. 32:47).

A preacher of a mathematical turn of mind once addressed his congregation in these words: "My friends, you make very free with your days; pray, how many do you expect to have? Let us consider: Seventy years of life yield 25,550 days. Remember that a period of twenty years is gone, almost before you begin to live. Deduction Number 1—7,300 days. Remainder—18,250 days. Then the one item sleep deducts 6,080 days, leaving 12,170 days. For recreation and occupations, we will deduct another third. Deduction Number 3—4,060 days. Remainder—8,110 days. Then deducting the time used in eating, drinking, dressing, bathing, etc., at a single blow will leave you not over 4,000 days in a long life in which to develop good things in your nature. Approximately eleven years. Think of it. That is to say, if we live out our allotted time; many do not. Does it look small and short? Indeed, brethren, it is. And it is priceless; nothing on earth can represent its true value. And yet what a glorious inheritance, for the Master commits this into your hands today with the great charge, 'Occupy till I come.'"

We prove the value which we attach to things by the time we devote to them. The kingdom of God asks our time. God has broken up our lifetime into day and night that we may learn to live a day at a time. Begin the day with God, and God will maintain His kingdom in your heart.—*Andrew Murray.*

The great use of a life is to spend it for something that outlasts it.
—*William James.*

> Not many lives, but only one have we—
>   One, only one;
> How sacred should that one life ever be—
>   That narrow span!
> Day after day filled up with blessed toil,
> Hour after hour still bringing in new spoil.
> —*Horatius Bonar.*

Rests in the divine symphony

"And on the seventh day God ended his work which he had made; and he rested" (Gen. 2:2).

In our whole life-melody the music is broken off here and there by "rests," and we foolishly think we have come to the end of the tune. God sends a time of forced leisure, sickness, disappointed plans, frustrated efforts, and makes a sudden pause in the choral hymn of our lives. We lament that our voices must be silent, and our part missing in the music which ever goes up to the ear of the Creator. How does the musician read the "rest"? See him beat the time with unvarying count, and catch up the next note, true and steady, as if no breaking-place had come between.

Not without design does God write the music of our lives. Be it ours to learn the tune, and not be dismayed at the "rests." They are not to be slurred over, not to be omitted, not to destroy the melody, not to change the keynote. If we look up, God Himself will beat the time for us. With the eye on Him, we shall strike the next note full and clear. If we sadly say to ourselves, "There is no music in a 'rest,'" let us not forget "there is the making of music in it."

—John Ruskin.

There's a song that God is writing on the staff for you and me,
And its melody is sweeter than the songs of earth could be;
For the major and the minor of this song of life sublime
Bring us nearer home to Heaven—when God beats time. . . .

There are "holds" and "rests" before us, and to pause it may be hard,
But we find a hidden meaning when we come to God's "retard";
He alone can give expression, make the song of life sublime,
If we only mind the pauses—when God beats time.

There are chords of minor music that we may not understand,
In this song of life unfolding, written by the Master's hand;
Yet how patiently He lingers till we catch the glory chime,
And the song is made the sweeter—when God beats time.

When at last the curtain's lifted, and the choirs of Heaven stand
In the Hallelujah greeting to the happy, blood-washed band,
Then our sharpest "accidental" with the angel notes will rhyme
In the chorus of redemption—when God beats time.

—F. M. Lehman.

"When God Beats Time," by F. M. Lehman. Copyright property of the Nazarene Publishing House, U.S.A. Used by permission.

164

In partnership with hindrances

"Thou shalt be in league with the stones of the field" (Job 5:23).
"Neither fear ye the people of the land; for they are bread for us"
(Num. 14:9).

The very things that are obstacles—stumbling-blocks in the way, may, when the chastening of God has had its way, be taken as helps instead of hindrances. We may take our very impediments into partnership in the work of our sanctification. Praise be to His Name!—*I. Lilias Trotter.*

When God is going to do something wonderful, He begins with a difficulty. If it is going to be something very wonderful, He begins with an impossibility.
—*Charles Inwood.*

A difficulty should always be interpreted as an invitation. If the Church be healthy a great task will always be an allurement. For difficulties are only rightly interpreted when they are regarded as promises. Every difficulty contains prospective wealth. Break it open, and the wealth is yours! We appropriate the strength of the enemy we vanquish. Overcome a difficulty, and its power henceforth enlists on our side. . . . Let us, therefore, look at difficulties as promises in the guise of tasks. They are treasure-houses presenting the appearance of bristling efforts. Break them open, I say, and the treasure is yours. To dare is to win!—*J. H. Jowett.*

No circumstances in which we can ever find ourselves can be called "impossible circumstances," while the God of the impossible is on our side and dwelling within.—*John Harrison.*

Nothing will ever be attempted if all possible objections must first be overcome.—*Dr. Samuel Johnson.*

If the Lord has a gigantic task to be performed, faith gets the contract.
—*Unknown.*

June 4

Conditions for effective prayer

"I will therefore that men pray every where, lifting up holy hands, without wrath and doubting": (1 Tim. 2:8).
"Ye ask, and receive not, because ye ask amiss" (James 4:3).
"Beloved, if our heart condemn us not, then have we confidence toward God"
(1 John 3:21).

Do you want to have your prayers answered? Walk so that your own heart condemns you not. The obedient child that lives in complacent affection with its parent has no fear in coming up to ask for favors. It knows it will get them. Its own heart does not condemn it. "If our heart condemn us not, then have we confidence toward God." I defy any man to separate confidence from obedience. If you will not be obedient, you cannot have confidence.

I challenge any Christian to tell me that he can go up to the throne of God in faith for any blessing when his own heart condemns him. He knows he cannot. He has first to get that state of condemnation taken away before he can exercise faith for any blessing. Walk in the light, and then you shall have fellowship with Him, and His blood will cleanse you from all sin. The Spirit will teach you how to pray, and what to pray for, which the great mass of professors know nothing about.—*Catherine Booth.*

> Why, why is Heaven silent still
> When I have prayed so long?
> Ah! answerless the silence speaks,
> And tells me that the heart that seeks,
> The heart, the heart is wrong.
> —*Paget Wilkes.*

The prayer-hour is left standing before God till the other hours come and stand beside it; then, if they are found to be a harmonious sisterhood the prayer is granted.—*George Bowen.*

166

Live so as to be missed

"I perceive that this is an holy man of God, which passeth by us continually"
(2 Kings 4:9).
"There is a man in thy kingdom, in whom is the spirit of the holy gods"
(Dan. 5:11).

Brethren, we should live so as to be missed—missed both in the church and in the world—when we are removed. Oh, how rapidly is the time hastening on! We should live in such a manner as that, if we were called hence, our dear brethren and sisters might feel our loss, and from their innermost souls exclaim, "Oh, that such an one were in our midst again!" We ought to be missed even by the world. Worldly persons should be constrained to say of us, "If ever there was a Christian upon earth, that man was one."—*George Müller.*

There is no glory halo round his devoted head,
No luster marks the sacred paths in which his footsteps tread.
Yet holiness is graven upon his thoughtful brow
And all his steps are ordered in the light of Heaven e'en now.

He often is peculiar and seldom understood,
And yet his power is felt by both the evil and the good,
For he lives in touch with Heaven, a life of faith and prayer,
His sympathies, his hopes, his joys, his all is centered there.

His body is God's temple, his heart the Master's shrine.
He lives, and thinks, and speaks, and acts, as moved by power divine.
His is the calm of Heaven, the faith that can be still,
For God revealeth unto such the secrets of His will.

He is a chosen servant among God's many sons;
He bears His sayings on his lips and on His errands runs.
No human frown he feareth, no earthly praise he seeks,
But in the dignity of Heaven his burning message speaks.

I've found him in the workshop and in the busy street,
The plainest, simplest, humblest man that one could wish to meet.
I've treasured up his sayings and marked his faithful ways
And oft to follow in his steps my longing spirit prays.

—*Unknown.*

God's choice brings rest

"Thou knowest my downsitting and mine uprising, thou understandest my thought afar off" (Psa. 139:2).
"But as for you, ye thought evil against me; but God meant it unto good"
(Gen. 50:20).

Never complain of your birth, your training, your employment, your hardships; never fancy that you could be something, if only you had a different lot and sphere assigned you. God understands His own plan, and He knows what you want a great deal better than you do. The very things that you most deprecate as fatal limitations or obstructions, are probably what you most want. What you call hindrances, obstacles, discouragements, are probably God's opportunities; and it is nothing new that the patient should dislike his medicines, or any certain proofs that they are poisons.

No! a truce to all such impatience! Choke that envy which gnaws at your heart because you are not in the same lot with others. Bring down your soul, or rather, bring it up to receive God's will, and do His work, in your lot, in your sphere, under your cloud of obscurity, against your temptations; and then you shall find that your condition is never opposed to your good, but really consistent with it.—*Horace Bushnell.*

There is a jewel which no Indian mine can buy,
No chemic art can counterfeit;
It makes men rich in greatest poverty,
Makes water wine, turns wooden cups to gold,
The homely whistle to sweet music's strain;
That much in little—all in nought—Content.
—*H. W. Longfellow.*

Fragrant giving of one's self

"Consecrate yourselves today to the Lord" (Exod. 32:29).
"And who then is willing to consecrate his service this day unto the Lord?"
(1 Chron. 29:5).

Said David Brainerd, the missionary to the North American Indians: "Here I am, Lord, send me, send me to the ends of the earth; send me to the rough savage pagans of the wilderness; send me from all that is called comfort in earth, or earthly comfort, send me even to death itself, if it be in Thy service, and to promote Thy kingdom."

This consecration seems all the more sacred when we realize under what circumstances it was written. This young missionary had labored for several years among the Indians, sleeping on bits of straw, suffering extreme loneliness, eating foods almost unpalatable. His labors had been rewarded by a revival, and he had been blessed with the love and friendship of a godly daughter of Jonathan Edwards, so that he now thought a settled abode possible. But at this point, he received a doctor's verdict that the disease against which he had been battling for years would soon end his life. Mounting his horse, he once again faced the roving, uncertain life of the wilderness to spend his few remaining days for the souls he longed to save.

He continues: "At the same time, I had as quick and lively a sense of the value of worldly comforts, as I ever had: but only saw them infinitely overmatched by the worth of Christ's kingdom, and the propagation of His blessed Gospel. A quiet settlement, a certain place of abode, the tender friendships of life, appeared as valuable to me, considered absolutely in themselves as ever before; but considered comparatively, they appeared nothing. Compared with the value and preciousness of an enlargement of Christ's kingdom, they vanished as stars before the rising sun. Sure I am, that although the comfortable accommodations of life appeared valuable and clear to me, yet I did surrender and resign myself, soul and body, to the service of God, and to the promotion of Christ's kingdom; though it should be in the loss of them all. I could not do any other, because I could not will or choose any other. I was constrained, and yet chose, to say, 'Farewell, friends, and earthly comforts, the dearest of them all, the very dearest, if the Lord calls for it. Adieu, adieu; I will spend my life, to my latest moments, in the caves and dens of the earth, if the kingdom of Christ may thereby be advanced.'"

June 8
Nourishment through the Word

"Man shall not live by bread alone, but by every word . . . of God"
(Luke 4:4).
"I have esteemed the words of his mouth more than my necessary food"
(Job 23:12).

Now all the athletic Christians—all those who can carry heavy loads, do thorough work and stand a long pull—are hungry feeders on God's Book. Nothing will impart sinew and muscle to your piety like the thorough study and digestion of your Bible. A good sermon must be digested or it will be of little use to you, and your daily bread of the Bible must go through the same process in order that it may be assimilated and taken into your spiritual fiber. "Thy words were found and I did eat them, and they were the joy of mine heart," said the old-time saint.

Every growing Christian is a ruminating animal. He chews Bible truth and nutritious sermons and wholesome books and other such provender as the cow cheweth her cud. One strong Bible text lodged in the memory, and turned over and over and well digested, will be a breakfast for your soul, and in the strength of it you go through the whole day.

A soldier is never in so good trim for battle as after a sound sleep and a square morning meal. It is not easy to fight or to march on an empty stomach. In like manner, every servant of Jesus Christ must recruit his or her spiritual strength by reading Christ's words, and thinking about them, by meditation, by prayer and soul converse with God. Martin Luther, in the thick of his campaigns with the Pope and the devil, said that he could not get on without two good hours each day for his private devotions. I have always observed that the light readers and light thinkers make light Christians, and those who neglect their Bibles and their closets soon dwindle into dwarfs. Having no depth of root their religion withers away.—*Theodore Cuyler.*

Most people give their bodies about ten hours a day in eating, and drinking, and dressing, and sleeping, and maybe a few minutes to their souls. We ought to give at least one solid hour every day to restful, loving devotion with Jesus over our open Bible, for the refreshing, developing and strengthening of our spiritual life. If we would do this, God would have an opportunity to teach, correct, inspire, and comfort us, reveal His secrets to us, and make spiritual giants of us. If we will not do this, we shall surely be spiritual weaklings all our days, however we may wish to be strong.—*Samuel Logan Brengle.*

Know your own size

"I say . . . to every man that is among you, not to think of himself more highly than he ought to think; but to think soberly, according as God hath dealt to every man the measure of faith" (Rom. 12:3).
"The tongue is a little member, and boasteth great things" (James 3:5).

One of the hardest phrases to utter in the English language is, "I don't know." Many people try to bluff their way through life and find themselves in all kinds of complications which at times takes something akin to white lies in order to extricate themselves. But the true man or woman of God will lose nothing but gain much by admitting what he does not know.

The celebrated Duval, librarian of Francis I, often answered questions by, "I don't know." An insolent man replied to him one day, "Why, sir, you ought to know. The Emperor pays you for your knowledge." Duval answered, "The Emperor pays me for what I know; if he was to pay me for what I don't know, all the treasures of his empire would not be sufficient."

> He who knows not and knows not that he knows not is a fool:
> Shun him!
> He who knows and knows not that he knows is asleep:
> Awake him!
> He who knows not and knows that he knows not is a child:
> Teach him!
> He who knows and knows that he knows is wise:
> Follow him!
> —*Arabian Proverb.*

When I was young I was sure of everything; in a few years, having been mistaken a thousand times, I was not half as sure of most things as I was before. At present I am hardly sure of anything, but what God has revealed to man.
—*John Wesley.*

June 10
Enriched by pain

"Yet learned he obedience by the things which he suffered" (Heb. 5:8).
"For as the sufferings of Christ abound in us, so our consolation also aboundeth by Christ" (2 Cor. 1:5).

One who had suffered a great deal through illness wrote to a friend:

"I can hardly say I am sorry for you, dear friend, although you tell me of suffering and trial, and although I feel very much for you in it; because I am so *sure* the Master is leading you by the right way, and only means it to issue in all the more blessing. What mistakes we should make if we had the choosing, and marked out nice smooth paths for our friends! It has struck me, too, very much lately, that the Lord's most used and blessed workers are almost always *weighted* in some way or other. I don't know one who, to our limited view, is not working under weights and hindrances of some sort, contrasting with mere professors who seem so much more favorably placed for what they *don't* do.

"I am so very glad that He did not answer prayer for my recovery all those eight months of illness; why I should have missed all sorts of blessing and precious teaching if He had!"—*Frances Ridley Havergal.*

Praise to God! He often crosses
    Plans and schemes poor self has form'd,
And for reckon'd gains have losses
    Sprung where God's dark purpose storm'd;
But I bless Him that His thunder
    Spake His grace into my soul,
And my heart melts at the wonder
    God has brought good from the whole.

Gourds have perish'd, but I would not
    Like impatient Jonah be;
God is God, and oh, I could not
    Trace my road so well as He!
Darkest hour before the dawning,
    Shadows thickest just before,
Lifting, show they're but the awning
    Drawn around our Father's door.

Bless His Name! He ever mindeth
    His Blood-Covenant with me;
And the soul that trusts Him findeth
    Good in all life's mysteries.
        —J. Robertson & R. F. Beveridge.

Happy believers

"But let all those that put their trust in thee rejoice: let them ever shout for joy, because thou defendest them: let them also that love thy name be joyful in thee" (Psa. 5:11).
"In thy presence is fulness of joy; at thy right hand there are pleasures for evermore" (Psa. 16:11).
"Now the God of hope fill you with all joy and peace in believing"
(Rom. 15:13).

The prayer is for fullness of joy and peace through believing. There are no happy doubters, no jubilant unbelievers. The highest joy grows on the topmost bough of faith. The seed of joylessness is unbelief. Hence the antidote for a lack of joy, that "fruit of the Spirit," is a little more faith in Jesus. Faith is the only doorway for God to enter the soul, leading the blessed procession of beatitudes—love, joy, and peace. How many try to admit them through the door of reason and fail. While His truth enters in through this door, He Himself can enter only through the door of faith. He is too large for our logic, but not for our faith.—*Daniel Steele.*

A heavenly mind is a joyful mind; this is the nearest and the truest way to comfort, and without this you must needs be uncomfortable. Can a man be at the fire and not be warm, or in the sunshine and not have light? Can your heart be in Heaven and not have comfort? What could make so many frozen, uncomfortable Christians, but living so far as they do from Heaven, and what makes others so warm in comforts, but their frequent access so near to God!
—*Richard Baxter.*

Ah, life is lonely without God—
A desert drear and wild;
One feels an exile far from home
And like an orphan child.

Though weak and sinful, God is found
By those who are sincere;
To hearts that hunger for His love
He tenderly draws near.

To know the Father and the Son
Is everlasting bliss;
Earth's fading joys cannot compare
With joy as pure as this!
—*Max I. Reich.*

Self-denying love

"Though he was rich, yet for your sakes he became poor, that ye through his poverty might be rich" (2 Cor. 8:9).
"Then said Jesus unto his disciples, If any man will come after me, let him deny himself, and take up his cross, and follow me" (Matt. 16:24).

On the whole, then, to deny ourselves is to deny our own will where it does not fall in with the will of God, and that however pleasing it may be. It is to deny ourselves any pleasure which does not spring from and lead to God; that is in effect to refuse going out of our way, though into a pleasant, flowery path; to refuse what we know to be deadly poison, though agreeable to the taste.

The great hindrance of our receiving or growing in the grace of God is always the want of denying ourselves or taking up our cross.

> He might have built a palace at a word
> Who sometimes had not where to lay His head;
> Time was when He Who nourished crowds with bread
> Would not one meal unto Himself afford.
>
> Twelve legions girded with angelic sword
> Were at His beck—tho' scorned and buffeted;
> He healed another's scratch; His own side bled,
> Side, feet, hand with cruel piercings gored.
>
> Oh, wonderful the wonders left undone!
> And scarce less wonderful than those He wrought!
> Oh, self-restraint passing all human thought
> To have all power and be as having none!
> Oh, self-denying love, which felt alone
> For needs of others, never for its own.
> —*Richard Chenevix Trench.*

The natural desire of all of us is to have better clothes, better food, better homes, more gadgets, more THINGS, but when we become a new creature in Christ our desires are reversed. Our passion then is to serve Christ, and to use as little of the things of this world as we can in order that God may have the more. That is when God will be able to evangelize the world—when His people will say, "I don't want to have more furniture, more money, more of this and that; I just want what I need. I'll spend as little as I can even on food, so that I can give as much as I can to God. I have only one life to live—I must give all of it to God for His work."—*Norman Grubb.*

Prayer vital to the Christian

"But thou, when thou prayest, enter into thy closet, and when thou hast shut thy door, pray to thy Father which is in secret; and thy Father which seeth in secret shall reward thee openly" (Matt. 6:6).
"I have set the Lord always before me: because he is at my right hand, I shall not be moved" (Psa. 16:8).

We know from much experience that the enemy does his utmost to prevent us from having a quiet hour. He is only too well aware of its importance in a healthy believer's life, and knows what wealth of overcoming power lies hidden for us there. Public worship, Bible-study circles, meetings, prayer meetings, are all good, and we should attend them whenever possible, but they can never take the place of the quiet hour. Moreover, our Lord Himself ordained these times of stillness when He said, "But thou, when thou prayest, enter into thy closet, and when thou hast shut thy door, pray to thy Father which is in secret; and thy Father which seeth in secret shall reward thee openly."

The Lord does not state explicitly what length of time we should spend in secret, but it is clear that He meant private prayer to be practiced in perfect seclusion and inner concentration. In a few hurried minutes this is impossible; we need time to wait in silence before God, and to speak with Him. If we need further proof of the import of this thing, we have our Lord's own silent watches on the mountain, in the early morning hours or in the quiet of the night, to convince us. If He, the Son of God, felt the need of solitude, He Who was never disturbed, never influenced by His surroundings, how much more do we need such times of quiet alone with God!—*Sister Eva.*

I would converse with Thee from day to day,
With heart intent on what Thou hast to say,
And through my pilgrim walk, whate'er befall,
Consult with Thee, O Lord! about it all.
Since Thou art willing thus to condescend
To be my intimate, familiar Friend,
Oh! let me to the great occasion rise,
And count Thy friendship life's most glorious prize!
—*J. R. Miller.*

175

June 14

Leave no duty undone

"Therefore to him that knoweth to do good, and doeth it not, to him it is sin"
(James 4:17).
"So did Joshua; he left nothing undone" (Josh. 11:15).

No matter what the form of the temptation may be, he who, when convinced of his duty, yet takes no corresponding action, is on the highroad to perdition. Inevitably this bondage grows stronger and stronger with every fresh trial of its strength.

Every time you are convinced of duty and yet resist that conviction and refuse to act in accordance with it, you become more and more helpless; you commit yourself more and more to the control of your iron-hearted master. Every fresh case renders you only the more fully a helpless slave.

—*Charles G. Finney.*

You will be judged in that great day of accounts not only for what you have done, but for what you have left undone. Your neglected opportunities will be taken into account.

> They do the least who talk the most,
> Whose good designs are all their boast.
> Let words be few.
>
> They do the most whose lives possess
> The sterling stamp of righteousness;
> For deeds are true.
> —*Unknown.*

Maxims from David Livingstone:

Fear God and work hard.

Anywhere, provided it be forward.

I am resolved to continue doing my duty whatever it cost.

I mean to open up the country or die in the attempt. I'll find a path or make one.

All that I am I owe to Jesus Christ, revealed to me in His divine Book. Here is the source of strength and the transforming power.

Keep a good conscience

"Herein do I exercise myself, to have always a conscience void of offence toward God, and toward men" (Acts 24:16).
"Holding faith, and a good conscience" (1 Tim. 1:19).

A good conscience is a palace for Christ, a temple for the Holy Ghost, a paradise of delight, and a standing Sabbath for the saint.—*St. Augustine.*

If a man has nothing to reproach himself with, he can bear anything.
—*Phillips Brooks.*

A Conscience:
　　So awake, that it cannot be surprised;
　　So just, that it cannot be bribed;
　　So pleased with that which is right, as to be a cause of constant joy;
　　So pained with what is wrong, that it is, so long as we are guided by its
　　　　dictates, impossible to sin;
　　A Conscience that will not give its consent, however enticed or
　　　　persuaded, to anything that is evil.—*John Hunt.*

The conscience is to man what the lighthouse is to the mariner except that the lighthouse continues to flash its warnings, but the conscience can be stifled and seared.

"Having their conscience seared with a hot iron" (1 Tim. 4:2).

　　　　　"Good-bye," I said to my conscience.
　　　　　　"Good-bye, for aye and aye."
　　　　And I put off her hands harshly,
　　　　　And I turned my face away;
　　　　And conscience smitten sorely
　　　　　Returned not from that day.

　　　　But a time came when my spirit
　　　　　Grew weary of its pace,
　　　　And I cried, "Come back, my conscience;
　　　　　I long to see thy face."
　　　　But conscience cried, "I cannot;
　　　　　Remorse sits in my place."
　　　　　　　　　　　—*Unknown.*

The Master's blueprint for me

"Be ye not unwise, but understanding what the will of the Lord is"
                                                                (Eph. 5:17).
*"Teach me to do thy will; for thou art my God: thy spirit is good; lead me into
the land of uprightness" (Psa. 143:10).*

Let it once be fixed that a man's one ambition is to fit into God's plan for
him, and he has a North Star ever in sight to guide him steadily over any sea,
however shoreless it seems. He has a compass that points true in the thickest
fog, and fiercest storm, and regardless of magnetic rocks.—*S. D. Gordon.*

> There was a time I had a plan for life,
> A cunning blueprint fashioned in a dream,
> And proudly would I build my structure great,
> With fame and fortune ever as my theme.
>
> High on a hill I thought that I would build,
> And watch the world below—its envious eyes
> Looking with tribute to my wealth and fame,
> And honor to the man who grew so wise.
>
> One day I stood there worshipping my plans,
> When suddenly I heard a Voice so true,
> "Give me those plans, for they must be destroyed.
> I've worked a plan and pattern out for you."
>
> I knew that Voice, I'd heard it oft before;
> Though still and small, it came to me again,
> A voice to touch the proud and boastful life,
> And melt the very hearts of haughty men.
>
> That day I turned my blueprints over to God.
> He gave another set for taking mine,
> With pages blank—I cannot tell you why—
> But every day He adds another line.
>   —*Esther Pritchard Moore.*

What God calls a man to do He will carry him through. I would undertake
to govern half a dozen worlds if God called me to do it, but I would not undertake
to govern half a dozen sheep unless God called me to do it.—*Edward Payson.*

The seriousness of wrong advice

"For our rejoicing is this, the testimony of our conscience, that in simplicity and godly sincerity, not with fleshly wisdom, but by the grace of God, we have had our conversation in the world, and more abundantly to you-ward"
(2 Cor. 1:12).
"Give therefore thy servant an understanding heart . . . that I may discern between good and bad" (1 Kings 3:9).

Counsel is good; any man that thinks he does not need it is a fool or worse. But counsel in order to be good must come from a reliable source.

I may be called a preacher of divine truth; I may be a teacher of the young; I may be a parent called to instruct my children in the things of God; I may be simply one friend giving advice to another in some perplexity of conscience, some difficulty of faith, some doubt as to the path of duty. In any of these capacities, it is sadly possible that I may only lead astray, unless I myself am unmistakably and consciously and continually taught of God.

Mistaken advice, even in questions of science or literature or art—the advice of an incompetent guide—may be serious in many of its effects. Yet these are only trifles compared with the danger of misleading souls in the matter of their relation to God.—*G. H. Knight.*

> Oh, if mine own thought should on Thy words falling,
> Mar the great message, and men hear not Thee,
> Give me Thy mind to grasp Thy mystery;
> So shall my heart throb, and my glad eyes glisten,
> Rapt with the wonders Thou dost shew to me.
> —*By a Missionary en route to his Field.*

Christ's witnesses

"Ye are my witnesses, saith the Lord" (Isa. 43:10).
"If thou shalt confess with thy mouth the Lord Jesus, and shalt believe in thine heart that God hath raised him from the dead, thou shalt be saved"
(Rom. 10:9).

A witness is presumed to know something, to have something to tell, and he is considered bound by all the solemnities of an oath to divulge whatever he knows touching the pending case. Accordingly God has placed every renewed man on the witness-stand, and He now bids him proceed with the story of His redemption. It is also recorded, "With the heart man believeth unto righteousness; and with the mouth confession is made unto salvation." Faith, which works by love, or interests the affections in the exercise of confiding trust, brings the blessing of righteousness; but salvation, full and continuous, is made to hinge upon confession from the lips. Smothered fire goes out, but live coals, exposed and swept by the winds of Heaven, will glow and kindle into a flame. It is so with experimental grace.

It has been the general belief of our people, that when reputed Christians cease to speak of the dealings of God with their souls, they are in the condition of the man, who, being asked, "Have you got religion?" replied, "None to speak of." It is the nature of religion to tell itself.

Testimony is the conveyance of facts, by speaking or writing, from those who have personal knowledge of them, to those who have not.—*I. Taylor.*

> Help me to sing, help me to sing!
> My captive heart is Thine!
> Thy love has sought me and has won
> The life I thought was mine.
>
> Now would I offer back to Thee
> One consecrated song,
> I would the music ever be
> Courageous, brave and strong.
> —*John Wright Follette.*

God has not retained many of us as lawyers, but He has subpoenaed all of us as witnesses.

A Bible Christian

"When ye received the word of God which ye heard of us, ye received it not as the word of men, but as it is in truth, the word of God, which effectually worketh also in you that believe" (1 Thess. 2:13).

Mrs. Phoebe Palmer wielded such a powerful influence on those around her that De Witt Talmage said, "I believe that one hundred Phoebe Palmers would bring the millennium tomorrow morning." She, however, learned the way into this useful, Spirit-filled life through the study of the Scriptures.

One night she dreamed she stood before the Judgment Seat of Christ, and was asked on what she based her hope of heavenly reward. She was speechless as she remembered how she had compared herself and her experience with other professing Christians around her, rather than going to God's Word for her guidance. Then the eyes of the stern Judge pierced her through. "You had My Word. Did you not use it?" He asked. "'The word that I have spoken, the same shall judge him in the last day.'" She awakened with a sense of relief that this terrible condemnation was not final and made this vow: "I will seek only to be fully conformed to the will of God, as recorded in His written Word. My chief endeavors shall be centered in the aim to be a humble Bible Christian."

> Blessed Bible! how I love it!
> How it doth my bosom cheer!
> What hath earth like this to covet?
> O, what stores of wealth are here!
> Man was lost and doomed to sorrow;
> Not one ray of light or bliss
> Could he from earth's treasure borrow,
> 'Til his way was cheered by this!
>
> Yes, I'll to my bosom press thee,
> PRECIOUS WORD, I'll hide thee here;
> Sure my very heart will bless thee,
> For thou ever sayest "good cheer":
> Speak, my heart, and tell thy ponderings,
> Tell how far thy rovings led,
> When THIS BOOK brought back thy wanderings,
> Speaking life as from the dead.
> —*Phoebe Palmer.*

Were I to live to be as old as Methuselah, and be brought into the most perplexing circumstances anyone could be brought into, I should ever find the light and guidance I need in the Bible.—*Phoebe Palmer.*

June 20
Don't avoid being unpopular

"If they have persecuted me, they will also persecute you" (John 15:20).
"Rejoicing that they were counted worthy to suffer shame for his name"
(Acts 5:41).

Oh, for an enthusiasm for Christ that will not endure to be popular when He is unpopular, but will be fired rather than be quenched when His claims are unrecognized and His Word is slighted; that will thrill us with joy if He allows us to share in the faintest measure in His dishonor and loneliness; that will set every pulse throbbing with exultation as we go forth unto Him.—*I. Lilias Trotter.*

> Measure your life by loss, and not by gain,
> Not by the wine drunk but by the wine poured forth;
> For love's strength standeth in love's sacrifice,
> And he who suffers most has most to give.
> *—Unknown.*

We are refining on Christian work—the whole tendency is in that direction. We are so refined that we send apologetic word to iniquity when we propose to attack it. With a sword, silver chased, presented by the ladies, we ride out on a white palfrey covered with embroidered housing, and we put spurs into the war charger just enough to make him dance gracefully, and then we send a missive, delicate as a wedding card, asking the old black giant of sin to surrender.

Christian women saved by the sacrifice of Christ, and with a glorious mission given them, sometimes staying at home from the Sabbath-school class because their new hat is not finished, and churches, which used to shake our cities with rousing revivals, sending around a committee to ask demonstrative worshippers if they will please to say "Amen" and "Hallelujah" a little softly. We are trying to baptize the Church of God in this day with Cologne and balm of a thousand flowers, when it wants a baptism of fire from the Lord God of Pentecost. O! we are so afraid somebody will criticize our sermons, or our prayers, or our exhortations, that we forget our desire for the world's conquest in the fear we shall get hurt.—*De Witt Talmage.*

Add your light

"I have set thee to be a light" (Acts 13:47).
"Now are ye light in the Lord: walk as children of light" (Eph. 5:8).

Dwight L. Moody used the following illustration of a great truth: "Away out in the prairie regions, when meetings were held at night in the log schoolhouse, the announcement of the meeting is given out in this way: 'A meeting will be held by early candlelight.' The first man who comes brings a tallow dip with him. It does not light the building much, but it is better than none at all. The next man brings his candle, and the next family brings their candles. By the time the house is full there is plenty of light. So if we all shine a little there will be a good deal of light. If we cannot all be lighthouses, any one of us can at any rate be a tallow candle."

> I am but one, but I am one.
> I cannot do everything,
> But I can do something.
> What I can do, I ought to do.
> What I ought to do,
> God helping me, I will do.
> —*Motto in an old church.*

Suppose we are beginning to feel the splendid conviction that, after all, our obscure life is not to be wasted; that having this ideal principle within it, it may yet be as great in its homely surroundings as the greatest human life—seeing that no man can do more with his life than the will of God—that though we may never be famous or powerful, or called to heroic suffering or acts of self-denial which will vibrate through history; that though we are neither intended to be apostles nor missionaries nor martyrs—but to be common people living in common houses, spending the day in common offices or common kitchens, yet doing the will of God there, we shall do as much as apostle, or missionary, or martyr—seeing that they can do no more than do God's will where they are, even as we can do as much where we are—and answer the end of our life as truly, faithfully and triumphantly as they.—*Henry Drummond.*

June 22
Moving God and men

"Ye also helping together by prayer for us" (2 Cor. 1:11).
"That which thou hast prayed to me . . . I have heard" (2 Kings 19:20).

Day by day you need communion with God if you are to resist the influences of the difficult days we are in, and of the world round about you. You must have day-by-day communion with God, and day by day a time of much prayer. When crossing the Atlantic, I went into the Marconi room, where wireless messages are sent and received. The operator is a man who can talk to someone hundreds of miles away. He is a most important man to the whole ship. He could talk to others miles away and bring help, if necessary. He could state where the ship was, and call for help in time of danger. The man who prays is the most important man in the kingdom and Church of God. He is a wireless operator, day by day dealing with the unseen, sending out messages, and at times an S O S message, that shall bring help and salvation perhaps to a whole townful of people.—*Barclay Buxton.*

> The day was long, the burden I had borne
> Seemed heavier than I could longer bear;
> And then it lifted—but I did not know
> Someone had knelt in prayer;
>
> Had taken me to God that very hour,
> And asked the easing of the load, and He
> In infinite compassion had stooped down
> And lifted the burden from me.
>
> We cannot tell how often as we pray
> For some bewildered one, hurt and distressed,
> The answer comes, and many times these hearts
> Find sudden peace and rest.
>
> Someone had prayed in faith, a lifted hand
> Reached up to God, and He reached down that day.
> So many, many hearts have need of prayer—
> Then, let us, let us pray.
> —*Unknown.*

Prayer is the power by which that comes to pass which would not otherwise take place.—*Unknown.*

Love—the cure for fear

"There is no fear in love; but perfect love casteth out fear: because fear hath torment. He that feareth is not made perfect in love" (1 John 4:18).
"For ye have not received the spirit of bondage again to fear; but ye have received the Spirit of adoption, whereby we cry, Abba, Father" (Rom. 8:15).

You cannot love and fear the same person, unless the love is of a very rudimentary and imperfect character. Remember that it is "perfect love" which "casts out fear." There are many professing Christian people who live all their days with a burden of shivering dread upon their shoulders and an icy cold fear in their hearts, just because they have not got close enough to Jesus Christ, nor kept their hearts with sufficient steadfastness under the quickening influences of His love, to have shaken off their dread as a sick man's distempered fancies. A little love has not mass enough in it to drive out thick, clustering fears.

There are hundreds of professing Christians who know very little indeed of that joyous love of God which swallows up and makes impossible all dread, who, because they have not a loving Father's loving will, tremble when they front in imagination, and still more when they meet in reality, the evils that must come, and who cannot face the thought of death with anything but shrinking apprehension. There is far too much of the old leaven of selfish dread left in the experiences of many Christians. "I feared thee, because thou wert an austere man, and so, because I was afraid, I went and hid my talent, and did nothing for thee" is a transcript of the experience of far too many of us.

See that you resort only to the sane, sound way of getting rid of the wholesome rational dread of which I have been speaking. There is only one wise thing to do, and that is, to make sure work of getting rid of the occasion of dread, which is the fact of sin. Take all your sin to Jesus Christ; He will—and He only can—deal with it. He will lay His hand on you, as He did of old, with the characteristic word that was so often upon His lips, and which He alone is competent to speak in its deepest meaning, "Fear not, it is I," and He will give you the courage that He commands.—*Alexander Maclaren.*

Temptation or sin

"The Lord knoweth how to deliver the godly out of temptations"
(2 Peter 2:9).
". . . Though now for a season, if need be, ye are in heaviness through manifold temptations" (1 Peter 1:6).

I am glad you seem able in some measure to distinguish between darkness and heaviness. Darkness implies sin, and is associated with condemnation. Heaviness frequently implies little more than temptation, though it may often arise from such innocent causes as disordered nerves, bad health, or the influence of the atmosphere and is consistent with confidence in God; such as Job felt when he said, "though he slay me, yet will I trust in him."

I allow, there may be at such times, great "searchings of heart," and "these try the sinews of the soul, and drill the heart to suffering," but "God is faithful." Hold on here, and you shall weather every storm of earth and hell.

—*James Caughey.*

Each day will bring just temptation enough and power enough to conquer it, and, as one says, "Temptations, with distinct deliverances from them, avail much." The unction of the Holy One is given to believers for this very end—to enable them to distinguish (which otherwise would be impossible) between sin and temptation. And this you will do, not by any general rule, but by listening to Him on all particular occasions and by your consulting with those that have experience in the ways of God.—*John Wesley.*

Satan is never permitted to block up our way without the providence of God making a way through the wall. God ever makes a breach in his otherwise impregnable fortification. Should an upright soul get into difficulties and straits, he may rest assured that there is a way out as there was a way in; and that the trial shall never be above the strength that God shall give him to bear it.

God not overtaxed in filling us

"Yet that valley shall be filled with water, that ye may drink, both ye, and your cattle, and your beasts. And this is but a light thing in the sight of the Lord" *(2 Kings 3:17-18).*
"He hath filled the hungry with good things; and the rich he hath sent empty away" (Luke 1:53).

When the Holy Ghost comes, our needs will be supplied, and the very remembrance of our sorrow and distress will leave us. So long as you are looking at the ditches and thinking of your desperate need, you are not filled with water. God wants so to fill you that He will even obliterate the remembrance of your sin and sorrow, and, as Job beautifully expressed it, you will remember your misery as waters that pass away.

Again, when the water came there was enough, not only for them to drink, but also for their cattle and their beasts; so when God fills your life with the Holy Spirit, the blessing overflows not only to every person around you, but the very beasts that serve you will be the better for your blessing. That truckman was not far astray when he said that his horse and his dog knew that he had been converted.

There is a very remarkable expression used respecting this glorious miracle of divine grace and bounty. "This is but a light thing in the sight of the Lord." This wonderful blessing was not, in God's estimation, anything extraordinary nor at all hard for Him to do. Nor is it a great or difficult thing for Him to baptize you and me with the Holy Ghost till all our wants are supplied and all our being is filled with His blessing. We are constantly thinking of it as though it cost Him some great effort. On the contrary, it is but a light thing for God to do, and is intended to mark rather the beginning than the close of a career of usefulness.—*A. B. Simpson.*

"They were all filled with the Holy Ghost" (Acts 4:31).

June 26
Not to progress is to regress

"The righteous also shall hold on his way, and he that hath clean hands shall be stronger and stronger" (Job 17:9).
"We beseech you . . . that ye increase more and more" (1 Thess. 4:10).

The Christian cannot cease to grow without danger. To keep any religion at all we must grow in grace.

The Christian who does not grow becomes peevish, fretful and unhappy, like a child that has ceased to grow. Is this not the reason why so many professors of religion have become weak, uneasy and dissatisfied? In nature, when growth ceases, decay and death are at hand. When a child ceases to grow, it starts for the grave. Not to progress is to regress, and regression is destruction.

—J. A. Wood.

"Yesterday was the best day of my life, but today is better." This is real Christian experience. Anything short of this kind of progression is backsliding.

"A man of genius," says Gilfillan, "is always a man of limitless growth, with a soul smitten with a passion for growth, and open to every influence that promotes it; who grows always like a tree, by day and by night, in calm and in storm, through opposition and through applause, in difficulty and in despair."

> The oak tree's boughs once touched the grass
> But every year they grew
> A little farther from the ground,
> And nearer toward the blue.
>
> So live that you each year may be,
> While time glides softly by,
> A little farther from the earth,
> And nearer to the sky.
> *—Unknown.*

"Out of the ground made the Lord God to grow every tree" (Gen. 2:9).

Scarred for Christ's sake

"I have fought a good fight" (2 Tim. 4:7).
"These are they which came out of great tribulation" (Rev. 7:14).

Jesus will stand there, scars on His hands, scars on His feet, scars on His brow, scars over His heart, won in the great battle of redemption, and all Heaven will sob aloud with emotion and gratitude. Ignatius will stand there and point to the marks where the tooth and the paw of the lion seized him in the Coliseum. John Huss will show where the coals first scorched his foot on that day when his spirit took wing of flame and rose from Constance. Hugh McKail will point to the mark on the neck where the axe struck him. McMillan and Campbell and Freeman, the American missionaries, who, with their wives and children perished in the awful massacre at Cawnpore, will show where the daggers of the Sepoys struck them. The Waldenses will show where their bones were broken on that day when the Piedmontese soldiery pitched them over the rocks. And all who have nursed the sick and cared for the poor will show the evidences of earthly exhaustion, and Christ shall wave His scarred hand over the scarred multitude, saying: "Ye suffered with Me on earth, now be glorified with Me in Heaven." And the great organs of eternity will take up the chant, and St. John will sweep the keys with his fingers: "These are they which came out of great tribulation, and washed their robes and made them white in the blood of the Lamb." But on that day what will be your chagrin and mine if it shall be told on the streets of Heaven that in this world we shrank back from all toil, from all hardship, from all fatigue? No battle-scars to show the glorified; not so much as one ridge on the palm of the hand to show that just once in all this great battle for God and the truth we clutched so tight and struck so hard that the hand clave to the sword.—*De Witt Talmage.*

My sword I give to him that shall succeed me in my pilgrimage, and my courage and strength to him that can get it. My marks and scars I carry with me, to be a witness for me that I have fought His battles Who will now be my Rewarder. . . . So he passed over, and all the trumpets sounded for him on the other side.—*John Bunyan.*

Faithfulness in small things

"He that is faithful in that which is least is faithful also in much" (Luke 16:10).
"And if ye have not been faithful in that which is another man's, who shall give you that which is your own?" (Luke 16:12).

Little faithfulnesses then are not only the preparation for great ones, but little faithfulnesses are in themselves the great ones. Observe the striking fact that our Lord does not say, "He that is faithful in that which is least *will be* faithful also in much," but "He that is faithful in that which is least *is* faithful also in much." The essential fidelity of the heart is the same whether it be exercised in two mites or in a regal treasury; the genuine faithfulness of the life is equally beautiful whether it be displayed in governing an empire or in writing an exercise. It has been quaintly said that if God were to send two angels to earth, the one to occupy a throne, and the other to clean a road, they would each regard their employments as equally distinguished and equally happy.

All of us may be, in St. Paul's high language, "fellow-laborers with God," and he who is that, be he slave or angel, can be nothing better or greater. The mountains cease to be colossal, the ocean tides lose their majesty, if you see what an atom our earth is in the starry space. Even so turn the telescope of faith to Heaven, and see how at once earth's grandeurs dwindle into nothingness, and Heaven's least interests dilate into eternal breadth. Yes, to be a faithful Christian is greater in God's sight than to be a triumphant statesman or a victorious emperor.—*Dean Farrar.*

I believe it matters little whether we are employed in gathering the sheaves or gleaning the straggling ears after the reaper; it is the *state of the soul* which fixes the value of the employment, not the employment itself; to glorify God is enough, in small or great things, according as the measure of ability and opportunity is ours. Let us try to fix our eye on this and aim at it alone.

—*Catherine Booth.*

There never has been a great and beautiful character which has not become so by filling well the ordinary and smaller offices appointed of God.

—*Horace Bushnell.*

Saved to serve

"This woman was full of good works and almsdeeds which she did"
(Acts 9:36).
"Every one that doeth righteousness is born of him" (1 John 2:29).

A great many professed Christians have no other idea of religion than that it is the means of getting to Heaven when they die. As to doing anything for God while they live, it does not enter into their plans. I tell you, my brethren, I do not believe there is one in five hundred of such professors that will reach Heaven; for there is a magnanimity in true religion that is above all such contemptible meanness.—*L. Beecher.*

Oh, turn me, mold me, mellow me for use;
Pervade my being with Thy vital force,
That this else inexpansive life of mine
May become eloquent and full of power,
Impregnated with life and strength divine.
Put the bright torch of Heaven into my hand
That I may carry it aloft
And win the eye of weary wanderers here below,
To guide their feet into the paths of peace.
I cannot raise the dead
Nor from this soil pluck precious dust,
Nor bid the sleeper wake,
Nor still the storm, nor bend the lightning back,
Nor muffle up the thunder,
Nor bid the chains fall from off creation's long enfettered limbs.

But I can live a life that tells on other lives
And makes this world less full of anguish and of pain;
A life that, like the pebble dropped upon the sea,
Sends its wide circle to a hundred shores.
May such a life be mine!
Creator of true life, Thyself the life Thou givest,
Give Thyself, that Thou mayest dwell in me, and I in Thee.
                                                    —*Horatius Bonar.*

God's love in us for others

"Behold, what manner of love the Father hath bestowed upon us"
(1 John 3:1).
"He that dwelleth in love dwelleth in God, and God in him" (1 John 4:16).
"The Lord direct your hearts into the love of God" (2 Thess. 3:5).

"Behold, what manner of love the Father hath bestowed upon us," not manifested or demonstrated, but bestowed, imparted, given to us as a gift. What a wonderful truth this is, that God's love for us shall be in us, and become our love to others! Was this not what our Lord asked for when He prayed, "that the love wherewith thou hast loved me may be in them, and I in them"? The truth declared is that God gives us His love to love with. He has made His love our property, absolutely given it to us, so that it is now ours. Who can tell all that this means? Inspiration itself can only find relief in adoring gratitude. "Behold what manner of love."

Perhaps we shall now better understand the new commandment to love "As I have loved you." On Calvary we see love stronger than death. There we learn what love really is, and what it can do. When that same love drives our chariot wheels, we shall be ready to do as He did. It is where sacrifice begins that the proof of love begins. We must not offer, either to God or man, what costs nothing. The noblest thing in God's world is a lavished life. Carnal, selfish men cannot understand the service and sacrifice of those "Who spend their lives for others, with no ends of their own."

But when our love is in kind like His, we cannot help doing it. Our "must" then is like the "must" of God. God must give His love, whether souls accept it or not. Let the love of Christ, the most sublime of all motives, and the glory of Christ, the most sublime of all ends, become the ruling principle of action, and who can help living magnanimously for man and for God?

(From *New Testament Holiness* by Thomas Cook. Used by permission of the Epworth Press).

> But the souls who love Him truly
>   Whether for woe or bliss,
> These will count their truest heart's blood
>   Not their own but His.
> Savior, Thou Who thus hast loved me,
>   Give me love like this.
>   —*Unknown.*

July 1
Restrained favors

"Therefore will the Lord wait, that he may be gracious unto you"
(Isa. 30:18).
"For the vision is yet for an appointed time, but at the end it shall speak, and not lie: though it tarry, wait for it; because it will surely come, it will not tarry" (Hab. 2:3).

Yet there are delays in the answers to our prayers. As the husbandman does not reap today that which he sowed yesterday, so neither do we always at once obtain from the Lord that which we seek from Him. The door of grace does open, but not to our first knocks. Why is this? It is because the mercy will be all the greater for being longer on the road. There is a time for every purpose under Heaven, and everything is best in its time. Fruit ripens in its season, and the more seasonable it is the better it is. Untimely mercies would be only half mercies, therefore the Lord withholds them till they have come to their perfection. Even Heaven itself will be all the better because it will not be ours till it is prepared for us, and we are prepared for it.

Love presides over the arrangements of grace, and strikes upon the bell when the best moment has arrived. God blesses us by His temporary delays, as well as by His prompt replies. We are not to doubt the Lord because His time has not yet come: that would be to act like petulant children, who must have a thing at the instant, or else they think they shall never have it. A waiting God is the true object of confidence to His waiting people. "Therefore will the Lord wait, that he may be gracious unto you" (Isa. 30:18). His compassions fail not even when His gracious operations appear to be suspended, and our griefs are deepened. Yea, it is because He loves us so much that He tries us by delaying His answers of peace. It is with our Father in Heaven even as it was with our Lord on earth: "Now Jesus loved Martha, and her sister, and Lazarus. When he had heard therefore that he was sick, he abode two days still in the same place where he was" (John 11:5-6). Love closes the hand of divine bounty, and restrains the outflow of favor, when it sees that a solid gain will ensue from a period of trial.—*C. H. Spurgeon.*

Ready for every good work

"If a man therefore purge himself from these, he shall be a vessel unto honour, sanctified, and meet for the master's use, and prepared unto every good work"
(2 Tim. 2:21).
"Be ready to every good work" (Titus 3:1).

PREPARED UNTO EVERY GOOD WORK.—This last characteristic means readiness for all sorts of service. The teaching is that holiness is the source of every kind of human excellence. It sets to work all our powers and in the best possible directions. It means the sanctification of hands, feet, brain, temper, pocket, the whole man inwardly and outwardly. The desire and aim then is to make a "good work" of whatever is given us to do, and to do it in the best and most perfect way, according to our light and knowledge; let it be the painting of a picture, the sweeping of a room, the managing of a business, or the preaching of a sermon. The meanest service is ennobled by its lofty motive when we work under the inspiration of the Cross. In estimating the value of Christian work we often think too much of our efforts and too little of our spirit and life, but character is really of more importance than our activities. "Words have a weight," says Thomas Carlyle, "when there is a man behind them," and when behind our efforts there is the fragrance of a holy and consistent life our labor cannot be in vain. "Holy living is the rhetoric that tells best in this age of facts." The measure of our holiness is the measure of our power. By this means and this only are we "prepared unto every good work."

Let us note the word "every," because we shall be many-sided when our hearts are cleansed from all sin. We are in danger of limiting our conceptions of duty to some particular sphere, repeating one note instead of a full chord, but the world is wide, the human need is great, and the best servants are the servants of all work. They are always on the alert for opportunities to do good, and ready even if the call comes suddenly, as it often does. It is not with them as with many who are not living with their loins girt, and who often let their opportunity pass before they have pulled themselves together. It is a grand thing to be "prepared unto every good work"—always ready. Chrysostom interprets the words to mean "ready for every emergency which would add to the glory of God, ready even for death, if needs be, or any other painful witness."

(From *New Testament Holiness*, by Thomas Cook. Used by permission of the Epworth Press).

Readiness for God means that we are ready to do the tiniest little thing or the great big thing, it makes no difference. . . . A ready person never has to get ready.

Sprinkle the salt discreetly

"And he went forth unto the spring of the waters, and cast the salt in there, and said, Thus saith the Lord, I have healed these waters; there shall not be from thence any more death or barren land" (2 Kings 2:21).

In the story of old when the water was bitter and the land was barren, the prophet took a cruse of salt and cast it into the spring. At once the fountain was healed, and the land became fruitful. Christ's true disciple is just such a cruse of salt in the Master's hand, one whose presence has power to heal life's bitterness, making the water of life sweet for those about us, and planting the waste and desolate places of life with a beauty like the garden of the Lord. Surely Heaven itself could have no fairer sight for our blessed Master than such a disciple here in the midst of our busy life, one whose noiseless influence is like a breath of Heaven, bringing wholesomeness, sweetness and strength. To come into contact with such an one is to find a healing virtue.

Think, then, how Christ is saddened and what a sense of failure hurts Him when anyone stands forth as His disciple, and yet brings no blessing, never healing the springs of bitterness or turning the barren places into beauty. The salt that is without savor is no salt at all. Fling it away! White it may be, and in the most orthodox of saltcellars, but if it is not sweetening the life about you, fling it away and cry to God for some better.

Salt, so needful, so wholesome, yet it is to be wisely used. There is a kind of good people who find it saves so much trouble to deal out religion in large doses, especially, perhaps, to servants and children, giving them a long and solemn lecture on religion at some solemn time, or when one is in the mood for it, or, still more likely, when some grave offense is committed, as if religion were only a supplementary punishment. No wonder such sufferers never like the taste of it again. Salt discreetly sprinkled over all the common dishes of life, giving all things a savor and sweetness—this our Master seeks to make us.—*Mark Guy Pearse.*

July 4
The cure for worldly anxiety

"To be spiritually minded is life and peace" (Rom. 8:6).
"To him that overcometh will I give to eat of the hidden manna" (Rev. 2:17).

Overcoming the world implies overcoming a state of worldly anxiety. You know there is a state of great carefulness and anxiety which is common and almost universal among worldly men. It is perfectly natural if the heart is set upon securing worldly good, and has not learned to receive all good from the hand of a great Father and trust Him to give or withhold with His own unerring wisdom. But he who loves the world is the enemy of God, and hence can never have this filial trust in a parental Benefactor, nor the peace of soul which it imparts. Hence worldly men are almost incessantly in a fever of anxiety lest their worldly schemes should fail. They sometimes get a momentary relief when all things seem to go well, but some mishap is sure to befall them at some point soon, so that scarce a day passes that brings not with it some corroding anxiety. Their bosoms are like the troubled sea which cannot rest, whose waters cast up mire and dirt.

But the man who gets above the world gets above this state of ceaseless and corroding anxiety. There is a worldly spirit and there is also a heavenly spirit; and one or the other exists in the heart of every man and controls his whole being. Those who are under the control of the world, of course have not overcome the world. No man overcomes the world till his heart is imbued with the spirit of Heaven.—*Charles G. Finney.*

There is a rest that God bestows,
Transcending pardon's peace,
A lowly, sweet simplicity,
Where inward conflicts cease.
—Unknown.

Give the Bible its place

"Come, I pray you, and hear what is the word that cometh forth from the Lord" (Ezek. 33:30).
"Let the word of Christ dwell in you richly in all wisdom" (Col. 3:16).

One must get at least half an hour daily when his mind is fresh. A tired mind does not readily *absorb.* This should be persisted in until there is a habitual spending of at least that much time daily over the Book, with a spirit at leisure from all else, so it can take in. Then the time should be given to *the Book* itself. If other books are consulted and read, as they will be, let that be *after* the reading of this Book. Let God talk to you direct, rather than through somebody else. Give Him first chance at your ears. This Book in the central place of your table, the others grouped about it. First time given to it.—*S. D. Gordon.*

This Revelation—holy, just and true—
Though oft I read, it seems forever new;
While light from Heaven upon its pages rests,
I feel its power, and with it I am blest.
To this blest treasure, O my soul, attend,
Here find a firm and everlasting friend—
A friend in all life's varied changes sure,
Which shall to all eternity endure.
Henceforth, I take thee as my future guide,
Let naught from thee my youthful heart divide;
And then, if late or early death be mine,
All will be well, since I, O Lord, am Thine.
—*Phoebe Palmer.*

What trouble people take to learn a foreign language in order to have access to its writers! Let no trouble be too great to understand the language of God, His Word, His Son. To learn a foreign language, I get someone who knows it to teach me. The language of God is heavenly, spiritual, supernatural—altogether divine; only the Holy Spirit can teach me to understand it, to think God's own thoughts. Let me take Him as my Teacher.

Watered gardens

"I the Lord do keep it; I will water it every moment: lest any hurt it, I will keep it night and day" (Isa. 27:3).

"He found him in a desert land, and in the waste howling wilderness; he led him about, he instructed him, he kept him as the apple of his eye"
(Deut. 32:10).

"And he shall be like a tree planted by the rivers of water, that bringeth forth his fruit in his season" (Psa. 1:3).

Oh, to have one's soul watered by the Holy Spirit, uniformly—every part of the garden having its own stream; plentifully—sufficient refreshment coming to every tree and herb, however thirsty by nature it may be; continually—each hour bringing not only its heat, but its refreshment; wisely—each plant receiving just what it needs! In a garden you can see by the verdure where the water flows, and you can soon perceive where the Spirit of God comes.

—C. H. Spurgeon.

I've found a great refreshing and a place of perfect rest,
Where waters, gushing, bubbling, spring up in my heart so blest;
Here trees of life are blooming, yielding fruit so rich and rare:
My soul is full of glory and my heart is free from care.

God fills me with His Spirit; I am cleansed in Jesus' blood;
The waters of salvation flow in rivers like a flood;
A channel for God's mighty pow'r my heart and life shall be;
I'll praise Him till my latest breath, then thro' eternity.

This world is like a desert, and the ground is parched and dry,
But Canaan's trees and rivers give one's soul a rich supply.
Men look and wonder how God's plants are kept so fresh and green;
They're watered, like a garden, by God's hand that is unseen.

—L. F. Mitchell.

Be an example

"Be thou an example of the believers, in word, in conversation, in charity, in spirit, in faith, in purity" (1 Tim. 4:12).
"In all things shewing thyself a pattern of good works" (Titus 2:7).

Once more, be sure your example exhorts as well as your words. Let them see you constant in all the duties you persuade them to. Let them see in your lives that superiority to the world which your lips recommend. Let them see, by your constant labors for Heaven, that you indeed believe what you would have them believe.

A holy and heavenly life is a continual pain to the consciences of sinners around you, and continually solicits them to change their course.

—Richard Baxter.

It is trite to say that men leave "footprints on the sands of time." Footprints! They do vastly more. They make or mar the generations which follow them. How many have been offered upon the altar of ambition because Napoleon lived! What numbers have sunk into the lees of sensuality because Byron sang! How many have been won to goodness by the eloquence of Howard's life! "No man liveth to himself," and a man's light words of today may fix the destiny of many who have never heard the speaker's name. It is impossible, therefore, to overrate the importance of the conversion of one soul to Christ, or of the hardening of one heart in sin. In both cases you have started a series of influences whose vibrations reach to the farthest land, and to the latest time.

—W. Morley Punshon.

We need not make so much effort to defend the Bible as to practice it.

—Unknown.

To speak well, is to sound like a cymbal, but to do well, is to act like an angel.—*Phillips Brooks.*

If you will convince a man that he does wrong, do right. Men will believe what they see.—*Thoreau.*

Strengthened through testings

*"We glory in tribulations also: knowing that tribulation worketh patience;
And patience, experience; and experience, hope" (Rom. 5:3-4).
"God left him, to try him, that he might know all that was in his heart"
(2 Chron. 32:31).*

A gentleman once asked George Müller how to have strong faith, and that mighty man of God, whose faith has for many years been a worldwide marvel, replied: "The only way to learn strong faith is to endure great trials." And then to this gem of spiritual truth he added, "I learned my faith by standing firm amid severe testings." James made the same statement when he wrote, "Count it all joy when ye fall into divers temptations." Why? "Knowing this, that the trying of your faith worketh patience." To what end? "That ye may be perfect and entire, wanting nothing." Perfect through perfect testings.

If we, indeed, desire our faith to be strengthened, we should not shrink from opportunities where our faith may be tried, and, therefore, through the trial, be strengthened. Even as believers, we have the same shrinking from standing with God alone—from depending upon Him alone—from looking to Him alone, and yet this is the very position in which we ought to be, if we wish our faith to be strengthened. The more I am in a position to be tried in faith with reference to my body, my family, my service for the Lord, my business, etc., the more shall I have opportunity of seeing God's help and deliverance, and every fresh instance, in which He helps and delivers me, will tend towards the increase of my faith.—*George Müller.*

It is said that Luther was qualified for eminent usefulness by three invaluable teachers: Prayer, Meditation and Temptation.

> I ask:
> What He would have this evil do for me?
> What is its mission? What its misery?
> What golden fruit lies hidden in its husk?
> How shall it nurse my virtue, nerve my will,
> Chasten my passions, purify my love,
> And make me in some goodly sense like Him
> Who bore the cross of evil while He lived,
> Who hung and bled upon it when He died,
> And now in glory wears the victor's crown?
> —*J. G. Holland.*

Bible standard of Christian joy

"And the disciples were filled with joy, and with the Holy Ghost" (Acts 13:52).
"And ye . . . received the word in much affliction, with joy of the Holy Ghost"
(1 Thess. 1:6).

Count those "joy" texts in the Bible. You will be surprised at their number, their beauty, their comprehensiveness, and the way in which they crop out of heavy, hard experiences, like diamonds out of a quartz rock.

Then take more time, and find out whether or not the joy of these Bible people matches yours. If not, why not? If you go grumbling where they are praising, if you are meeting persecution, trials, hardships, privations, necessities, sorrows, with grit, dogged endurance, a sense of hard duty, or anything except the grace and joy of the Holy Spirit, with all the perfect fruits of righteousness, which the Spirit produces, you can't spend the rest of your time any better than in getting on praising ground. Get filled with the Spirit, and you must, you will, rejoice at all times.—*Elizabeth S. Brengle.*

As lilies of the valley pour forth perfume, so good hearts pour forth thanksgiving. No mercy is too small to provoke it, no trial too severe to restrain it. As Samson got honey from the carcass of the lion he slew, and as Moses got water from the flinty rock, so the pure in heart are possessed of a sort of heavenly alchemy, a divine secret by which they get blessing out of all things, and for which there is giving of thanks.—*Samuel Logan Brengle.*

Sorrow with his pick mines the heart, but he is a cunning workman; he deepens the channels whereby happiness may enter, and hollows out new chambers for joy to abide in when he is gone.—*Mary Cholmondeley.*

July 10
Let the Christ-mind be in you

"For who hath known the mind of the Lord, that he may instruct him? But we have the mind of Christ" (1 Cor. 2:16).
"Let this mind be in you, which was also in Christ Jesus" (Phil. 2:5).
"Forasmuch then as Christ hath suffered for us in the flesh, arm yourselves likewise with the same mind: for he that hath suffered in the flesh hath ceased from sin" (1 Peter 4:1).

We can only enter into this mind of Christ when He has entered into us—when the mind of the old Adam, the covetous mind that wants to be something, has been condemned and deprived of its rights that it may be put to death on the Cross. Then we can receive the Son of God into the center of our lives so that we become partakers of His mind, the mind which denies itself and its own things, ever responding "Yea, Father" to the will of God, and stands at His disposal in life and action, in doing and letting be, in work and suffering.

Oh, how this mind of Christ transforms us and our relation to our surroundings! When it has taken possession of us it gives us an inner contentment with the way God leads us. All worry over our own way and will is at an end. "I delight to do thy will, O my God" becomes the watchword of a soul that is filled with the mind of Christ. The least, most insignificant place, which might be compared to the home in Nazareth, is big enough to show forth the glory of God in such a life. Work in the stables, in the scullery, in the laundry, or wherever it may be, will be transfigured into holy divine service, since the Father will be glorified through the mind of the Son.

But when anyone who has this mind stands alone, or has to live and serve among others who have the old selfish disposition, he has glorious opportunities to exalt the victory of self-renouncing love, and through daily dying to bear fruit in a life of voluntary sacrifice. He will be triumphant even in misunderstandings and persecution, and will finally prove the truth of the words: "Blessed are the meek, for they shall inherit the earth." The wonder of this blessed life lies in this, that he who loses finds, and he who dies lives, he that humbles himself is exalted, he who humbly gives up his own rights is raised to a divine position of authority, he who possesses nothing has all things, and whatsoever we surrender for Christ's sake, we find again, transfigured and glorified in Him.—*Sister Eva.*

The zest of uncertainty

"And he went out, not knowing whither he went" (Heb.11:8).

"The wind bloweth where it listeth, and thou hearest the sound thereof, but canst not tell whence it cometh, and whither it goeth: so is every one that is born of the Spirit" (John 3:8).

"It doth not yet appear what we shall be" (1 John 3:2).

We are apt to look upon uncertainty as a bad thing, because we are all too mathematical and common sense. The nature of spiritual life is that we are certain in our uncertainty, consequently we do not make our "nests" anywhere spiritually. Immediately we make a "nest" out of an organization or a creed or a belief, we come across the biggest of all calamities, the fact that all certainty brings death. G. K. Chesterton, that insurgent writer, pronounces all certainties "dead certainties."

All through the Bible the realm of the uncertain is the realm of joy and delight; the certainty of belief brings distress. Certainty of God means uncertainty in life; while certainty in belief makes us uncertain of God. Certainty is the mark of the common-sense life; gracious uncertainty is the mark of the spiritual life, and they must both go together. "It is not yet made manifest what we shall be"—we are gloriously uncertain of the next step, but we are certain of God. Immediately we abandon to God and do the duty that lies nearest, He packs our lives with surprises all the time; whereas if we become the advocates of a set creed, something dies. All certainty brings death to something. When we have a certain belief we kill God in our lives, because we do not believe Him, we believe our beliefs about Him. The helplessness of professional religion is that there is no room for surprise; we tie God up in His laws and in denominational doctrines and orders of services, consequently we do not see God at all. We cannot corner God or spiritual life, to think we can is the curse of denominational belief—we have all the "stock" and no one can have it except in our way. Jesus Christ says: "Except ye become as little children . . ." A little child is certain of its parents, but uncertain about everything else, therefore it lives a perfectly delightful healthy life.—*Oswald Chambers.*

Deliver God's messages

"Thou shalt go to all that I shall send thee, and whatsoever I command thee thou shalt speak. Be not afraid of their faces: for I am with thee to deliver thee, saith the Lord" (Jer. 1:7-8).
*"Then the Lord put forth his hand, and touched my mouth. And the Lord said unto me, Behold, I have put **my words** in thy mouth" (Jer. 1:9).*

There comes a day when all voices, soft or terrible, that man has heard, grow still, to let henceforth only one be heard, which cries to him: "Go! go now and be a witness of the things you have heard! Go! I send you forth as lambs among wolves! Go! I send you toward men whose brow is harsh, whose heart is wicked! Fear nothing, I shall embolden your face. I shall give you a heart of brass and a forehead of diamond."

When that moment has come, one must, in order to remain faithful to his mission, remember that after all he is only a voice. Truth does not belong to us; it is we who belong to truth! Woe to him who possesses it and treats it as something that belongs to himself. Happy is he who is possessed by it! No preference, no kinship, no sympathy counts here. Alas! it is not thus that men understand it. It is for this reason that they degrade truth and that it becomes without power in their hands. Instead of winging its way heavenward in vigorous flight, it crawls along the earth, like an eagle whose wings have been broken. Nothing is sadder than to see how those who ought to lend their voice to truth, turn it to their own uses and play with it.—*Charles Wagner.*

> For truth with tireless zeal they sought;
> In joyless paths they trod—
> Heedless of praise or blame they wrought,
> And left the rest with God.
>
> The lowliest sphere was not disdained;
> Where love could soothe or save
> They went, by fearless faith sustained,
> Nor knew their deeds were brave.
> —*Unknown.*

Absolute surrender

"My lord, O king, . . . I am thine, and all that I have" (1 Kings 20:4).
"Present your bodies a living sacrifice, . . . which is your reasonable service"
(Rom. 12:1).

What Benhadad asked was absolute surrender, and what Ahab gave was what was asked of him—absolute surrender. I want to use these words: "My lord, O king, according to thy saying, I am thine and all that I have," as the words of absolute surrender, with which every child of God ought to yield himself to his Father.

Absolute surrender—let me tell you where I got that word. I have used it myself often before, and you have heard it numberless times. But, ten days ago, in Scotland, I was in a company where we were talking about the condition of Christ's Church, and what the great need of the Church and of believers is. There was in our company a godly worker who has much to do in training workers, and I asked him what he would say was the great need of the Church, and the message that ought to be preached. He answered very quietly and simply and determinedly: "Absolute surrender to God is the one thing." The words struck me as never before. And that man began to tell how, in the workers with whom he had to deal, he finds that if they are sound on that point, even though they be backward, they are willing to be taught and helped, and they always improve; whereas, others who are not sound there very often go back and leave the work. The condition for obtaining God's full blessing is absolute surrender to Him.

You know in daily life what absolute surrender is. You know that everything has to be given up to its special, definite object and service. I have a pen in my pocket, and that pen is absolutely surrendered to the one work of writing, and that pen must be absolutely surrendered to my hand if I am to write properly with it. If another holds it partly, I cannot write properly. And now, do you expect that in your immortal being, in the divine nature that you have received by regeneration, God can work His work, every day and every hour, unless you are entirely given up to Him?—*Andrew Murray.*

In Wesley's day the Bishop of London, hearing of their strange enthusiasm and open-air preaching, said: "Those young rawheads, what can they attempt?" Wesley's reply was a noteworthy one: "We can attempt to be that in the hands of God that a pen is in the hands of a man."

July 14
The absurdity of pride

"For if a man think himself to be something, when he is nothing, he deceiveth himself" (Gal. 6:3).
"Mind not high things, but condescend to men of low estate. Be not wise in your own conceits" (Rom. 12:16).

"Pride," says Ruskin, "is at the bottom of all great mistakes. Nor does it require experience of life to prove the truth of the dictum. The worst of it, however, is that pride seems to blind its victims. They are unconscious of any responsibility for the wreckage around them. The callous self has the eyes of the heart fast closed to what is obvious to the onlooker. So, locked up in steel, the proud soul wounds and knows it not; alienates and wonders at the shrinking; struts through life, losing and unconscious of its loss; instructing, but uninstructed. For herein does Nature avenge herself upon the man who erects himself above his kind. The proud heart and lofty mountain are always barren."

Two little raindrops were born in a shower,
And one was so pompously proud of his power,
He got in his head an extravagant notion
He'd hustle right off and swallow the ocean.
A blade of grass that grew by the brook
Called for a drink, but no notice he took
Of such trifling things. He must hurry to be
Not a mere raindrop, but the whole sea.
A stranded ship needed water to float,
But he could not bother to help a boat.
He leaped in the sea with a puff and a blare—
And nobody even knew he was there!

But the other drop as along it went
Found the work to do for which it was sent;
It refreshed the lily that drooped its head,
And bathed the grass that was almost dead.
It got under the ships and helped them along,
And all the while sang a cheerful song.
It worked every step of the way it went,
Bringing joy to others, to itself content,
And welcomed the sea as an old-time friend.
"An ocean," it said, "there could not be
Except for the millions of drops like me."
—*Joseph Morris.*

206

The Word necessary to prayer

"If ye abide in me, and my words abide in you, ye shall ask what ye will, and it shall be done unto you" (John 15:7).
"I have done all these things at thy word. Hear me, O Lord, hear me. . . . Then the fire of the Lord fell" (1 Kings 18:36-38).

The verse before us shows the important connection existing between a full knowledge of the Word of God and successful prayer. Those prayers only will be answered which are in harmony with the revealed will of God. Many of us have heard earnest, but ignorant believers praying for things clearly contrary to the revealed purposes of God. Again a full knowledge of the Word will often bring to our recollection appropriate promises, and thus enable us to pray with faith and confidence.

Abiding in Christ and feeding upon His Word will lead to a Christ-like walk, which will assure our hearts before God.

We *must* take time to be holy. It is not so much the quantity of Scripture we read, as the subjects for meditation which we find in it, that measure the nourishment we gain. On the other hand, our reading must not be too limited, for as the whole Paschal Lamb was to be eaten, so the whole Word of God is profitable and necessary "that the man of God may be perfect, throughly furnished unto all good works." We would earnestly recommend the consecutive reading of the whole Word of God to all who do not so read it; and to all who are able to do so that the whole Bible be read over in the course of the year. Where this cannot be done prayerfully and thoughtfully, rather let a shorter portion be taken for daily reading, still going through the whole of the Word consecutively.—*Hudson Taylor.*

What would He think of me
If when I saw Him, I should say,
"I was too busy every day
To read what Thou didst write to me;
I really hadn't time for Thee!"
—*Martha Snell Nicholson*
(*Evangelical Christian*).

July 16
Faithful witnessing rewarded

"Go, stand and speak in the temple to the people all the words of this life"
(Acts 5:20).
"Be not thou therefore ashamed of the testimony of our Lord" (2 Tim. 1:8).

Some years ago, during a revival meeting, a very timid lady felt moved to go and speak to a couple of young men whom she saw in the back part of the church. It was a great cross to her to do it, but in the Name of Him Who had worn the crown of thorns for her, she arose and started. When she came to them, and began to talk about Jesus, they burst out laughing in her face. Utterly crushed and humiliated to the lowest degree, she went back to her seat and sat down in sorrow. She felt that her mission had failed, and almost resolved that she would never again speak to anybody about salvation. It happened that those two young men were roommates. In the small hours of the night, one of them heard the other sobbing.

"What's the matter, Ed.? Are you sick?" he asked.

"No, but I despise myself for the way I insulted that dear old lady. It was a dreadful hard thing for her to come to us as she did, but she wanted to do us good, and to think that I was mean enough to laugh in her face makes me hate myself. I never would have believed that I could have been so mean. If anybody should insult my mother in that way I would thrash him if it was the last thing I ever did."

"That's just my case exactly," responded the first speaker. "My heart looks blacker to me than it ever did before. I wish I were a Christian."

It wasn't long until those boys crawled out of bed and began to hold a prayer-meeting. The result was that they were both converted before morning, and they have remained that way ever since. They have both been valiant workers for God from that day to this, and have done great good in His service. The timid little woman who was laughed at that evening for Christ's sake, was made almost too happy to live the next day when the joyful tidings came to her.

"If they had stood in my counsel, and had caused my people to hear my words, then they should have turned them from their evil way, and from the evil of their doings" (Jer. 23:22).

Beautify your corner

"Worship the Lord in the beauty of holiness" (Psa. 29:2).
"Let the beauty of the Lord our God be upon us: and establish thou the work of our hands" (Psa. 90:17).

Believe in yourself—that you, even you, can do some of the work which He would like done, and that unless you do it, it will remain undone. How are you to begin? As Christ did. First, He looked at the city; then He wept over it; then He died for it.

Where are you to begin? Begin where you are. Make that one corner, room, house, office, as like Heaven as you can. Begin? Begin with the paper on the walls, make that beautiful; with the air, keep it fresh; with the very drains, make them sweet; with the furniture, see that it be honest. Abolish whatever worketh abomination—in food, in drink, in luxury, in books, in art; whatsoever maketh a lie—in conversation, in social intercourse, in correspondence, in domestic life. This done, you have arranged for a heaven, but you have not got it. Heaven lies within, in kindness, in humbleness, in unselfishness, in faith, in love, in service. To get these in, get Christ in. Teach it not as a doctrine, but as a discovery, as your own discovery. Live your own discovery.—*Henry Drummond.*

Let me not die before I've done for Thee
My earthly work, whatever it may be;
Call me not hence with mission unfulfilled;
Let me not leave my space of ground untilled;
Impress this truth upon me, that not one
Can do my portion that I leave undone.

Then give me strength all faithfully to toil,
Converting barren earth to fruitful soil.
I long to be an instrument of Thine
For gathering worshipers into Thy shrine:
To be the means one human soul to save
From the dark terrors of a hopeless grave.
—*Unknown.*

The question is not "What can you do?" but "What can you and God together do?"—*Abbott.*

July 18
Blessings of adverse criticism

"Esteeming the reproach" (Heb. 11:26).
"Fear ye not the reproach of men, neither be ye afraid" (Isa. 51:7).

An enemy is always more interested in our faults and shortcomings than in our excellences, and frequently takes pain to discover them and spread them abroad. If, instead of letting this excite us to anger, we use it as a means for restraining those faults—if we are more concerned in the endeavor to avoid the misdeeds for which we are criticized than the criticism itself—then our enemies, in trying to harm us, will have done us a great good. If in those very points in which they depreciate us we prove ourselves spotless, their testimony against us will lose weight, and their influence in our disfavor will die away. But, if we are merely indignant at the detraction, and wrathful with the detractor, we shall confirm his evil report in the minds of those who have heard it.

Someone has aptly said, "When men speak ill of thee, live so that nobody may believe them." This reminds us of the case of the blacksmith who had been grossly slandered. A friend advised him to bring a suit against the evildoer. He declined with the remark that he could go into his shop and hammer out a better character in six months than all the courts in Christendom could give him. An intelligent enemy is worth more than an ignorant friend.—*Unknown.*

> Never you fear, but go ahead
> In God-relying strength;
> What matters it that malice said,
> "We've found it out at length"?
> Found out! Found what? An honest man
> Is open as the light;
> Go search as keenly as you can,
> You'll only find—all right.
>
> Aye! Blot him black with slander's ink,
> He stands as white as snow;
> You serve him better than you think,
> And kinder than you know.
> Yes! be the scandal what you will,
> Or whisper what you please;
> You do but fan his glory still
> By whistling up a breeze.
> —*Unknown.*
>
> Assailed by scandal and the tongue of strife,
> His only answer was—a blameless life.
> —*William Cowper.*

Create silence for God's voice

"Stand still, and I will hear what the Lord will command" (Num. 9:8).
"I will hear what God the Lord will speak" (Psa. 85:8).

How silent are God's voices. How few men are strong enough to be able to endure silence, for in silence God is speaking to the inner ear.

> Let us then labor for an inward stillness—
> An inward stillness and an inward healing;
> That perfect silence where the lips and heart
> Are still, and we no longer entertain
> Our own imperfect thoughts and vain opinions,
> But God alone speaks in us, and we wait
> In singleness of heart, that we may know
> His will, and in the silence of our spirits,
> That we may do His will, and do that only.
> —*H. W. Longfellow.*

It is pathetic what a time God has getting a hearing down here. He is ever speaking, but even where there may be some inclination to hear, the sounds of earth are choking in our ears the sound of His voice. God speaks in His Word. The most we know of God comes to us here. . . . What He says will utterly change what you will say.—*S. D. Gordon.*

There is hardly ever a complete silence in our souls. God is whispering to us well-nigh incessantly. Whenever the sounds of the world die out in the soul or sink low, then we hear these whisperings of God. He is always whispering to us, only we do not always hear, because of the noise, hurry and distraction which life causes as it rushes on.—*F. Faber.*

A flock of sheep once broke away from a shepherd who from the hillside above was trying in vain to direct his faithful sheep dog. The frightened animals were rushing here and there as waiting motorists tooted their horns. A fussy little terrier was making things worse by barking at the wrong time or in the wrong place. The sheep dog tried again and again to interpret his master's instructions, but the noise was too great and the distractions were too many. Finally, in desperation, he ran up the hill leaving all the confusion far below. With his eye and ear open only to the shepherd's commands, all became changed. Down he rushed, knowing exactly what to do. In a few moments, the sheep, grouped together, were herded up away from the road. And all was order and quiet. How like the faithful dog we are! Among earth's distractions, the Master's commands cannot clearly reach us. But when we go alone with Him, we are sure to return to a prompt completion of our God-directed task.

God guides and protects

"Lead me, O Lord, in thy righteousness because of mine enemies; make thy way straight before my face" (Psa. 5:8).
"And the Lord went before them by day in a pillar of a cloud, to lead them the way; and by night in a pillar of fire, to give them light; to go by day and night" (Exod. 13:21).

The pillar of cloud by day went before Israel to direct the way forward, to avoid bypaths, and to prevent Israel's getting ahead of God's leadings. The pillar of fire by night was behind to protect His people from the enemy in the rear and to prevent their lagging behind through a reluctance or disinclination to obey divine leadership.

> Thou seest I cannot journey on
>   Till Thou the lingering cloud remove,
> And make the destined action known,
>   And lead me by the fire of love.
>
> My every choice, desire, design
>   I now implicitly submit;
> My will is fixed to follow Thine,
>   And lies indifferent at Thy feet.
>
> Loosed and detached, I cease from man;
>   Opinions, names, are clean forgot;
> This all my aim, and all my plan,
>   To do, and be—I know not what.
>
> But wilt Thou not at last appear,
>   Make darkness light before my face,
> And crooked straight, and doubtful clear,
>   And show, and shine on all my ways?
>   —*Charles Wesley.*

Our Lord gives me the grace of keeping me in His peace. I find this: the more I plan and arrange to do a great deal in this place or that, the less gets done. But if I commit all my work to God much more gets done. Therefore I will let Him work.—*Marquis de Renty.*

Concealed treasures

"The Lord shall open unto thee his good treasure" (Deut. 28:12).
"Again, the kingdom of heaven is like unto treasure hid in a field"
(Matt. 13:44).

There is said to be a very remarkable iron egg preserved in the city of Dresden. There is a legend connected with it to the following effect: On a certain occasion a prince sent this egg to his betrothed. When she received it, she looked at it, and being disgusted with it, she flung it on the ground. As it struck the earth, a secret spring was touched, and lo, a silver yolk rolled from the egg. As she gathered up the yolk she touched another secret spring, and lo, a golden chicken came forth. She took the chicken in both hands, and in doing so she touched another secret spring, and lo, a ruby crown appeared. She now touched another secret spring in the crown, and lo, her eyes were blest with the sight of a magnificent marriage diamond ring.

The religion of Jesus Christ comes to some men as this iron egg, without much external beauty, and at first, perhaps, they treat it with disdain, but when upon second thoughts they take it into their personal examination and practice, it discovers to them one good after another, until they find within it an eternal union with the beautiful and preeminent King of Heaven. It unfolds to them repentance, faith, pardon, peace, purity, glory. The despised and rejected at first, ultimately becomes the Pearl of Great Price, the Precious Treasure, the Excellency of excellencies. As from dark depths are brought the jewels that sparkle in a monarch's crown, so in the depths of that religion which at first seemed dark, you find those graces that "adorn you as a bride for the bridegroom," and make you like the "king's daughter, all glorious within."

—*John Bate.*

Arise, my soul, on wings sublime,
Above the vanities of time;
Let faith now pierce the veil, and see
The glories of eternity.

Born by a new celestial birth,
Why should I grovel here on earth?
Why grasp at vain and fleeting toys,
So near to Heaven's eternal joys?

To dwell with God, to taste His love,
Is the full Heaven enjoyed above;
The glorious expectation now
Is heavenly bliss begun below.
—*Thomas Gibbons.*

Find God's purpose in trial

"As ye are partakers of the sufferings, so shall ye be also of the consolation"
(2 Cor. 1:7).

"Who comforteth us in all our tribulation, that we may be able to comfort them which are in any trouble by the comfort wherewith we ourselves are comforted of God" (2 Cor. 1:4).

It must be somewhere in my grief that the help of the grief is hidden. It must be in some discovery of the divine side of the sorrow that the consolation of the sorrow will be found. It is a wondrous change when a man stops asking of his distress, "How can I throw this off?" and asks instead, "What did God mean by sending this?"—*Phillips Brooks.*

If you would to another heart a source of comfort be,
Skilled to administer *true* balm, and show real sympathy:
If you would dry another's tears in deepest grief or woe,
O, marvel not then if today your own heart's blood must flow!

If you would in life's stress and strain, courage and strength impart
To those who 'neath life's burden oft might droop with sinking heart—
You too must know the pressure keen, the spirit sorely tried,
Draw for yourself the strength from God that *never* is denied.

If you would tell the words of power to lives that well might tire
With suffering prolonged, that still God shares the "furness fire"—
O, you must prove then for yourself His pressure surely there,
But marvel not if trials keen today your soul must bear!

Would you equipped for service be, where'er your path may lie?
God has His training school *on earth*, learn *here* your calling high—
When pain or joy shall to you come, perceive His coming too
To train you even now for work He has for you to do.
                                                    —*Unknown.*

Look rather to God's end in afflicting than at the measure and degree of thy afflictions.—*Unknown.*

Resolved to improve afflictions to the utmost.—*Jonathan Edwards.*

Unconscious influence

"So they ran both together: and the other disciple did outrun Peter, and came first to the sepulchre . . . yet went he not in. Then cometh Simon Peter following him, and went into the sepulchre . . . then went in also that other disciple which came first to the sepulchre, and he saw, and believed" (John 20: 4-8).

Little does Peter think, as he comes up where his doubting brother is looking into the sepulcher, and goes straight in, after his peculiar manner, that he is drawing in his brother apostle after him. As little does John think, when he loses his misgivings and goes into the sepulcher after Peter, that he is following his brother.

And just so unawares to himself, is every man, the whole race through, laying hold on his fellowman, to lead him where he otherwise would not go. We overrun the boundaries of our personality—we flow together. A Peter leads a John, a John goes after a Peter, both of them unconscious of any influence exerted or received.

There are then, you will perceive, two sorts of influence belonging to man; that which is active or voluntary, and that which is unconscious; that which we exert purposely or in the endeavor to sway another, as by teaching, by argument, by persuasion, by threatenings, by offers and promises—and that which flows out from us unawares to ourselves, the same which Peter had over John when he led him into the sepulcher.—*Horace Bushnell.*

O, blessed is that man of whom some soul can say,
"He was an inspiration along life's toilsome way;
A well of sparkling water, a fountain flowing free,
Forever like his Master, in tenderest sympathy."
—*Unknown.*

The people who influence us most are not those who buttonhole us and talk to us, but those who live their lives like the stars in Heaven and lilies in the field, perfectly, simply, and unaffectedly. Those are the lives that mold us. If you want to be of use to God, get rightly related to Jesus Christ and He will make you of use unconsciously every moment you live.

July 24
Greater achievement

"Seek that ye may excel to the edifying of the church" (1 Cor. 14:12).
"I press toward the mark for the prize of the high calling of God in Christ Jesus" (Phil. 3:14).

Sad will be the day for any man when he becomes satisfied with the life he is living, with the thoughts he is thinking, and the deeds he is doing; when there is not beating at the doors of his soul a desire to do something greater which he knows he was meant to do because he is a child of God.—*Phillips Brooks.*

High hearts are never long without hearing some new call, some distant clarion of God, even in their dreams, and soon they are observed to break up the camp of ease and start on some fresh march of faithful service. And, looking higher still, we find those who never wait till their moral work accumulates, and who reward resolution with no rest; with whom, therefore, the alternation is instantaneous and constant; who do the good only to see the better, and see the better only to achieve it; who are too meek for transport, too faithful for remorse, too earnest for repose; whose worship is action, and whose action is ceaseless aspiration.—*James Martineau.*

> Work for the good that is nighest;
> Dream not of greatness afar;
> That glory is ever the highest
> Which shines upon men as they are.
> Work, though the world would defeat you;
> Heed not its slander and scorn;
> Nor weary till angels shall greet you
> With smiles through the gates of the morn.
> —*Unknown.*

Christian, awake

"Wherefore he saith, Awake thou that sleepest, and arise from the dead, and Christ shall give thee light" (Eph 5:14).
"Awake, awake; put on thy strength, O Zion" (Isa. 52:1).
"And that, knowing the time, that now it is high time to awake out of sleep: for now is our salvation nearer than when we believed" (Rom. 13: 11).

How can a Christian sleep in such an age as ours? When life grows grander every year, by the increased knowledge and extended facilities for achieving great results for God and humanity! When so many harvest fields of labor invite the sturdy arm and glowing heart! When the wails of a world's sorrow rise on every gale! To sleep through such a period of the world's history is a fearful crime. Truly it is a sin against Heaven, to have no pulse that beats in palpitations of an age which trembles with the footsteps of an advancing God.
—*Theodore Cuyler.*

> To be alive in such an age—
> To live in it,
> To give in it!
> Rise, soul, from thy despairing knees.
> What if thy lips have drunk the lees?
> Fling forth thy sorrows to the wind,
> And link thy hope with humankind!
> The passion of a larger claim
> Will put thy puny grief to shame.
> —*Unknown.*

It is our work to arise; God will make us stand.—*Catherine Booth.*

It is not once in a hundred times that a lazy man ever becomes a Christian. There is but little hope for the man who has nothing to do.—*De Witt Talmage.*

Life eased by a yoke

"Take my yoke upon you, and learn of me; for I am meek and lowly in heart: and ye shall find rest unto your souls. For my yoke is easy, and my burden is light" (Matt. 11:29-30).

Did you ever stop to ask what a yoke is really for? Is it to be a burden to the animal which wears it? It is just the opposite. It is to make its burden light. Attached to the oxen in any other way than by a yoke, the plow would be intolerable. Worked by means of a yoke, it is light. A yoke is not an instrument of torture; it is an instrument of mercy. It is not a malicious contrivance for making work hard; it is a gentle device to make hard labor light. It is not meant to give pain, but to save pain. And yet men speak of the yoke of Christ as if it were a slavery and look upon those who wear it as objects of compassion.

And what was the "burden"? It was not some special burden laid upon the Christian, some unique infliction that he alone must bear. It was what all men bear. It was simply life, human life itself, the general burden of life which all must carry with them from the cradle to the grave. Christ saw that men took life painfully. To some it was a weariness, to others a failure, to many a tragedy, to all a struggle and a pain. How to carry this burden of life had been the whole world's problem. It is still the whole world's problem. And here is Christ's solution: "Carry it as I do. Take life as I take it. Look at it from My point of view. Interpret it upon My principles. Take My yoke and learn of Me, and you will find it easy. For My yoke is easy, works easily, sits right upon the shoulders, and therefore My burden is light." Christ's yoke is simply His secret for the alleviation of human life, His prescription for the best and happiest method of living.—*Henry Drummond.*

Blessed is any weight, however overwhelming, which God has been so good as to fasten with His own hand upon our shoulders.—*F. W. Faber.*

Prayer in time of need

"The eyes of the Lord are upon the righteous, and his ears are open unto their cry" (Psa. 34:15).
"In my distress I called upon the Lord, and cried unto my God: he heard my voice out of his temple, and my cry came before him, even into his ears"
(Psa. 18:6).

Trouble and fear are very spurs to prayer. I, in anguish of mind and vehement tribulation and affliction, called to the Lord, when not only the ungodly, but even my faithful brethren, yes, and my own self judged my cause irremediable. Therefore dare I be bold, in the verity of God's Word, to promise that, notwithstanding the vehemency of trouble, the long continuance thereof, the desperation of all men, the fearfulness, danger, trouble and anguish of our own hearts, if we call constantly to God, that beyond expectation of all men, He shall deliver.—*John Knox.*

When the busy world about me seems so filled with toil and care,
    That the Spirit's gentle voice is quite unknown,
Oft I slip into my closet and my Savior meets me there,
    And we spend an hour before the Father's throne.

When perplexing questions face me, and I know not where to turn,
    And the evil one would tempt my heart to groan,
I have found there's not a problem that I really want to learn
    That we cannot solve before the Father's throne.

When affliction adds its burden to the load already borne,
    And my cherished hopes by adverse winds are blown,
It is there I seek the Savior, for His heart like mine was torn,
    And we spend an hour together at the throne.

Yes, it's true we have our troubles, and our little trials, too,
    And our souls the tempter ne'er will leave alone;
But the blessed Lord has told us there is grace to help us through,
    If we'll only spend an hour before the throne.

Oh, the happy, secret hour! For His presence I do yearn,
    What communion there have I with Christ alone!
Now my heart is caused to shout by the lessons that I learn
    In that happy, secret hour before the throne!
                              —*Unknown.*

Do they see Jesus?

"Christ in you, the hope of glory" (Col. 1:27).
"Beholding . . . the stedfastness of your faith in Christ" (Col. 2:5).

Dannecker, a celebrated sculptor, spent eight years making a statue of Jesus. After having spent two years on it he brought a little child into his studio and asked, "My dear, who is that?"

The little girl looked up at the wonderful work and replied, "It is a great man."

The sculptor was smitten with disappointment. He said to himself, "This will never do. The statue must be a truer likeness of Christ than this."

And so he turned his chisel and his mallet for two or three years longer. He prayed in the vigils of the night, asking God to help him to reproduce the likeness of Christ upon the face of the marble.

Once more he brought a little child into his studio, and said, "Who is that?"

The child looked at the masterpiece in silence, and bursting into tears exclaimed, "Suffer the little children to come unto me."

The sculptor said, "I have gained it! This is a work of inspiration."

My friends, when little children look at you, whom do they see?

> Has someone seen Christ in you today?
> Christian, look to your heart, I pray;
> The little things that you've done or said—
> Did they accord with the way you prayed?
> Have your thoughts been pure, your words been kind;
> Have you sought to have the Savior's mind?
> The world with a criticizing view
> Has watched—but did it see Christ in you?
>
> Has someone seen Christ in you today?
> Oh, Christian, be careful, watch and pray.
> Look up to Jesus in faith, and then
> Lift up unto Him your fellowmen;
> Upon your own strength you cannot rely;
> There's a fount of grace and strength on high,
> Go to that fount and your strength renew
> And the life of Christ will shine through you.
> —*C. B. Hopkins.*

Results through suffering

"He laid down his life for us: and we ought to lay down our lives for the brethren" (1 John 3:16).
"Neither will I offer . . . unto the Lord my God of that which doth cost me nothing" (2 Sam. 24:24).

I have observed during all those years of evangelistic labor, that invariably when I have enjoyed most blessing in the work, I have suffered the greatest hardships; and, on the other hand, when I have been dined, and feasted, and carried shoulder high, there has been little good done.—*Duncan Matheson.*

We do real good to others only at cost of self. Christ blessed the world, not by an easy, pleasant, prosperous life in it, but by suffering and dying in it and for it; and we can never bless the world merely by having a good time in it.

Work for others that costs us nothing is scarcely worth doing. At least it takes heart's blood to heal hearts. Too many of us are ready to work for Christ and do good to our fellowmen only so long as it is very easy, and requires no self-sacrifice or self-denial. But if we stop there, we stop just where our service is likely to become of use.

This saving of life proves, in the end, the losing of it. It is they who sow in tears that shall reap in joy. We may take easy work, if we will, work that costs us nothing, that involves no pain or self-denial, but we must not then be surprised if our hands are empty in the great harvest time.

> Christ leads me through no darker rooms
> Than He went through before;
> He that into God's kingdom comes,
> Must enter by His door.
> Come, Lord, when grace has made me meet
> Thy blessed face to see;
> For if Thy work on earth be sweet,
> What will Thy glory be?
> —*Richard Baxter.*

Commit thy way and trust

"Commit thy way unto the Lord; trust also in him; and he shall bring it to pass" (Psa. 37:5).
"For we which have believed do enter into rest" (Heb. 4:3).

We must understand that *faith is rest*. In the beginning of the faith-life, faith is struggling; but as long as faith is struggling, faith has not attained its strength. But when faith in its struggling gets to the end of itself, and just throws itself upon God, and rests on Him, then comes joy and victory.

—*Andrew Murray.*

Commit thy way unto the Lord—and trust!
Ah! it is here we fail. We give the wheel
Of our small bark to Him; but then we thrust
Our hand upon His hand,
And dare to stand
Beside our Master, lest He wreck our keel.

Commit thy way unto the Lord—and trust!
There is an "also" we too oft forget,
And so are plagued and worried. Oh, we must
"Trust also," then our soul
Shall cease to roll
In restlessness and reason and regret.

Commit thy way unto the Lord and trust!
Leave all to Him; believe He knows thy course,
Thy dangers and thy safety—all—then just
Abandon all to Him.
So shalt thou skim,
Borne briskly on before the Spirit's force.

Trust Him to manage all that thou dost now
Commit to Him—the ship—the sails—the sea—
The sailors, thy strange crew. And ask not how
He will do all for thee,
But trustful be.
Lie down and rest from anxious worry free.
—*William Luff (Evangelical Christian).*

"The Lord on high is mightier than the noise of many waters, yea, than the mighty waves of the sea" (Psa. 93:4).

The Bible—a treasure

"I have rejoiced in the way of thy testimonies, as much as in all riches"
(Psa. 119:14).

The editor of a magazine sent out a questionnaire to "the hundred greatest men in Britain," asking: "If for any reason you were to spend a year absolutely alone (in a prison, for instance), and could select from your library three volumes as your companions during your retirement, please inform us what those three books would be."

In the answers, it was found that ninety-eight of the hundred named the Bible first in the list of the three books to be chosen.

> This holy Book I'd rather own
> Than all the gold and gems
> That e'er in monarch's coffers shone,
> Than all their diadems.
>
> Nay, were all the seas one chrysolite,
> The earth one golden ball,
> And diadems all the stars of night,
> This Book outweighs them all.
>
> Ah, no, the soul ne'er found relief
> In glittering hoards of wealth;
> Gems dazzle not the eye of grief,
> Gold cannot purchase health.
> —*Unknown.*

The Bible is a treasure. It contains enough to make us rich for time and eternity. It contains the secret of happy living. It contains the key of Heaven. It contains the title deeds of an inheritance incorruptible, and that fadeth not away. It contains the pearl of great price. It contains the Savior and the living God Himself.—*James Hamilton.*

The Bible walks the ways of all the world with familiar feet and enters land after land to find its own everywhere. Children listen to its stories with wonder and delight, and wise men ponder them as parables of life. The wicked and the proud tremble at its warnings, but to the wounded and the penitent it has a mother's voice. It has woven itself into our dearest dreams; so that love, friendship, sympathy, devotion, memory, hope, put on the beautiful garments of its treasured speech. No man is poor or desolate who has this treasure for his own.—*Henry Van Dyke.*

August 1
God knows our possibilities

"And Moses said unto God, Who am I, that I should go unto Pharaoh, and that I should bring forth the children of Israel out of Egypt?" (Exod. 3:11).
"Oh my Lord, wherewith shall I save Israel? Behold, my family is poor in Manasseh, and I am the least in my father's house" (Judges 6:15).
"I cannot speak: for I am a child. But the Lord said unto me, Say not, I am a child" (Jer. 1:6-7).

Do we not come to feel how almost absolutely worthless are men's descriptions of their own impossibilities. I used to be imposed on by such statements. When a man said any of these things about himself, it seemed as if it might be true, as if here might be a man in whom this one capacity of manhood had been left out. But so constantly the flowers have broken out of such unlikely soils, so often the darkest heavens have burst forth in unexpected stars, that it has come to seem as if no man's assertion of his own deficiency were trustworthy. "God knew things of him that he did not know of himself," we say when some new life opens upon a man who thought he had exhausted his capacity of living. Let us expect surprise out of the bosom of a life which God made, and which you whom He has set to live in it only half realize—as a tenant who came but yesterday into a palace only half knows the mystery and richness of the great house where he has been sent to live.—*Phillips Brooks.*

Great occasions do not make heroes of cowards; they simply unveil them to the eyes of men.—*Canon Westcott.*

There is always something over when we, from the Father's hand,
Take our portion with thanksgiving, praising for the path He planned.
Satisfaction, full and deepening, fills the soul, and lifts the eye,
When the heart has trusted Jesus all its need to satisfy.

There is always something over when we tell of all His love;
Unplumbed depths still lie beneath us, unsealed heights rise far above;
Human lips can never utter all His wondrous tenderness,
We can only praise and wonder, and His Name forever bless.
—*Margaret E. Barber.*

The microscope of love

"God that performeth all things for me" (Psa. 57:2).
"I have all, and abound" (Phil. 4:18).

He not only makes all things work together for good, but does more: "performeth all things for me." And if we did but open our eyes and *notice*, we should see Him at work for us. Every day is full of miracles when the Holy Spirit really opens our eyes to see God working them, and I often think it is the very little things which most magnify His loving-kindness. We talk about the telescope of faith, but I think we want even more the microscope of watchful and grateful love. Apply this to the little bits of our daily lives, in the light of the Spirit, and how wonderfully they come out! We see these little things in their true greatness, and in the beauty of their fitness as parts of His own perfect plan of our lives, which He is working out for us hour by hour. Don't wait for tomorrow; take this day, the morning hours past, the evening ones to come, and apply this microscope, and see if you don't find you are walking in the midst of miracles of love, and that all things are for your sakes.

—Frances Ridley Havergal.

This is what Hester Ann Rogers says she saw through this microscope:
"I was deeply penetrated with His presence, and stood as if unable to move, and was insensible to all around me. While thus lost in communion with my Savior, He spake these words to my heart: 'All that I have is thine. I am Jesus, in Whom dwells all the fullness of the Godhead bodily. I am thine. My Spirit is thine. My Father is thine. They love thee as I love thee. The whole Deity is thine. He even now overshadows thee. He now covers thee with a cloud of His presence.' All this was so realized to my soul in a manner I cannot explain, that I sank down motionless, being unable to sustain the *weight* of His glorious presence and *fullness* of love."

Changed into the same image

"We all with unveiled face beholding, as in a mirror, the glory of the Lord, are transformed into the same image" (2 Cor. 3:18—R.V.).
"And ye became followers . . . of the Lord . . . so that ye were ensamples to all that believe" (1 Thess. 1:6-7).

When the old Hebrews wanted to describe a man who reached their ideal in religious life, they used the simple but comprehensive phrase, "He walked with God." To them there was nothing higher than unbroken and unclouded communion with their Maker. That was, in their view, the secret of all holiness, and the New Testament has nothing higher than that to reveal. "We all with unveiled face beholding, as in a mirror, the glory of the Lord, are transformed into the same image." When we sit before the camera, and have our portraits taken, our picture is printed on the prepared film, but when we behold and continue to behold the image of Christ we become the camera, and His image is printed on our souls. The teaching is, that we become like those with whom we keep company.

> Go with me, Master, by the way,
>   Make every day a walk with Thee;
> New glory shall the sunshine gain,
>   And all the clouds shall lightened be.
> Go with me on life's dusty road
> And help me bear the weary load.
>   —*Annie Johnson Flint.*

Who has not watched some old couple come down life's pilgrimage hand in hand with such gentle trust and joy in one another that their very faces wore the selfsame look? These were not two souls; it was a composite soul. Half a century's companionship had told upon them. They were changed into the same image! What glorious possibilities are here suggested to those whom God hides in the secret of His presence? Who can think mean thoughts, or speak ungenerous words, in the presence of Christ? His mere presence must suggest immediately the right thing in the controlling passion, the subsiding of pride, and the overcoming of selfishness. In His company, who could help but always be at his best, and if this influence is perpetuated, what could not life become?

(From *New Testament Holiness* by Thomas Cook. Used by permission of the Epworth Press.)

Faith and action

"Who through faith subdued kingdoms, wrought righteousness, obtained promises, stopped the mouths of lions" (Heb. 11:33).

We walk by faith. Do we? What record is there on high of things that by faith we have obtained? Is each step each day an act of faith? Do we, as children of God, really believe the Bible? —*Hudson Taylor.*

> *Passive* faith accepts the word as true—
> But never moves.
> *Active* faith begins the work to do,
> And thereby proves.

Passive faith says, "I believe it! Every word of God is true.
Well I know He hath not spoken what He cannot, will not, do.
He hath bidden me go forward! But a closed-up way I see;
When the waters are divided, soon in Canaan's land I'll be.
I hear His voice commanding, 'Rise and walk; take up thy bed'—
And I know that He can help me to arise as He hath said.
When I am a little stronger, then I know I'll surely stand;
When there comes a thrill of healing, use with ease my other hand.
Yes, I know that 'God is able,' and full willing all to do;
I believe that every promise, sometime, will to me come true."

Active faith says, "I believe it! And the promise now I take,
Knowing well, as I receive it, God each promise real will make.
So I step into the waters, finding there an open way;
Onwards press, the land possessing; nothing can my progress stay.
Yea, I rise at His commanding, walk straightway, and joyfully;
This, my hand, so sadly shriveled, as I reach, restored shall be.
What beyond His faithful promise would I wish or do I need?
Looking not for 'signs or wonders' and full willing all to do—
I believe that every promise at this moment can come true!"

> *Passive* faith but praises in the light,
> When the sun doth shine.
> *Active* faith will praise in darkest night—
> Which faith is thine?

—*Unknown.*

August 5
The noblest course in sorrow

"Let us run with patience the race that is set before us" (Heb. 12:1).
"Strengthened with all might, according to his glorious power, unto all patience" (Col. 1:11).

To run with patience is a very difficult thing. Running is apt to suggest the *absence* of patience, the eagerness to reach the goal. We commonly associate patience with lying down. We think of it as the angel that guards the couch of the invalid. And, indeed, for those who *are* invalids patience is the angel-virtue, the crown of spiritual ripeness. Yet, I do not think the invalid's patience the hardest to achieve. There is a patience which I believe to be harder—the patience that can run. To lie down in the time of grief, to be quiet under the stroke of adverse fortune, implies a great strength. But I know of something that implies a strength greater still; it is the power to *work* under the stroke. To have a great weight at your heart and still to run, to have a big grief in your soul and still to work, to have a deep anguish in your spirit and still to perform the daily task—it is a Christ-like thing! Many of us could nurse our grief without crying if we were *allowed* to nurse it. The hard thing is that most of us are called to exercise our patience, not in bed, but in the street. We are called to bury our sorrow, not in lethargic quiescence, but in active service—in the exchange, in the countinghouse, in the workshop, in the hour of social intercourse, in the contribution to another's joy. There is no burial of sorrow so difficult as that; it is the "*running* with patience."—*George Matheson.*

Patience may lack, often does lack, one at least of its ingredients; there might be a waiting which has no submission; which, on the contrary, was indolence, was procrastination, was dallying, the man sitting still, and letting alone, and waiting upon chances which are no grace at all, but the opposite; or there might be a submission which was no enterprise, and waiting upon Providence with more or less of the resignation which is the ape and shadow of patience, which has in it no doing nor daring for Christ, no present running and fighting, and, therefore, no future crown. But who shall speak the praises of the real Gospel, Christian, spiritual patience?—*Dean Vaughan.*

O divine Master, grant that I may not so much seek to be consoled, as to console; to be understood, as to understand; to be loved, as to love.

—*St. Francis of Assisi.*

Alone with God

"Come ye yourselves apart" (Mark 6:31).
"And he took him aside from the multitude" (Mark 7:33).
"And Jacob was left alone" (Gen. 32:24).

The Lord filled me with desire, and made me feel that I must be as much with Him alone as with souls in public.—*Andrew Bonar.*

> Alone with Thee! Alone with Thee!
> O Friend divine!
> Thou Friend of friends, to me most dear,
> Though all unseen, I feel Thee near;
> And, with the love that knows no fear,
> I call Thee mine. . . .
>
> Alone with Thee! Alone with Thee!
> In Thy pure light
> The splendid pomps and shows of time,
> The tempting steeps that pride would climb,
> The peaks where glory rests sublime,
> Pale on my sight. . . .
>
> Alone with Thee! Alone with Thee!
> There not alone,
> But with all saints the mighty throng,
> My soul unfettered, pure and strong,
> Her high communings shall prolong
> Before Thy throne.
> —*Ray Palmer.*

It has been said that no great work in literature or in science was ever wrought by a man who did not love solitude, and we may lay it down as an elemental principle of religion that no large growth of holiness or real and continuous success in Christian work, was ever gained by one who did not take time to be often and long alone with God. Someone spoke to John Nelson, making unfavorable comparison of John Wesley with a prominent religious teacher of the day. Nelson replied, "He has not stayed in the upper room like John Wesley." It is there where we get our message, and where we win our battles before they are fought.

Our Gideons must Isaiahs be, visions first—then victory.

(From *New Testament Holiness* by Thomas Cook. Used by permission of the Epworth Press.)

August 7
Don't neglect the small duties

"If the prophet had bid thee do some great thing, wouldest thou not have done it?" (2 Kings 5:13).
"Thou hast been faithful in a very little" (Luke 19:17).

We think that conspicuous events, striking experiences, exalted moments have most to do with our character and capacity. We are wrong. Common days, monotonous hours, wearisome paths, plain old toils and everyday clothes tell the real story. Good habits are not made on birthdays, nor Christian character at the New Year. The workshop of character is everyday life. The uneventful and commonplace hour is where the battle is won or lost.

> Little by little all tasks are done;
> So are the crowns of the faithful won,
> So is Heaven in our hearts begun.
> With work and with weeping, with laughter and play,
> Little by little, the longest day
> And the longest life are passing away—
> Passing without return, while so
> The new years come, and the old years go.
> —*Unknown.*

Who neglects a thing which he suspects he ought to do, because it seems to him too small a thing, is deceiving himself. It is not too little, but too great for him, that he doeth it not.—*E. P.*

> "Master, where shall I work today?"
>   (My love flowed warm and free);
> He pointed out a tiny plot,
>   And said: "Tend that for me."
> I answered quickly, "Oh, no, not there;
>   Not anyone could see,
> No matter how well my task was done—
>   Not that little place for me."
> His voice when He spoke—it was not stern.
>   He answered me tenderly.
> "Little one, search that heart of thine,
>   Are you working for them or Me?
> Nazareth was just a little place,
>   And so was Galilee."
> —*Unknown.*

Responsibility for others

"None of us liveth to himself, and no man dieth to himself" (Rom. 14:7).
"He that is not with me is against me; and he that gathereth not with me scattereth abroad" (Matt. 12:30).

Mary Lyon was in charge of one of the first colleges for women in the New England States. She encountered much opposition for advocating higher female education. Such was the example and teaching of her life, and such high Christian character and conduct marked her young women that it was the highest reference in itself to have been to her college. Her young women were sought to fill positions all over the United States. These striking words on influence are from her pen:

"Spread out before me was a solemn and awful view of personal responsibility. I saw the folly and delusion of those who are ever striving to secure for some of their steps a middle path between the service of Christ and the service of His enemy. . . . I saw that each one's life must be devoted to the salvation of men, or its influence be felt for their eternal destruction. Everything about me seemed written all over with the Savior's words, 'He that is not with me is against me; and he that gathereth not with me scattereth abroad.' I seemed to hear a mighty harp of a thousand strings vibrating at the least touch of the hand, at the least breath of the lips. Its every tone seemed to echo and re-echo, and ceased not till it mingled in the songs of the New Jerusalem, or till it waked up a deep wail in the bottomless pit.

"O, who can strike with a careless, heedless hand the chords of such a harp? Who does not tremble to live, to walk, to speak in such a world as this? How distressing is the mere apprehension of having by accident administered a fatal cup of poison to a fellow-being. But infinitely more distressing must be the certainty of having, by neglect or self-indulgence, destroyed a never-dying soul. My heart exclaimed, 'Let the past of my life suffice me in the work of death; henceforth let me live only for the salvation of men.' I looked up to the God of my salvation and cried, 'Lord, grant that I may never again spend aught of my time or of my possessions without seeking guidance and direction from above; grant that I may never again spend aught of earth's treasures on myself without the united approval of the Word of God, and providence of God, and the Spirit of God.'"

August 9

The right measurement of time

"Lord, make me to know . . . the measure of my days" (Psa. 39:4).
"Time is short" (1 Cor. 7:29).

Said General Mitchell to an army officer who apologized for a few moments' delay: "Only a few seconds! Why, man, I am in the habit of calculating the thousandth part of a second." John Bradford used to say, "I count that hour lost in which I have done no good, either by tongue or pen." Seneca held that time was the only thing of which it was excusable to be covetous. Dr. Cotton Mather sometimes expressed his regret when a guest departed after merely visiting, and thus wasting his time. "I should rather have given him my money than my time," he would say. Henry Martyn has been called "the man who never wasted an hour."

> Heart gazing mournfully
> Back through past years—
> Bringing sad memories,
> Laden with tears—
> Life's hours wasted,
> Talents abused,
> Bright opportunities
> Blindly refused—
> Close up the record
> Fraught with such pain;
> Years that have vanished
> Return not again.
> Grasp now the Present,
> Be earnest and bold—
> Fleeting its moments,
> More precious than gold.
> —*Unknown.*

Lost, somewhere between sunrise and sunset, two golden hours, each set with sixty diamond minutes. No reward is offered, for they are gone for ever.
—*Horace Mann.*

Why are Time's feet so swift and ours so slow!—*Unknown.*

Joy is of God

"The Lord had made them joyful" (Ezra 6:22).
"Your joy no man taketh from you" (John 16:22).

There are few things more attractive than joy, and few more communicative. We are instinctively drawn to persons possessed of a happy countenance and a bright, cheery manner. Over the young especially, a joyful countenance and cheerful manner exert a powerful influence. True wisdom is "rejoicing always before Him," and neutralizing the devil's lie, that the service of God is a gloomy thing.

It is one of the striking evidences of the love of God that He has so secured the existence and wide diffusion of joy, that even in this sin-stricken world it is everywhere to be found. The young of all animals are naturally joyous; health and vigor make even toil a pleasure; and the lawful exercise of every faculty with which God has endowed us tends to the increase of our joy. The birds of the air, the flowers of the field, the wild rolling ocean, and the stable, glorious hills are all sources of joy; and every social and domestic relationship of life tends to increase the sum of human happiness. It is quite clear that the God of creation would have His creatures joyful.

Not only does nature teach us that it must be the will of our Father that His children especially should be a joyful family, but the Old and New Testaments are full of encouragements, and even commands, to lead rejoicing lives. In the revival recorded in Nehemiah we find that the people were overwhelmed by the contrast between their individual and national lives and the requirements of God. But those who taught the people said, "This day is holy unto the Lord your God; mourn not, nor weep. . . . Go your way, eat the fat and drink the sweet, and send portions unto them for whom nothing is prepared . . ." And the people went their way and rejoiced accordingly. Joy is of God.—*Hudson Taylor.*

August 11
Opposition before victory

"A great door and effectual is opened . . . and there are many adversaries"
(1 Cor. 16:9).

As soon as a man begins to enlarge his life his resistances are multiplied. Let a man tear out of his soul the petty selfish purpose and enthrone a world-purpose, the Christ-purpose, and his suffering will be increased on every side. Every addition to spiritual ambition widens the exposure of the soul, and sharpens its perception of the world's infirmity and the sense of its own restraints.—*J. H. Jowett.*

Wesley said, "The Lord increases His work in proportion to the opposition it meets with."

If you meet opposition, it may indicate that you are doing something that counts. In digging wells, Isaac had no opposition from the Philistines until he struck water.

Did I ever feel so? Yes, I think just as bad as any mortal could feel—empty, inside and out, as though I had nothing, human or divine, to aid me, as if all hell were let loose upon me! But I have generally felt the worst before the best results, which proves it was Satanic opposition. And it has been the same with many of God's honored instruments.

It stands to sense, if there is a devil, that he should desperately withstand those whom he sees are going to be used of God. Supposing you were the devil, and had set your heart on circumventing God, how would you do it but by opposing those who were bent on building up His kingdom? He tries the wilderness experience on every true son of the Father, depend on it. He hopes to drive us from the field by blood and fire and vapor and smoke. But our Captain fought and won the battle for us, and we have only to hold on long enough and victory is sure.—*Catherine Booth.*

Filled

"That ye might be filled with all the fulness of God" (Eph. 3:19).
"The fulness of him that filleth all in all" (Eph. 1:23).
"Till we all come in the unity of the faith, and of the knowledge of the Son of God, unto a perfect man, unto the measure of the stature of the fulness of Christ" (Eph. 4:13).

To be filled with God is a great thing; to be filled with the fullness of God is still greater; to be filled with all the fullness of God is greatest of all. This utterly bewilders the senses, and confounds the understanding; by leading us at once to consider the immensity of God, the infinity of His attributes, and the absolute perfection of each.

By the fullness of God we are to understand all the gifts and graces which He has promised to bestow on man in order to his full salvation here, and his being fully prepared for the enjoyment of glory hereafter. What God fills neither sin nor Satan can fill or in anywise occupy. For, if a vessel be filled with one fluid substance, not a drop or particle of any other kind can enter it, without displacing the same quantum of the original matter.—*William Bramwell.*

> Make me lonely for Thy presence, every earthly friend above;
> Make me thirst for Thine indwelling, make me hungry for Thy love;
> Till in full and free surrender I shall yield my life to Thee,
> Only then, in full perfection, canst Thou give Thyself to me.
>
> All the beauty that I seek for, every treasure I would own,
> Thou art these in rich completeness, they are found in Thee alone;
> All the loveliness I long for, all the best that I would be,
> I can never find them elsewhere than in Thee, Lord, just in Thee.
>
> Empty me of all my glory, all my boasting, all my pride;
> Let my righteousness, my wisdom, on Thy cross be crucified;
> Fill me, then, with all Thy fullness, all Thy will work Thou for me;
> In Thyself is nothing lacking; make me, Lord, complete in Thee.
> —*Annie Johnson Flint.*

The fullness of the Spirit will not bring any satisfied feeling of nothing more to be done or to be received, but rather fresh hungerings and thirstings for more. We are filled only in the sense of a flowing river: it is full and yet ever receiving and ever passing on all it receives.—*John Harrison.*

August 13
With the few on the right road

"Then all the disciples . . . fled" (Matt. 26:56).
"Many of his disciples went back, and walked no more with him" (John 6:66).

"What everybody says must be false," says an old proverb, and I do not dispute it. What most people say is, I think, most often false. And that is true about conduct, as well as about opinion. It is very unsafe in regard to matters of opinion; it is even more unsafe in regard to matters of conduct. That there are many on a road is no sign that the road is a right one. It is rather an argument the other way, looking at the gregariousness of human nature, and how much people like to save themselves the trouble of thinking and decision, and to run in ruts. So the fact that, if you are going to be Christlike Christians you will be in the minority, is a reason for being such.—*Alexander Maclaren.*

"I will not be afraid of ten thousands of people, that have set themselves against me round about" (Psa. 3:6).

When you are in the right, stand up for it, no matter if the heavens fall; if you lose every friend you have, God will raise up others who will be better.
—*D. L. Moody.*

I am not bound to win, but I am bound to be true. I am not bound to succeed, but I am bound to live up to the light I have. I must stand with anybody that stands right—stand with him while he is right, and part with him when he goes wrong.—*Abraham Lincoln.*

At home you can never know what it is to be alone—absolutely alone, without one friend, with everyone looking on you with curiosity, with contempt, with suspicion or with dislike. Thus to learn what it is to be despised and rejected of men, thus to learn what it is to have nowhere to lay your head, and then to have the love of Jesus applied to your heart by the Holy Spirit—to know more of Him, and the power of His resurrection, and the fellowship of His sufferings, being made conformable unto His death. The flesh would say, "Use not this prayer, you know not what you ask,"—but "God is love."
—*Hudson Taylor.*

Our greatest trials, struggles, and victories are experienced—alone.

God asks for our best

"The first of the firstfruits of thy land thou shalt bring into the house of the Lord thy God" (Gen. 23:19).

"Because thou hast done this thing, and hast not withheld thy son, thine only son: that in blessing I will bless thee" (Gen. 22:16-17).

Very often what we would offer to God is not what He calls upon us to relinquish. What He demands of us is often what we most cherish; it is this Isaac of our hearts, this only son, this well-beloved, that He commands us to resign. It is His will that we should yield up all that is most dear, and short of this obedience we have no repose. "Who is he that has resisted the Almighty, and been at peace?" Give up everything to Him, and the God of peace will be with you.—*Fénelon.*

Christ wants the best. He in the far off ages
Once claimed the firstlings of the flock, the finest of the wheat,
And still He asks His own, with gentlest pleading,
To lay their brightest hopes, their richest talents at His feet.
He'll not forget the feeblest service, humblest love,
He only asks that of our store we give to Him
            The best we have.

Christ gives the best. He takes the hearts we offer,
And fills them with His glorious beauty, joy and peace;
And in His service as we're growing stronger
The calls to grand achievements still increase.
The richest gifts on earth or in the Heaven above
Are hid in Christ. In Jesus we receive
            The best we have.

And is our best too much? Ah, friends, let us remember
How once our Lord poured forth His soul for us,
And in the prime of His mysterious manhood
Gave up His precious life upon the cross.
The Lord of lords, by Whom the worlds were made,
Through bitter grief and tears gave us
            The best He had.

                                            —*Unknown.*

August 15
Sincere prayer

"The righteous cry, and the Lord heareth, and delivereth them out of all their troubles" (Psa. 34:17).
"In the day when I cried thou answeredst me, and strengthenedst me with strength in my soul" (Psa. 138:3).

For real business at the Mercy Seat give me a homemade prayer, a prayer that comes out of the depths of my heart, not because I invented it, but because God the Holy Ghost put it there and gave it such a living force that I could not help letting it out.

Though your words are broken and your sentences disconnected, if your desires are earnest, if they are like coals of juniper, burning with vehement flame, God will not mind how they find expression.

If you have no words, perhaps you will pray better without them than with them. There are prayers that break the backs of words; they are too heavy for any human language to carry.—*C. H. Spurgeon.*

I often say my prayers;
But do I ever pray?
And do the wishes of my heart
Go with the words I say?

I may as well kneel down
And worship gods of stone,
As offer to the living God
A prayer of words alone,

For words without the heart
The Lord will never hear;
Nor will He to those lips attend
Whose prayers are not sincere.
—*John Burton.*

God hears the heart without words, but He never hears the words without a heart.—*Unknown.*

Poor yet rich

"As having nothing, and yet possessing all things" (2 Cor. 6:10).
"There is that maketh himself rich, yet hath nothing: there is that maketh himself poor, yet hath great riches" (Prov. 13:7).
"All things that the Father hath are mine" (John 16:15).

Sister Eva, the daughter of wealthy parents, disappointed her father's hopes by her work among the orphans and elderly while still very young. Eventually she obtained his consent and soon consumed all her personal wealth in her work among poor and needy. When she died, she left a large deaconess order known as the Friedenshort Sisterhood. Here then is a personal testimony from one who knew both wealth and poverty:

"Early in life the Spirit of God taught me to love poverty and awakened in me the desire for uttermost self-denial. I sought to regard whatever was entrusted to me as only borrowed. Personal possessions seemed to me like an injustice against the many who live in want, and it was only because it provided me with the possibility of giving, that I became reconciled to the heavy burden and responsibility of the stewardship of earthly goods. I did not have to bear the weight of that burden long. There was enough want in the world to give me an early opportunity of being freed from my wealth, and I was allowed to go the easy and blessed way of voluntary poverty.

"And yet—strange paradox—with all this longing to have nothing, to possess nothing, I find within myself an intense and large delight in the thought of the universal wealth which I share with all my brethren in Christ as the child and heir of my heavenly Father.

"Mine is the earth, and the worlds in their fullness,
Mine every ocean, and mountain, and hill;
Mine are the stars in the firmament's stillness,
Mine are the clouds as they wander at will.

"Oh, the unsearchable, incomprehensible, infinite riches that I may call mine in the realm of nature and in the realm of grace! Everything belongs to me, and the more I receive and enjoy, share and give again, the richer I become and the richer all others. As I think of it, my heart is flung wide and set free and filled with audacity, the audacity as of a child, who, pointing to his father's house and garden and field, says: 'All this is mine!'"

If He has given us all things, have we any business to live as spiritual paupers? Half the reason why we don't praise Him as we ought is because we don't really believe what great things He has given us. Oh, "consider what great things he hath done for you" (1 Sam. 12:24).—*Frances Ridley Havergal.*

Guard the tongue

"Set a watch, O Lord, before my mouth; keep the door of my lips"
(Psa. 141:3).
"The mouth of the righteous speaketh wisdom, and his tongue talketh of judgment" (Psa. 37:30).

Give not thy tongue too great liberty, lest it take thee prisoner. A word unspoken is like the sword in the scabbard, thine; if vented, thy sword is in another's hand. If thou desire to be held wise, be so wise as to hold thy tongue.

RECIPE FOR GOSSIP

Take a grain of falsehood, a handful of runabout, a sprig of herb of backbite, a teaspoonful of don't you tell it, six drachms of malice, and a few drops of envy. Stir well, and let simmer for an hour. Add a little discontent and jealousy, then strain through a bag of misconstruction. Cork it in a bottle of malevolence and hang it on a skein of street yarn. Shake it occasionally for a few days and it will be ready for use. Take a few drops before going out a walk, and you will succeed.

I pray every morning that He will keep me from evil-speaking through the day, and yesterday the Spirit's prompting stopped me short from telling something which while strictly true, and not unkind, was still unnecessary. When one comes to think of it, there is no sin so universal as that of evil-speaking—and this among good people as well as bad. By God's grace I'll be one Christian who will obey His will. It seems the highest resolve I have ever made, but there is power in my Savior to enable me to live up to it.—*Elizabeth S. Brengle.*

If any man . . . bridleth not his tongue . . . this man's religion is vain. . . .
The tongue is a little member,
And boasteth great things.
Behold how great a matter a little fire kindleth!
And the tongue is a fire, a world of iniquity:
So is the tongue among our members, that it defileth the whole body,
And setteth on fire the course of nature;
And it is set on fire of hell.
But the tongue can no man tame;
It is an unruly evil, full of deadly poison.
Therewith bless we God, even the Father;
And therewith curse we men, which are made after the similitude of God.
Out of the same mouth proceedeth blessing and cursing.
My brethren, these things ought not so to be (James 1:26, 3:5, 6, 8-10).

Helps to better health

"But they that wait upon the Lord shall renew their strength; they shall mount up with wings as eagles; they shall run, and not be weary; and they shall walk, and not faint" (Isa. 40:31).

"My son, attend to my words; incline thine ear unto my sayings. Let them not depart from thine eyes; keep them in the midst of thine heart. For they are life unto those that find them, and health to all their flesh" (Prov. 4:20-22).

In the sickroom of the heart He may say little, but His radiant personality transforms it. Where He is, abounding life is, and that life is overflowing into us. Where He is there is perfect love, for in the depths of His being He is love. And to wait on God is not to ask for benefits; it is something anterior to that. It is to maintain the consciousness that He is here. That is how waiting upon God renews strength. The restorative medicine is Himself. "Whom have I in heaven but thee, and there is none upon earth that I desire beside thee." To maintain the consciousness through broken days that in Him we live and move and have our being is to escape as a bird out of the fowler's snare.—*G. H. Morrison.*

It is noted that George Müller, though a man always of delicate constitution physically, began evangelistic tours at the age of seventy, involving a period of seventeen years, and of travel aggregating a distance of eight times around the world. He continued to carry much of the responsibility of the Orphanage besides, until beyond the age of ninety. As a young man his frequent illness and general debility had apparently disqualified him for all military duty, and many prophesied early death or hopeless succumbing to disease, yet at the age of ninety-two he is quoted as saying, "I have been able, every day and all the day, to work, and that with ease, as seventy years since." He ascribed his marvelous preservation to three causes: (1) The exercising himself to have always a conscience void of offense both toward God and toward men; (2) To the love he felt for the Scriptures, and the constant recuperative power they exercised upon his whole being (Prov. 4:20); and (3) To the happiness he felt in God and His work, which relieved him of all anxiety and needless wear and tear in his labors.

August 19
The test of true humility

"Learn of me; for I am meek and lowly in heart: and ye shall find rest unto your souls" (Matt. 11:29).
"Walk humbly with thy God" (Micah 6:8).

Has the meekness and lowliness of Jesus captured your heart? The following points from an old French author will only increase your assurance if this is so. There are times when Satan will accuse the humblest soul of pride; times, too, when jealous friends will hurl insinuations to make it appear that your very best efforts are prompted by pride, rather than zeal for God and truth. How can you know whether these accusations are true or sent to test you? The following list of tests will help you to know:

The grand rule is to sound sincerely the ground of our hearts when we are not in the hurry of temptation. For if on enquiry:

We find it loves obscurity and silence;

That it dreads applause and distinction;

That it esteems the virtue of others and excuses their faults with mildness;

That it easily pardons injuries;

That it fears contempt less and less;

That it sees a falsehood and baseness in pride and a true nobleness and greatness in humility;

That it knows and reveres the inestimable riches of the cross and the humiliations of Jesus Christ;

That it fears the luster of those virtues which are admired by men and loves those that are more secret;

That it draws comfort even from its own defects through the abasement which they occasion;

Then you may trust that all the motions you feel tending to pride or vanity, whether they are sudden or are thrust against you for some time, are not sin, but temptation. And then it may be the best to turn from and despise them, instead of giving them weight by fixing your attention to them.

Glad acceptance of suffering

"If I must needs glory, I will glory of the things which concern mine infirmities"
(2 Cor. 11:30).
"For I reckon that the sufferings of this present time are not worthy to be compared with the glory which shall be revealed in us" (Rom. 8:18).

Pain has come to me, but in it I have always found some secret pleasure and compensation. Sorrow and bereavement have thrown me back upon God and deepened and purified my joy in Him. Agony, physical and mental, have led to some unexpected triumph of grace and faith, some enlargement of sympathy and of power to understand and bless others. Loss and gain, loneliness and love, light and darkness, trials and things hard or impossible to understand—everything has brought its own blessing as my soul has bowed to and accepted the yoke of Jesus and refused to murmur or complain, but has received the daily providences of life as God's training school for faith, for patience, for steadfastness and love.—*Samuel Logan Brengle.*

> Smite on! It doth not hurt me now;
> The spear hath lost its edge of pain;
> And piercing thorns, that bound my brow,
> No longer leave their bleeding stain.
>
> What once was woe is chang'd to bliss;
> What once was loss is now my gain;
> My sorrow is my happiness;
> My life doth live by being slain.
>
> The birth-pangs of those dreadful years
> Are like the midnight chang'd to morn;
> And daylight shines upon my tears,
> Because the soul's great life is born.
>
> The piercing thorns have chang'd to flowers;
> The spears have grown to scepters bright;
> And sorrow's dark and sunless hours
> Become eternal days of light.
> —*Thomas C. Upham.*

What we do from fear, and without love, is always wearisome, hard, grievous, oppressive. What we do out of love, from persuasion, with a free will, however hard to the senses, becomes pleasant. A desire to please God because we love Him makes us love to suffer, and what we suffer for love's sake ceases to be suffering.—*Fénelon.*

August 21

Our stops ordered by God

"Stand thou still a while, that I may show thee the word of God"
(1 Sam. 9:27).
"They . . . were forbidden of the Holy Ghost to preach the word in Asia"
(Acts 16:6).
"They assayed to go into Bithynia: but the Spirit suffered them not"
(Acts 16:7).

The stops of a good man, as well as his steps, are ordered by the Lord.
—*George Müller.*

Next to knowing when to seize an opportunity the most important thing in life is to know when to forego an advantage.—*Disraeli.*

It may be that the sphere of some of you is that of endurance rather than of enterprise. You are not called to aggress, but to resist. The power to work has reached its limit for a while—the power to wait must be exerted. There are periods in our history when Providence shuts us up to the exercise of faith, when patience and fortitude are more valuable than valor and courage, and when any "further struggle would but defeat our prospects and embarrass our aims."

Murmur not, then, if in the inscrutable allotments of Providence you are called to suffer rather than to do. There is a time to labor, and there is a time to refrain. The completeness of the Christian character consists in energetic working when working is practicable, and in submissive waiting when waiting is necessary.—*W. Morley Punshon.*

The humble offering
Of quiet, folded hands,
Costly with suffering,
He only understands;
To God more dear may be
Than eager energy.

And He is here, my song,
That I may learn of Him.
What though the days are long!
What though the way is dim!
'Tis He Who says: "Lie still!"
And I adore His will.
—*Anna Boobbyer.*

What is your influence?

"For as by one man's disobedience many were made sinners, so by the obedience of one shall many be made righteous" (Rom. 5:19).
"Your zeal hath stirred up very many of them" (2 Cor. 9:2—R. V.).

Books and sermons may be resisted; even tears and entreaties may be despised; but the silent and unostentatious influence of holy lives will speak a language to the heart it cannot easily gainsay, a language which will sound on when we sleep in the dust. The dim tracery of words will be washed away and effaced from memory, but the deep lines of a beautiful example, chiseled into the heart, will remain forever. It is holiness, not the profession of it, that will give us influence both with God and men, winging our prayers with faith, and our counsels with wisdom, deriving power from above, and sending out from us currents of influence through the earth.—*Unknown.*

Chrysostom said that one single man, inflamed by holy ardor, could change an entire neighborhood. This has been proved true by men in different circumstances. A Boston newspaper once wrote that Phillips Brooks brightened an entire community when he went through it. Men felt their hearts warm as if the sun had broken through the murk and dim alleys of the city.

Marquis de Renty, the French nobleman who was so devout, had such an influence that his mere presence sufficed often to rebuke without a word being spoken. He once passed a house during the carnival season, where loud noise and carousing and dancing was heard. He went in and looked on, standing silently. The revelers were unable to go on, and began to weep. As a result a number of them began a new life.

Charles Finney, during his revival efforts, one time walked through a factory. One young woman passed a trifling, foolish remark to another and laughed. Finney looked at her, and she became confused, breaking a thread with which she was working. Then she began to weep. Finney spoke to her, and sensed she was convicted. Conviction spread rapidly through the entire factory so that the owner, who was accompanying Finney, gave permission for work to cease. The prayer-meeting which followed was the beginning of a revival.

Redeeming the time

"Remember how short my time is" (Psa. 89:47).
"Redeeming the time, because the days are evil" (Eph. 5:16).

We are all great people, or at least we think so, until we come to Time, but Time makes everybody look small. When the morning comes, it is soon twelve o'clock, and very little done, and the day has soon gone. When Saturday comes it appears to most of us as if Saturday were here two days ago. . . . How small Time makes us! Even our pleasures are measured by Time: "pleasures of sin for a season" (Heb.11:25). We are all very great people, until we place ourselves by the side of Time! The hours are flying over our heads; the days, weeks, months, and years, are gliding silently but swiftly away. A few more sunsets over the dark hills of Time, a few more springs, summers, autumns, winters, and Time will have left us in Eternity!

"Tomorrow," he promised his conscience,
    "Tomorrow I'll do as I should;
Tomorrow I'll think as I ought to;
    Tomorrow I mean to be good;
Tomorrow I'll conquer the habits
    That hold me from Heaven away";
But ever his conscience repeated
    One word—and one only—"Today."
Tomorrow, tomorrow, tomorrow—
    Thus day after day it went on;
Tomorrow, tomorrow, tomorrow—
    Till Youth like a vision was gone;
Till age and his passions had written
    The message of fate on his brow,
And forth from the shadows came Death
    With pitiless syllable—"Now."
                              —Unknown.

Much of life is lost in getting ready to live.*—Unknown.*

"Make the very most of your time." (Mof.) Are we really doing this? How much frittering away in selfish ends and wasteful talk! The very word "redeemed" indicates a price to be paid for this. The other translators (Wey. and Rhm.) definitely state "buy." If investing money you had a chance of, say, 7.5% or 10% in one scheme and only 1% and 2% in others, which way would you act? Then what is yielding the greatest profit now? There is no time for prayer. No, you will not find it, you must take it from something else less vital.*—John Harrison, (successor to C. T. Studd).*

Expecting answers to prayer

"For the weapons of our warfare are not carnal, but mighty through God to the pulling down of strong holds" (2 Cor. 10:4).

"And this is the confidence that we have in him, that, if we ask anything according to his will, he heareth us: And if we know that he hear us, whatsoever we ask, we know that we have the petitions that we desired of him"

(1 John 5:14-15).

There are no impossibilities to these intercessors, for they have to do with the God of all power and might to Whom nothing is impossible. Heaven and earth are there to serve them, and they are full of joyous faith. Angels, men and powers of the universe consciously and unconsciously work together for the fulfillment of their petitions.

The intercessor must often wait for a time in the outer court before he gains access to the Holiest of all. When this is so he must tarry and knock till the inner door opens to him, and he is granted admission to the Throne-room. When once he has entered, the cause is all but won. What had been at first weary work in prayer becomes easy, the divine stream lays hold of and floods his heart, his horizon widens. The consciousness of his own weakness and nothingness is outweighed by an overwhelming sense of the glory of God and of the grace of being allowed to draw near to Him in the Name of Christ. In that Name, the Name of our great High Priest, the Father grants everything. He has been granted an audience with the King of Heaven. With growing joy that is mingled with a thanksgiving and worship, the intercessor presents his petition. He is certain of acceptance. He has believed the promises and received the assurance of their fulfillment, and when the hour so graciously granted is over, he is sure that he has obtained what he has asked, even though the tangible fulfillment may be long in coming. It will come in God's time.—*Sister Eva.*

> Thou art coming to a King,
> Large petitions with thee bring;
> For His grace and pow'r are such,
> None can ever ask too much.
> —*John Newton.*

August 25
The power of faith

"Now faith is the substance of things hoped for, the evidence of things not seen" (Heb. 11:1).
"Abraham believed God, and it was accounted to him for righteousness"
(Gal. 3:6).

Faith makes all evil good to us, and all good better; unbelief makes all good evil to us, and all evil worse. Faith laughs at the shaking of the spear; unbelief trembles at the shaking of a leaf. Faith finds food in famine, and a table in the wilderness. In greatest danger faith answers, "I have a great God"; when outward strength is broken, faith pulls out the sting of trouble, and draws out the wormwood of every affliction.

This is the Christian's privilege, that he lives in a larger world than other men. He sees things that are hid from their eyes. Behind the chaos of good and bad just about us, behind the seeming defeat of the right, behind disaster and loss and doubt, there stands up to his sight the figure of Infinite Love, controlling all things. Beyond the imperfections of life lies the fullness of Heaven.

> A tender child of summers three,
> Seeking her little bed at night,
> Paused on the dark stairs timidly.
> "O, mother, take my hand," said she,
> "And then the dark will all be light."
>
> We older children grope our way
> From dark behind to dark before;
> And only when our hands we lay,
> Dear Lord, in Thine, the night is day,
> And there is darkness nevermore.
>
> Reach downward to the sunless days,
> Wherein all guides are blind but Thee,
> And faith is small and hope delays;
> Take Thou the hands of prayer we raise,
> And let us feel the light of Thee.
> —*J. G. Whittier.*

It is a little thing to trust God as far as we can see Him, so far as the way lies open before us, but to trust Him when we are hedged in on every side and can see no way to escape, this is good and acceptable with God.—*John Wesley.*

The heavenly lodestone

"Sir, thou hast nothing to draw with" (John 4:11).
"And I, if I be lifted up from the earth, will draw all men unto me" (John 12:32).

The greatest compliment you can pay to man or woman is to say that they attract without adornment. There are some who would reveal their birth in any garb—in the meanest, in the poorest. You might clothe them in rags; you might lodge them in hovels; you might surround them with the humblest furniture, but their speech would betray them to be "not of Galilee." They have nothing to draw with, but they themselves draw.

So it is with Thee, Thou Son of the Highest. Thou hast nothing to attract but Thine own beauty. Thou hast put off the best robe of the Father; Thou hast assumed the dress of the prodigal son. It is in a soiled garment that Thou hast solicited my love. Thou hast come to me footsore and weary—a Man of sorrows and acquainted with grief. Thou hast asked me to share Thy poverty. Thou hast said: "Wilt thou come with Me to the place where the thorns are rifest, to the land where the roses are most rare? Wilt thou follow Me down the deep shadows of Gethsemane, up the steep heights of Calvary? Wilt thou go with Me where the hungry cry for bread, where the sick implore for health, where the weary weep for rest? Wilt thou accompany Me where pain dwells, where danger lurks, and alleys where the poor meet and struggle and die? Wilt thou live with Me where the world passes by in scorn, where fashion pauses not to rest, where even disciples have often forsaken Me and fled? Then is thy love complete, My triumph perfected. Then have I reached the summit of human glory; for thou hast chosen Me for Myself alone, and without the aid of earth I have drawn thy heart to Heaven."—*George Matheson.*

A Man of sorrows, of toil and tears,
An outcast Man and a lonely;
But He looked on me, and through endless years
Him must I love—Him only.

And I would abide where He abode,
And follow His steps for ever;
His people my people, His God my God,
In the land beyond the river.

And where He died would I also die,
For dearer a grave beside Him,
Than a kingly place amongst living men,
The place which they denied Him.
                                        —*Unknown.*

August 27
Undeveloped or mature—which?

"Therefore leaving the principles of the doctrine of Christ, let us go on unto perfection" (Heb. 6:1).
"For when for the time ye ought to be teachers, ye have need that one teach you again which be the first principles of the oracles of God" (Heb. 5:12).

There are two classes of babes—they who are just born, and they who have never grown. The former are ever sources of exquisite pleasure; the latter are the cause of much pain. A parent feels that a fountain of purest satisfaction is opened when God in tender love puts a babe into her arms. How fondly she watches that helpless one, and how gratefully she thanks God for that choice gift. But she does not wish that child ever to remain a babe, but to grow in physical stature, and mental culture, and spiritual completeness, and is only satisfied when these results are secured.

We ought to be equally earnest to grow in the divine life. An overgrown babe—that is, one who has the stature of a man, but the spirit and tastes of a babe; one who has the age of a man, but the manners and the weakness of a babe—is, whether found in the Church or out of it, a most uninteresting spectacle. (When the stunting of the child is physical, our feelings are of unmixed sympathy, but the spiritual baby is to be deplored because his lack of development could have been avoided.)

How many Christians there are who have never grown for twenty years. They are no more loving, no more earnest, no more devoted; they have no more control over themselves; they have no more influence over the world, no more power with God than they had twenty years ago. They would take their child from the school in which he never got beyond his alphabet. They would fling upon the rubbish heap the plant that only just kept alive and never grew into symmetry and beauty of form. They would laugh at that society which just started into existence, but never accomplished the work for which it was called into being.—*The King's Highway.*

When courage is needed

"He took courage, and put away the abominable idols out of all the land of Judah" (2 Chron. 15:8).
"Be of good courage, and let us play the men for our people, and for the cities of our God: and the Lord do that which seemeth him good"
(2 Sam. 10:12).

If I profess with the loudest voice and clearest exposition every portion of the truth of God except precisely that little point which the world and the devil are at that moment attacking, I am not confessing Christ, however boldly I may be professing Christ. Where the battle rages, there the loyalty of the soldier is proved, and to be steady on all the battlefield besides, is mere flight and disgrace if he flinches at that point.—*Martin Luther.*

Whomsoever I please or displease, I will be faithful to God, to the people, and to my own soul.—*Francis Asbury.*

Cowardice asks, Is it safe? Expediency asks, Is it politic? Vanity asks, Is it popular? But Conscience asks, Is it right?—*Unknown.*

Who walks with God must take His way
Across far distances and gray
To goals that others do not see,
Where others do not care to be.
Who walks with God must have no fear
When danger and defeat appear,
Nor stop when every hope seems gone,
For God, our God, moves ever on.

Who walks with God must press ahead
When sun or cloud is overhead,
When all the waiting thousands cheer,
Or when they only stop to sneer;
When all the challenge leaves the hours
And naught is left but jaded powers.
But he will some day reach the dawn,
For God, our God, moves ever on.
—*Unknown.*

Live today

"I must walk today" (Luke 13:33).
"Give us THIS DAY our daily bread" (Matt. 6:11).

Apprehension sometimes comes from looking too far ahead. How few of us really live in the present! Most of us are perpetually saddened by looking back upon the past, or filled with apprehensions from looking forward into the dim and shadowy future. We are crippled in our exertions because we fail to seize vigorously upon the present. Let us learn to live now. What calmness of mind it produces, what weight of character—"I do one thing at a time."

No longer forward, nor behind,
I look in hope and fear;
But grateful, take the good I find,
The best of now, and here.

I plow no more a desert land
For harvest, weed and tare;
The manna dropping from God's hand
Rebukes my painful care.

I break my pilgrim staff, I lay
Aside the toiling oar,
The angel sought so far away
I welcome at my door.
—*J. G. Whittier.*

A Christian can no more take in a supply of grace for the future than he can eat enough today to last him for the next six months, or take sufficient air into his lungs at once to sustain life for a week to come. We must draw upon God's boundless stores of grace from day to day, as we need it.—*D. L. Moody.*

Tomorrow you have no business with. You steal if you touch tomorrow. It is God's. Every day has in it enough to keep any man occupied, without concerning himself with the things beyond.—*Henry Ward Beecher.*

The Word, a powerful weapon

"For the word of God is quick, and powerful, and sharper than any two-edged sword, piercing even to the dividing asunder of soul and spirit, and of the joints and marrow, and is a discerner of the thoughts and intents of the heart" (Heb. 4:12).

"O earth, earth, earth, hear the word of the Lord" (Jer. 22:29).

In our Protestant land where the Bible is taken for granted, we are apt to forget the impact the first simple reading of the Gospel story can have. Is it not possible for us today to read its simple passages expecting it to affect us and others as powerfully as it did the persons in the following story?

The story is told of a colporteur in Sicily, trudging along the road in the gloaming with still a few miles to travel to his destination. A black-cloaked rider came cantering up behind him and demanded to know what was in his bag. He had fallen into the hands of one of Sicily's brigand chiefs! The bag was opened and the books displayed. "Ah ha! You are the man who sells pestilential books which corrupt the morals of simple people. I have heard about you. I'll burn the accursed books though, and then I'll shoot you dead!" The colporteur thought and prayed very hard for a moment; then he said, "Sir, before you burn my books and shoot me, I will ask one thing. Let me read some passages from them." The brigand agreed to this last request, and the colporteur took out a Gospel of St. Luke. "A certain man was going down from Jerusalem to Jericho and he fell among thieves . . ." The brigand listened carefully, and when the story was finished he said he liked it, and agreed that that book at least needn't be burned. The colporteur selected another, reading this time from the Sermon on the Mount: then another, reading the thirteenth chapter of 1 Corinthians; and so it went on until he had read something from every one of his books, and each time the brigand had been pleased, and had agreed that such a book could not corrupt anyone's morals. He was most surprised to find that there were no more books left, and felt in the bag and in the colporteur's pockets to make sure. Then he let the colporteur go on his way, which he did, praising God for his escape.

Years afterwards the colporteur received a letter from America. "My dear friend, do you remember the brigand who stopped you one night on the road? I am he, but a brigand no longer. I have never forgotten you nor the words you read to me. They saved me from an evil life, thank God."

Soul-savers or self-savers

"When thou art converted, strengthen thy brethren" (Luke 22:32).
"Follow me, and I will make you fishers of men" (Matt. 4:19).

Living to save others is the condition of saving ourselves. No man is truly converted who does not live to save others. Every truly converted man turns from selfishness to benevolence, and benevolence surely leads him to do all he can to save the souls of his fellowmen. This is the changeless law of benevolent action.

The self-deceived are always to be distinguished by this peculiarity—they live to please themselves. This is the chief end of their religion. All their religious efforts and activities tend toward this sole object. If they can secure their own conversion so as to be pretty sure of it, they are satisfied. Sometimes the ties of natural sympathy embrace those who are especially near to them, but selfishness goes commonly no further, except as a good name may prompt them on.—*Charles G. Finney.*

We ourselves are "saved to save," and are made to give. The pebble takes in all the rays of light that fall upon it, but the diamond flashes them out again; every little facet is a means, not simply of drinking it in, but of giving more out. The unearthly loveliness of the opal arises from the same process carried on within the stone; the microscope shows it to be shattered through and through with numberless fissures that catch and refract and radiate every ray they can seize. Yes, there lies before us a beautiful possible life—one that shall have a passion in giving, that shall be poured forth to God—spent out for man: that shall be consecrated "for the hardest work and the darkest sinners."

—*I. Lilias Trotter.*

When I am dying, how glad I shall be
That the lamp of my life has been blazed out for Thee;
I shall not mind whatever I gave,
In labor, or money, one soul to save;
I shall not mind that the way has been rough,
That Thy dear feet led the way was enough—
When I am dying, how glad I shall be
That the lamp of my life has been blazed out for Thee.

—*Unknown.*

September 1
God's badge of honor

"And who is he that will harm you, if ye be followers of that which is good? But and if ye suffer for righteousness' sake, happy are ye: and be not afraid of their terror, neither be troubled" (1 Pet. 3:13-14).

The devil's growls and the world's sneers are God's marks of high honor. There are far greater calamities than to be unpopular and misunderstood. There are far worse things than to be found in the minority. Many of God's greatest blessings are lying behind the devil's scarecrows of prejudice and misrepresentation. The Holy Ghost is not ashamed to use the unpopular people, and if He uses them what need they care for men?

There was once a captain promoted for merit, but despised by aristocratic companions. One day the colonel found it out and determined to stop it, so he called on the young officer, and they walked up and down the parade ground, the other captains meanwhile being obliged to salute both him and his companion every time they passed. That settled the new captain's standing. After that there were no cuts or sneers. It was enough that the commanding officer had walked by his side.

Oh, to have God's recognition, when man's notice will count for little. He will give us all the human help and praise we need.

Expect contradiction and opposition, together with crosses of various kinds. Consider the words of St. Paul, "Unto you it is given in the behalf of Christ"— for His sake, as a fruit of His death and intercession for you—"not only to believe on him, but also to suffer for his sake."

It is given. God gives you this opposition or reproach; it is a fresh token of His love. And will you disown the Giver, or spurn His gift and count it a misfortune? Will you not rather say, "Father, the hour is come that Thou shouldst be glorified; now Thou givest Thy child to suffer something for Thee, do with me according to Thy will"?—*John Wesley.*

September 2
The soul's need of quiet

"In returning and rest shall ye be saved; in quietness and in confidence shall be your strength" (Isa. 30:15).
"Ye ought to be quiet, and to do nothing rashly" (Acts 19:36).
"Be still, and know that I am God" (Psa. 46:10).

I seem to hear a deep sigh from the heart of many a true servant of God, "faint yet pursuing," whose soul is athirst for the Living God and for the calm and the silence in which he may hear the divine voice, but who sees no way of escape from the pressing claims of earthly duty. The case of such (which has also been my own) calls forth my deepest sympathy. "With God all things are possible." Cease from conflict with circumstances, from this "toiling in rowing," from this breathless swimming against the tide. Put the matter into His hands. "There was silence in heaven about the space of half an hour" at His command; silence even of the angelic voices. He can create a silence around you, and trace a clear path for your feet to enter into the Holy of Holies, where you shall find Him and hear His voice.—*Josephine Butler.*

Lord, what a change within us one short hour
Spent in Thy presence would prevail to make!
What heavy burdens from our bosoms take,
What parched grounds revive, as with a shower;
We kneel, and all around us seems to lower;
We rise, and all, the distant and the near
Stands forth in sunny outline brave and clear.

We kneel, how weak! We rise, how full of power!
Why, therefore, should we do ourselves this wrong,
Or others, that we are not always strong;
That we are ever overborne with care;
That we should ever weak or heartless be,
Anxious or troubled, when with us is prayer,
And joy and strength and courage are with Thee?
                    —*Richard Chenevix Trench.*

Too much taken up with our work, we may forget our Master. It is possible to have the hand full, and the heart empty. Taken up with our Master we cannot forget our work; if the heart is filled with His love, how can the hands not be active in His service?—*A. Monod.*

Music under pressure

"Thy hand presseth me sore" (Psa. 38:2).
"Humble yourselves therefore under the mighty hand of God, that he may exalt you in due time" (1Peter 5:6).

God knows what keys in the human soul to touch, in order to draw out its sweetest and most perfect harmonies. They may be the minor strains of sadness and sorrow; they may be the loftiest notes of joy and gladness. God knows where the melodies of our nature are, and what discipline will call them forth. Some with plaintive song, must walk in the lowly vales of life's weary way; others, in loftier hymns, shall sing of nothing but joy, as they tread the mountain tops of life. But they all unite without a discord or jar, as the ascending anthem of loving and believing hearts finds its way into the chorus of the redeemed in Heaven.

God presses me hard, but He gives patience, too!
And I say to myself, "'Tis no more than my due,"
And no tone from the organ can swell on the breeze
Till the organist's fingers press down on the keys.
—*Unknown.*

It does not matter how great the pressure is, it only matters where the pressure lies; whether it comes between you and God, or whether it presses you closer to His heart.—*Hudson Taylor.*

In the still air the music lies unheard;
In the rough marble beauty hides unseen:
To wake the music and the beauty, needs
The master's touch, the sculptor's chisel keen.

Great Master, touch us with Thy skillful hand,
Let not the music that is in us die;
Great Sculptor, hew and polish us, nor let
Hidden and lost, Thy form within us lie.

Spare not the stroke, do with us as Thou wilt;
Let there be nought unfinished, broken, marred;
Complete Thy purpose, that we may become
Thy perfect image, O our God and Lord!
—*Horatius Bonar.*

Let love expel self

"The fruit of the Spirit is love" (Gal. 5:22).
"And the greatest of these is love" (1 Cor. 13:13—R.V.).

"The fruit of the Spirit is love." Why? *Because nothing but love can expel and conquer our selfishness.* Self is the great curse, whether in its relation to God, or to our fellowmen, or to fellow Christians; thinking of ourselves and seeking our own. Self is our greatest curse. But, praise God, Christ came to redeem us from self. We sometimes talk about deliverance from the self-life— and praise God for every word that can be said about it to help us. But I am afraid some people think deliverance from the self-life means this: Now I am going to have no longer any trouble to myself in serving God; and they forget that *deliverance from the self-life means to be a vessel overflowing with love to everybody all the day.*

And there you have the reason why many people pray for the power of the Holy Ghost, and they get something, but, oh, so little, because they prayed for power for work, and power for blessing, but they have not prayed for power for full deliverance from self. That means not only the righteous self in intercourse with God, but the unloving self in intercourse with men. But there is deliverance. "The fruit of the Spirit is love." I bring you the glorious promise of Christ, that He is able to fill our hearts with love.—*Andrew Murray.*

> Thy mighty Love, O God, constraineth me,
> As some strong tide it presseth on its way,
> Seeking a channel in my self-bound soul,
> Yearning to sweep all barriers away.
>
> Shall I not yield to that constraining power?
> Shall I not say, O tide of Love, flow in?
> My God, Thy gentleness hath conquered me,
> Life cannot be as it hath hither been.
>
> Break through my nature, mighty, heavenly Love,
> Clear every avenue of thought and brain,
> Flood my affections, purify my will,
> Let nothing but Thine own pure life remain.
>
> Thus wholly mastered and possessed by God,
> Forth from my life, spontaneous and free,
> Shall flow a stream of tenderness and grace—
> Loving, because God loved, eternally.
> —*E. May Grimes.*

Christ where we live and work

"Surely the righteous shall give thanks unto thy name: the upright shall dwell in thy presence" (Psa. 140:13).
"One thing have I desired of the Lord, that will I seek after; that I may dwell in the house of the Lord all the days of my life" (Psa. 27:4).

"One thing have I desired, that will I seek after; that I"—in my study; I, in my shop; I, in my parlor, kitchen, or nursery; I, in my studio; I, in my lecture-hall—"may dwell in the house of the Lord all the days of my life." In our "Father's house are many mansions." The room that we spend most of our lives in, each of us at our tasks or our worktables, may be in our Father's house, too; and it is only we that can secure that it shall be.

The Psalmist longed to break down the distinction between sacred and secular; to consecrate work, of whatever sort it was. He had learned what so many of us need to learn far more thoroughly, that if our religion does not drive the wheels of our daily business, it is of little use; and that if the field in which our religion has power to control and impel is not that of the trivialities and secularities of our ordinary life, there is no field for it at all.

And if we have, in our lives, things over which we cannot make the sign of the cross, the sooner we get rid of them the better. If there is anything in our daily work, or in our characters, about which we are doubtful, here is a good test: does it seem to check our continual communion with God, as a ligature round the wrist might do the continual flow of the blood, or does it help us to realize His presence? If the former, let us have no more to do with it; if the latter, let us seek to increase it.—*Alexander Maclaren.*

> Lord try us, lest our holy creed
> We hold in word but not in deed;
> Or hold mere forms of godliness
> Without a Christlike holiness.
>
> Lord halt us, lest with bigot tread
> We live a name and yet are dead
> Or lest in fighting error's pen
> We smirch, not heresies, but men.
>
> Lord keep us true, but ever kind,
> With Thine own gentleness of mind;
> With Thine own wisdom from above,
> Whose strongest argument is love.
> —*Unknown.*

September 6
Deeds live forever

"Every man shall receive according to his own labour" (1 Cor. 3:8).
"Surely he shall not be moved for ever: the righteous shall be in everlasting remembrance" (Psa. 112: 6).
"The memory of the just is blessed: but the name of the wicked shall rot"
(Prov. 10:7).

Gladly away from this toil would I hasten,
    Up to the crown that for me has been won;
Unthought of by man in rewards or in praises,
    Only remembered by what I have done.

Up and away, like the odors of sunset
    That sweeten the twilight as darkness comes on—
So be my life—a thing felt but not noticed,
    And I but remembered by what I have done.

Yes, like the fragrance that wanders in freshness
    When the flowers that it came from are closed up and gone—
So would I be to this world's weary dwellers,
    Only remembered by what I have done.

Not myself, but the truth that in life I have spoken,
    Not myself, but the seed that in life I have sown
Shall pass on to ages—all about me forgotten,
    Save the truth I have spoken, the things I have done.

So let my living be, so be my dying;
    So let my name lie, unblazoned, unknown;
Unpraised and unmissed, I shall still be remembered;
    Yes—but remembered by what I have done.
            —*Horatius Bonar.*

Every true Christian is a tree of righteousness, whose fruits are good and profitable unto men. He is glad to help and to comfort others. He is diligent and industrious. He speaks to edification, dwells in peace, and gentleness, and love. He reproves what is wrong by an excellent example, and recommends by his own practice what is pleasing to God.—*Unknown.*

The world will little note, nor long remember, what we say here; but it can never forget what they did here.—*Abraham Lincoln.*

Every man his brother's keeper

"Am I my brother's keeper?" (Gen. 4:9).
"But a certain Samaritan, as he journeyed, came where he was: and when he saw him, he had compassion on him" (Luke 10:33).

Here comes the demand that every man should be the keeper of his brother-man. That means, that whatever may be the care which a man takes of his own life, however he watches it and tends it, he has not done his duty, he has not filled out his existence, unless he also has, just as far as he possesses the ability and chance, watched and protected and helped the lives of other people.

Are there not in the world very many intelligent people who do not in the least believe that they have any responsibility for other people? Somebody has, they think. There are the ministers. There are the managers of philanthropic institutions. There is the "benevolent public." But they have no such responsibility. They are nobody's keepers but their own.

Men have been too apt to think of helpfulness to their brother-man as an accidental privilege or an exceptional duty of human life, and not as a true and essential part of humanity, without whose presence humanity is not complete. See what I mean. A beautiful voice is an exceptional privilege of a few extraordinary people among mankind. It does not belong to this man because he is a man, in very virtue of his manhood. Other men are destitute of it, and cannot sing any more than the stone upon the hillside, and yet they are as truly men as he. But a man has two arms. They are not the exception. They are the constant human rule. It is not a privilege to have them. The man who has one arm or none—he is the exception. He is not a total man. The loss may come nobly, by some great self-exposure which it was glorious for him to make. Nevertheless, he has suffered a detraction from the completeness of his humanity. Not to have the beautiful voice is to lack a lovely ornament and decoration of the life; not to have two arms is to lack a portion of the life itself.

Helpfulness to our fellowman has been put in a wrong class. It has seemed to be like the beautiful voice, a special, splendid privilege and gift; not like the two arms, a test and proof of humanity.—*Phillips Brooks.*

September 8

The joy supreme

"They that turn many to righteousness shall shine as the stars for ever and ever" (Dan. 12:3).
"Let him know, that he which converteth the sinner from the error of his way shall save a soul from death, and shall hide a multitude of sins" (James 5:20).

Even if I were utterly selfish and had no care for anything but my own happiness, I would choose if I might, under God, to be a soul winner; for never did I know perfect, overflowing, unutterable happiness of the purest and most ennobling order till I first heard of one who had sought and found the Savior through my means. No young mother ever so rejoiced over her firstborn child, no warrior ever was so exultant over a hard-won victory.—*C. H. Spurgeon.*

"I would think it a greater happiness to gain one soul to Christ," declared Matthew Henry, "than mountains of silver and gold to myself. If God suffers me to labor in vain, though I should get hundreds a year by my labor, it would be the constant grief and trouble of my soul. And if I do not gain souls, I shall enjoy all my other gains with very little satisfaction."

Dr. Doddridge wrote to a friend: "I long for the conversion of souls more sensibly than anything else. Methinks I could not only labor but die for it with pleasure. The love of Christ constraineth me."

While lying on what was his deathbed, David Brainerd said: "My greatest joy and comfort has been to do something for promoting the interests of religion, and the souls of particular persons, and now in my illness, while I am full of pain and distress, from day to day, all the comfort I have is in being able to do some little char (or small piece of work) for God, either by something that I say, or by writing, or by some other way."

We bear the torch that, flaming, fell from the hands of those
Who gave their lives proclaiming that Jesus died and rose;
Ours is the same commission, the same glad message ours,
Fired by the same ambition, to Thee we yield our powers.

O Father, Who sustained them! O Spirit Who inspired!
Savior, Whose love constrained them to toil with zeal untired,
From cowardice defend us, from lethargy awake!
Forth on Thine errands send us to labor for Thy sake.
                                        —*Bishop Houghton.*
                                        (*Evangelical Christian*).

The sacrifice of our will

"I seek not mine own will" (John 5:30).
"We ceased, saying, The will of the Lord be done" (Acts 21:14).

There are no disappointments to those whose wills are buried in the will of God.—*F. Faber.*

Absolute resignation to Divine Will baffles a thousand temptations, and confidence in our Savior carries us sweetly through a thousand trials.
—*John Fletcher.*

> Laid on Thine altar, O my Lord divine,
>   Accept my will this day, for Jesus' sake;
> I have no jewels to adorn Thy shrine,
>   Nor any world-proud sacrifice to make;
> But here I bring within my trembling hand
>   This will of mine—a thing that seemeth small;
> And Thou alone, O God, canst understand
>   How, when I yield Thee this, I yield my all.
>
> Hidden therein, Thy searching gaze can see
>   Struggles of passion—visions of delight—
> All that I love, and am, and fain would be—
>   Deep loves, fond hopes and longings infinite.
> It hath been wet with tears and dimmed with sighs,
>   Clinched in my grasp, till beauty hath it none.
> Now, from Thy footstool where it vanquished lies,
>   The prayer ascendeth, "May Thy will be done."
>
> Take it, O Father, ere my courage fail,
>   And merge it so in Thine own will, that e'en
> If, in some desperate hour, my cries prevail
>   And Thou give back my will, it may have been
> So changed, so purified, so fair have grown,
>   So one with Thee, so filled with love divine,
> I may not see or know it as my own,
>   But, gaining back my will, may find it Thine.
> —*Unknown.*

The will is the keystone to the arch of man's being. It is the foundation stone of his whole mental and moral superstructure. If this is given up, or consecrated, all else will be laid on the altar with it.—*Lewis R. Dunn.*

263

September 10
Anxious care forbidden

"Be careful for nothing; but in every thing by prayer and supplication with thanksgiving let your requests be made known unto God" (Phil. 4:6).
"Hast thou not known? hast thou not heard, that the everlasting God, the Lord, the Creator of the ends of the earth, fainteth not, neither is weary? there is no searching of his understanding" (Isa. 40:28).

The command, "Be careful for nothing," is unlimited, and so is the expression, "casting all your care upon him." If we cast our burdens upon another, can they continue to press upon us? If we bring them away with us from the throne of grace, it is evident that we do not leave them there.

With respect to myself, I have made this one test of my prayers. If, after committing anything to God, I can, like Hannah, come away and have my countenance no more sad, my heart no more pained or anxious, I look upon it as one proof that I prayed in faith. But if I bring away my burden, I conclude that faith was not in exercise.—*Edward Payson.*

But where is the room for care, when in everything we may make our requests unto God? Let the requests be large. Let them embrace perfect purity of life and perfect obedience in all things, and this command will be easily fulfilled. Think to Whom thou dost make thy request.

Were Christianity only useful in liberating men from care, it ought to earn the liveliest gratitude of the entire universe. Ever since sin came into our world, care has pressed upon our race with awful force. The wrinkled brows, the stooping gait, and the anxious countenances of thousands, tell of an amount of care that can be comprehended only by God. But by the wonderful provision made for us in the Gospel of Jesus Christ, we may be freed from all care. Indeed, if we put trust in Jesus for full salvation, we shall be freed from all care.

To profess to be a follower of the Lord Jesus, and yet to be full of care, casts a sad reflection on the goodness of our heavenly Father. Has He not made fullest provision for our wants? Has He not distinctly forbidden care? Has He not urged us to make Him a confidant, and open our hearts in grateful recognition of His goodness, and trust in His continued guidance to help?—*King's Highway.*

Oh, if men would but give God credit for sincerity!—*Hewitson.*

It is not work that kills men; it is worry. Work is healthy; you can hardly put more on a man than he can bear. But worry is rust upon the blade. It is not movement that destroys the machinery, but friction.—*Henry Ward Beecher.*

Unrecorded battles

"Verily, verily, I say unto you, He that believeth on me, the works that I do shall he do also; and greater works than these shall he do; because I go unto my Father. And whatsoever ye shall ask in my name, that will I do, that the Father may be glorified in the Son" (John 14:12-13).

There is no greater power in the world than prayer. True prayer can do anything—the prayer that is wrought by the Spirit and is presented at the throne of the omnipotent God in the Name of Christ. The greatest promises in the Bible concern prayer. Jesus Christ, the supreme Intercessor, gave to His followers the privilege of prayer, and none can tell the immensity of the sphere He opened to them (John 14:12-15). In the life of individuals, and indeed of the whole human race, prayer has often been the guiding power, the connecting link, or the molding factor both in little everyday happenings and in important crises. Behind closed doors, far away from the busy scenes of life, deeds are done, doors are opened, conditions are created, power is liberated, promises are obtained, decisions are made. Who can estimate the extent of the influence, or fully grasp the significance of such prayer? True prayer, the prayer of faith in the power of the Holy Spirit, brings the intercessor into immediate touch with God.—*Sister Eva.*

> Believers have a silent field to fight,
> And their exploits are veiled from human sight;
> They are God's secret ones, whose warfare is unseen;
> And in some nook where, little known, they dwell,
> Kneel, pray in faith, and route the hosts of hell.
> There, unfatigued, their fervent spirits labor.
> There they fight and there obtain fresh triumphs,
> And never-withering wreaths, compared with which
> The laurels that a Caesar reaped were weeds.
> —*Unknown.*

Prayer is the hand that moves the world, but the fingers of that hand are consecrated men and women.—*Robert Moffat.*

265

Bring self to God's crucible

"The fining pot is for silver, and the furnace for gold: but the LORD trieth the hearts" (Prov. 17:3).
"He shall purify the sons of Levi, and purge them as gold and silver, that they may offer unto the Lord an offering in righteousness" (Mal. 3:3).

No vessel of gold is molded without the fire. Shrink not from the flames of divine love. If you would be molded you must be melted.

Take my heart, Thou Blacksmith of the ages,
  Try me in the furnace Thou hast planned;
Place me in the white-heat of affliction,
  And fashion with the hammer of Thy hand.

Make of my else worthless self, a girder,
  Tempered with Thy Spirit from above;
And when Thou hast finished, build me firmly
  Into the princely temple of Thy love.
                                        —*Nathaniel Krum.*

It is the fire which refines the gold. Men dig it from the earth, and bring it to the crucible. If it is not put in the flame, it will not be refined. The fire does not refine the gold unless it be brought; the bringing does not refine. It must be brought, and the fire must exert its agency. The soul is not sanctified by means, nor in the absence of them. The means are necessary to bring it to God, and when it is brought, God does the work. Remember this, seeking soul, and now having employed the means, expect God to touch you, and accomplish His promise. Look now away from the means. Look away from self. Trust in Him; yea, trust now! Fall at His feet, and He will make thee whole.
                                        —*R. S. Foster.*

God's furnace doth in Zion stand;
  But Zion's God sits by,
As the refiner views his gold
  With an observant eye.
His thoughts are high, His love is wise,
  His wounds a cure intend;
And though He does not always smile,
  He loves unto the end.
                —*Countess of Huntingdon.*

Peace amid turmoil

"And the peace of God, which passeth all understanding, shall keep your hearts and minds through Christ Jesus" (Phil. 4:7).
"Peace I leave with you, my peace I give unto you" (John 14:27).

And there was calm! O Savior, I have proved
That Thou to help and save art really near.
How else this quiet rest from grief, and fear,
And all distress? The cross is not removed;
I must go forth to bear it as before,
But leaning on Thine arm, I dread its weight no more.
—Frances Ridley Havergal.

Nothing for a moment broke the serenity of Christ's life on earth. Tempest and tumult met Him everywhere, until outwardly His life was one of the most troubled that was ever lived. But the inner life was a sea of glass. The highest tranquility, serenity and peace of mind were always there. It was at the very time when the bloodhounds were dogging Him in the streets of Jerusalem, that He turned to His disciples and offered them, as a last legacy, "My peace." If the meagerness of human language fails to convey to a blind man the vastness of that ocean which lies in the hollow of the Creator's hand, how much more is its poverty seen when it attempts to set forth, in an inexperienced soul, all that is meant by God's perfect peace.

It is the deep tranquility of a soul resting wholly upon God, in contrast with the unrest and anxiety engendered by a self-centered and worldly spirit. Jesus calls it, "My peace," in contrast with the hollowness of what the world calls peace. The world's peace is determined by outward things, and is as changeable as external conditions. But the peace of God changes not. It is not fitful and transient, but an abiding and ever-increasing reality. Ecstatic joy fluctuates like the waves of the sea, but peace flows on without interruption, like a river ever flowing and full.

(From *New Testament Holiness* by Thomas Cook. Used by permission of the Epworth Press).

Like a river glorious
Is God's perfect peace,
Over all victorious
In its bright increase;
Perfect, yet it floweth
Fuller ev'ry day:
Perfect, yet it groweth
Deeper all the way.
—F. R. Havergal.

September 14

Religion—doleful or delightful?

"Ye shall rejoice in all that ye put your hand unto" (Deut. 12:7).
"Alway rejoicing" (2 Cor. 6:10).

Some people think that there is no joy in religion—it is a gloomy thing. When a young person becomes a Christian, they would say, "Alas! he must bid farewell to pleasure—farewell to the joys of youth, farewell to a merry heart. He must exchange these pleasures for reading of the Bible and dry sermon books—for a life of gravity and preciseness." This is what the world says. What does the Bible say? "I sat down under his shadow with great delight." Ah! let God be true, and every man a liar. Yet no one can believe this except those who have tried it.

Ah! be not deceived, my young friends; the world has many sensual and many sinful delights—the delights of eating and drinking, and wearing gay clothes—the delights of revelry and the dance. No man of wisdom will deny that these things are delightful to the natural heart; but, oh! they perish in the using, and they end in an eternal hell. But to sit down under the shadow of Christ, wearied with God's burning anger, wearied with seeking after vain saviors, at last to find rest under the shadow of Christ, ah! this is great delight. Lord, evermore may I sit under this shadow! Lord, evermore may I be filled with this joy!

Some people are afraid of anything like joy in religion. They have none themselves, and they do not love to see it in others. Their religion is something like the stars, very high, and very clear, and very cold. When they see tears of anxiety, or tears of joy, they cry out, "Enthusiasm, enthusiasm!" Well, then, to the law and to the testimony. "I sat down under his shadow *with great delight.*" Is this enthusiasm? O Lord, evermore give us this enthusiasm! May the God of hope fill you with all joy and peace in believing! If it be really in sitting under the shadow of Christ, let there be no bounds to your joy. Oh, if God would but open your eyes, and give you simple, childlike faith to look to Jesus, to sit under His shadow, then would songs of joy rise from all our dwellings. Rejoice in the Lord always, and again I say, Rejoice!

—*Robert Murray McCheyne.*

God's will for my career

"Make you perfect in every good work to do his will" (Heb. 13:21).
"The God of our fathers hath chosen thee, that thou shouldest know his will" (Acts 22:14).

But there is a will for career as well as for character. There is a will for *where*—in what place, viz., in this town or another town—I am to become like God. There is a will for where I am to be, and what I am to be, and what I am to do tomorrow. There is a will for what scheme I am to take up, and what work I am to do for Christ, and what business arrangements to make, and what money to give away. This is God's private will for me, for every step I take, for the path of life along which He points my way: God's will for my *career.*

If I have God's will in my character, my life may become great or good. It may be useful and honorable, and even a monument of the sanctifying power of God. But it will only be a life. However great and pure it be it can be no more than a life. And it ought to be a mission. There should be no such thing as a Christian life; each life should be a mission.

God has a life-plan for every human life. In the eternal counsels of His will, when He arranged the destiny of every star, and every sand-grain and grass-blade, and each of those tiny insects which live but for an hour, the Creator had a thought for you and me. Our life was to be the slow unfolding of this thought, as the cornstalk from the grain of corn, or the flower from the gradually opening bud. It was a thought of what we were to be, of what we might become, of what He would have us do with our days and years, our influence and our lives. But we all had the terrible power to evade this thought, and shape our lives from another thought, from another will, if we chose. The bud could only become a flower, and the star revolve in the orbit God has fixed. But it was man's prerogative to choose his path; his duty to choose at all has always seemed more to him than his duty to choose in God, so, for the most part, he has taken his life from God and cut his career for himself.

It comes to pass, therefore, that there are two great classes of people in the world of Christians today: (1) Those who have God's will in their character; (2) Those who have God's will likewise in their career. The first are in the world to live. They have a *life*. The second are in the world to minister. They have a *mission.—Henry Drummond.*

September 16
The Scripture gold mine

"These were more noble than those in Thessalonica, in that they received the word with all readiness of mind, and searched the scriptures daily, whether those things were so" (Acts 17:11).
"Search the scriptures; . . . they are they which testify of me" (John 5:39).

Precious things are deeply hidden. Pebbles and stones and autumn leaves abound everywhere, but gold and silver and precious stones are hidden deep in the bowels and rocky ribs of the earth; shells cover the seashore, but pearls are hidden in its depths. And so with truth. Some truths may lie on the surface of the Bible, but those that will altogether satisfy and distinguish us and make us wise unto salvation are found only after diligent search, even as for hid treasure.—*Samuel Logan Brengle.*

I open it, my fingers trace the lines
That Wesley's, Moody's, Spurgeon's eyes have scanned.
Beneath my fingertips a promise shines,
A diamond unearthed by my seeking hand,
A gem that countless saints have touched before
And left among this jewel casket's store.

I searched as one who searches long for gold,
And oh, what gleaming nuggets I unearthed.
All that my seeking heart and hands can hold
I gather, and I know their precious worth.
And strange, the vein has never failed, though man
Has mined its channel since the world began.

The Holy Book, that gives its wealth unpriced
To every seeker after God and Christ.
> —*Grace Noll Crowell.*
> (*Evangelical Christian*).

God in routine

"I will dwell in them, and walk in them" (2 Cor. 6:16).
"Walk in the Spirit" (Gal. 5:25).

Oh, how it helps and comforts us in the plod of life to know that we have a Christ Who spent the first thirty years of His life in the carpenter shop at Nazareth, swinging the hammer, covered with sweat and grimy dust, physically weary as we often are, and able to understand all our experiences of drudgery and labor, One Who still loves to share our common tasks and equip us for our difficult undertakings of hand and brain!

Yes, humble sister, He will help you at the washboard and the kitchen-sink as gladly as at the hour of prayer. Yes, busy mechanic, He will go with you and help you to swing the hammer, or handle the saw, or hold the plow in the toil of life. You shall be a better mechanic, a more skillful workman, and a more successful man, because you take His wisdom for the common affairs of life. The God we serve is not only the God of the Sabbath, and of the world of sentiment and feeling; but He is the God of Providence, the God of Nature, and Author and Director of the whole mechanism of human life. There is no place nor time where He is not able and willing to walk by our side, to work through our hands and brains, and to unite Himself in loving and all-sufficient partnership with all our needs and tasks and trials, and to prove our all-sufficiency for all things.

Blessed Holy Spirit—our Wisdom and our Guide! Let us enlarge the sphere of His operations. Let us take Him into partnership in all the length and breadth of our human life, and let us prove to the world that:

> "We need not bid for cloistered cell,
> Our neighbor and our work farewell.
> The daily round, the common task,
> Will furnish all we need to ask,
> Room to deny ourselves, a road
> To bring us daily more of God."
> —*John Keble.*

—*A. B. Simpson.*

God's purposes of affliction

"And the afflicted people thou wilt save" (2 Sam. 22:28).
"For they verily for a few days chastened us after their own pleasure: but he for our profit, that we might be partakers of his holiness" (Heb. 12:10).

How should we regard ourselves when causes of great sorrow fall upon us? First of all, we should carefully inquire whether these providences have come down from God out of Heaven, as judgments for wrongdoing, or as merely disciplinary trials of faith, and seek unto God accordingly. In neither case should we lose heart, or hope, or faith in God. We should conclude, at once, that God sees in us something which He desires to refine and perfect into a thing of beauty and perfection, for His own glory and ours, too; that He sees in us undeveloped capacities for good—capacities which He desires to perfect for the reception of those great and eternally enduring joys which He has prepared for us. Why should we be afraid of causes of sorrow, when, if we hold fast our integrity and faith in God, they are only the birth-throes of everlasting consolations, and deep and ever-enduring joys otherwise impossible to us.

—*Asa Mahan.*

Is not the way to heavenly gain
Through earthly grief and loss?
Rest must be won by toil and pain—
The crown repays the Cross.
As woods, when shaken by the breeze,
Take deeper, firmer root,
As winter's frosts but make the trees
Abound in summer fruit;
So every Heaven-sent pang and throe
That Christian firmness tries,
But nerves us for our work below,
And forms us for the skies.

—*Henry Francis Lyte.*

272

Christ enthroned in the heart

"My son, give me thine heart, and let thine eyes observe my ways"
(Prov. 23:26).
"That Christ may dwell in your hearts by faith" (Eph. 3:17).
"I will put my laws into their mind, and write them in their hearts"
(Heb. 8:10).

It is instructive to note that Christ dwells only in the vital center of our being, not in the tongue, which would produce only a mouth religion, not in the hand, which would make a lifeless routine of works, but in the heart, which rules the tongue, the hands, the feet, making them the instruments of a glad and willing service. He never takes up His abode in the brain alone, but it is His purpose, after taking possession of the heart, to extend His conquest to the head. A Christ flitting through the intellect now and then gives no such repose of soul as the Christ Who becomes a permanent resident in the heart, year after year, and decade after decade. The beauty of this is, that he who carries Him through life will have His presence in death.—*Daniel Steele.*

> Enthrone the great Jehovah in thine heart,
>   Let all thine homage unto Him be paid;
> Suffer no idol to usurp in part
>   The glory due to Him Who all things made.
> In thought, word, deed, thy life to Him be given,
> Thou shalt be blest on earth, and saved in Heaven.
>   —*Unknown.*

Collins, the infidel, once meeting a plain countryman, inquired where he was going.
"To church, sir."
"What to do there?"
"To worship God."
"Pray tell me, is your God a great or little God?"
"He is so great, sir, that the heavens cannot contain Him, and so little that He can dwell in my heart."
Collins afterwards declared that this simple yet sublime answer had more effect on his mind than all the volumes he had ever read.

September 20
Shut in with God

"Enter into thy closet, and when thou hast shut thy door, pray to thy Father"
(Matt. 6:6).
"I was left alone, and saw this great vision" (Dan. 10:8).

We need a place for prayer. Oh! you can pray anywhere, on the street, in the store, traveling, measuring dry goods, hands in dishwater—where not. But you are not likely to unless you have been off in some quiet place shut in alone with God. The Master said: "Enter into thine inner chamber, and having shut thy door;" that door is important. It shuts out, and it shuts in. "Pray to thy Father who is in secret." God is here in this shut-in spot. One must get alone to find out that he never is alone. The more alone we are as far as men are concerned the least alone we are so far as God is concerned.

The quiet place and time are needful to train the ears for keen hearing. A mother will hear the faintest cry of her babe just awaking. It is upstairs perhaps; the tiniest bit of a sound comes; nobody else hears, but quick as a flash the mother's hands are held quiet, the head alert, then she is off. Her ears are trained beyond anybody's else—love's training. We need trained ears. A quiet place shuts out the outer sounds, and gives the inner ear a chance to learn other sounds.

A man was standing in a telephone booth trying to talk, but could not make out the message. He kept saying, "I can't hear, I can't hear." The other man by and by said sharply, "If you'll shut that door you can hear." *His* door was shut and he could hear not only the man's voice but the street and store noises too. Some folks have gotten their hearing badly confused because their doors have not been shut enough. Man's voice and God's voice get mixed in their ears. They cannot tell between them. The bother is partly with the door. If you'll shut that door you can hear.—*S. D. Gordon.*

> Lord, I have shut my door!
> Come Thou and visit me: I am alone!
> Come as when doors were shut Thou cam'st of yore
> And visited Thine own.
> My Lord, I kneel with reverence, love, and fear,
> For Thou art here.
> —*Mary Ellen Atkinson.*

Every day a fresh opportunity

"So teach us to number our days, that we may apply our hearts unto wisdom"
(Psa. 90:12).
"As we have therefore opportunity, let us do good" (Gal. 6:10).

All the days seem alike, as they come to us. But each day comes with its own opportunities, its own duties, its own privileges—holding out hands offering us radiant gifts. The day passes and never returns again. Other days as bright may come, but that day never comes a second time. If we do not take just then the gifts it offers, we shall never have another chance to get them, and shall always be poorer for what we have missed.—*J. R. Miller.*

> I think not of tomorrow,
>   It's trial or its task;
> But still, with childlike spirit,
>   For present mercies ask.
> With each returning morning
>   I cast old things away;
> Life's journey is before me;
>   My prayer is for today.
>   —*Unknown.*

One of the illusions is that the present hour is not the critical, decisive hour. Write it on your heart that every day is the best day in the year.

Don't waste life in doubts and fears; spend yourself on the work before you, well assured that the right performance of this hour's duties will be the best preparation for the hours or ages that follow it.—*R. W. Emerson.*

> But once I pass this way
> And then, no more.
> So while I may
> I will essay
> Sweet comfort and delight
> To all I meet upon the Pilgrim Way
> For no man travels twice,
> The Great Highway
> That climbs through Darkness up to Light—
> Through Night
> To Day.
>   —*John Oxenham.*

Cheerful service

"I will very gladly spend and be spent for you" (2 Cor. 12:15).
"Serve the Lord with gladness" (Psa. 100:2).
"Freely ye have received, freely give" (Matt. 10:8).

Dole not thy duties out to God,
But let thy hand be free.
—*F. W. Faber.*

As you do His will, do not go about it with a groan and a murmur, but do it with a desire to be well-pleasing in His sight. Sometimes your boy does what you tell him to do, but he does it with such a dark face, and moaning over it all the time. At another time he is glad to do what you tell him, with a bright face and a smile, and that sort of work is worth ten times the other kind. God promised us a spirit like that, not merely that we shall do His will, but do it rejoicing all the time; working in us what is well-pleasing in His sight, and what is well-pleasing is serving the Lord with gladness.—*Barclay Buxton.*

Not in dumb resignation
We lift our hands on high;
Not like the nerveless fatalist,
Content to do and die.
Our faith springs like the eagle
Who soars to meet the sun,
And cries, exulting, unto Thee,
"O Lord, Thy will be done!"
—*John Hay.*

Thus infectious is the gladness of a life wholly harmonized with God. Surely this acceptance of the will of God was the yoke which the Son of Man carried and which He invites us to bear with Him. In the will of God He found rest, and He promises that rest to those who bear the same yoke. For the yoke on the ox, which looks so heavy, in reality makes light the hard toil of the plow or laden cart. In that yoke Christ found joy and satisfaction, even when the will of God brought to Him base ingratitude, callous rejection, bitter opposition from the very cities He had most graced with His presence and blessed with His gifts.—*Unknown.*

Courage necessary to nobility

"The Lord is on my side; I will not fear: what can man do unto me?"
(Psa. 118:6).
"So that we may boldly say, The Lord is my helper, and I will not fear what man shall do unto me" (Heb. 13:6).

Luther, when making his way into the presence of Cardinal Cajetan, who had summoned him to answer for his heretical opinions at Augsburg, was asked by one of the cardinal's minions where he should find a shelter if his patron, the Elector of Saxony, should desert him? "Under the shield of Heaven!" was the reply. The silenced minion turned round, and went his way.

> A wonderful comrade is Courage,
>   He tears the black bandage of fear
> From the eyes of the frightened and stumbling,
>   And lets in the sunshine of cheer;
> He rejoices in all that is righteous,
>   He claims the Almighty as Friend,
> And "Forward!" is always his motto,
>   As he leads on toward Heaven at the end.
> *—Unknown.*

I would have you regard courage as nearly the supreme quality in character. One may get rich without it; one may live a good easy life without it; but one cannot live a full and noble life without it. It is the quality by which one rises in the line of each faculty; it is the wings that turn dull plodding into flight. It is the courage especially that redeems life from the curse of commonness.
—T. T. Munger.

The true hero is the man whose soul is armed by truth and supported by the smile of God; he who meets life's perils with a cautious but tranquil spirit, dies, if he is called to die, as a Christian victor at the post of duty. And if we must have heroes, and wars wherein to make them, there is not so brilliant a war as a war with wrong, no hero so fit to be sung as he who has gained the bloodless victory of truth and mercy.—*Horace Bushnell.*

September 24
Greatness in lowliness

"But made himself of no reputation, and took upon him the form of a servant, and was made in the likeness of men" (Phil. 2:7).
"He humbled himself, and became obedient unto death" (Phil. 2:8).

When the Holy Guest abides within, the soul does not shun the way of the Cross, or seek great things for itself. It is content to serve in lowly as in lofty ways, in obscure and hidden places as in open and conspicuous places where waits applause. To wash a poor disciple's feet is as great a joy as to command an army, to follow as to lead, to serve as to rule—when the Holy Guest abides within the soul. Then the soul does not contend for or grasp and hold fast to place and power.

When after having been a Methodist pastor, I joined the Salvation Army; in the Training College I was set to black the boots of ignorant Cadets. I was tempted to feel it was a dangerous waste of my time, for which my Lord might hold me to account as He did the man who buried his talent, instead of putting it out at usury. Then the Holy Guest whispered to me of Jesus, and pointed me to Him washing the weary and soiled feet of His lowly disciples, and as I saw Jesus, I was content. Any service for Him and His lowly ones, instead of abasing, exalted me.—*Samuel Logan Brengle.*

> Think not too highly of thyself, O man!
> 'Tis but one little thing thou hast to do;
> Then if He find thee diligent and true,
> New tasks await thee and a wider span.
> Perhaps a better knowledge of the plan
> Of that great web on which thy hands have wrought.
> And be not thou too lowly in thy thought;
> No man before thee, since the world began,
> Could do the work that lies upon thy loom;
> If thou neglect or slight it, it is loss
> To all the world, in all the time to come.
> What is thy kinship to the Savior worth
> If thou demean thee as the sons of earth:
> And what if Jesus had despised His cross?
> —*Unknown.*

Unafraid because of trust

"I will trust, and not be afraid" (Isa. 12:2).
"What time I am afraid, I will trust in thee" (Psa. 56:3).

One Christian Scotsman said to another, "Man, I got a most comforting text today. Listen to this: 'What time I am afraid, I will trust in thee.'" The other smiling, answered, "I have found one better. 'I will trust and not be afraid.'"

The secret of such a trust is revealed in the following incident as told by Vaughan: "A military officer being in a dreadful storm, his lady, who was sitting in the cabin near him, and filled with alarm for the safety of the vessel, was so surprised at his composure that she cried out, 'My dear, are you not afraid? How is it possible you can be so calm in such a storm?' He arose from a chair lashed to the deck and drew his sword. Pointing it to his wife's breast he said, 'Are you not afraid?' She instantly replied, 'No, certainly not.' 'Why?' 'Because I know the sword is in the hand of my husband, and he loves me too well to hurt me.' 'Then,' said he, 'remember, I know Whom I have believed, and He holds the winds in His fist, and the waters in the hollow of His hand.'"

> Afraid? Of what?
> To feel the spirit's glad release?
> To pass from pain to perfect peace,
> The strife and strain of life to cease?
> Afraid—of that?
>
> Afraid? Of what?
> Afraid to see the Savior's face,
> To hear His welcome, and to trace
> The glory gleam from wounds of grace?
> Afraid—of that?
>
> Afraid? Of what?
> A flash—a crash—a pierced heart;
> Darkness—light—O Heaven's art!
> A wound of His a counterpart!
> Afraid—of that?
>
> Afraid? Of what?
> To do by death what life could not—
> Baptize with blood a stony plot,
> Till souls shall blossom from the spot?
> Afraid—of that?
> —*E. H. Hamilton.*

(The above poem was a favorite of John and Betty Stam who gave their lives for Christ in China).

September 26
Read the Bible and grow

"As newborn babes, desire the sincere milk of the word, that ye may grow thereby" (1 Peter 2:2).
"But his delight is in the law of the Lord. . . . And he shall be like a tree planted by the rivers of water" (Psa. 1:2-3).

Newspapers, and circulating libraries, and magazines, and little religious books—very good in their way, but secondary and subordinate—have taken the place that our fathers used to have filled by honest reading of God's Word. And that is one of the reasons, and I believe it is a very large part of the reason, why so many professing Christians do not come up to this standard; and instead of *"running* with patience the race that is set before them," walk in an extraordinarily leisurely fashion, by fits and starts, and sometimes with long intervals, in which they sit still on the road, and are not a mile farther at a year's end than they were when it began. There never was, and there never will be, vigorous Christian life unless there be an honest and habitual study of God's Word. There is no shortcut by which Christians can reach the end of the race. Foremost among the methods by which their eyes are enlightened and their hearts rejoiced are application to the eyes of their understanding of that eye-salve, and the hiding in their hearts of that sweet solace and fount of gladness, the Word of Christ's patience, the revelation of God's will. The trees whose roots are laved and branches freshened by that river have leaves that never wither, and all their blossoms set.—*Alexander Maclaren.*

We search the world for truth, we cull
The good, the pure, the beautiful
From graven stone and written scroll,
From the old flower-fields of the soul,
And, weary seekers for the best,
We come back laden from our quest,
To find that all the sages said
Is in the Book our mothers read.
—*J. G. Whittier.*

Reminding men of Christ

"Now when they saw the boldness of Peter and John, and perceived that they were unlearned and ignorant men, they marvelled; and they took knowledge of them, that they had been with Jesus" (Acts 4:13).
"And when the sons of the prophets which were to view at Jericho saw him, they said, The spirit of Elijah doth rest on Elisha" (2 Kings 2:15).

Men are all mosaics of other men. No man can meet another on the street without making some mark upon him. We say we exchange words when we meet; what we exchange is souls. There was a savor of David about Jonathan and a savor of Jonathan about David.

There are some men and some women in whose company we are always at our best. All the best stops in our nature are drawn out by their intercourse, and we find a music in our souls that was never there before. Suppose even that influence prolonged through a month, a year, a lifetime, and what could not life become? Here, even on the common plane of life, talking our language, walking our streets, working side by side, are sanctifiers of souls; here, breathing through common clay, is Heaven.

If to live with men diluted to the millionth degree with the virtue of the Highest, can exalt and purify the nature, what bounds can be set to the influence of Christ? To live with Socrates—with unveiled face—must have made one wise; with Aristides, just. Francis of Assisi must have made one gentle; Savonarola, strong. But to have lived with Christ?

A few raw, unspiritual, uninspiring men were admitted to the inner circle of His friendship. The change began at once. Day by day we can almost see the first disciples grow. They do not know how it is, but they are different men. One day they find themselves like their Master, going about and doing good. To themselves it is unaccountable, but they cannot do otherwise.

But the people who watch them know well how to account for it—"They have been," they whisper, "with Jesus." Unparalleled phenomenon, that these poor fishermen should remind other men of Christ! Stupendous victory and mystery of regeneration, that mortal men should suggest to the world, GOD!

—Henry Drummond.

September 28

God prepares our work

"For we are his workmanship, created in Christ Jesus unto good works, which God hath before ordained (prepared) that we should walk in them"
(Eph. 2:10).

When the Lord says to us, "Prepare thy work," we have the comfort of recollecting that He has prepared our works for us (Eph. 2:10, marg.). Why not take the comfort of this as to any untried work which we may be "called unto"? That sphere did not make itself, neither did man form it into just what it is at his own will. It was God Who prepared it for the worker whom He intended for it, and if there is sufficient evidence that you are called to it, then you may rest assured that He "prepared" it and "ordained" it for you. Do not let us dwell *only* on our side of the preparation. Let us recollect that He Who prepares the workers prepares the works too, and prepares them for us to walk in, i.e., just to go on *step by step*; for that is "walking."

Then, for our own side, let us recollect, "Thou also hast wrought all our works in us," or, as the very striking margin has it, "for us." So we see that He has wrought in us, and for us, every bit of work we have ever succeeded in doing as yet; therefore to Him be all the glory! And no less evidently, it will be He Himself Who will work in us and for us every single bit that we shall yet do; therefore in Him be all our trust! And yet (oh, wonderful condescension!), though it is all His own doing from beginning to end, "your work shall be rewarded." "Every man" (just think, every one of us poor workers!) "shall receive his own reward," not a general premium all round. And this, too, by the hand of our Mediator, knowing that *of the Lord* ye shall receive the reward of the inheritance, for ye serve the "Lord Christ."

May we, all through the year, be so many individual illustrations of St. Paul's sevenfold desire for his converts as to "every good work."

May we—

1. Be "*prepared* unto every good work."
2. "Be *ready* to every good work."
3. Be "*throughly furnished* unto all good works."
4. "*Abound* in every good work."
5. "Being *fruitful* in every good work."
6. Be *stablished* "in every good word and work."
7. Be made "*perfect* in every good work."

—Frances Ridley Havergal.

Daily strength through prayer

"Seek the Lord and his strength, seek his face continually" (1 Chron. 16:11).
"God is my strength" (Hab. 3:19).

Prayer is the conduit-pipe between my soul and Heaven. It is the outlet upwards for gratitude and yearning desires for blessing; it is the inlet through which the supplies of grace pour downwards into the heart. Prayer is just as vital to my spiritual life as water is to the "monthly rose" whose leaves are now dripping from the refreshing of the pitcher. Alas for the Christian who has broken his connection with Christ!

I do not believe that there is such a thing in the history of God's kingdom as a prayer offered in a right spirit that is forever left unanswered.
—Theodore Cuyler.

Prayer has been my source of help when burdens have pressed so heavily upon me that they threatened to crush my spirit; when disappointment, misrepresentation almost overwhelmed me, prayer has brought strength and comfort, a courage that could face a world of bitterness and scorn. I have proved that prayer will enable me to retain the substance of holiness. Prayer enables me to retain a passion for souls; keeps it burning in the hours of disappointment and failure, indifference and hardness, when men and devils rise in power against me.—*Kate Lee.*

Prayer is so mighty an instrument that no one ever thoroughly mastered all its keys. They sweep along the infinite scale of man's wants and God's goodness.—*Hugh Miller.*

The mother of Moses laid the ark in the flags by the river's brink. Aye, but before doing so, she laid it on the heart of God! She could not have laid it so courageously upon the Nile if she had not first devotedly laid it upon the care and love of God. We are often surprised at the outward calmness of men who are called upon to do unpleasant and most trying deeds; but could we have seen them in secret we should have known the prayerful preparation which they underwent before coming out to be seen by men.—*Joseph Parker.*

September 30
Daring to act alone

"Every man . . . shall leave me alone: and yet I am not alone" (John 16:32).
"At my first answer no man stood with me, but all men forsook me"
(2 Tim. 4:16).

There is a cowardice in this age which is not Christian. We shrink from the consequences of truth. We look round and cling dependently. We ask what men will think; what others will say; whether they will stare in astonishment. Perhaps they will, but he who is calculating that, will accomplish nothing in this life. The Father, the Father Who is with us and in us—what does He think? God's work cannot be done without a spirit of independence. A man has got some way in the Christian life when he has learned to say humbly, and yet majestically, "I dare to be alone."

The strength that is in a man can only be learnt when he is thrown upon his own resources and left alone. What a man can do in conjunction with others does not test the man. Tell us what he can do alone. It is one thing to defend the truth when you know that your audience are already prepossessed, and that every argument will meet a willing response; and it is another thing to hold the truth when truth must be supported, if at all, alone—met by cold looks and unsympathizing suspicion. It is one thing to rush on to danger with the shouts and sympathy of numbers; it is another thing when the lonely chieftain of the sinking ship sees the last boat-full disengage itself, and folds his arms to go down into the majesty of darkness, crushed, but not subdued.—*F. W. Robertson.*

> Here, who follows Him the nearest,
> Needs must walk alone.
> —*T. P.*

AS FOR ME, I am resolved not to follow a multitude to do evil. I will keep to the old faith, and the old way, if I never find a comrade between here and the celestial gates!—*C. H. Spurgeon.*

Moral courage is obeying one's conscience, and doing what one believes to be right in the face of a hostile majority; and moral cowardice is stifling one's conscience, and doing what is less than right to win other people's favor.
—*Dr. John Watson.*

October 1
The joy of sacrifice

"Esteeming the reproach of Christ greater riches than the treasures in Egypt: for he had respect unto the recompence of the reward" (Heb. 11:26).
"For the joy that was set before him endured the cross, despising the shame" (Heb. 12:2).

People talk of the sacrifice I have made in spending so much of my life in Africa. Can that be called a sacrifice which is simply paid back as a small part of a great debt owing to our God, which we can never repay? Is that a sacrifice which brings its own best reward in healthful activity, the consciousness of doing good, peace of mind, and a bright hope of a glorious destiny hereafter?

Away with the word in such a view, and with such a thought! It is emphatically no sacrifice. Say rather it is a privilege. Anxiety, sickness, suffering or danger now and then, with a foregoing of the common conveniences and charities of this life, may make us pause, and cause the spirit to waver and the soul to sink, but let this only be for a moment. All these are nothing when compared with the glory which shall hereafter be revealed in and for us.

—David Livingstone.

The moment you can make a very simple discovery, viz., that obligation to God is your privilege and is not imposed as a burden, your experience will teach you many things—that duty is liberty, that repentance is a release from sorrow, that sacrifice is gain, that humility is dignity, that the truth from which you hide is a healing element that bathes your disordered life.

—Horace Bushnell.

The evening before C. T. Studd parted with his family to go to Africa, a young fellow said to them, "Is it a fact that at fifty-two you mean to leave your country, your home, your wife, and your children?"

"What?" said C. T. Studd, "have you been talking of the sacrifice of the Lord Jesus Christ tonight? If Jesus Christ be God and died for me, then no sacrifice can be too great for me to make for Him."

October 2

We must fight to conquer

"Blessed be the Lord my strength, which teacheth my hands to war, and my fingers to fight" (Psa. 144:1).
"Waxed valiant in fight" (Heb. 11:34).

We need more of the spirit that animated General Foch during the first World War. This was the message he sent to General Joffre when surrounded on all sides: "Outflanked on the right; outflanked on the left. Situation on the whole excellent. I am going to advance."

We are to attack Satan, as well as secure ourselves; the shield in one hand and the sword in the other. Whoever fights with the powers of hell will need both. How shall we conquer if we do not fight?—*John Wesley.*

> Stand forth, my soul, and grip thy woe,
> Buckle the sword and face thy foe.
> What right hast thou to be afraid
> When all the universe will aid;
> Ten thousand rally to thy name,
> Horses and chariots of flame.
> Do others fear, do others fail?
> My soul must grapple and prevail.
> My soul must scale the mountainside
> And with the conquering army ride—
> Stand forth, my soul!
> —*Angela Morgan.*

God could have kept Daniel out of the lions' den. He could have kept Paul and Silas out of jail. But God has never promised to keep us out of hard places. What He has promised is to go with us through every hard place, and to bring us through victoriously.—*Hannah W. Smith.*

Let the North wind blow

"Awake, O north wind; and come, thou south; blow upon my garden, that the spices thereof may flow out. Let my beloved come into his garden, and eat his pleasant fruits" (Cant. 4:16).
"He bringeth the wind out of his treasuries" (Psa. 135:7).

A good gardener, it is true, prunes the lower parts of his trees as far as he can, but the higher parts he must leave to the North wind. It shakes and shakes until all the dead, useless branches and twigs and the old leaves are thrown down. We also need, now and again, to be thoroughly shaken. Even if He sends the "North wind" as in the form of human beings, we need not be terrified. They come to us as from the hand of a wise, loving Father for our good.

When the North wind has done his work, then the South wind comes. The North wind may be compared to the judgment storms of God, and the South to the gentle movings of the Holy Spirit. The South wind must blow through the garden so that it can drop its sweetness. The North wind bends the boughs to the earth, and then comes the South wind which lifts up and renews. It is the breath of the living God Himself, His breath of life.—*Sister Eva.*

All as God wills, who wisely heeds
    To give or to withhold,
And knoweth more of all my needs
    Than all my prayers have told.

Enough that blessings undeserved
    Have marked my erring track;
That, wheresoe'er my feet have swerved,
    His chastening turned me back.

That all the jarring notes of life
    Seem blending in a psalm,
And all the angles of its strife
    Slow rounding into calm.

And so the shadows fall apart,
    And so the West winds play:
And all the windows of my heart
    I open to this day.
            —*J. G. Whittier.*

October 4
The Christian is singular

"For my thoughts are not your thoughts, neither are your ways my ways, saith the Lord. For as the heavens are higher than the earth, so are my ways higher than your ways, and my thoughts than your thoughts" (Isa. 55:8-9).

Now, God's views of almost every object differ widely from those of men. He Himself says, "My thoughts are not your thoughts: you judge according to the outward appearance, but My judgment is according to truth; the things which are highly esteemed among men are in My sight an abomination." Now if the views of God differ thus widely from those of men, and if He imparts His own views to every person whom He favors with His gracious presence, then it follows that the new views with which such a person is favored must differ widely from those of all other men. And so far as he is influenced by these views, he will pursue a path different from them, for how can two walk together unless they be agreed? He will look at things unseen and eternal, but they live without God in the world. He will seek and follow the narrow way to life, but they are following the broad road to destruction. As these paths lead in opposite directions, those who follow one must be separated from those who walk in the other.—*Edward Payson.*

When I was at Oxford, I never was afraid of any but the almost Christians. If you give way to them and their prudence an hair's breadth, you will be removed from the hope of the Gospel.

If you are walking as the generality of men walk, you are walking to the bottomless pit! Are many wise, many rich, many mighty, or noble, traveling with you in the same way? By this token, without going any farther, you know it does not lead to life. Here is a chart, a plain, an infallible rule. In whatever profession you are engaged, you must be singular, or be damned! The way to hell has nothing singular in it, but the way to Heaven is singularity all over. If you move but one step toward God, you are not as other men are.—*John Wesley.*

Precious fragments of time

"This is the day which the Lord hath made" (Psa. 118:24).
"This day have I payed my vows" (Prov. 7:14).

Every day is a little life, and our whole life is but a day repeated. Those, therefore, that dare lose a day are dangerously prodigal; those that dare misspend it, desperate.—*Joseph Hall.*

> Oh, waste them not! the minutes God has given—
> Use them to soothe poor hearts by sorrow riven,
> Use them to teach whom ignorance has 'slaved,
> Use them to warn the wayward and depraved,
> To lift the crushed, and bravely right the wronged—
> Use them to learn thy God, and how to blend
> Thy will with His—grow like Him. Life's end
> Draws daily near—'tis short, man's earthly lot:
> Fragments of time! O mortal, waste them not.
>
> Oh, waste them not! the powers that God has given
> To work on earth, to press on up to Heaven—
> It may be that thou dost in trembling stand,
> With failing health, and fears on either hand:
> Yet hast thou something left of life and power,
> Oh, fail not to employ it, 'tis God's dower:
> Use it until He takes it all away.
> Let nought be lost of gifts so costly—stay
> Not in regrets, back-glancing o'er thy lot:
> Fragments of health and power! Oh, waste them not.
> —*Unknown.*

Let us then, each morning, resolve to send the day into eternity in such a garb as we shall wish it to wear for ever. And at night let us reflect that one more day is irrevocably gone, indelibly marked.—*Adoniram Judson.*

October 6
Deliverance from self

"Where sin abounded, grace did much more abound" (Rom. 5:20).
"For he that is dead is freed from sin" (Rom. 6:7).

The ruin of human souls can never be achieved by enemies from without unless they be aided by traitors from within.

We need not wonder where the demons dwell
To find the foes of Christ; we need not seek
The shining haunts of sensual men to find
The foe of peace and purity. In self
Sin reigns, inciting man against Thy sway,
O Christ, Thou blessed King of kings! Sin reigns
With ruthless pow'r within the heart; sin blinds
The eyes to things of God, and turns the gaze
On self. Come, Spirit, come! Be Thou my guide
To Him Who, in the flames of love,
Surrendered self. O gentle Dove! be Thou
My guide to Calvary, and I may see
Where death to sin begins, where self will meet
With crucifixion, and where life is found.
　　　　　　　　　　—*John Livingstone.*

God, harden me against myself,
This coward with pathetic voice,
Who craves for ease, and rest, and joys.

My self, arch-traitor to myself;
My hollowest friend, my deadliest foe,
My clog whatever road I go.

Yet One there is can curb myself,
Can roll this strangling load from me,
Break off the yoke and set me *free.*
　　　　　　　　　　—*Christina Rossetti.*

The Spirit seemed to lead me into the inmost sanctuary of my soul—into those chambers where I had before discovered such defilement, and showed me that all was cleansed, that the corruptions which had given me such distress were dead, taken away, that not one of them remained. I felt the truth of the witness; it was so; I was conscious of it, as conscious as I ever had been of my conversion.—*Bishop Foster.*

Love with God's love

"The love of God is shed abroad in our hearts by the Holy Ghost which is given unto us" (Rom. 5:5).
"That the love wherewith thou hast loved me may be in them, and I in them" (John 17:26).

"The love of God is shed abroad in our hearts." It has often been understood in this sense: It means the love of God to me. Oh, what a limitation! That is only the beginning. The love of God always means the love of God in its entirety, in its fullness as an indwelling power; a love of God to me that leaps back to Him in love, and overflows to my fellowmen in love—God's love to me, and my love to God, and my love to my fellowmen. The three are one; you cannot separate them. Do believe that the love of God can be shed abroad in your heart and mine, so that we can love all the day.

"Ah!" you say, "how little I have understood that!" Why is a lamb always gentle? Because that is its nature. Does it cost the lamb any trouble to be gentle? No. Why not? It is so beautiful and gentle. Has a lamb to study to be gentle? No. Why does that come so easy? It is its nature. And a wolf—why does it cost a wolf no trouble to be cruel, and to put its fangs into the poor lamb or sheep? Because that is its nature. It has not to summon up its courage; the wolf-nature is there.

And how can I learn to love? Never until the Spirit of God fills my heart with God's love, and I begin to long for God's love in a very different sense from which I have sought it so selfishly, as a comfort and a joy and a happiness and a pleasure to myself. Never until I begin to learn that "God is love," and to claim it, and receive it as an indwelling power for self-sacrifice. Never until I begin to see that my glory, my blessedness, is to be like God and like Christ, in giving up everything in myself for my fellowmen.—*Andrew Murray.*

O Lord, that I could waste my life for others,
    With no ends of my own,
That I could pour myself into my brothers,
    And live for them alone.
              —Unknown.

October 8
Be definite in prayer

"Ask, and it shall be given you; seek, and ye shall find; knock, and it shall be opened unto you" (Matt. 7:7).
"Therefore I say unto you, What things soever ye desire, when ye pray, believe that ye receive them, and ye shall have them" (Mark 11:24).

Be definite in prayer to God. How wearisome indefiniteness is! Some of you who stand behind the counters in drapers' shops know what a nuisance an indefinite woman is. She comes and looks at half-a-dozen articles, and turns everyone of them over, but she cannot find what she wants. At last she does find what she wants, but she cannot make up her mind to pay the price for it. Oh, let us be businesslike with God in this matter. He has paid the price, all we have to do is to "ask and receive."—*Reader Harris.*

> I am watching for the answers to the prayers which
> I have made.
> I am eagerly expecting all the things for which
> I prayed!
> But I know if they appear not in the form I
> Thought they would,
> It is just that He is planning for me
> Something extra good!
> Aye, I'm certain, and I trust Him;
> He has heard, and He will give.
> Let me then "Pray without ceasing"
> And in "watching" ever live.
>
> *—F. M. N.*

Mr. Finney tells of a church in which there was a continuous revival for thirteen years. At last the revival stopped, and everybody feared and questioned why, till one day a tearful man arose and told how for thirteen years he had prayed every Saturday night till after midnight for God to glorify Himself and save the people. But two weeks before, he had stopped this praying, and then the revival had stopped. If God will answer prayer like that, what a tremendous responsibility rests on us all to pray!—*Samuel Logan Brengle.*

Prayer is the key to Heaven; the Spirit helps faith to turn the key.—*T. Watson.*

We are the world's Bible

"Edify one another, even as also ye do" (1 Thess. 5:11).
"Follow that which is good, both among yourselves, and to all men"
(1 Thess. 5:15).

Every individual makes an impression by his conduct, and witnesses either for one side or the other. His looks, dress, whole demeanor make a constant impression on one side or the other. He cannot help testifying for or against religion. He is either gathering with Christ or scattering abroad.

Every moment of your lives you are exerting a tremendous influence which will tell on the immortal interests of souls all around you. Are you asleep, while all your conduct is exerting such an influence?

If you show pride, levity, bad temper and the like, it is like tearing open the wounds of the Savior. Your spirit and deportment produce an influence on the world against religion. How shall the world believe religion when the witnesses are not agreed among themselves, and the sum of their whole testimony is, There is no need of being pious?

Oh, how guilty! Perhaps hundreds of souls will meet you in the Judgment, and curse you—if they are allowed to speak—for leading them to hell by practically denying the truth of the Gospel.—*Charles G. Finney.*

A holy life has a voice. It speaks when the tongue is silent, and is either a constant attraction or a perpetual reproof.—*Hinton.*

> We are the only Bible
>> The careless world will read;
> We are the sinner's gospel,
>> We are the scoffer's creed;
> We are the Lord's last message,
>> Given in deed and word;
> What if the type is crooked?
>> What if the print is blurred?
>
> What if our hands are busy
>> With other work than His?
> What if our feet are walking
>> Where sin's allurement is?
> What if our tongues are speaking
>> Of things His lips would spurn?
> How can we hope to help Him
>> And hasten His return?
>> —*Annie Johnson Flint.*

October 10
Fountains of joy

"For the kingdom of God is not meat and drink; but righteousness, and peace, and joy in the Holy Ghost" (Rom. 14:17).
"And the ransomed of the Lord shall return, and come to Zion with songs and everlasting joy upon their heads: they shall obtain joy and gladness, and sorrow and sighing shall flee away" (Isa. 35:10).

The reason why Christians are not overflowing with joy is because they are not filled with the Holy Ghost. "The Kingdom of God is . . . righteousness, and peace, and joy in the Holy Ghost." When the blessed Comforter fills the heart of a believer, He opens such a fountain of joy within him, so sweet, so full and so lasting as to utterly extinguish all desire for base delights. "I am dwelling," wrote the seraphic Payson in one of his letters, "in the land of Beulah, the celestial city is in full view. I can hear its song; I am gazing at its sunshine; I am breathing its sweet odors. Oh, that I had only known what I now know twenty-five years ago! I might have walked all my days in the light of Heaven."

The Spirit-filled Christian has an artesian well of joy in his heart, a miraculous spring opened in his breast, which fills, floods and overwhelms his soul with joy unspeakable all the year round. Common surface wells are soon dry, but artesian wells, even in dry weather, have plenty of water.

(From *New Testament Holiness* by Thomas Cook. Used by permission of the Epworth Press).

The joy of the Holy Ghost: it is supernatural—an out-gushing fountain from a rock stricken by the rod of a greater than Moses. It is a joy not springing up in the course of nature, but handed down from Heaven, and implanted in the believing soul. It is really a miraculous spring opened by the Holy Spirit in the Sahara of the human breast.—*Daniel Steele.*

> Thou Who givest of Thy gladness
> Till the cup runs o'er—
> Cup whereof the pilgrim weary
> Drinks to thirst no more—
> Not a-nigh me, but within me
> Is Thy joy divine;
> Thou, O Lord, hast made Thy dwelling
> In this heart of mine.
> —*Gerhardt Tersteegen.*

Live by the Bible

"Holding forth the word of life; that I may rejoice in the day of Christ, that I have not run in vain, neither laboured in vain" (Phil. 2:16).

We have our responsibility for God's Holy Word. If this is the inspired Word of God, how solemn and supreme its claims! Let us believe it implicitly; let us believe it without compromise or questioning. Let us not try to eliminate the supernatural and bring it down to the plane of our own reason and knowledge, but let us bow submissively before the throne of Him Who speaks from Heaven, and say with every fiber of our being, "It means just what it says."

But let us also obey. Believe means to "live by." Our faith has two sides: one is faith, the other is faithfulness. One is trust, the other is trustworthiness. They are the two wings that bear us above the dark abyss; they are the two oars that carry us through the dangerous rapids; they are the two hands that grasp and hold fast forever the eternal covenant. Obedience is always the condition of faith. Only as we live by this blessed Book can we fully claim its promises and rest upon its words of grace. Let us live up to the fullness of our Bible. Let us translate every word of it into our lives. Let each of us be a new edition and a new version of the Scriptures, translated into flesh and blood, words and acts, holiness and service.—*A. B. Simpson.*

A Chinese Mandarin was once asked if he had read the Bible. He brought out a book into which he had copied Bible verses which he admired, and then laying his hand on the book said, "If only the people who profess this religion were to live in accordance with its precepts, this religion would spread all over the world."

> You can stick up the placards all over the wall,
> But here is the word I announce:
> It is not the motto that hangs on the wall,
> But the motto you live that counts.
> —*Unknown.*

"Ye are manifestly declared to be the epistle of Christ" (2 Cor. 3:3).

October 12

The Master's touch

"For he must reign" (1 Cor. 15:25).
"The Lord shall reign for ever and ever" (Exod. 15:18).

A village organist in Germany was once practicing a piece by that master-musician—Mendelssohn. He was not a great expert, and stumbled somewhat through it. While he was playing, a stranger quietly entered the church and sat in one of the back pews.

As the organist was finishing, the stranger approached and asked to be allowed to play his instrument. The organist gruffly refused, saying, "Certainly not, I never allow anyone to touch the organ but myself."

A second time the stranger begged to be allowed to play, but permission was not given. And yet a third request was made, and this time most grudgingly it was granted. The stranger sat down, pulled out the stops, and on the same instrument began to play, but with what a difference! The organ, now under the control of the stranger, gave forth the most beautiful music. The organist, in wonderment at the new results, asked the stranger who he was. Very modestly he replied, "My name is Mendelssohn."

"What!" replied the organist, "did I refuse you permission to play on my organ?"

Shall we make the Lord Jesus King of our lives now? Can we say, "The Lord reigneth"?—*George S. Ingram.*

> Strike, Thou the Master, we Thy keys,
> The anthem of the destinies!
> The minor of Thy loftier strain,
> Our hearts shall breathe the old refrain,
> Thy will be done!
> —*J. G. Whittier.*

The reign of Christ on earth is nothing more nor less than the subjection of the whole soul to Himself. Alas, the world is opposed to this reign. Many pray, "Thy will be done in earth, as it is in heaven." But they are unwilling to be crucified to the world.

It is my only desire to abandon myself into the hands of God, without scruples, without fears. Since I am there, O Lord, how can I be otherwise than happy? When divine love has enfranchised the soul, what power can make it falter?

How small the world appears to a heart that God fills with Himself! I love Thee, my Lord, not only with a sovereign love, but it seems to me I love Thee alone, and all creatures only for Thy sake. Thou art so much the soul of my life, that I have no other life than Thine.—*Madam Guyon.*

Speak out

"Be not afraid, but speak, and hold not thy peace" (Acts 18:9).
"He that speaketh truth sheweth forth righteousness: but a false witness deceit" (Prov. 12:17).

I find it impossible to avoid offending guilty men, for there is no way of avoiding it but by our silence or their patience; and silent we cannot be because of God's command, and patient they cannot be because of their guilt.

—Martin Luther.

When men supplant the sacred page,
With errors from a darkened age,
And with God's truth a warfare wage—
    Speak out!

When men great saints would seem to be,
And ape the ancient Pharisee,
And judge themselves from failings free—
    Speak out!

When men feel not affliction's rod,
And shun the path their fathers trod,
And cast aside their faith in God—
    Speak out!

When men live unprepared for death,
And give the world their latest breath,
And heed not what the Scripture saith—
    Speak out!

—Unknown.

Wait not until you are backed by numbers; the fewer the voices on the side of truth, the more distinct and strong must be your own.—*William Channing.*

October 14
Christians make life tasty

"Ye are the salt of the earth: but if the salt have lost his savour, wherewith shall it be salted?" (Matt. 5:13).
"Can that which is unsavoury be eaten without salt?" (Job 6:6).

Christ says to certain people, "Ye are the salt of the earth." Mark, it is not, "Your sound doctrine, your splendid churches, your excellent ritual, your prayers, your charity, your preaching, is the salt of the earth, the light of the world." These things are in no way to be disparaged. They are, or may be, most acceptable to God, but they are not "the salt of the earth." The salt of the earth, the light of the world, are YE. Whom then does YE embrace? The answer is, those whose character has just been described in the preceding verses, the citizens of the kingdom of Heaven.

Of what use is *salt*? First of all, it makes many things agreeable to the taste, which without it are tasteless, *insipid*. Because earnest Christians do not delight themselves in many worldly amusements, those who give themselves to these things often suppose the life of a Christian to be dull, uninteresting, and insipid. How completely is this the opposite of the truth! To the Christian the commonest duty is interesting. He has discovered the secret of the great happiness that infallibly follows doing good to others. His ordinary conversation is far more interesting than that of others. . . .

To live so as to please God, to make known Christ and His salvation, to make human hearts glad around us, to make homes more sweet and bright, and by the Christian life on earth to prepare for the better life to come—

"'Tis worth living for this,
To administer bliss
And salvation through Jesus' Name."

—Benjamin Hellier.

Salt of the earth. It is the noiseless power of a good life, making all about us pure and blessed, not by great fuss and ado, not even by preaching, still less by scolding, but just by being Christ-like. Yet by no means a weak amiability that is scarcely felt: salt—a very quick and sharp unpleasantness to those whose moral life is chapped and cracked, dreadfully in the way of those who want to be wrong.

Salt of the earth. He who thinks that religion has nothing to do with politics, with business, with pleasure, is ignorant of the whole meaning of religion. It is a power right in the midst of all these, sweetening and purifying them all. Think of this as holiness—not rapture, not glowing and glorious experiences, but in Christ's strength and for Christ's sake, setting ourselves to sweeten and purify the life about us.—*Mark Guy Pearse.*

Everything found in Christ

"His name shall be called Wonderful, Counsellor, The mighty God, The everlasting Father, The Prince of Peace" (Isa. 9:6).
"It pleased the Father that in him should all fulness dwell" (Col. 1:19).

Oh! my dear friends, let us rest more upon the truth as it is in Jesus. Of late, I have been brought to feed more upon Jesus as the truth. I see more in Him in that character than I ever did. I see Christ the truth of my life, friends, relations, sense, food, raiment, light, fire, resting-place. All out of Him are but shadows. All in Him are blessed sacraments—I mean visible signs of the fountain, or vehicles to convey the streams of inward grace.—*John Fletcher.*

IN CHRIST WE HAVE . . .
Love that can never be fathomed.
Life that can never die.
Righteousness that can never be tarnished.
Peace that can never be understood.
Rest that can never be disturbed.
Joy that can never be diminished.
Hope that can never be disappointed.
Glory that can never be clouded.
Light that can never be darkened.
Strength that can never be enfeebled.
Happiness that can never be defiled.
Beauty that can never be marred.
Resources that can never be exhausted.
Wisdom that can never be baffled.
—*War Cry.*

Take a long look at Jesus—often, often. If you wanted to know a man again you would take an intense look at his face. Look then at Jesus—deeply, intensely—till every feature is graven on your heart.
—*Robert Murray McCheyne.*

When Rutherford was in prison he dated his letter from "Christ's Palace in Aberdeen." He made the remark to some friend, "Do you know I thought of Jesus till every stone in the wall of my cell glowed like a ruby."

October 16
Riches through impoverishment

"With what measure ye mete, it shall be measured to you again" (Matt. 7:2). "But this I say, He which soweth sparingly shall reap also sparingly; and he which soweth bountifully shall reap also bountifully" (2 Cor. 9:6).

Life is not enriched by selfishness, but by sacrifice. Life only becomes fruitful when it becomes sacrificial. This is true concerning our influence upon one another; it seems ordained that life has to attain a certain fervor of sacrifice before it can become contagious and multiply itself throughout the race. On the cold planes of calculation and selfishness life is unimpressive, and its products leave the general life unmoved. It is even so with a poem, a painting, a sermon, or with a courtesy. The measure of its impressiveness is just the measure of the sacrifice of which it is the shrine. What is there in it? What "virtue" has gone out of him? Just so much will be the measure of healing. Just what he lost will be our gain; he becomes fruitful where he touches sacrifice.

But let us say more—the poet himself is the gainer by so much as he lost. The spirit of sacrifice not only impresses others, it fertilizes self. In the fervent atmosphere of sacrifice buried seeds of possibility awake into life, which in an air of cold calculation remain in their graves—powers of perception, of resolution, of effort; in the tropical heat of sacrifice they spring into strength and beauty. I say, therefore, that the spirit of sacrifice enriches self, while yet it fertilizes others. Our giving is our getting.—*J. H. Jowett.*

> Where is the school for each and all,
> Where men become as children small,
> And little ones are great?
> Where love is all the task and rule,
> The fee our all, and all at school,
> Small, poor, of low estate?
>
> Where to unlearn all things I learn,
> From self and from all others turn,
> One Master hear and see?
> I learn and do one thing alone,
> And wholly give myself to One
> Who gives Himself to me.
>
> My task, possessing nought, to give;
> No life to have, yet ever live—
> And ever losing, gain. . . .
>   —*Gerhardt Tersteegen.*

Importance of prayer

"And when he had sent them away, he departed into a mountain to pray"
(Mark 6:46).
"But so much more went there a fame abroad of him: and great multitudes
came together to hear, and to be healed by him of their infirmities. And he
withdrew himself into the wilderness, and prayed" (Luke 5:15-16).

The struggle to maintain a quiet time alone is great, and the godliest people have been most aware of it. Satan opposes a true prayer life more than any other spiritual activity. Andrew Bonar aptly pictures this struggle:

"Satan, like the lapwing, drew me away from the real object (prayer and fellowship with God) by suggesting every now and then something about some other part of my work . . . and so the best hours of yesterday were in a great measure lost, so far as 'prayer and transfiguration' might have been."

On the brink of eternity, prayer will assume its right perspective. We busy Christians can well afford to heed the warning of a reformer, Josephine Butler, who did much for her own sex:

"Many continue to postpone and to subordinate the claims of the spiritual life to the constantly pressing claims (sacred claims also) of their fellow-creatures, and of the good works in which they are engaged. At the last, when earth's claims are fading and the spirit is called into the presence of God, conscience will speak, and the poor soul may reproach itself in the spirit of the lament which Shakespeare put into the mouth of Wolsey in his last moments: 'O, Cromwell, Cromwell! Had I but served my God with half the zeal that I have served my king!'

"In the clear light of eternity all things assume their right proportion. We have worked, we have slaved for duty, we have worn ourselves out in the service of humanity. That is good, that is noble; yet an inward voice will tell us in some silent hour that we should have worked better and served humanity better had we possessed the moral force to withdraw at times from life's crowded avenues, had we firmly refused some of the thousand claims which pressed upon us in order that our speech and our action might have possessed more of the Divine, more of 'spirit and of life.'"

October 18
God's oaks

"After that ye have suffered . . . strengthen, settle you" (1 Peter 5:10).
"I was strengthened as the hand of the Lord my God was upon me"
(Ezra 7:28).

When God means to grow an oak the acorn is not cast into a hothouse. It is flung into the outdoor earth and struggles bravely upward through the mountain sod. It strikes its roots far below the surface and takes mighty hold, as with subterranean cables. The winter comes down oft and again upon it. The tempest wrestles with its brawny boughs. And through the regimen of storm and gale it earns its imperial place—the monarch of the forest. God leaves the old tree to "try" it, and it comes out an oak!

So when God would have an oak-like Christian, He exposes that Christian to a discipline of toil or of trial—or of both combined. But out from these terrible trials comes the triumphant child of God—wet with the baptism of suffering and radiant as "mercy" rising from the river of death to the pearly gates. And as she cometh out she exclaims with adoring gratitude, "Oh, my God! Thou hast tried me—but when Thou didst try me, I came forth as gold!" For:

> "The deepest trials that we know
> A higher grace discloses;
> Men saw the thorns on Jesus' brow
> But angels saw the roses!"
>
> *—Theodore Cuyler.*

I find in all Christians who have passed through much tribulation, a certain quality or ripeness which I am of the opinion can be formed in no other school. Just as a certain degree of solar heat is necessary to bring the finest fruits to perfection, so is fiery trial indispensable for ripening the inner man.—*Tholuck.*

Right use of time

"There is . . . a time to every purpose" (Eccles. 3:1).
"Are there not twelve hours in the day?" (John 11:9).

When Drexelius was asked by his friend Faustinius how he could do so much as he had done, he answered, "The year has three hundred and sixty-five days, or eight thousand, seven hundred and sixty hours; in so many hours great things may be done; the slow tortoise made a long journey by losing no time." The man who hasn't the time to do the things that are worth while is probably doing some things that are not.

The length of a life is not to be estimated by the winters over which it has spread. Some lives are brief at seventy, for their record is a blank and dreary vacancy; others are protracted at twenty-five, for a history has been compressed within the space.

"Men live in deeds, not years; in thoughts, not breaths;
In feelings, not in figures on a dial."
—*W. Morley Punshon.*

Have you ever settled anything about your time, whether any of it belongs to God, and if so, how much of it belongs to God? Did you ever sit down and make an honest division with God of your time—I will give God so much every week? John Wesley, a grander man than whom never lived, sat down and divided the twenty-four hours of the day into equal parts, and said, "Eight hours a day I give to sleep and recreation; eight hours I give to my business, and eight hours I give to God." When I look at Wesley's life, and see how many sermons he preached, I'm astonished that he had any time to travel; and when I look at the number of miles he traveled on horseback, I'm astonished that he had time to preach; and when I look at the number of books he left behind him, I say, "Well, well, how did Wesley have time for writing and preaching?" And the whole life of that great man, the most laborious life almost of any century, was made successful and extensive because he divided up rightly with God.—*S. Jones.*

October 20

Am I usable?

"If a man therefore purge himself from these, he shall be a vessel unto honour, sanctified, and meet for the master's use, and prepared unto every good work"
(2 Tim. 2:21).
"Be ready to every good work" (Titus 3:1).

I was talking with a Christian merchant a while ago, who expressed a great and important truth. He said: "People are crying to God to use them, but He cannot. They are not given up to Him; they are not humble, and teachable, and holy. There are plenty of people who come to me and want to work in my store, but I cannot use them; they are not fit for my work. When I must have some one, I have to go and advertise, and sometimes spend days in trying to find a man who will fit into the place I want him for; and then I have to try him and prove him to know whether he will suit me or not."

The fact is, God is using everybody that He can, and using them to the full extent of their fitness for His service. So instead of praying so much to be used, people should search themselves to know whether they are usable.

God cannot use anybody and everybody who comes along any more than the merchant could. It is only those who are "sanctified and meet for the master's use," and "prepared unto every good work," that He can bless with great usefulness.

God wants men and women, and He is hunting for them everywhere, but, like the merchant, He has to pass by hundreds before He finds the right individuals. The Bible says: "The eyes of the Lord run to and fro throughout the whole earth, to show himself strong in the behalf of them whose heart is perfect toward him."—*Samuel Logan Brengle.*

My little girl is only three—a tiny little miss,
But a lesson she has taught me, now list to what it is.
"Help me to write my name," she said, and placed her hand in mine;
And so we wrote across the page a neat and careful line.
And then she gripped the pencil tight and wouldn't let me lead.
The page became all scribbled up with marks we couldn't read.

It is the same in life, I thought, we want to have our way;
We cannot be content to stay alone with Him each day.
Relax your hand in God's, Oh friend, don't hold on quite so tight;
Just let Him lead across the page, your life will then be right.
                                        —*Doris Gainder.*

Don't go overloaded

"Take therefore no thought for the morrow: for the morrow shall take thought for the things of itself. Sufficient unto the day is the evil thereof"
(Matt. 6:34).
"Take heed to yourselves, lest at any time your hearts be overcharged with surfeiting . . . and cares of this life" (Luke 21:34).

In order to make "good speed" in your day's journey, do not go overloaded. I do not refer so much to your undertaking too many things as to your carrying too many cares. Honest work is strengthening; but worry frets and fevers us. The temptation to worry should be resisted as a temptation of the devil; to yield to it is a sin against our own peace, and a reproach upon our Christian character. The journey made by any pedestrian is simply a succession of steps. In accomplishing your day's work you have simply to take one step at a time. To take that step wisely is all that you need to think about. If I am climbing a mountain, to look down may make me dizzy; to look too far up may make me tired and discouraged.

Take no anxious thought for the morrow. Sufficient for the day—yes, and for each hour in the day—is the toil or the trial thereof. There is not a child of God in this world who is strong enough to stand the strain of today's duties and all the load of tomorrow's anxieties piled upon the top of them. Paul himself would have broken down if he had attempted the experiment. We have a perfect right to ask our heavenly Father for strength equal to the day; but we have no right to ask Him for one extra ounce of strength for anything beyond it. When the morrow comes, grace will come with it sufficient for its tasks or for its troubles.—*Theodore Cuyler.*

Why should this anxious load
Press down your weary mind?
Haste to your heavenly Father's throne
And sweet refreshment find.
—*Philip Doddridge.*

Rest from self

"And he said, My presence shall go with thee, and I will give thee rest"
(Exod. 33:14).
"Let us therefore fear, lest, a promise being left us of entering into his rest,
any of you should seem to come short of it" (Heb. 4:1).
"There remaineth therefore a rest to the people of God" (Heb. 4:9).

"And I will give you rest"—so said my Lord.
   I heard His word,
I started, sighed. "Dear Lord," I cried,
     "My heart is sick and sore;
     No peace dwells in my breast.
     Give me this guest—Thy rest
     For evermore."

With tender, instant touch out of my heart
   The sting, the smart,
The secret, native source of pain He drew,
     And held it up to view.
     I looked. The smart, the sting
     Was SELF! The deadly thing
     Forthwith I knew.

"Wilt thou," said He, "consent to part with this—
   The bane of bliss?
Peace cannot dwell within if self is there."
     "Dear Lord," I quick replied, "I see
     If self is slain
     My loss is glorious gain:
     Self I resign to Thee."

He smiled a gracious smile, and with a breath
   Smote self to death.
And then surprising sweet He entered in!
     Himself my peace, my rest from sin!
     He is my other self, and I
     Serve Him alone in free captivity,
     Delighting in His wondrous discipline.
              —*W. T. G.*

The Bible our soul's food

"Thy words were found, and I did eat them; and thy word was unto me the joy and rejoicing of mine heart" (Jer. 15:16).
"Man doth not live by bread only, but by every word that proceedeth out of the mouth of the Lord doth man live" (Deut. 8:3).

It has pleased the Lord to teach me a truth, the benefit of which I have not lost for more than fourteen years. The point is this: I saw more clearly than ever that the first great and primary business to which I ought to attend every day was, to have my soul happy in the Lord. The first thing to be concerned about was not how much I might serve the Lord, but how I might get my soul into a happy state, and how my inner man might be nourished. For I might seek to set the truth before the unconverted, I might seek to benefit believers, I might seek to relieve the distressed, I might in other ways seek to behave myself as it becomes a child of God in this world; and yet, not being happy in the Lord, and not being nourished and strengthened in my inner man day by day, all this might not be attended to in the right spirit. Before this time my practice had been, at least for ten years previously, as an habitual thing, to give myself to prayer after having dressed myself in the morning. Now I saw that the most important thing I had to do was to give myself to the reading of the Word of God, and to meditate on it, and thus my heart might be comforted, encouraged, warmed, reproved, instructed; and that thus by means of the Word of God, whilst meditating on it, my heart might be brought into experimental communion with the Lord.

I began, therefore, to meditate on the New Testament from the beginning, early in the morning. The first thing I did, after having asked in a few words the Lord's blessing upon His precious Word, was to begin to meditate on the Word of God, searching, as it were, into every verse to get a blessing out of it, not for the sake of the public ministry of the Word, not for the sake of preaching on what I had meditated upon, but for obtaining good for my own soul.

The result I have found to be almost invariably this: that after a very few minutes my soul has been led to confession, or to thanksgiving, or to intercession, or to supplication; so that, though I did not, as it were, give myself to prayer, but to meditation, yet it turned almost immediately more or less into prayer.

—*George Müller.*

The godly shall suffer

"Yea, and all that will live godly in Christ Jesus shall suffer persecution"
(2 Tim. 3:12).
"But let none of you suffer as a murderer . . . or as an evildoer, or as a
busybody in other men's matters. Yet if any man suffer as a Christian, let him
not be ashamed; but let him glorify God on this behalf" (1 Peter 4:15-16).

All that live godly in this world shall suffer persecution. Do not let us be surprised if we are persecuted, but remember that the faithful people of God have always been so treated in the past. Neither let us groan or grumble, but rather "rejoice, and be exceeding glad."

At the same time let us see well to it that the opposition we encounter is to our holiness and not to our sourness; that the persecution we suffer is for righteousness' sake and not for any less glorious cause. Satisfied on these points, let us be careful to go on enjoying and preaching and witnessing to full salvation quite irrespective of the treatment we may be receiving. Our God has promised with every temptation or trial to make a way for our escape. Let us expect Him to do so. Nay, more than this, let us claim that the scene of every such attack shall become the place of victory.—*Reader Harris.*

God does not often, as He easily could, cut off persecutions at a stroke. But He provides a hiding place for His people, and by methods not less effectual, though less pompous, preserves them from being swept away, even when the enemy comes in like a flood.—*John Wesley.*

> Then learn to scorn the praise of men,
> And learn to lose with God;
> For Jesus won the world through shame,
> And beckons thee His road.
>
> God's glory is a wondrous thing,
> Most strange in all its ways,
> And, of all things on earth, least like
> What men agree to praise.
>
> As He can endless glory weave
> From what men reckon shame,
> In His own world He is content
> To play a losing game.
> —*F. Faber.*

Making or marring other lives

"Let us therefore follow after the things . . . wherewith one may edify another"
(Rom. 14:19).
"Let . . . no man put a stumblingblock or an occasion to fall in his brother's
way" (Rom. 14:13).

No human being can come into this world without increasing or diminishing the sum total of human happiness, not only of the present, but of every subsequent age of humanity. No one can detach himself from this connection. There is no sequestered spot in the universe, no dark niche along the disc of nonexistence to which he can retreat with his relations to others; where he can withdraw the influence of his existence upon the moral destiny of the world. Everywhere his presence or absence will be felt, everywhere he will have companions who will be better or worse for his influence.

It is an old saying, and one of fearful and fathomless import, that we are forming characters for eternity. Forming characters! Whose? Our own or others? Both, and in that momentous fact lies the peril and responsibility of our existence. Who is sufficient for such a thought? Thousands of my fellow-beings will yearly enter eternity with characters differing from those they would have carried thither, had I never lived. The sunlight of that world will reveal my finger marks in their formations, and in their successive strata of thought and life.—*Unknown.*

> The smallest bark on life's tumultuous ocean
> Will leave a track behind forevermore;
> The lightest wave of influence, once in motion,
> Extends and widens to the eternal shore.
> We should be wary, then, who go before
> A myriad yet to be, and we should take
> Our bearings carefully where breakers roar
> And fearful tempests gather: one mistake
> May wreck unnumbered barks that follow in our wake.
> —*Sarah Knowles Bolton.*

It is a high, solemn and almost awful thought for every individual man that his earthly influence which has had a commencement will never, through all ages, were he the very meanest of us, have an end.—*T. Carlyle.*

October 26
Find a place alone with God

"Study to be quiet" (1 Thess. 4:11).
"When the evening was come, he was there alone" (Matt. 14:23).

Souls sing their finest songs and utter their sublimest truths under difficulties, frustration, and trials. This was certainly the case with Mrs. Phoebe Brown, a mother of four small children, who was anxious to find a place where she could get alone with God. She found that by walking in the twilight in the countryside near her house, she could pray undisturbed. One unfrequented lane especially suited her, with elms planted on either side and which led to the beautiful garden of a wealthy neighbor. Here she enjoyed uninterrupted communion with her heavenly Father until the owner of the garden noticed her rambles and her condescending manner made Mrs. Brown feel that she must abandon them.

"I had four small children, a small unfinished house," she tells us, "a sick sister in the only furnished room; and there was not a place above or below where I could go as in former days. I have often thought Satan had tried his best to prevent me from prayer, by depriving me of a place in which to pray."

But Mrs. Brown found an outlet for her frustration. Putting the older children to bed, she sat down in the kitchen with the baby in her arms. Taking out her pen and paper, she gave vent to her oppressed heart in the following poem:

My Apology For My Twilight Rambles

"I love to steal awhile away
        From little ones and care,
And spend the hours of setting day
        In gratitude and prayer.

"I love to feed on Nature's scenes
        When falls the evening dew,
And dwell upon the silent themes,
        Forever rich and new.

"I love this silent twilight hour
        Far better than the rest;
It is of all the twenty-four
        The happiest and best.

"Thus, when life's toilsome day is o'er,
        May its departing ray
Be calm as this impressive hour,
        And lead to endless day."

310

Increase through giving

"There is that scattereth, and yet increaseth; and there is that withholdeth more than is meet, but it tendeth to poverty" (Prov. 11:24).
"Let no man seek his own, but every man another's wealth" (1 Cor. 10:24).
"Look not every man on his own things, but every man also on the things of others" (Phil. 2:4).

Wisely and mercifully are we commanded to care for the things of others. It is the surest way to grow in grace and in the knowledge of Christ; for it nurtures charity, the best of all graces, and likens us to Christ in the largeness of His views and the opulence of His sympathy. Such Christians are never cold, and they never backslide. They are identified with the Savior in all His plans. They exult in His triumphs and rejoice in His joys. Their vision and their prayers embrace the whole earth, and they become familiar with the largest plans and the most stirring enterprises.

In the midst of such interests and employments there is little room for sloth or stagnation. Christians of this stamp outstrip all others in the race. They speedily attain the highest moral efficiency and the clearest spiritual perceptions, unusual vigor, and steadiness of faith and power in prayer. I think it may be announced as a maxim in religion, that they who devote themselves most eagerly to the salvation of others are ever in the most favorable position for working out their own salvation.—*Stephen Olin.*

While you are thus feeding God's lambs, He will lead you into rich pastures.—*John Wesley.*

> God's love hath to us wealth upheaped;
> Only by giving it is reaped.
> The body withers, and the soul,
> If love of self is all the goal;
> Then give your strength, your thought, your deeds,
> Give love, give tears, give till you bleed;
> Who gives not, shrivels up and dies;
> Who gives not, misses Heaven's prize.
> > The more we give,
> > The more we live.
>
> —*Adapted.*

October 28
God expects fruit

"Behold . . . I come seeking fruit" (Luke 13:7).
"For he shall be as a tree planted by the waters, and that spreadeth out her roots by the river, and shall not see when heat cometh, but her leaf shall be green; and shall not be careful in the year of drought, neither shall cease from yielding fruit" (Jer. 17:8).

A farmer goes to the agricultural fairs, and he says, "I have a farm that I want to put in competition. It has not a weed on it—not one; it has not a Canada thistle; it has no purslain; it has not a dock; it has no plantain; it has not any mullein. There is not a weed on it, absolutely."
"Well," it is asked him, "what are your crops?"
"Oh, I—I—."
"Have you any wheat?"
"No."
"Any corn?"
"No."
"Any grafts in the orchard?"
"No; I have nothing of that kind—but I've got no weeds." And that is all!
There are a great many people who seem to think that religion is not doing wrong. As if a knitting machine that never knit any stockings would be considered good because it never "misknit"!—*Henry Ward Beecher.*

God has no more use for a fruitless Christian than a farmer for a stalk of corn without an ear, a flock of hens without eggs or a herd of cows without milk. It is by fruits we verify our faith.—*F. H. Sparks.*

DO YOU BEAR FRUIT? Without holy fruit all evidences are vain. How vain would it be to prove to a farmer that his fields were good and productive, if they produced no corn! You might say to him, "Neighbor, your land is good; the soil is dry and well trenched." "Oh! but," he would say, "where is the yellow grain—where are the full ears falling before the sickle of the reaper?"
—*Robert Murray McCheyne.*

If I were fruitless, it mattered not who commended me, but if I were fruitful, I cared not who did condemn.—*John Bunyan.*

Charmed by Christ

"Thine eyes shall see the king in his beauty" (Isa. 33:17).
"We beheld his glory, the glory as of the only begotten of the Father"
(John 1:14).

The world—oh, what a bubble, what a trifle it is! Friends are nothing, fame is nothing, health is nothing, life is nothing; Jesus, Jesus is all!

Oh! what will it be to spend an eternity in seeing and praising Jesus! To see Him as He is, to be satisfied with His likeness! Oh, I long, I pant, I faint with desire to be singing, "Worthy is the Lamb!"—to be extolling the riches of sovereign grace—to be casting the crown at the feet of Christ! And why may we not do all this on earth?—*Edward Payson.*

Leave me Jesus, only Jesus—let the lights of earth grow dim;
I shall miss no other radiance, looking ever unto Him.
Put away my earthly idols; let them crumble; let them fall;
Leave me Jesus, only Jesus; let me keep my All-in-all.
While the changeful years are passing, bearing from my heart away
Many treasures, loved and cherished—only let Him stay.
Other joys no more may bless me; other friends may leave my side;
Only let me hold His friendship; only let Him still abide.
Let the chill mists fall about me; let the lights of earth grow dim;
Leave me Jesus, only Jesus; I am satisfied with Him.

—Unknown.

I have sometimes heard of spells and charms to excite love, and have wished for them, when a boy, that I might cause others to love me. But how much more do I now wish for some charm which should lead men to love the Savior! What would I not give for the power to make sinners love Him, for the faculty of describing His beauties and glories in such a manner as to excite warmer affections toward Him in the hearts of Christians! Could I paint a true likeness of Him, methinks I should rejoice to hold it up to the view and admiration of all creation and be hid behind it for ever. It would be Heaven enough to hear Him.

I have no heart to speak or write about anything but Jesus; and yet I have little patience to write about Him in our miserably defective language, unsuitable to speak His praises and describe His glory and beauty! But they cannot be described—they cannot be conceived; for "no man knoweth the Son, but the Father." What a wonderful idea does that text give us of the Son! Saints in Heaven do not know Him perfectly; even the angels do not. None but the Father is able to comprehend all His excellence. Yet, various, great, unsearchable, infinite as are His excellencies, they are all ours; for He is our Savior, our Head.—*Edward Payson.*

The mightiness of meekness

"Blessed are the meek: for they shall inherit the earth" (Matt. 5:5).
"A man's pride shall bring him low: but honour shall uphold the humble in spirit" (Prov. 29:23).

Pride was Nebuchadnezzar's downfall—"Is not this great Babylon which I have builded?" Do we take glory from God after doing some small service for Him? Can God trust us with success or are we like the vain woodpecker in the following story?

"A certain woodpecker flew up to the top of a high pine tree and gave three hard pecks on the side of the tree as woodpeckers are wont to do. At that instant a bolt of lightning struck the tree, leaving it on the ground, a heap of splinters. The woodpecker had flown to a tree nearby where it clung in terror and amazement at what had taken place. There it hung expecting more to follow, but as all remained quiet, it began to chuckle to itself saying, 'Well, well, well! Who would have imagined that just three pecks of my beak could have such power as that!'"

Pride is a natural trait in man; humility comes only with grace from God. "In all the copious language of the Greeks," says John Wesley, "there was not one word for humility till it was made by the great apostle Paul. The whole Roman language, even with all the improvements of the Augustan age, does not afford so much as a name for HUMILITY (the word from whence we borrow this, as is well known, bearing in Latin a quite different meaning)."

It is the best filled stalk of corn that bends its head the lowest.—*Unknown.*

Oh, the mightiness of meekness. There are thousands whom God is yearning to use, in the soul-winning work, but dare not. Success would turn their heads and be their ruin.—*Catherine Booth.*

> Humility, the fairest, loveliest flower
> That bloomed in paradise, and the first that died.
> It is so frail, and delicate a thing
> That if it look upon itself it's gone;
> And he who ventures to esteem it his
> Shows by that very thought he has it not.
> —*Caroline Fry.*

314

God's way of guidance

"And I will bring the blind by a way that they knew not; I will lead them in paths that they have not known: I will make darkness light before them, and crooked things straight. These things will I do unto them, and not forsake them" (Isa. 42:16).

"And thine ears shall hear a word behind thee, saying, This is the way, walk ye in it, when ye turn to the right hand, and when ye turn to the left"
(Isa. 30:21).

Do we inquire whether the Lord directs His children still as in old time? Undoubtedly He does, though not by any audible voice, yet with equal certainty and evidence. This He does commonly by closing up inwardly or outwardly all other ways, and leaving only one open to us. And is not this equivalent to our hearing a voice behind us? When He inwardly leads us, He impresses a Scriptural conviction on the judgment as to what we ought to do, and it is scarcely possible for us any longer to hesitate. Would our feelings lead us a different course? Then peace immediately departs and such disquietude arises within us, that we are compelled to retrace our steps. When He outwardly leads us, He brings us into such circumstances, connections, situations, that only one way remains open, for we see every other obstructed by visible providences.—*James Caughey.*

I believe that if you and I were to heed the whispers of our Father, we should not need so many of His thunders.—*J. H. Evans.*

If we have not learned the habit of committing the daily steps to the Lord, we shall find it very hard to seek His help when we come to a fork in the road.—*Spiritual Life.*

> He guided by paths that I could not see,
>   By ways that I had not known;
> The crooked was straight and the rough made plain
>   As I followed the Lord alone. . . .
>
> There is light for me on the trackless wild,
>   As the wonders of old I trace,
> When the God of the whole earth went before
>   To search me a resting place.
> Has He changed for me? Nay, He changes not.
>   He will bring me by some new way,
> Through fire and flood and each crafty foe,
>   As safely as yesterday.
>   —*Evangelical Christian.*

315

November 1
Increase through trial

"Thou, which hast shewed me great and sore troubles, shalt quicken me again. . . . shalt increase my greatness, and comfort me on every side" (Psa. 71:20-21). "O thou afflicted, tossed with tempest . . . behold, I will lay thy stones with fair colours, and lay thy foundations with sapphires" (Isa. 54:11).

If by the enlargement of my life I let in human sorrow I also let in divine consolation. A big, holy purpose makes me more sensitive toward the sin and hostility of man, but it also makes me more sensitive toward God. If the sufferings abound, "so our comfort aboundeth also." If I said nothing more than this, this alone would suffice: if we suffer with Christ, Christ Himself becomes a great reality. When life is a picnic we play with theology: when life becomes a campaign we grope for religion.—*J. H. Jowett.*

> The tears we shed are not in vain;
>   Nor worthless is the heavy strife;
> If, like the buried seed of grain,
>   They rise to renovated life.
> It is through tears our spirits grow;
>   'Tis in the tempest souls expand,
> If it but teaches us to go
>   To Him Who holds it in His hand.
> Oh, welcome, then, the stormy blast!
>   Oh, welcome, then, the ocean's roar!
> Ye only drive more sure and fast
>   Our trembling bark to Heaven's bright shore.
>   —*Thomas C. Upham.*

Now, as I look back over my own life, I can discover that some of the richest mercies my heavenly Father has ever bestowed have come in the shape of bitter disappointments. It has been truly remarked that "disappointment never means wreck when God's hand is in it. There is often a lift in that ugly thing." Disappointment, like fire, has a double power; it may scorch and crisp and blast a man, or else it may thaw out his blood, and quicken his life.

        —*Theodore Cuyler.*

Accomplish something

"And he trembling and astonished said, Lord, what wilt thou have me to do?"

(Acts 9:6).

"Speak; for thy servant heareth" (1 Sam. 3:10).

"What shall I do, Lord?" is the keynote of St. Paul's whole Christian life—activity and not a selfish quietism. It indicates that he did not have that conception of the new birth in which the sinner is passive, or rather, passive in fulfilling its conditions. That form of piety in which the Christian devotes himself exclusively to coddling himself, to constant morbid introspections of frames and feelings, will not be found in the writings of St. Paul.

—*Daniel Steele.*

Not by mere moods, not by how I feel today or how I felt yesterday, may I know whether I am indeed living the life of God, but only by knowing that God is using me to help others. No mood is so bright that it can do without that warrant. No mood is so dark that, if it has that, it need despair. It is good for us to think no grace or blessing truly ours till we are aware that God has blessed someone else with it through us.—*Phillips Brooks.*

In a tear-off calendar recently, I was interested to read about a conversation Mr. Charles M. Alexander had had on one occasion with a critical friend. "I admire your sincerity, Mr. Alexander," the man had said, "but I do not like the way you do your personal work." "No, I don't like it very much either," replied Mr. Alexander, "but tell me, how do you do yours?" The man was a bit taken aback, and hesitatingly replied, "Well,... er... I am afraid I don't do very much in the way of personal work." "Then," said Mr. Alexander, "I like the way I do mine, better than the way you don't do yours!"

> Do, please, be busy, for time flieth fast,
>   Soon it will all be gone;
> Soon will our season of service be past,
>   Soon will our day be done.
> Somebody near you needs now a kind word;
> Someone needs help such as you can afford;
> Haste to assist in the Name of the Lord,
>   There may be a soul to be won.
>   —*Unknown.*

November 3
Abiding in Christ

"Ye shall know that I am in my Father, and ye in me, and I in you"
(John 14:20).
"If a man love me, he will keep my words: and my Father will love him, and we will come unto him, and make our abode with him" (John 14:23).
"Abide in me, and I in you" (John 15:4).

I have thought and thought and thought of Jesus in Bethlehem, and of Jesus on Calvary, and of Jesus upon the throne, and I have worshiped and loved and rejoiced exceedingly in Him, but all the time I wanted something better and something deeper and something nearer. . . .

The presence of Jesus by the Holy Ghost is meant to be unbroken, continual, and for ever. Is not that what your heart longs for?—*Andrew Murray.*

> Abide in me, I pray, and I in Thee;
>> From this good hour, oh! leave me nevermore:
> Then shall the discord cease, the wound be healed,
>> The lifelong bleeding of the soul be o'er.
>
> Abide in me; o'ershadow by Thy love
>> Each half-formed purpose and dark thought of sin
> Quench, e'er it rise, each selfish, low desire,
>> And keep my soul as Thine, calm and divine.
>
> As some rare perfume in a vase of clay
>> Pervades it with a fragrance not its own,
> So, when Thou dwellest in a mortal soul,
>> All Heaven's own sweetness seems around it thrown.
>
> Abide in me. There have been moments blest
>> When I have heard Thy voice and felt Thy power:
> Then evil lost its grasp; and passion, hushed,
>> Owned the divine enchantment of the hour.
>
> These were but seasons beautiful and rare;
>> Abide in me, and they shall ever be:
> Fulfill at once Thy precept and my prayer;
>> Come and abide in me, and I in Thee.
>> >   —*Harriet Beecher Stowe.*

Possibility of prayer

"The effectual fervent prayer of a righteous man availeth much"
(James 5:16).
"Elias was a man subject to like passions as we are, and he prayed earnestly that it might not rain: and it rained not on the earth by the space of three years and six months" (James 5:17).

Prayer has many, many times brought opportune supplies, and cleared away serious difficulties. I know that faith can fill a purse, provide a meal, change a hard heart, procure a site for a building, heal sickness, quiet insubordination, and stay an epidemic. Like money in the worldling's hand, faith in the hand of the man of God "answereth all things." All things in Heaven, and earth, and under the earth, answer to the command of prayer. Faith is not to be imitated by a quack, nor simulated by a hypocrite, but where it is real, and can grasp a divine promise with a firm grip, it is a great wonderworker.

How I wish that my reader would so believe in God as to lean upon Him in all the concerns of his life! This would lead him into a new world, and bring to him such confirmatory evidence as to the truth of our holy faith that he would laugh skeptics to scorn. Childlike faith in God provides sincere hearts with a practical prudence, which I am inclined to call sanctified common sense. The simpleminded believer, though laughed at as an idiot, has a wisdom about him which cometh from above, and effectually baffles the cunning of the wicked. Nothing puzzles a malicious enemy like the straightforward unguardedness of an out-and-out believer.—*C. H. Spurgeon.*

Prayer can obtain everything. It can open the window of Heaven, and shut the gates of hell. It can put a restraint upon God, and detain an angel till he leave a blessing. It can open the treasures of rain, and soften the iron ribs of rock till they melt into a flowing river. It can unclasp the girdles of the North; it can arrest the sun in its course and the winds upon their errand. What may not the saints have for asking?—*Jeremy Taylor.*

> I trust the Lord, and He replies,
> In things both great and small.
> He honors faith with prompt supplies;
> Faith honors Him in all.
> —*Unknown.*

November 5
The day of small things

"For who hath despised the day of small things?" (Zech. 4:10).
"There is a lad here, which hath five barley loaves, and two small fishes: but what are they among so many?" (John 6:9).

Small things, little incidents, trifles, go to make up our lives. Carelessness as to trifles leads to grievous falls; attention to trifles makes us developed men and women.

It is the little things, the minor duties that are constantly occurring, that form our characters and augment our powers. If we despise the small, we shall fall by the small; but if we are faithful in little, we shall be faithful in much. A word fitly spoken may seem a trifle, but it is full of joy and blessing; a trifling handshake may be a benediction; a cup of cold water shall not lose its reward.

Accomplish the little things well. Do your best; simply, sweetly, quietly, and quickly; do it not for self, but to the Lord. Strive not after great things, not after that which is self-love and desire of applause, and is not pleasing to God.

—*Stephen Merritt.*

Letters joined make words,
　　And words to books may grow
As flake on flake, descending,
　　Forms an avalanche of snow.
A single utterance may good
　　Or evil thoughts inspire;
One little spark, enkindled,
　　May set a town on fire.
What volumes may be written
　　With little drops of ink!
How small a leak, unnoticed,
　　A mighty ship will sink!
A tiny insect's labor
　　Makes the coral strand,
And mighty seas are girdled
　　With grains of golden sand. . . .
Our life is made entirely
　　Of moments multiplied,
As little streamlets, joining,
　　Form the ocean's tide.
Our hours and, aye, our months and years,
　　Are in small moments given:
They constitute our time below,
　　Eternity in Heaven.

—*Unknown.*

Treasure in Heaven's bank

"Lay not up for yourselves treasures upon earth, where moth and rust doth corrupt, and where thieves break through and steal: But lay up for yourselves treasures in heaven, where neither moth nor rust doth corrupt, and where thieves do not break through nor steal: For where your treasure is, there will your heart be also" (Matt. 6:19-21).

There is such a thing as laying up as truly in Heaven as there is laying up on earth; if it were not so, our Lord would not have said so. Just as persons put one sum after another into the bank, and it is put down to their credit, and they may use the money, afterwards; so truly the penny, the shilling, the pound, the hundred pounds, the ten thousand pounds given, for the Lord's sake and constrained by the love of Jesus, to poor brethren, or in any way spent in the work of God, He marks down in the book of remembrance. He considers it is laid up in Heaven. The money is not lost, it is laid up in the bank of Heaven; yet so that whilst an earthly bank may break, or through earthly circumstances we may lose our earthly possessions, the money which is thus secured in Heaven cannot be lost.

Treasures laid up in Heaven never give care. Treasures laid up on earth never can afford spiritual joy. Treasures laid up in Heaven bring along with them peace and joy in the Holy Ghost even now. Treasures laid up on earth, in a dying hour cannot afford peace and comfort, and when life is over, they are taken from us. Treasures laid up in Heaven draw forth thanksgiving, that we were permitted and counted worthy to serve the Lord with the means with which He was pleased to intrust us as stewards. And when life is over we are not deprived of what was laid up there, but when we go to Heaven we go to the place where our treasures are, and we shall find them there.—*George Müller.*

There is no so certain way of increase, as to lend or give to the Owner of all things.—*Bishop Hall.*

> We lose what on ourselves we spend,
> We have, as treasure without end,
> Whatever, Lord, to Thee we lend,
> Who givest all.

> Whatever, Lord, we lend to Thee,
> Repaid a thousandfold will be;
> Then gladly will we give to Thee,
> Who givest all.
> —*Unknown.*

November 7
Rejoicing or resigned?

"But rejoice inasmuch as ye are partakers of Christ's sufferings; that, when his glory shall be revealed, ye may be glad also with exceeding joy"
(1 Peter 4:13).
"Rejoice ye in that day, and leap for joy: for, behold, your reward is great in heaven: for in the like manner did their fathers unto the prophets"
(Luke 6:23).

Joy is "the fruit of the Spirit"—not a counterfeit, but real, with supernatural and divine power. The Lord Jesus Christ told His disciples that hard times meant blessing. This is what He said: "Blessed are ye, when men shall hate you, and when they shall separate you from their company, and shall reproach you, and cast out your name as evil, for the Son of Man's sake."

And how did the Lord say the disciples should take these experiences when they came? With resignation? God forbid! This is what He said: "Rejoice ye in that day, and leap for joy." They were to look upon these experiences with thanksgiving and exultation, as an investor would look upon an investment that was going to bring him inordinately large returns, and returns absolutely guaranteed by resources that never could fail. "For," continued the Lord, "behold, your reward is great in heaven."

It is good to remember, every time some fresh affliction comes, that we are making an investment with assured returns of 100 or 1,000 or even a greater percentage in dividends. There is nothing to be resigned about in having investments that are making us rich beyond words. Therefore, "Rejoice in the Lord always: and again I say, Rejoice."

It is better to rejoice than to be resigned. The word "resigned" is not found in the Bible, but "rejoice" runs through the Scriptures like a great carillon of music. There is danger of self-pity in resignation—and self-pity is a deadly poison. There is no danger that we may be pitying ourselves while we are rejoicing with "joy unspeakable and full of glory." Resignation often means a certain mock piety—perhaps unconsciously so, but none the less real. Frances Havergal once said that with her the will of God used to be a sigh, but now it was a song.—*E. C. W. Boulton.*

Life-giving channels

"He that believeth on me, as the scripture hath said, from within him shall flow rivers of living water" (John 7:38—R.V.).
"Every thing shall live whither the river cometh" (Ezek. 47:9).

Everyone has the great responsibility devolved upon him or her to win as many souls as possible to Christ. This is the great privilege and the great duty of all the disciples of Christ. There are a great many departments in this work. But in every department we may and ought to possess this power; that whether we preach, or pray, or write, or print, or trade, or travel, take care of children, or administer the government of the State, or whatever we do, our whole life and influence should be permeated with this power. Christ says: "He that believeth on me . . . out of his belly shall flow rivers of living water"—that is, a Christian influence, having in it the element of power to impress the truth of Christ upon the hearts of men, shall proceed from him. The great want of the Church at present is, first, the realizing conviction that this commission to convert the world is given to each of Christ's disciples as his life-work. I fear I must say that the great mass of professing Christians seem never to have been impressed with this truth. The work of saving souls they leave to ministers.

Speaking of this baptism: it is not a thing into which people can gradually grow by forming habits of persuasion and conversation. It is a gift—an anointing, instantaneously received, and that may be enlarged or diminished as the possessor of it uses it more or less faithfully and intensely for the purposes for which it was given. It is oftentimes possessed and then lost, or its manifestation suspended by something that quenches the light of the Spirit in the soul. I have myself seen striking examples of this.—*Charles G. Finney.*

Spirit-filled believers carry life, and satisfaction and gladness wherever they go. Their presence is life-giving, fructifying, refreshing, even as a river which blesses as it flows. "Every thing shall live whither the river cometh." The weakest, feeblest member of the body of Christ may be so instinct with the most vigorous life that there shall come forth from him a holy river-like abundance to the blessing of the souls of others.

(From *New Testament Holiness* by Thomas Cook. Used by permission of the Epworth Press).

God's love to us immeasurable

"His great love wherewith he loved us" (Eph. 2:4).
"For God so loved the world, that he gave" (John 3:16).
"To know the love of Christ, which passeth knowledge" (Eph. 3:19).

Oh! if the tenderest mother were possessed
Of all the love (within her single breast)
Of all the mothers since the world began—
'Tis nothing to the love of God to man.
—*John Byrom.*

The love of God is an ocean, and no line can sound its depths. It is a sky of unknown dimensions, and no flying machine can reach its heights. It is a continent of unexplored distance, and no tape can measure its length. It is a width of unsurpassed country, and no survey can find its boundary. It is a mine of wealth, and no delving of man can estimate or exhaust its riches. It is a pole of attraction, which no explorer can discover. The love of God is a forest of beauty, and no botanist can find or describe its variety and glory.

Go, count the sands that form the earth,
    The drops that make the mighty sea;
Go, count the stars of heavenly birth,
    And tell me what their numbers be;
    And thou shalt know Love's mystery.

No measurement hath yet been found,
    No lines or numbers that can keep
The sum of its eternal round,
    The plummet of its endless deep,
    Or heights to which its glories sweep.

Yes, measure Love, when thou canst tell
    The lands where seraphs have not trod,
The heights of Heaven, the depths of hell,
    And lay thy finite measuring-rod
    On the Infinitude of God!
    —*Thomas C. Upham.*

Influenced and influencing

"Thou shalt not follow a multitude to do evil" (Exod. 23:2).
"Walk worthy of the vocation wherewith ye are called" (Eph. 4:1).

In some degree, upon all, conscious or unconscious, we shall exert an influence. We cannot help it. It is not a question of whether we will or will not, but of what shall be the influence that we exert.

A flower may not know how sweet it is, but it is sweet; and the perfume is wafted from it perpetually. A candle does not know what it is doing, nevertheless its light is going out all the time, in every direction. A magnet has no volition, yet it is forever searching and drawing objects to itself. So it is with the human soul; it is put together and tempered in such a way that it is constantly radiating influences. Man is a double creature, and which is the more wonderful of the two sides we cannot tell—namely, the capacity to receive endless influences and appreciate them, or the capacity to give out endless influences, consciously and unconsciously.

The bell when struck does not ring because it chooses to, but because it cannot help itself. And when a man beholds a noble trait, he admires it not because he wills to do it, but because he is so constituted that he must do it.

—Henry Ward Beecher.

Our many deeds, the thoughts that we have thought,
They go out from us thronging every hour;
And in them all is folded up a power
That on the earth doth move them to and fro;
And mighty are the marvels they have wrought
In hearts we know not, and may never know.
—F. Faber.

The slightest breeze that ever blew,
Some slender grass has wavered;
The smallest life I ever knew,
Some other life has flavored.
We cannot live our lives alone,
For other lives we touch
Are either strengthened by our own
Or weakened just as much.
—Finch.

November 11

Possess your possessions

"Whereby are given unto us exceeding great and precious promises"
(2 Peter 1:4).
"So will I bring upon them all the good that I have promised" (Jer. 32:42).

The promises of God are not enclosures to be the private property of this saint or that, but they are an open common for all the dwellers in the parish of Holy Faith. No doubt there are persons who would, if they could, make a freehold of the stars, and a personal estate out of the sun and moon. The same greed might put a ring-fence around the promises, but this cannot be done. As well might misers hedge in the songbirds and claim the music of a lark and thrush as their own sole inheritance, as propose to keep promises all to themselves. No, not the best of the saints can, even if they wished to do so, put a single word of the God of grace under lock and key. The promise is not only "unto you, and to your children," but also "to all that are afar off, even as many as the Lord our God shall call." What a comfort is this! Let us take up our common rights, and possess by faith what the Lord has made ours by a covenant.

Lastly, *talk about the promises.* Tell the King's household what the King has said. Never keep God's lamp under bushels. Promises are proclamations; exhibit them on the wall; read them aloud at the market-cross. Oh, that our conversation were more often sweetened with the precious promises of God! After dinner we often sit for half-an-hour, and pull our ministers to pieces, or scandalize our neighbors. How often is this the Sunday's amusement! It would be far better if we said, "Now, friend, quote a promise," and the other replied, "And you mention a promise too."—*C. H. Spurgeon.*

Take to yourself the promises
Found in His Holy Word,
Bring to your mind His messages,
Have faith that you are heard
When in your need you pray to Him
To strengthen you just there,
Claim His most precious promises,
You'll find God answers prayer.
—*Clara Simpson.*

Our best is our all

"She of her want did cast in all that she had" (Mark 12:44).
"Make me thereof a little cake first, and bring it unto me, and after make for thee and for thy son . . . and she, and he, and her house did eat many days"
(1 Kings 17:13, 15).

Let us ever remember that God is glorified in the full consecration of *what we have*, be it *small or great.* He desires not the increase of five talents for the loan of one, but a full, perfect consecration of that one to His own honor; and whoever renders this, He pronounces as hearty a "Well done" upon, as upon him who has received ten. I have often erred here. I will try to remember in future that *all I have* is all He wants.—*Catherine Booth.*

He couldn't sing and he couldn't play,
He couldn't speak and he couldn't pray.
He'd try to read, but he'd break right down,
Then sadly grieve at smile or frown.

While some with talents ten begun,
He started out with only one.
"With this," he said, "I'll do my best,
And trust the Lord to do the rest."

His trembling hand and tearful eye
Gave forth a world of sympathy;
When all alone with one distressed,
He whispered words that calmed that breast.

And little children learned to know,
When grieved and troubled, where to go.
He loved the birds, the flowers, the trees,
And, loving him, his friends loved these.

His homely features lost each trace
Of homeliness, and in his face
There beamed a kind and tender light
That made surrounding features bright.

When illness came, he smiled at fears,
And bade his friends to dry their tears.
He said, "Good-bye," and all confess
He made of life a grand success.
—*Unknown.*

November 13

Bear misunderstandings

"Blessed are ye, when men shall revile you, and persecute you, and shall say all manner of evil against you falsely, for my sake. Rejoice, and be exceeding glad: for great is your reward in heaven: for so persecuted they the prophets which were before you" (Matt. 5:11-12).

Be not disheartened because the eye of the world is constantly and earnestly fixed upon you to detect your errors and to rejoice in your halting. But rather regard this state of things, trying as it may be, as one of the safeguards which a kind Father has placed around you, to keep alive in your own bosom an antagonist spirit of watchfulness, and to prevent those very mistakes and transgressions which your enemies eagerly anticipate.—*Thomas C. Upham.*

To be misunderstood, even by those whom one loves, is the cross and bitterness of life. It is the secret of that sad and melancholy smile on the lips of great men which so few understand. It is the cruelest trial reserved for self-devotion. It is what must have oftenest wrung the heart of the Son of Man, and if God could suffer, it would be the wound we should be for ever inflicting upon Him. He also—He, above all—is the great misunderstood, the least comprehended. "He was accustomed to this," says Henry Drummond. "'Tis because He was accustomed to walk by a light that others could seldom see. All His life He had been misunderstood—by His disciples, by His relations, by His enemies, by His friends. Yes, and He could even remember a bitterer time than all, when His own mother said He was mad."

Alas! alas! never to tire, never to grow cold; to be patient, sympathetic, tender; to look for the budding flower and the opening heart; to love always—this is duty.

Martin Luther said, "I am persuaded that for the last hundred years, there has not existed a man whom the world at large hated more than it hates me. You cannot know how delighted I am, at seeing day after day my adversaries rising higher in their fury against me. I never feel prouder, more full of lofty daring than when I hear from time to time, their denunciations upon me."

Yesterday's heretics often become today's saints.—*Unknown.*

Quiet times with God

"And he said unto them, Come ye yourselves apart into a desert place, and rest a while: for there were many coming and going, and they had no leisure so much as to eat" (Mark 6:31).
"And Jesus said, Make the men sit down" (John 6:10).
"And he took them, and went aside privately into a desert place" (Luke 9:10).

> How good the heart's still chamber thus to close
>   On all but God alone—
> There in the sweetness of His love repose,
>   His love unknown!
> All else for ever lost—forgotten all
>   That else can be;
> In rapture undisturbed, O Lord, to fall
>   And worship Thee.
>   —*Gerhardt Tersteegen.*

I want you to notice, with regard to this blessedness of a pause in the outflowing energy of life, that it applies not merely to what we call our secular occupations, but to our sacred and religious ones as well. Indeed it often seems as if there were a sense in which it might be said that nothing so tended to keep God out of our lives as work for God done in a wrong and superficial spirit. . . . How religious work tries to push out religious thought and to kill the soul's receptivity. The more earnestly you are at work for Jesus, the more you need time when what you are doing for Him passes totally out of your mind, and the only thing worth thinking of seems to be what He is doing for you.—*Phillips Brooks.*

> Allured into the desert,
>   With God alone apart,
> There spirit meeteth spirit,
>   There speaketh heart to heart.
> Far, far on that untrodden shore,
>   God's secret place I find,
> Alone I pass the golden door,
>   The dearest left behind.
>   —*Gerhardt Tersteegen.*

Through God's threshing mill

"For verily, when we were with you, we told you before that we should suffer tribulation; even as it came to pass, and ye know" (1 Thess. 3:4).
"These are they which came out of great tribulation, and have washed their robes, and made them white in the blood of the Lamb" (Rev. 7:14).

We all know, in a general way that this word "tribulation" which occurs not seldom in Scripture and in the Liturgy, means affliction, sorrow, anguish, but it is quite worth our while to know how it means this, and to question the word a little closer. It is derived from the Latin "tribulum"—that word signifying the thrashing instrument, or roller, by which the Roman separated the corn from the husks; and "tribulatio," in its primary significance, was the act of this separation. But some Latin writer of the Christian Church appropriated the word and image for the setting forth of a higher truth; and sorrow, and distress, and adversity being the appointed means for the separating in men of their chaff from their wheat, of whatever in them was light, and trivial, and poor, from the solid and the true, therefore he called these sorrows and griefs, "tribulations," threshings, that is, of the inner spiritual man.

—*Richard Chenevix Trench.*

The three Hebrew children were wonderfully preserved, not only from destruction, but even from the smell of fire upon their garments. All they lost were the bands which bound them. So are Christ's people graciously kept in the hour of their affliction from the destroying power of their enemies. The Son of God is with them as He was with the Hebrew worthies. They lose nothing but the evils of their nature, which have hitherto been entanglements to them. They come forth with freedom and purity for the service of God, either on earth or in Heaven.—*John Bate.*

> Tho' in affliction's furnace tried,
> Unhurt, on snares and death I'll tread;
> Tho' sin assail, and hell, thrown wide,
> Pour all its flames upon my head,
> Like Moses' bush I'll mount the higher,
> And flourish, unconsumed, in fire.
> —*Charles Wesley.*

There goes a Christian

"These men are the servants of the most high God, which shew unto us the way of salvation" (Acts 16:17).
"Then this Daniel was preferred above the presidents and princes, because an excellent spirit was in him; and the king thought to set him over the whole realm" (Dan. 6:3).

Such was the influence of Ron Davies, the missionary who was later killed in Kashmir, that his mere passing through a coffee-room caused a university undergraduate of pronounced Unitarian views to exclaim: "There goes a Christian." The most prejudiced had to admit the loveliness of his life.

Morley Punshon has aptly said: "Don't let the question ever be asked about you, 'Is such an one a Christian?' The very necessity to ask suggests a negative answer. Some painters in the rude times of art are said to have put under their works, 'This is a horse.' Of course! it was necessary for no one could possibly recognize it without being told. But it is a poor sign when either a work of art or a work of grace needs to be labeled. Who thought of asking where Moses had been when he came down from the mount? They looked at him, and they saw the glory. Let your consistency be thus steadfast and pure. If you know that the 'writing is signed' which will throw you upon the world's pity or cruel scorn because you will keep your conscience inviolate, take heart from the example of Daniel. Don't shut your lattice-window. Men may ridicule you, but they will respect you notwithstanding. And if they do not, you can afford to do without their good opinion, while God looks down upon you with complacency, and the light of His countenance shines, broad and bright upon your soul."

> From scheme and creed the light goes out,
> The saintly fact survives;
> The blessed Master none can doubt
> Revealed in holy lives.
> —*J. G. Whittier.*

November 17
No place for self-pity

"If God be for us, who can be against us?" (Rom. 8:31).
"All these things are against me" (Gen. 42:36).

Do not let us simply bemoan our circumstances. In some cases the believer's testimony is, "All things are against me." That was old Jacob's testimony. Then he added, "Joseph is dead"—but he was not!—"Simeon is dead"—but he was not!—"and now they are going to take Benjamin." Now Jacob, yield all to God; leave it all in God's hands. And if you do, you will hear the returning cavalcade, which will bring you the news that Joseph is not dead, but is the governor of Egypt; that Simeon is in the spare bedroom of the palace; that Benjamin is in the seat of honor; and there is a warm place for the old man.
—*Reader Harris.*

Ye fearful saints, fresh courage take;
The clouds ye so much dread
Are big with mercy and shall break
In blessings on your head.
—*William Cowper.*

Difficulties on all sides confronted the missionaries in Burma. And now Adoniram Judson was being taken to prison. As he was being led along, a man spat at him out of the darkness and sneeringly said, "How bright are the prospects of your mission now?" "As bright as the promises of God, my friend," came the saintly reply. That is true faith that can believe God's wonderful promises when all is dark without and there is little outward evidence of the great success we have been promised in our ventures for God.

If the Lord lifts up the light of His countenance upon you as He has done upon me this day, all your mountains will become molehills.—*Samuel Pearce.*

Our words echo down the years

"Let the words of my mouth, and the meditation of my heart, be acceptable in thy sight, O Lord" (Psa. 19:14).
"How forcible are right words" (Job 6:25).

Peter Ainslie, in his little book, *God and Me*, says: "It has been estimated that the average person consumes about five hours a day in conversation, covering about fifteen octavo pages an hour, the space covered by the ordinary public speaker, from which it is concluded that the average person makes a weekly volume of 525 pages and, covering 70 years, the conversation of one person would make a library of 3,640 octavo volumes. What an immense individual library! What is it worth? If I have left on those pages thoughts of God, forgiveness, longsuffering, kindness, meekness, be my life ever so obscure and insignificant, I shall have made a library grander than the Congressional in Washington, or the British Museum in London, or the National in Paris, or the Imperial in St. Petersburg, or the Royal in Berlin."

> When I have gone from earth, though soon or late,
> The years will come and go, nor hesitate
> In their calm passing. This, my universe,
> Will turn on its unhurried way, no worse
> In order with me gone than with me here;
> But the words once spoken cling to heart and mind
> To echo down the years. O tongue, be sure
> In speaking that which strangely will endure
> After the one who utters it has gone
> Beyond the sunset, and beyond the dawn.
> O lips, be quick to stay the hasty speech—
> Too far, too far its influence will reach,
> Clinging to life as words have ever clung.
> —*Grace Noll Crowell.*
> *(Evangelical Christian).*

November 19

Build on the enduring Word

"Heaven and earth shall pass away: but my words shall not pass away"
(Luke 21:33).
"But the word of the Lord endureth for ever" (1 Peter 1:25).

If you plant for a year, plant grain.
If you plant for ten years, plant trees.
If you plant for a hundred years, plant men.
If you plant for ETERNITY, PLANT THE WORD.

We can trust men too much, but we can never do so towards God. It is the surest thing that has been, or that can ever be. To believe His Word is to believe what none can fairly question. Has God said it? Then so it must be. Heaven and earth will pass away, but God's Word will never pass away. The laws of nature may be suspended; fire may cease to burn, the water to drown, for this would involve no unfaithfulness to God. But for His Word to fail would involve a dishonoring variableness in the character and nature of the Godhead, and this can never be. Let us set to our seal that God is true, and never suffer a suspicion of His veracity to cross our minds.—*C. H. Spurgeon.*

A strange, mysterious life pervades the Bible, which makes it not only an inexplicable mystery, but an indestructible Book. It is also life-giving. Its Living Waters make everything to live, wherever the river of God cometh. The living Spirit of God here speaks to the responsive spirit of man. And so down through the ages this Book continues to go, a mighty miracle worker, forever undying in itself, and carrying to the nations a message and a power which are both Divine.—*Dr. A. T. Pierson.*

Oh, wonderful, wonderful Word of the Lord!
　　True wisdom its pages unfold;
And though we may read them a thousand times o'er,
　　They never, no never, grow old.
Each line hath a treasure, each promise a pearl,
　　That all if they will may secure;
And we know that when time and the world pass away,
　　God's Word shall for ever endure.
　　　　　　　　　　　　　—Julia Sterling.

Danger of ungodly alliances

"Quit you like men, be strong" (1 Cor. 16:13).

> God give us men! A time like this demands .
> Strong minds, great hearts, true faith, and ready hands.
> Men whom the lust of office does not kill;
> Men whom the spoils of office cannot buy;
> Men who possess opinions and a will;
> Men who have honor and who will not lie;
> Men who stand before a demagogue
> And scorn his treacherous flatteries without winking;
> Tall men, sun-crowned, who live above the fog,
> In public duty, and in private thinking.
> —*J. G. Holland.*

Some are too prudent—rascally prudent!—*Unknown.*

We have, alas, traveled far from apostolic Christianity. Just imagine the mayor and corporation of Ephesus calling a conference of religion and inviting Alexander the Jew, Demetrius the silversmith, and Paul, to have a friendly conference as to the best method of producing religious feeling and good morality among the townsfolk! Imagine Paul on the receipt of such an invitation! But of course those benighted days are gone! We are noted "back numbers" unless we are prepared to smile at those solemn words of Paul that the things which the Gentiles sacrifice they sacrifice to devils. Oh, for a breath from Heaven that shall scatter these despicable compromises!—*Paget Wilkes.*

"Shouldest thou help the ungodly, and love them that hate the Lord?"
(2 Chron. 19:2).

The men who move the world are the ones who do not let the world move them.—*Unknown.*

Willing to do His will

"If any man will do his will, he shall know of the doctrine, whether it be of God" (John 7:17).
"If ye be willing and obedient, ye shall eat the good of the land" (Isa. 1:19).

It is not, If any man *do*, he shall know; but if any man *is willing* to do, he shall know. He does not need to do His will in order to know, he only need be willing to do it. For "will" is not at all the sign of the future tense as it looks. It is not connected with the word *do* at all, but a separate verb altogether, meaning, "is willing," or "wills." If any man wills, or if any man is willing to do, he shall know.

Now, notice the difference this makes in the problem. Before, it looked as if the doing were to come first and then knowing His will; but now another element is thrown in at the very beginning. The being willing comes first, and then the knowing; and thereafter the doing may follow—the doing, that is to say, if the will has been sufficiently clear to proceed.

The whole stress of the passage therefore turns on this word "will." And Christ's answer to the question, How to know the will of God? may be simply stated thus: "If any man is willing to do God's will he shall know," or, in plainer language still, "If any man is sincerely trying to do God's will he shall know."

A heart not quite subdued to God is an imperfect element in which His will can never live; and the intellect which belongs to such a heart is an imperfect instrument and cannot find God's will unerringly—for God's will is found in regions which obedience only can explore.

The connection of all this with obedience is just that being willing is the highest form of obedience. It is the spirit and essence of obedience. There is an obedience in the world which is no obedience, because the act of obedience is there, but the spirit of submission is not.—*Henry Drummond.*

Effective praying

"Let thine ear now be attentive, and thine eyes open, that thou mayest hear the prayer of thy servant, which I pray before thee" (Neh. 1:6).
"Thy prayer is heard" (Acts 10:31).

The story is related of a poor but exceedingly pious colored woman, who felt keenly the need of her people having a church. She went about accordingly to have the neighbors meet for prayer-meeting at an old unused house. When the evening came, the woman took her lantern and went to the place of appointment, but no one else came. Nothing daunted, the woman prayed and sang, and then went home. The week following, the woman went again. Some were curious to know where the woman went, and followed. Outside they listened to a fervent prayer, and in time grew interested. After some time one or two ventured into the house that they might the better hear. One, more bold than the rest, asked the woman if she was not discouraged over the failure of others to come.

"The Lord and I makes a 'jority," was the simple answer.

After a while there were others to pray besides the old colored woman, for her faithfulness and earnest prayers had led them to Christ.

In three years from the time the woman began holding meetings within the unused house, there were enough Christians to build a neat church upon the site of the old building where the prayers had been offered.

If the effectual fervent prayer of one righteous man avails so much with God, how much more the united prayers of your entire church! "If one sigh of a true Christian," says an old divine, "wafts the bark to the desired haven, or stirreth Zion's ship, how much more a gale of sighs, breathed by hundreds of believers. If one trumpet sounds so loudly in the ears of God, how much more a concert of all the silver trumpets in Zion sounding together! Where so many hands are lifted up, how many blessings may they not pull down from Heaven!"—*James Caughey.*

Tell God all the truth

"Behold, thou desirest truth in the inward parts" (Psa. 51:6).
"The law of truth was in his mouth" (Mal. 2:6).

Beware of unintentional lying to God. We so often tell the Lord what is untrue! We say we would follow Him—that we desire to be holy and wholehearted and that we are seeking God, when in reality, if we knew our own hearts, we should confess that we were after happiness and not holiness, that we wanted peace and joy and power, and not God Himself.

But there can be no progress in divine things, no believing unto realization, until we tell Him all the truth. Caroline Fry, the author of "Christ our Example," affords a striking illustration of this. Possessed of wealth, position, and beauty, she was a gay woman of the world until, when still quite young, she grew utterly tired of life. Urged by an unconverted friend to seek consolation in religion, she set herself to this task. Being of a shrewd and keen intelligence, and illumined by the Spirit of God, she discovered that in all her seeking she had no true desire for the Lord Himself. She then told God the truth. She confessed her true state, and was stripped of all her supposed righteousness. This is how she prayed:

"O God, if Thou art a God, I do not love Thee. I do not seek Thee. I do not believe there is any happiness in Thee, but I am miserable as I am. Give me what I do not seek, do not want. If Thou canst, make me happy; I am tired of this world. If there is anything better, give it me."

God answered her prayer in one moment. She was immediately saved. Oh, that we would give up telling God what appears to us as the good desires and aspirations of our hearts, and begin to tell Him without fear the bad and unmanageable things within. How soon should we be freed!—*Paget Wilkes.*

"Neither shall a deceitful tongue be found in their mouth" (Zeph. 3:13).

I caught a flash of truth one day—
    How daring ignorance can be!—
And shut it up within my heart,
    A flame that danced and sang for me.

It scorched hypocrisy and sham
    And from earth bondage set me free;
Its beauty searched my trembling soul
    And bared my inner self to me.
            —*John Wright Follette.*

Salvation from worry

"To you who are troubled rest with us" (2 Thess. 1:7).
"Now the Lord of peace himself give you peace always by all means"
(2 Thess. 3:16).

> Couldst thou love Me when creeds are breaking,
>> Old landmarks shaking
>> With wind and sea?
> Couldst thou restrain the earth from quaking,
>> And rest thy heart in Me?
>
> Couldst thou love Me when storms are roaring,
>> Their torrents pouring
>> O'er mart and lea?
> Couldst thou on larger wings be soaring,
>> And hear all calm in Me?
>
> Couldst thou love Me when death is nearing,
>> A mist appearing
>> In all but Me?
> If then thy heart cast out its fearing,
>> Thy love shall perfect be.
>> *—Unknown.*

Salvation from worry is no small thing, especially in the case of one whose views of life are strongly tinged with indigo. Fear and faith cannot keep house together. When one enters the other departs. I believe that Jesus, Who is head over all things to His Church, has the program of my best possible future, which involves these two elements:

1. His highest glory through me.
2. My highest happiness in Him.

It is the mission of the Comforter to lead me, step by step, through this program, till Christ's ideal of my earthly life is fully realized. My only anxiety, moment by moment, is this: Am I now led by the Spirit of God? Just what the hidden plan of my future is, so long as it is the will of Jesus, is no concern of mine. The veil that hides it is woven by the fingers of Mercy.—*Daniel Steele.*

> Ill that He blesses is my good,
>> And unblest good is ill;
> And all is right that seems most wrong,
>> If it be His sweet will!
>> *—F. Faber.*

November 25
God's shaping process

"What I do thou knowest not now; but thou shalt know hereafter" (John 13:7).
"Beloved, now are we the sons of God, and it doth not yet appear what we shall be" (1 John 3:2).
"Now I know in part; but then shall I know even as also I am known"
(1 Cor. 13:12).

A man who had heard a piano for the first time was so thrilled and enraptured with the wondrous melody that he determined to see the factory where pianos were made. When he arrived, instead of hearing many mingling strains of music, he found only the whirl and buzz of machinery, the rasping sound of saws, the clatter of hammers, the patter of hurrying feet, and dust and din, and stroke and shout, as the work went on.

As he went on from room to room the uproar continued, and he despaired and questioned whether he had really found a piano factory. Not until he had reached the last room was he able to hear the finished piano's lovely music.

So many persons who desire the "beauty of holiness" become discouraged as God works upon their carnal hearts in sawing, shaping, planing, polishing and constructing the true character of holiness by divine process; they draw away from the very processes that God planned for them in preparation for the incoming of the Sanctifier. But they who patiently endure . . . at last come forth in the "beauty of holiness."

> The hammer of Thy discipline, O Lord,
> Strikes fast and hard. Life's anvil rings again
> To Thy strong strokes. And yet we know 'tis then
> That from the heart's hot iron all abroad
> The rich glow spreads. Great Fashioner divine,
> Who spareth not, in Thy farseeing plan,
> The blows that shape the character of man,
> Or fire that makes him yield to touch of Thine,
> Strike on, then, if Thou wilt! For Thou alone
> Canst rightly test the temper of our will,
> Or tell how these base metals may fulfill
> Thy purpose—making all our life Thine own.
> Only we do beseech Thee, let the pain
> Of fiery ordeals through which we go
> Shed all around us such a warmth and glow,
> Such cheerful showers of sparks in golden rain,
> That hard hearts may be melted, cold hearts fired,
> And callous hearts be taught to feel and see
> That discipline is more to be desired
> Than all the ease that keeps us back from Thee.
> —*Unknown.*

Let your light shine

"Ye are the light of the world. A city that is set on an hill cannot be hid. Neither do men light a candle, and put it under a bushel, but on a candlestick; and it giveth light unto all that are in the house. Let your light so shine before men, that they may see your good works, and glorify your Father which is in heaven" (Matt. 5:14-16).

The Bible calls the good man's life a light, and it is the nature of light to flow out spontaneously in all directions, and fill the world unconsciously with its beams. So the Christian shines, I would say, not so much because he will, as because he is a luminous object. Not that the active influence of Christians is made of no account in the figure, but only that this symbol of light has its propriety in the fact that their unconscious influence is the chief influence, and has the precedence in its power over the world.

An earthquake, for example, is to them a much more vigorous and effective agency. Hear how it comes thundering through the solid foundations of nature. It rocks a whole continent. The noblest works of man—cities, monuments and temples—are in a moment leveled to the ground, or swallowed down the opening gulfs of fire. Little do they think that the light of every morning, the soft and genial and silent light, is an agent many times more powerful. But let the light of the morning cease and return no more, let the hour of morning come and bring with it no dawn—the outcries of a horror-stricken world would fill the air, and make, as it were, the darkness audible.

Such is the light, which revisits us in the silence of the morning. It makes no shock or scar. It would not wake an infant in his cradle. And yet it perpetually new creates the world, rescuing it each morning as a prey from night and chaos. So the Christian is a light, even "the light of the world," and we must not think that, because he shines insensibly or silently, as a mere luminous object, he is therefore powerless. The greatest powers are ever those which lie back of the little stirs and commotions of nature; and I verily believe that the insensible influences of good men are more potent than what I have called their voluntary or active, as the great silent powers of nature are of greater consequence than her little disturbances.—*Horace Bushnell.*

A cause of dissatisfaction

"If ye be willing and obedient, ye shall eat the good of the land" (Isa. 1:19).
"It is hard for thee to kick against the pricks" (Acts 9:5).

Unsurrendered Christians are the unhappiest Christians on earth. And they are only on earth—there are none in Heaven. But why should we cheat ourselves of the happiness that God wants us to have? Full surrender to the unconditional mastery of our Lord Jesus Christ means a fully satisfied life. My way means misery; His way means happiness; why should it take us long to decide? A Christian woman whose messages in verse have enriched these pages wrote to *The Sunday School Times* several years ago: "The little editorial paragraphs on the first page flash with the Sword of the Spirit, so that when I was cherishing in the secret nook of my heart something that God would have me surrender, I could not bear to read those passages. But now that I, always a poor tenant, have moved out, and He has come in, and every room and cupboard and hidden drawer are His alone, these words are like Jacob's present to Joseph, balm and honey, spices and myrrh. Thank you." Any call to do God's will is unpleasant reading when we are refusing to do God's will. And it is the most blessed, precious call on earth when we have given in to Him and His will is our will. Shall we settle it now?—*Sunday School Times.*

The secret of an unsatisfied life too often is an unsurrendered will.
—*Hudson Taylor.*

Utterly abandoned to the Holy Ghost!
Seeking all His fullness at whatever cost;
Cutting all the shorelines, launching in the deep
Of His mighty power—strong to save and keep.

Utterly abandoned to the Holy Ghost!
Oh! the sinking, sinking, until self is lost!
Until the empty vessel lies broken at His feet;
Waiting till His filling shall make the work complete. . . .

Utterly abandoned! 'tis so sweet to be
Captive in His bonds of love, yet so wondrous free;
Free from sin's entanglements, free from doubt and fear,
Free from every worry, burden, grief or care. . . .

Lo! He comes and fills me, Holy Spirit sweet!
I in Him am satisfied; I in Him complete!
And the light within my soul shall never more grow dim
While I keep my covenant—abandoned unto Him!
—*Unknown.*

How Christian soldiers are made

"Thou therefore endure hardness, as a good soldier of Jesus Christ"
(2 Tim. 2:3).
"This charge I commit unto thee . . . that thou by them mightest war a good warfare" (1 Tim. 1:18).

The Lord trains His soldiers, not by allowing them to lie on feather beds, but by turning them out, and using them to forced marches and hard service. He makes them ford through streams, and swim through rivers, and climb mountains, and walk many a long march with heavy knapsacks of sorrow on their backs.

This is the way in which He makes them soldiers, not by dressing them up in fine uniforms, to swagger at the barrack gates, and to be fine gentlemen in the eyes of the loungers in the park. God knows that soldiers are only to be made in battle; they are not to be grown in peaceful times.

We may grow the stuff of which soldiers are made, but warriors are really educated by the smell of powder, in the midst of whizzing bullets and roaring cannonades, not in soft and peaceful times.

Well, Christian, may not this account for it all? Is not thy Lord bringing out thy graces and making them grow? Is He not developing in you the qualities of the soldier by throwing you into the heat of the battle, and should you not use every appliance to come off conqueror?—*C. H. Spurgeon.*

From silken self, O Captain free
Thy soldier, who would follow Thee:
From subtle love of softening things,
From easy choices, weakenings,
From all that dims Thy Calvary,
O Lamb of God, deliver me.
—*Amy Carmichael.*

Each heart must pass through the furnace for itself. To hear of the refining of others has no lasting effect on the heart's own alloy.—*Florence Barclay.*

God allures through affliction

"Behold, I will allure her, and bring her into the wilderness, and speak comfortably unto her" (Hos. 2:14).
"With lovingkindness have I drawn thee" (Jer. 31:3).

Thus God attracts us, showing us His love and His Word, and bringing us unto Himself, alluring us, not scolding us. God does not scold. He allures and draws us and attracts us. That has been His dealing with every soul (Jer. 31:3). Because He loves us, He draws us to Himself. As we look back on our past, it may be that some lives have been hedged up with thorns (Hos. 2:6), and there have been difficulties and trials and troubles, because you have forgotten Him, and gone after other things. But God has allured you unto Himself. He wanted you to feel the hopelessness of all those other things, in which you hoped to find pleasure and satisfaction.—*Barclay Buxton.*

> He bade me leave the things I love the best;
>   I held them back from His entreating hand;
> He offered peace; I chose my own unrest,
>   And would not understand.
>
> And still His patience never knew decay,
>   And still He waited for the certain end;
> There came a storm that swept my joys away,
>   And then I knew my Friend.
>
> And finding One in Whom my soul can trust,
>   I turned my face from dreams that proved untrue,
> Leaving old relics crumbling in the dust;
>   For Christ makes all things new.
>   —*Sarah Doudney.*

I always find that there is more hazard in sailing upon smooth water. When the winds blow and the seas rage, even sleepers will rise and call upon God.
                     —*John Wesley.*

Call for laborers

"Then saith he unto his disciples, The harvest truly is plenteous, but the laborers are few" (Matt. 9:37).
"Let me now go to the field, and glean" (Ruth 2:2).

Pray the Lord of the harvest to send forth laborers into His harvest—laborers! Men with coats off and sleeves rolled up, and with grace, grit and gumption, to do exploits for the Master!—*John Harrison.*

> Use me, God, in Thy great harvest field,
>> Which stretcheth far and wide like a wide sea;
> The gatherers are so few; I fear the precious yield
>> Will suffer loss. Oh, find a place for me!
> A place where best the strength I have will tell;
>> It may be one the older toilers shun;
> Be it a wide or narrow place, 'tis well,
>> So that the work it holds be only done.
>> —*Christina Rossetti.*

"The fields are white unto harvest. Thrust in the sickle, for the harvest is ripe." But the Lord wants reapers. Who of you will go out, sickle in hand, to meet Him? The harvest is ripe; shall it droop in heavy and neglected masses, for want of reapers to gather it in? To you, the young, in your enthusiasm—to you, the aged, in your wisdom—to you, men of daring enterprise and chainless ardor—to you, heirs of the rare endurance, and strong affection of womanhood—to you, the rich, in the grandeur of your equalizing charity—to you, the poor, in the majesty of your ungrudging labor, the Master comes and speaks. Does not the whisper thrill you? "Why stand ye here all the day idle?" Up, there's work for you all—work for the lords of broad acres, work for the kings of two hands. Ye are born, all of you, to a royal birthright.—*W. Morley Punshon.*

A young woman puzzled about the call of God once asked Ron Davies, a missionary home on furlough, "Please, Mr. Davies, what is a call?" His face lit up. He beamed at her and took up his Bible. Turning the pages of it, he found Mark 16:15, showed it to her, and read aloud the words, "'Go ye into all the world, and preach the Gospel to every creature!' The call! That is the call," he said. "God expects every Christian to go somewhere with the Gospel. All you have to do is to find out just where He wants you to go. It may be here in your own home town, or it may be He wants you to go to Africa, to China, or to Kashmir. If you are a Christian, you must preach Christ somewhere!"
—*Jock Purves.*

December 1
God's power ours through prayer

"Without me, ye can do nothing" (John 15:5).
"If ye abide in me, and my words abide in you, ye shall ask what ye will, and it shall be done unto you" (John 15:7).

Prayer is the chalice in which we fetch the water from the rock. It is the ladder on which we climb up to pick the grapes hanging over the wall of Heaven. It is the fire that warms the frigid soul. It is the ship that carries away our wants, and comes back with a return cargo of divine help. Archimedes said if he could only find a fulcrum for his lever, he could move the world. Ah! we have found it! Prayer is the lever. The divine promise is the fulcrum. Pushing down on such a lever, we move not only earth, but also Heaven.

—De Witt Talmage.

Prayer is the touch of an infant—but on the arm of the Almighty.

—Thomas Scott.

Say, what is prayer, when it is prayer indeed?
The mighty utterance of a mighty need.
The man is praying who doth press with might
Out of his darkness into God's own light.

White heat the iron in the furnace won;
Withdrawn from thence 'twas cold and hard anon.
Flowers, from their stalk divided, presently
Droop, fall, and wither in the gazer's eye.

The greenest leaf, divided from its stem,
To speedy withering doth itself condemn.
The largest river, from its fountain head
Cut off, leaves soon a parched and dusty bed.

All things that live from God their sustenance wait,
And sun and moon are beggars at His gate.
All skirts extended of thy mantle hold,
When angel hands from Heaven are scattering gold.

—Richard Chenevix Trench.

Am I a temple of God?

"Know ye not that ye are the temple of God, and that the Spirit of God dwelleth in you?" (1 Cor. 3:16).

"And what agreement hath the temple of God with idols? for ye are the temple of the living God; as God hath said, I will dwell in them, and walk in them; and I will be their God, and they shall be my people" (2 Cor. 6:16).

How have I kept Thy temple, Guest divine—
The house that Thou hast deigned to call Thy shrine,
And bought, at such a price, to make it Thine?

How have I watched beside its fivefold gate
Against the crafty foes that lie in wait
And never let their vigilance abate? . . .

Scourge from its courts whatever can defile,
Malice and wrath and selfish greed and guile,
Each word and act on which Thou canst not smile;

For Thou Thyself must cleanse Thy dwelling-place,
Illumine with the brightness of Thy face,
And furnish with Thine all-sufficient grace.

Enter Thou in and make me all Thine own,
In spirit, soul and body reign alone
Without a rival on my being's throne.
—Annie Johnson Flint.

God's presence dwelt in Solomon's temple in Old Testament times. A prayer uttered toward the temple could be assured of being heard. Trespasses, failures could be confessed, lack of rain, sickness, blighting and war could be entreated for with hands spread toward the temple, and God would hear. Daniel in captivity prayed facing Jerusalem and the temple, so confident was he of God's presence.

But after the day of Pentecost, Stephen filled with the Holy Ghost uttered the new truth, "the most High dwelleth not in temples made with hands." And Paul numbers of times startles his correspondents with that grand truth that each of us are "temples of the Holy Ghost."

And will the mighty God
Whom Heaven cannot contain,
Make me His temple and abode,
And in me live and reign?
—George Rawson.

347

December 3
Joy preserves spiritual life

"Therefore with joy shall ye draw water out of the wells of salvation"
(Isa. 12:3).
"Wilt thou not revive us again: that thy people may rejoice in thee?"
(Psa. 85:6).

Rejoicing is the salt of our salvation. It keeps it. Joy is almost the first blessing that comes with the new birth. Relief from anguish may precede it; peace may forerun it, but as soon as the soul can be trusted with it, the gracious joy of God comes streaming into the soul. Joy in the Name of the Lord! It is even more than the birthright of salvation; it is an integral part of it. And so when joy in God wavers or disappears, we must look to our soul's safety.

Whatever His love may take from us, He must always leave us Himself, and while He is the God of all comfort, of hope, of consolation, of peace, He can always fill us with joy while we believe.—*Elizabeth S. Brengle.*

And notice what joy is. It is the cataract in the stream of life. Peace is the gentle even flowing of the river. Joy is where the waters go bubbling, leaping with ecstatic bound, and forever after, as they go on, making the channel deeper for the quiet flow of peace. Paul had put his no-worry rules through the crucible of experience. He follows the Master in that. These three rules really mean living ever in that Master's presence. When we realize that He is ever alongside, then it will be easier to be:

Anxious for nothing,
Thankful for anything,
Prayerful about everything.—*S. D. Gordon.*

The other day a dull, professing Christian met a young man who was shouting, "Hallelujah to the Lamb Who died on Calvary," and making the hills resound. "Are you drunk this morning," asked the professor coldly, "that you are making such a noise?" "Ah, you would be drunk too, if you had been where I have been, and had what I have had this morning." "Where have you been?" "I've been to Calvary, and seen Jesus bearing all my sins away; and if you had been there, you would have been as intoxicated with joy as I am."

Now I would face the world with my new life,
With my new crown.
How soon a smile of God can change the world.
How we are made for happiness—how work
Grows play, adversity a winning fight!
—*R. Browning.*

Tiring zigzagging

"This one thing I do, forgetting those things which are behind, and reaching forth unto those things which are before" (Phil. 3:13).
"Ye shall not turn aside to the right hand or to the left. Ye shall walk in all the ways which the Lord your God hath commanded you, that ye may live, and that it may be well with you, and that ye may prolong your days in the land which ye shall possess" (Deut. 5:32-33).

The old farmer unconsciously taught a great truth when he told about his dog, which had just returned with the carriage from a little drive and seemed thoroughly exhausted as he lay down on the grass panting for breath: "'Taint the road that tired him," said the farmer, "but the zigzagging. The team has only gone about ten miles, but he's run more than fifty. There wasn't a gate open on the way but he had to go in and examine the whole premises. There wasn't a cat appeared, but he had to chase it. There wasn't a dog barked but he just wore himself out barking back again and showing fight, so that while we were keeping on the road he was running over the whole country. No," he concluded, "'taint the straight traveling, but the zigzagging that tires him."

How true the old farmer's words are about many of our spiritual walks. The real tasks and trials of life are not too hard to bear, but the roundabouts that we make for ourselves, the cares we imagine, the needless waste of life and energy in things we have no need to say or do, this is where the wear and the worry come. Most of us are like the old lady who said she had had many trials in life, especially those that never came. Beloved, God is able to keep you from stumbling, to lead you in a straight path and to save you from "zigzagging."

> Behind my back I fling,
> Like an unwanted thing,
>   My former self and ways,
> And reaching forward far,
> I seek the things that are
>   Beyond time's lagging days.
>
> Oh! may I follow still,
> Faith's pilgrimage fulfill,
>   With steps both sure and fleet;
> The longed-for good I see,
> Jesus waits there for me,
>   Haste! haste! my weary feet.
>   —*A. N. Groves.*

December 5

Indifference to man's opinions

"It is a very small thing that I should be judged of you, or of man's judgment"
(1 Cor. 4:3).
"Not with eye service, as menpleasers; but as the servants of Christ, doing the will of God from the heart; With good will doing service, as to the Lord, and not to men" (Eph. 6:6-7).

They who have overcome the world are no longer careful either to secure its favor or avert its frown, and the good or the ill opinion of the world is to them a small matter. "To me," said Paul, "it is a small thing to be judged of man's judgment." So of every real Christian; his care is to secure the approbation of God; this is his chief concern, to commend himself to God and to his own conscience. No man has overcome the world unless he has attained to this state of mind. Almost no feature of Christian character is more striking or more decisive than this—indifference to the opinions of the world.

—Charles G. Finney.

There is no commoner danger than that of accepting the code of the society in which you live as the rule of right.—*Bishop Temple.*

Strive all your life to free men from the bondage of custom and self, the two great elements of the world that lieth in wickedness.—*Charles Kingsley.*

Life is simplified when our only thought is to please God. Our friends and neighbors have such varying ideas and opinions that life would be burdensome were we to try and please man. Some people are forever busy running here and there endeavoring to reconcile and straighten up false rumors. Henry Ward Beecher expressed it thus: "Life would be a perpetual flea hunt if a man were obliged to run down all the innuendos, inveracities, insinuations, and misrepresentations which are uttered against him." How restful to leave our reputation in God's hands. "What I *must* do," says Emerson, "is all that concerns me, not what the people think. This rule . . . is harder, because you will always find those who think they know what is your duty better than *you* know it."

Seeking daily counsel

"If any of you lack wisdom, let him ask of God, that giveth to all men liberally, and upbraideth not; and it shall be given him. But let him ask in faith, nothing   wavering" (James 1:5-6).
". . . His candle shined upon my head, . . . by his light I walked through darkness" (Job 29:3).

I have not sufficient wisdom to meet these difficulties so as to be able to know what steps to take, but He is able to direct me. What I have, therefore, to do is this: in simplicity to spread my case before my heavenly Father and my Lord Jesus. Then I have to believe that God will do so, and go with good courage to my business, and expect help from Him in the next difficulty that may come before me. I have to look for guidance, I have to expect counsel from the Lord, and, as assuredly as I do so, I shall have it. I shall find that I am not nominally, but really in partnership with the Father and with the Son.

—George Müller.

Being perplexed, I say,
        "Lord, make it right,
Night is as day to Thee,
        Darkness is light.
I am afraid to touch
Things that involve so much:
My trembling hand may shake,
My skill-less hand may break,
Thine can make no mistake,
        Lord, make it right!"

Being in doubt, I say,
        "Lord, make it plain,
Which is the true, safe way,
        Which would be vain.
I am not wise to know,
Nor sure of foot to go:
My poor eyes cannot see
What is so clear to Thee—
Lord, make it clear to me,
        Lord, make it plain!"
                —Anna Warner.

December 7
Strengthened hands

"O God, strengthen my hands" (Neh. 6:9).
"And he touched her hand, and the fever left her: and she arose, and ministered unto them" (Matt. 8:15).

One morning on waking, a woman charged with the care of a home began thinking of the day's simple duties. And as she thought they seemed to magnify and pile up. There was her little daughter to get off to school with her luncheon. Some of the church ladies were coming that morning for a society meeting, and she had been planning a dainty luncheon for them. The maid in the kitchen was not exactly ideal—yet. And as she thought into the day her head began aching.

After breakfast, as her husband was leaving for the day's business, he took her hand and kissed her good-bye. "Why," he said, "my dear, your hand is feverish. I'm afraid you've been doing too much. Better just take a day off." And he was gone. And she said to herself, "A day off! The idea! Just like a man to think that I could take a day off." But she had been making a habit of getting a little time for reading and prayer after breakfast. . . .

Now she slipped to her room and, sitting down quietly, turned to the chapter in her regular place of reading. It was the eighth of Matthew. As she read she came to the words, "And he touched her hand, and the fever left her; and she arose, and ministered unto them." And she knelt and breathed out the soft prayer for a touch of the Master's hand upon her own. And it came as she remained there for a few moments. And then with much quieter spirit she went on into the day.

The luncheon for the church ladies was not quite so elaborate as she had planned. There came to her an impulse to tell her morning's experience. She shrank from doing it. It seemed a sacred thing. They might not understand. But the impulse remained, and she obeyed it, and quietly told them. And as they listened there seemed to come a touch of the Spirit's presence upon them all. And so the day was a blessed one. Its close found her husband back again. And as he greeted her he said quietly, "My dear, you did as I said, didn't you? The fever's gone."—*S. D. Gordon.*

> My hands were growing feverish,
>   And cumbered with much care;
> Trembling with haste and eagerness,
>   Nor folded oft in prayer.
> The Master came and touched my hands
>   (With healing in His own),
> And calm and still to do His will
>   They grew—the fever gone.
> "I must have quiet hands," said He,
> "Wherewith to work My works through thee."
>   —*Unknown.*

352

How much should we love?

"Thou shalt love the Lord thy God with all thy heart" (Matt. 22:37).
"Love is the fulfilling of the law" (Rom. 13:10).

"With all thy heart," is the command. Our love-power may be very limited, but so long as it is fully employed in loving God, we fulfill the divine requirement just the same as those who have the larger capacities. A thimble may be as full as a bucket. To love God with more than all our heart—beyond our power or capacity—would be impossible, and to love Him less than to the full measure of our power to love, would be short of His requirement. "He that does as well as he can, does well: angels can do no better, and God requires no more."
(From *New Testament Holiness* by Thomas Cook. Used by permission of the Epworth Press).

> God measures souls by their capacity
> For entertaining His best Angel, Love.
> Who loveth most is nearest kin to God,
> Who is all Love, or Nothing.
>
> He who sits and looks out on the palpitating world,
> And feels his heart swell in him large enough
> To hold all men within it, he is near
> His great Creator's standard, though he dwells
> Outside the pale of churches, and knows not
> A feast-day from a fast-day, or a line
> Of Scripture even. What God wants of us
> Is that outreaching bigness that ignores
> All littleness of aims, or loves, or creeds,
> And clasps all Earth and Heaven in its embrace.
> —*Ella Wheeler Wilcox.*

The love of Christ is my study, but I am frequently at a loss to understand how it is that my love to Him is so small. . . . Could I die for Thee? Could I suffer long, and still love with a passion like Thine? I am crying to God daily, hourly, constantly, to receive a thousand times more love.—*William Bramwell.*

My present capacity for the love of God is filled, but so precious is the treasure that I am coveting a vessel a thousand times larger. Hence with Charles Wesley I daily exclaim:

> "Insatiate to this spring I fly;
> I drink, and yet am ever dry;
> Ah! who against Thy charms is proof?
> Ah! who that loves can love enough?"
> —*Daniel Steele.*

Service that costs but triumphs

"They loved not their lives unto the death" (Rev. 12:11).
"So will I go in unto the king, which is not according to the law: and if I perish, I perish" (Esther 4:16).

The life of the Church becomes fruitful when it becomes sacrificial. When the Church is easeful she loses her power to redeem. I remember the old story of Pope Innocent IV and Thomas Aquinas, who were standing together as bags of treasure were being carried in through the gates of the Lateran.

"You see," observed the Pope, with a smile, "the day is past when the Church could say, 'Silver and gold have I none.'"

"Yes, Holy Father," was the saint's reply, "and the day is past when the Church could say to the lame man, 'Rise and walk.'"

When the Church's life is lived on the plane of ease, and comfort, and bloodless service, she has no power to fertilize the dry and barren places of earth. When the Church becomes sacrificial she becomes impressive. The sacrificial things in history are the influential things today. It is the men and the women who have given away their being, the bleeding folk, who are our present inheritance. "They loved not their lives unto the death." "And they overcame . . . by the blood of the Lamb."

The woman who gave the two mites still works as a factor in the life of the race. Sir John Kelynge—have you ever heard of him?—the brutal, cynical justice who thrust John Bunyan for twelve years into Bedford jail, his very name is now a conundrum! John Bunyan, the sacrificial martyr, is still fertilizing the field of common life with energies of rich inspiration. The finders have lost. The apparent losers are at the winning post! The sacrificial are the triumphant.—*J. H. Jowett.*

> The spirit of self-sacrifice
> Stays not to count the price.
> Christ did not of His mere abundance
> Cast into the empty treasury of man's store:
> The First and Last gave
> Until even He could give no more.
> His very living—
> Such was Christ's giving.
> —*Anna E. Hamilton.*

Lean on God's Word

"So then faith cometh by hearing, and hearing by the word of God"
(Rom. 10:17).
"Whatsoever is not of faith is sin" (Rom. 14:23).

What is faith? In the simplest manner in which I am able to express it, I answer: Faith is the assurance that the thing which God has said in His Word is true, and that God will act according to what He has said in His Word. This assurance, this reliance on God's Word, this confidence is faith. No impressions are to be taken in connection with faith. Impressions have neither one thing nor the other to do with faith. Faith has to do with the Word of God. It is not impressions, strong or weak, which will make any difference. We have to do with the written Word and not ourselves or our impressions.

Probabilities are not to be taken into account. Many people are willing to believe regarding those things that seem probable to them. Faith has nothing to do with probabilities. The province of faith begins where probabilities cease and sight and sense fail. A great many of God's children are cast down and lament their want of faith. They say that they have no impressions, no feelings, they see no probability that the thing they wish will come to pass. Appearances are not to be taken into account. The question is—whether God has spoken it in His Word.

And now, beloved Christian friends, you are in great need to ask yourselves whether you are in the habit of thus confiding, in your inmost soul, in what God has said in His Word, and whether you are in earnest in seeking to find whether the thing you want is in accordance with what He has said in His Word.

—*George Müller.*

When the great missionary, John G. Paton, was translating the Scriptures for his South Sea Islanders, apparently there was no word for "believe" in their native tongue. For a long while he was well-nigh baffled. One day a native came into his study, and, tired out, flung himself down on a chair, rested his feet on another chair, and lay back full length, saying as he did so something about how good it was to lean his whole weight on those chairs. Instantly Dr. Paton noted the word the man had used for "lean his whole weight on." The missionary had his word thereafter in translating the Scriptures. Try it for yourself and see, in any verse that uses the word "believe."

December 11

Cross-bearing proves the disciple

"He that taketh not his cross, and followeth after me, is not worthy of me"
(Matt. 10:38).
"Come, take up the cross, and follow me" (Mark 10:21).

One fruitful cause of failure might be called "Shrinking the Cross." We use the word "cross" in a general sense. Good men have given their various ideas as to just what the cross is, in the life of today. Without giving it any specific meaning, we might define it as any exercise, more or less distasteful and irksome to the natural, carnal man, which, if carried out heartily and consistently, yields spiritual benefits. Taken in this light, it is evident that different individuals have different crosses. What may be a cross for one person may be perfectly easy and convenient for his neighbor.

It is evident that service to God which is so convenient as to demand no exertion, is a poor test of virtue; hence it remains for the crosses which stretch and strain the moral fiber, to prove the strength of heart-affections for Christ. The idea is simply this: a real Christian willingly goes through "hard things" for Christ's sake, and like his Captain, is made "perfect" through suffering.

—Howard B. Bitzer.

All those who challenge the enemies of mankind, and draw their swords against all evil must expect to be struck back, to be wounded—nay, they must be prepared to die. When therefore difficulty and persecution come, instead of giving up, the Christian should say, "This is what I expected; this proves I am in the right place. I have promised God I would bear the cross, and here it is; therefore, I will take it up and carry it. Now I have a chance of proving that I am made of the right stuff." He should always bear in mind for his encouragement that his reward will not be according to the measure of his visible success, but the character of his fightings.—*General William Booth.*

Let us take up the cross,
Till we the crown obtain;
And gladly reckon all things loss,
So we may Jesus gain.
—Charles Wesley.

To take up the cross of Christ is no great action done once for all; it consists in the continual practice of small duties which are distasteful to us.
—J. H. Newman.

356

The power I possess

"A little leaven leaveneth the whole lump" (1 Cor. 5:6).
"For what knowest thou, O wife, whether thou shalt save thy husband? or how knowest thou, O man, whether thou shalt save thy wife?" (1 Cor. 7:16).

The stone flung from my careless hand into the lake splashed down into the depths of the flowing water, and that was all. No, it was not all. Look at those concentric rings rolling their tiny ripples among the sedgy reeds dipping the overhanging boughs of yonder willow and producing an influence slight but conscious, to the very shores of the lake itself. That hasty word, that word of pride or scorn, flung from my lips in casual company produces a momentary depression, and that is all. No, it is not all. It deepened that man's disgust at godliness, and it sharpened the edge of that man's sarcasm, and it shamed that half-converted one out of his penitent misgivings, and it produced an influence slight but eternal on the destiny of an immortal life.

Oh, this power that I have—this power of influence, and it clings to me. I cannot shake it off. It is born with me. It has grown with my growth and strengthened with my strength. It speaks, it walks, it moves; it is powerful in every look of my eye, in every word of my lips, in every act of my life. I cannot live to myself. I must either be a light to illumine, or a tempest to destroy. I must either be an Abel, who by his immortal righteousness being dead yet speaketh, or an Achan, the saddest continuance of whose otherwise forgotten name is the fact that man perishes not alone in his iniquity.

O brethren, this necessary element of power belongs to you all. Thy sphere may be contracted, thine influence may be small, but a sphere and an influence you have.—*W. Morley Punshon.*

A note so low that none but Echo heard,
    Was sung into the world one Summer day;
The singer died,—the song went on its way,
At first as faint as call of sleeping bird,
While Echo carried it in rhythmic word
    From rock to rock, until it went astray
    Into the outer space, where Freedom lay,
And all the world then listened and was stirred.
And none could name or trace its humble birth,
    Not even Echo, who had simply known
It as a broken note of little worth;—
    So many voices now had swelled the tone,
It floated far beyond the bounds of earth
    And blended with the songs around the Throne.
              —*Mary A. Mason.*

December 13
Connection with the vine

"And nothing shall be impossible unto you" (Matt. 17:20).
"I can do all things through Christ which strengtheneth me" (Phil. 4:13).

At a certain agricultural school in Western United States, one of the professors recently made some interesting experiments with a growing squash (a vegetable similar to a marrow). He fitted a harness of strap iron over the squash in such a way that, as the vegetable grew, the expanding iron harness would register the strength that the squash exerted upon it. Thus harnessed, the squash lifted at different stages of its growth weights of sixty, five hundred, eleven hundred, and eventually three thousand pounds. And all this marvelous power was made possible through just one thing—the connection of the squash with the vine.

One of the most amazing things in life is the power for burden-bearing that apparently weak and almost helpless men and women often manifest. . . . We marvel that they do not go down beneath their loads. Instead, they accept them with patience and cheerfulness; day after day they fare courageously onward.

There is an explanation. If the secret of the inner life of these people could be known, the explanation of their strength would be found in just one thing— connection with the Vine. They are in constant contact with Him Who said, "I am the true vine." "I can do all things," wrote the great Apostle, "through Christ which strengtheneth me."

> Would He speak more clearly, fully,
>   If we listened more;
> If we waited at His footstool,
>   In a hush unknown before?
>
> Would His guidance seem more certain,
>   On this uphill way,
> If our hands held His more closely,
>   If we never looked away?
>
> O I think we miss the pathway,
>   Go unsatisfied,
> Just by failing to remember
>   That the Master said, "Abide."
>   —*Edith Hickman Divall.*

Wanted—deeds, not words

"Son, go work today in my vineyard" (Matt. 21:28).
"I will arise and go" (Luke 15:18).
"Go, and do thou likewise" (Luke 10:37).

We must insist on instant activity. We need less dress parade, less reviews, more results. Rust is killing off tens of thousands. The vineyard suffers for lack of workers. The harvest needs laborers. We have a thousand well-wishers where we have a score of real soul-savers.—*Reader Harris.*

I have seen nearly twenty set at liberty. I believe I should have seen many more, but I cannot yet find one pleading man. There are many good people, but I have found no wrestlers with God.—*William Bramwell.*

> Wanted: deeds,
> Not words of winning note,
> Not thought from life remote,
> Not fond religious airs,
> Not sweetly languid prayers,
> Not love of cant and creeds;
> Wanted: deeds.
> —*Duncan Macgregor.*

I am sick of opinions. . . . Give me a humble, gentle lover of God and man; a man full of mercy and good fruits, without partiality and without hypocrisy; a man laying himself out in the works of faith, the patience of hope and the labor of love.—*John Wesley.*

What proportion of people do you suppose have ever tried to take the teachings of Christ seriously in any given century? My guess is a very small percentage. Most people who have troubled themselves to learn what Jesus Christ really said and did, don't do anything about it. So how can you be surprised when the result is so poor? Christianity—the real thing—has never failed. But it hasn't been given a fair chance to work, by most people. Don't blame Christianity for the mess the world is in. Blame people—maybe yourself.—*J. B. Phillips.*

December 15
Every man's life a plan of God

"And the Lord looked upon him, and said, Go . . . have not I sent thee?"
(Judges 6:14).
"Who hath . . . called us with an holy calling, not according to our works, but according to his own purpose and grace" (2 Tim. 1:9).

God has a definite life-plan for every human person, girding him visibly or invisibly, for some exact thing which it will be the true significance and glory of his life to have accomplished. Many persons never even think of any such thing. They suppose that, for most men, life is a necessarily stale and common affair. What it means for them they do not know. They complain, venting heavy sighs, that, while some few are set forward by God to do great works and fill important places, they are not allowed to believe that there is any particular object in their existence.

What do the Scriptures show us, but that God has a particular care for every man, a personal interest in him and a sympathy with him and his trials. God watches for the use of his one talent as attentively and kindly, and approves him as heartily, in the right employment of it, as if He had given him ten.

—Horace Bushnell.

> Thou cam'st not to thy place by accident,
>   It is the very place God meant for thee;
>   And shouldst thou then small scope for action see,
> Do not for this give room to discontent,
> Nor let the time thou owest to God be spent
>   In idly dreaming how thou mightest be,
>   In what concerns thy spiritual life more free
> From outward hindrance or impediment.
> *—Richard Chenevix Trench.*

Tell me that I have received my ministry from man, and I shall take one view of the difficulties which may beset it. But tell me that that ministry has been imposed upon me from Heaven, and that I am called and the elect of God to do a certain work; and whatever may be the impediments round about me, there shall be sunshine in my heart, there shall be deep, inexplicable peace in my soul; I shall regard the difficulties of the present occasion as but momentary, and the strength upon which I rest shall be nothing less than the omnipotence of God.

Whose servants are we, then? Who has called us to this Christian work? We are called of God, we are not called of men, and we must take our orders from Heaven, and not from earth.—*Joseph Parker.*

Glory in reproach

"We are made a spectacle unto the world, and to angels, and to men. We are fools for Christ's sake" (1 Cor. 4:9-10).

"Blessed are ye, when men shall . . . reproach you, and cast out your name as evil, for the Son of man's sake" (Luke 6:22).

Do not be deterred from this fullness of spiritual life by the fact that the world has long since pronounced every one of its possessors a madman. The world has some good ground for its verdict. A madman is one who sees, or thinks he sees, what others see not, and seeing such things walks accordingly. Under the intense illumination of the Father, Son, and Holy Spirit abiding with the believer (John 14:16-23), he sees what the blind world sees not, and shapes his conduct in accordance with the heavenly light. Hence, those who see not what he sees must think him beside himself, and express their pity that reason has been dethroned. If you are unwilling to be an unintelligible and sadly misunderstood person in the eye of the world, an enigma to your best friends, who know not the experience of the indwelling Spirit, we advise you to wait till you have conquered the world in so far as to live without its good opinion. By the grace of God the thing can be done. "Be of good cheer," says the great Representative and Exemplar, "I have overcome the world."—*Daniel Steele.*

Trials may come, but they are all good. I have not been so tried for many years. Every week, and almost every day, I am bespattered in the public papers. Many are in tears on the occasion; many terribly frightened and crying out, "Oh, what will the end be?" What will it be? Why, glory to God in the highest, and peace and goodwill among men.—*John Wesley.*

It is not the many who reform the world, but the few who rise superior to that public opinion which crucified our Lord many years ago.

—*Charles Kingsley.*

December 17
Salute to the handicapped

"Therefore I take pleasure in infirmities . . . in distresses for Christ's sake"
(2 Cor. 12:10).

The authors of the following selections did their greatest work for God and man without their sight. Your handicap may not be so obvious to others—but whatever it is, allow God to sanctify it to you and the door of blessing and fruitfulness will be opened.

O merciful One!
When men are farthest, then Thou art most near;
When friends pass by, my weaknesses to shun,
Thy chariot I hear.

Thy glorious face
Is leaning toward me, and its holy light
Shines in upon my lonely dwelling-place—
And there is no more night.

On my bended knee
I recognize Thy purpose, clearly shown;
My vision Thou hast dimm'd that I may see
Thyself, Thyself alone.

I have nought to fear;
This darkness is the shadow of Thy wing;
Beneath it I am almost sacred—here
Can come no evil thing.

Give me now my lyre!
I feel the stirrings of a gift divine,
Within my bosom glows unearthly fire
Lit by no skill of mine.

—*John Milton.*

I once thought the ills of life were messages of vengeance—the thunderbolts of a vindictive God. But when Christ mounted my heart's throne, the thunderbolts became musical. Death was a chariot to bear me Home. Pain was an operation to heal disease. Bereavement was a lifting of my treasures to a safer bank. Poverty was the test of my love. Clouds were the trial of my faith. Surprise was the proof of my patience. The fires of life were the cleansing of the golden chain.—*George Matheson.*

"Fear none of those things which thou shalt suffer" *(Rev. 2:10).*

Known by our fruits

"Ye shall know them by their fruits. . . . Every good tree bringeth forth good fruit; but a corrupt tree bringeth forth evil fruit. . . . Wherefore by their fruits ye shall know them" (Matt. 7:16-17, 20).

What is the use of an apple tree if it never bears any apples?

And what is the use of calling yourself a Christian if there is no fruit in your life, no change in your conduct?

A boy went home from a meeting one evening, and told his little sister that he had got a new heart.

"Have you?" she innocently replied, "then please show it to me!"

And that is just what all Christians have to do, to show in their changed life and conduct that they have a new heart.—*Unknown.*

Actions speak louder than words, because they commonly cost more; we usually test the utterances of the lips by the conduct of the life. The words of promise spoken at the marriage altar are weighed in the scales of wedlock; they may prove to be solid gold, or they may be lighter than a feather. We test the solemn confessions and covenants made by many of you before this pulpit by the lives you are now leading before the world. Our Master's own challenge is, "by their fruits ye shall know them." The religious truth contained in a book, or in a creed, or in a discourse, is only a theory. The same truth, if wrought out into noble deeds and godly character becomes certified by experiment.

Christianity, attested by its fruits, is unanswerable. If it purifies the human heart; if it elevates the affections; if it conquers sinful lusts, and subdues evil passions; if it prompts to generous sympathies and noble deeds; if it sweetens the home and cleanses society; if it lifts fallen humanity up toward God; and if it makes its possessors the better, stronger, purer and holier—then doth it vindicate its divine origin and establish its divine authority. Such a religion no scoffer can laugh down, and no philosopher can silence.—*Theodore Cuyler.*

December 19

Strength in joy

"The joy of the Lord is your strength" (Neh. 8:10).
"These things have I spoken unto you, that my joy might remain in you, and that your joy might be full" (John 15:11).

The gladdest, brightest, happiest thing in all the universe is the Christian religion. There is so much trouble in the world; business men have so many anxieties; toiling men have so many fatigues; orphans have so many desolations. If there be any bright places on earth, show it to them. Let the Church of Jesus Christ be the most cheerful spot on earth.

Remember that your physical health is closely allied to your spiritual. The heart and the liver are only a few inches apart, and what affects the one affects the other. A historian records that by the sound of great laughter in Rome, Hannibal's assaulting army was frightened away in retreat. And there is in the great outbursting joy of a Christian's soul that which can drive back any infernal besiegement. Rats love dark closets, and Satan loves to burrow in a gloomy soul.—*De Witt Talmage.*

> Joy is a fruit that will not grow
> In nature's barren soil;
> All we can boast, till Christ we know,
> Is vanity and toil.
>
> But where the Lord has planted grace,
> And made His glories known,
> There fruits of heavenly joy and peace
> Are found, and there alone.
>
> A bleeding Savior seen by faith,
> A sense of pard'ning love;
> A hope that triumphs over death,
> Give joys like those above. . . .
>
> These are the joys which satisfy,
> And sanctify the mind;
> Which make the spirit mount on high,
> And leave the world behind.
> —*John Newton.*

If there is no sunshine in your religion, do not be surprised if nobody wants it.—*Unknown.*

Unselfish prayers

"I exhort therefore, that, first of all, supplications, prayers, intercessions, and giving of thanks, be made for all men" (1 Tim. 2:1).
"Brethren, my heart's desire and prayer to God for Israel is, that they might be saved" (Rom. 10:1).

The unselfish desires for others, that exhale from human hearts under the influence of the love which Christ plants in us, do come down in blessings on others, as the moisture drawn up by the sun may descend in fructifying rain on far-off pastures of the wilderness. We help one another when we pray for one another.—*Alexander Maclaren.*

There are innumerable people who have reached a crisis in their life; they are "white already to harvest." We find them everywhere, not only in the foreign field, but in the people living beside us, and the way we discern it is not by intellect, not by suggestions, but by prayer. Think of the countless crises in people's lives at this time; they are at the parting of the ways. "Say not ye, There are yet four months, and then cometh harvest? behold, I say unto you, Lift up your eyes, and look on the fields; for they are white already to harvest." "Pray ye therefore the Lord of the harvest, that he will send forth labourers into his harvest."—*Oswald Chambers.*

> Not for My name thy prayer was made,
> Not for My sake thy praises paid.
> My gift is sacrifice; My blood
> Was shed for human brotherhood,
> And till thy brother's woe is thine
> Thy heartbeat knows no throb of Mine.
> Come, leave thy selfish hopes, and see
> The birthright of humanity!
> Shun sorrow not; be brave to bear
> The world's dark weight of sin and care;
> Spend and be spent, yearn, suffer, give,
> And in thy brethren learn to live.
> —*Unknown.*

December 21
Doing that counts

"Therefore whosoever heareth these sayings of mine, and doeth them, I will liken him unto a wise man, which built his house upon a rock" (Matt. 7:24). "Not every one that saith unto me, Lord, Lord, shall enter into the kingdom of heaven; but he that doeth the will of my Father which is in heaven"
(Matt. 7:21).

Do is still the keynote of the chapter. He that doeth righteousness is righteous. He that doeth the will of the heavenly Father, he and he only shall enter into the kingdom of Heaven. By this we are to know false prophets, testing their doctrine by their deeds. Holiness is not in saying, "Lord, Lord!" Pious phrases, pious tones, pious looks, pious professions, count for nothing, unless there is the doing of the Father's will. He that heareth and doeth not, builds his house upon the sand; he that heareth and doeth, builds his house upon a rock.

Then our Lord closes the sermon with the parable of the two builders: he that heareth and doeth; and he that heareth and doeth not. The figure continues the line of thought which immediately precedes the parable. Each house was a doing—a labor. Probably, building on the sand is the greater labor of the two. But the wise man's labor was to get on to the Rock. As soon as that was his foundation the Rock gave its strength to the whole building. Every stone in it was firm, because the foundation was good. THAT ROCK WAS CHRIST.
—*Mark Guy Pearse.*

What we do should be done to purpose; effect something; not only move ourselves, but move others—out of their sins to Christ; move the Church, and better it, and not be at an everlasting standstill.

Erasmus tells us of a man, named Rabirius, who wanted his servant, Syrus, to get up, and called to him to move.

"I do move," replied Syrus.

"I see you move," rejoined the master, "but you move nothing!"

Now, there may be much religious activity, and yet not a sinner moved out of his sins, and the Church very little advanced in holiness. When we move, we should move to some purpose, and accomplish something!—*James Caughey.*

Kindly reproof

"Rebuke a wise man, and he will love thee" (Prov. 9:8).
"Brethren, if any of you do err from the truth, and one convert him; Let him know, that he . . . shall save a soul from death, and shall hide a multitude of sins" (James 5:19-20).

Speak the truth, by all means! Speak it so that no man can mistake the utterance. Be bold and fearless in your rebuke of error and in your keener rebuke of wrongdoing; all Christ's witnesses are bound to be thus "valiant for the truth," but be human, and loving, and gentle, and brotherly, the while. If you must deliver the Redeemer's testimony, deliver it with the Redeemer's tears. Look, straight-eyed, and kindly, upon the vilest, as a man ought to look upon a man, both royal, although the one is wearing, and the other has pawned his crown.—*W. Morley Punshon.*

> They are slaves who fear to speak
> For the fallen and the weak.
> They are slaves who will not choose
> Hatred, scoffing, and abuse,
> Rather than in silence shrink
> From the Truth they needs must think.
> —*Unknown.*

It often happens that friends need remonstrance and even reproof. When these are administered in a kindly spirit they ought to be taken in good part. But somehow or other there is truth in what friend Terence says in his Andria: "Compliance gets us friends, plain speaking hate."

Plain speaking is the cause of trouble, if the result of it is resentment, which is poison to friendship; but compliance is really the cause of much more trouble, because by indulging his faults it lets a friend plunge into headlong ruin. But the man who is most to blame is he who resents plain speaking and allows flattery to egg him on to his ruin.

If we remonstrate, it should be without bitterness; if we reprove, there should be no word of insult. . . . But if a man's ears are so closed to plain speaking that he cannot bear to hear the truth from a friend, we may give him up in despair. This remark of Cato's, as so many of his did, shows great acuteness: "There are people who owe more to bitter enemies than to apparently pleasant friends: the former often speak the truth, the latter never." Besides, it is a strange paradox that the recipients of advice should feel no annoyance where they ought to feel it, and yet feel so much where they ought not. They are not at all vexed at having committed a fault, but very angry at being reproved for it.—*Cicero.*

December 23

The Bible my guide

"Thou shalt guide me with thy counsel, and afterwards receive me to glory"
(Psa. 73:24).
"Do not my words do good to him that walketh uprightly?" (Micah 2:7).

To candid, reasonable men, I am not afraid to lay open what have been the inmost thoughts of my heart. I have thought, I am the creature of a day, passing through life, as an arrow through the air. I am a spirit come from God, and returning to God, just hovering over the great gulf, till, a few moments hence, I am no more seen! I drop into an unchangeable eternity. I want to know one thing, the way to Heaven: how to land safely on that happy shore. God Himself has condescended to teach the way; for this very end He came from Heaven. He hath written it down in a Book. At any price, give me the Book of God! I have it; here is knowledge enough for me.—*John Wesley.*

> It is so sweet to trust Thy Word alone:
>   I do not ask to see
> The unveiling of Thy purpose, or the shining
> Of future light on mysterious untwining;
> Thy promise roll is all my own—
>   Thy Word is enough for me!
>   —*Frances Ridley Havergal.*

Let us read the Bible as we never read it before. We must go forth, we must live above the world, if we would wish to enjoy the pure humanity which it fetters. And how? We cannot go without a guide, that were self-conceited; but what guide shall we take? Oh, I am sick of doctors and divines! Books! There is no end of them: mud, fire, acids, alkalies, every foreign ingredient contaminating pure truth. Shall we listen to the voice of God's Spirit alone? Yes! but where? Has He not spoken to those very bookmakers? And hath not every man his own gift? Each hero the appointed witness of some peculiar truth? Then, must we plunge again into that vast, muddy, blind, contradictory book-ocean? No! Is there not one immutable book? One pure written wisdom? The Bible, speaking of God's truth in words meant for me. There may be other meanings in that Book besides the plain one. But this I will believe, that whatever mysticism the mystic may find there, the simple human being, the lover of his wife, the father of children, the lover of God's earth, glorying in matter and humanity, not for that which they are, but that which they ought to be and will be, will find in the Bible the whole mystery solved—an answer to every riddle, a guide in every difficulty.—*Charles Kingsley.*

Life's inn still full

"There was no room . . . in the inn" (Luke 2:7).
"The foxes have holes, and the birds of the air have nests; but the Son of man hath not where to lay his head" (Matt. 8:20).

What Christ is ever seeking is room. The Bethlehem Inn was too full to receive Him, and lost its greatest opportunity. To each of us, in our Inn of Life, comes the same Christ, seeking "room." Are we too crowded to give admission to the King of kings?

> No room!
> No room!
> No room for Thee,
> Thou Man of Galilee!
> The house is full,
> Yea, overfull.
> There is no room for Thee,
> Pass on! Pass on!
>
> Nay—see!
> The place is packed.
> We scarce have room
> For our own selves,
> See how shall we
> Find room for Thee,
> Thou Man of Galilee—
> Pass on! Pass on!
>
> But—if Thou shouldst
> This way again,
> And we can find
> So much as one small corner
> Free from guest,
> Not then in vain
> But now—
> The house is full.
> Pass on!
>
> Christ passes
> On His ceaseless quest,
> Nor will He rest
> With any,
> Save as Chiefest Guest.
> —*Unknown.*

The loveliness of Christ

"Whom have I in heaven but thee? and there is none upon earth that I desire beside thee" (Psa. 73:25).

"But he was wounded for our transgressions, he was bruised for our iniquities: the chastisement of our peace was upon him; and with his stripes we are healed" (Isa. 53:5).

He became Son of Man that we might become sons of God. He came from Heaven to earth that we might go from earth to Heaven. He was rich, yet for our sakes He became poor.

He lived in poverty and was reared in obscurity. He had no formal education. His relatives were inconspicuous and uninfluential.

In infancy He startled a king; in boyhood He puzzled the doctors; in manhood He walked upon the billows and hushed the sea to sleep. He healed the multitudes without medicine and made no charge for His services. He never wrote a book, yet not all the libraries of the country could hold the books that could be written about Him. He never wrote a song, yet He has furnished the theme of more songs than all the song-writers combined. He never founded a college yet all the schools together cannot boast of as many students as He has. Great men have come and gone, yet He lives on. Death could not destroy Him, the grave could not hold Him.

All failed, but He never. The ever-perfect One, He is Chief among ten thousand. He is altogether lovely.

> Majestic sweetness sits enthroned
> Upon the Savior's brow;
> His head with radiant glories crowned,
> His lips with grace o'erflow. . . .
>
> No mortal can with Him compare,
> Among the sons of men;
> Fairer is He than all the fair
> That fill the heavenly train.
>
> He saw me plunged in deep distress,
> He flew to my relief;
> For me He bore the shameful cross,
> And carried all my grief. . . .
>
> Since from His bounty I receive
> Such proofs of love divine,
> Had I a thousand hearts to give,
> Lord, they should all be Thine.
> —*Samuel Stennett.*

God's hidden purpose

"It is not in man that walketh to direct his steps" (Jer. 10:23).
"His going forth is prepared as the morning" (Hosea 6:3).

The purposes of God seemed hidden to Mrs. Studd when her husband left for Africa, leaving his loved ones behind. Norman Grubb quotes a letter written by Mrs. Studd revealing her struggle and victory:

"As I thought of all that was going to happen to me, I began to weep. I do not often weep, but I wept sore that night. Then I thought, 'This will never do . . . I shall be ill tomorrow, and unable to help anyone.' Going up in the train that day to Waterloo, I had been reading a book in which there were two references, one was Psalm 34, and the other Daniel 3:29. . . so I opened my Bible. The very first words seemed almost to knock me down. The first was, 'I will,' it means determination, it means grit, courage; 'I will bless'—I will make the Lord happy—and that was not to be attained by weeping. 'I will bless the Lord at all times'—now! And before I got to the end of that verse, the tears were gone, and I got to that point where I could say, 'I will make the Lord happy now.'

"Then I read on, 'I sought the Lord, and he heard me, and delivered me from all my fears.' 'This poor man cried, and the Lord heard him, and saved him out of all his troubles' and then the last was the most astonishing of all: 'He keepeth all his bones, not one of them is broken.'. . . I just felt every fear was gone; all my fears, all my troubles, all that 'left alone' was going to mean, all the fears of malarial fever and the poisoned arrows of the savages; and I went to bed rejoicing. I just laughed 'the laugh of faith' that night. I rose from my knees and wrote the experience to my husband and posted it to Marseilles, though he had not yet left this country."

God is working out His purpose even tho' we go alone:
It may take us from our loved ones, lead us far away from home;
It will be the greatest pleasure just to feel His presence near,
And to know that God is working out the purpose to Him dear.

God is working out His purpose; never murmur or repine;
For our future's in His keeping, gladly to His will resign.
When at last the veil is lifted and the shadows flee away,
We shall understand His purpose thro' one glad, eternal day. . . .

—*Mrs. F. W. Suffield.*

December 27

God gives us grace, but we build character

"And beside this, giving all diligence, add to your faith virtue; and to virtue knowledge; And to knowledge temperance; and to temperance patience; and to patience godliness; And to godliness brotherly kindness; and to brotherly kindness charity. For if these things be in you, and abound, they make you that ye shall neither be barren nor unfruitful in the knowledge of our Lord Jesus Christ" (2 Peter 1:5-8).

Reputation is what men say we are: Character is what God says we are.

Christ's reputation took Him to the Cross, His character to the Throne.

When wealth is lost, nothing is lost; when health is lost, something is lost; when character is lost, all is lost.—*Motto over the walls of a school in Germany.*

> I have to live with myself, and so
> I want to be fit for myself to know;
> I don't want to stand, with the setting sun
> And hate myself for the things I've done.
> I want to go out with my head erect;
> I want to deserve all men's respect;
> But here in the struggles for fame and self
> I want to be able to like myself.
> I don't want to look at myself and know
> That I'm bluster and bluff and empty show.
> Whatever happens, I want to be
> Self-respecting and conscience-free.
> —*Unknown.*

The great question is not what you will get, but what you will become. The greatest wealth you ever can get will be in yourself.—*Horace Bushnell.*

Every man is a joint architect with God to make his own future. God makes capacity, man makes character. You cannot dream yourself into a character, you must forge yourself one.—*J. G. Carter.*

Prayer before work

"Watch and pray, that ye enter not into temptation: the spirit indeed is willing, but the flesh is weak" (Matt. 26:41).
"And there is none that calleth upon thy name, that stirreth up himself to take hold of thee" (Isa. 64:7).

There have been few men more faithful in prayer than George Müller. What better authority could we have, therefore, than his testimony as to the temporary loss of inward peace and power when prayer was neglected even a few days:

"I would offer here a word of warning to my fellow-believers. Often the work of the Lord itself may be a temptation to keep us from that communion with Him that is so essential to the benefit of our own souls. On the 19th I had left Dartmouth, conversed a good deal that day, preached in the evening, walked afterwards eight miles, had only about five hours sleep, traveled again the next day twenty-five miles, preached twice, and conversed very much besides, went to bed at eleven and rose before five. All this shows that my body and spirit required rest, and, therefore, however careless about the Lord's work I might have appeared to my brethren, I ought to have had a great deal of quiet time for prayer and reading the Word, especially as I had a long journey before me that day, and as I was going to Bristol, which in itself required much prayer. Instead of this I hurried to the prayer-meeting after a few minutes' private prayer. But let none think that public prayer will make up for closet communion.

"Then again, afterwards, when I ought to have withdrawn myself, as it were, by force, from the company of beloved brethren and sisters, and given my testimony for the Lord (and, indeed, it would have been the best testimony I could have given them), by telling them that I needed secret communion with the Lord: I did not do so, but spent the time, till the coach came, in conversation with them. Now, however profitable in some respects it may have been to those whom I was with on that morning, yet my own soul needed food, and not having had it, I was lean, and felt the effects of it the whole day, and hence I believe it came that I was dumb on the coach."

And, again, George Müller says:

"These last three days I have had very little real communion with God, and have therefore been very weak spiritually, and have several times felt irritability of temper. May God in His mercy help me to have more secret prayer."

If I had only prayed more; Oh, that I had prayed a hundredfold more.

—Andrew Bonar.

December 29
The price of enlargement

"After that ye have suffered a while, make you perfect, stablish, strengthen, settle you" (1 Peter 5:10).
"That I may know him, and the power of his resurrection, and the fellowship of his sufferings" (Phil. 3:10).

The range of our possible sufferings is determined by the largeness and nobility of our aims. It is possible to evade a multitude of sorrows by the cultivation of an insignificant life. Indeed, if it be a man's ambition to avoid the troubles of life the recipe is perfectly simple: let him shed his ambitions in every direction, let him cut the wings of every soaring purpose, and let him assiduously cultivate a little life, with the fewest correspondences and relations. By this means a whole continent of afflictions will be escaped and will remain unknown.

Cultivate negations, and large tracts of the universe will cease to exist. For instance, cultivate deafness, and you are saved from the horrors of discords. Cultivate blindness, and you are saved from the assault of the ugly. Stupefy a sense, and you shut out a world. And therefore it is literally true that if you want to get through the world with the smallest trouble you must reduce yourself to the smallest compass. That is why so many people, and even so many professedly Christian people, get through life so easily, and with a minimum acquaintance with tribulation. It is because they have reduced their souls to a minimum, that their course through the years is not so much the transit of a man as the passage of an amoeba. They have no finely organized nervous system, for they have deadened and arrested the growth of one nerve after another; they have cut the sensitive wires which bind the individual to the race, and they are cosily self-contained, and the shuddering sorrow of the world never disturbs their seclusion.—*J. H. Jowett.*

> Who liveth best? Not he whose sail
> Swept on by favoring tide and gale,
> Swift wins the haven fair;
> But he whose spirit strong doth still
> A victory wrest from every ill;
> Whose faith sublime
> On every cloud a rainbow paints—
> 'Tis he redeems the time.
> —*Unknown.*

The quickening Word

"Enquire, I pray thee, at the word of the Lord to day" (2 Chron. 18:4).
"Thy word hath quickened me" (Psa. 119:50).

The man of one book is always formidable, but when that book is the Bible he is irresistible.—*W. M. Taylor.*

There is no feature more noticeable in Bunyan's character than the *devout earnestness with which he studied the Divine Word,* and the *reverence which he cherished for it* throughout the whole of his life.

In the time of his agony, when "a restless wanderer after rest," he battled with fierce temptation, and was beset with Antinomian error, he gratefully records, "The Bible was precious to me in those days." After deliverance it was his congenial life-work to exalt its honor, and to proclaim its truths.

Is he recommending growth in grace to his hearers? The Word is to be the aliment of their life. "Every grace is nourished by the Word, and without it there is no thrift in the soul."

Has he announced some fearless exposition of truth? Hark how he disarms opposition and challenges scrutiny! "Give me a hearing: take me to the Bible, and let me find in thy heart no favor if thou find me to swerve from the standard."

Is he uplifting the Word above the many inventions of his fellows? Mark the racy homeliness of his assertion: "A little from God is better than a great deal from men. What is from men is often tumbled over and over. Things that we receive at God's hand come to us as things from the minting-house. Old truths are always new to us if they come with the smell of Heaven upon them."

Is his righteous soul vexed with the indifference of the faithful, or with the impertinence of the profane? How manfully he proclaims his conviction of a pressing want of the times! "There wanteth even in the hearts of God's people a greater reverence for the Word of God than to this day appeareth among us; and this let me say, that want of reverence for the Word is the ground of all the disorders that are in the heart, life, conversation, or Christian communion."

—*W. Morley Punshon.*

December 31
Taking inventory

"Examine yourselves, whether ye be in the faith; prove your own selves"
(2 Cor. 13:5).
"But let every man prove his own work, and then shall he have rejoicing in himself alone, and not in another" (Gal. 6:4).
"Examine me, O Lord, and prove me" (Psa. 26:2).

I believe this is about the time of the year in which men take account of stock, in everything except their souls. In the shoe and leather business they know just how much has come and how much has gone, and where they are. In the book business they know the whole account. So in every great concern and establishment of various businesses. They want to know how they stand as it regards riches. But alas! where is your bookkeeper and your cashier, that shall take account of stock so that you may know whether you have been gaining in knowledge or idling away your time; whether you have gained in a stable conscience, or have let your conscience be like a weather-vane, blown about by custom or by the breath of men; whether you have been brought nearer to men, and into more loving relations with them, or whether you have been disintegrating?—*Henry Ward Beecher.*

> To leave the old with a burst of song,
> To recall the right and forgive the wrong;
> To forget the thing that binds you fast
> To the vain regrets of the year that's past;
> To have the strength to let go your hold
> On the not worthwhile of the days grown old;
>
> To dare go forth with a purpose true,
> To the unknown task of the year that's new;
> To help your brother along the road,
> To do his work, and lift his load;
> To add your gift to the world's good cheer,
> Is to have and to give a Glad New Year.
> —*Words and Deeds.*

OTHER BOOKS BY HARVEY

Amazing Book, The, Vol. 1
Amazing Book, The, Vol. 2
Asking Father
Call Back 1: Illness
Call Back 2: Loneliness
Call Back 3: Frustration
Call Back 4: Opposition 1
Call Back 5: Opposition 2
Call Back 6: Handicaps 1
Call Back 7: Handicaps 2
Call Back 8: Old Age
Christian's Daily Challenge, The
Covetousness
Father Calling
Him or It?
Household Foes
How They Prayed 1: Household Prayers
How They Prayed 2: Ministers' Prayers
How They Prayed 3: Missionaries and Revival
King's Diamond, The
Kneeling We Triumph 1
Kneeling We Triumph 2
Let My People Go!
New Creation, The
Royal Counsel
Royal Exchange
Royal Insignia
Royal Pilgrimage
Royal Purposes
Soul Sculpture
They Knew Their God 1
They Knew Their God 2
They Knew Their God 3
They Knew Their God 4
They Knew Their God 5
They Knew Their God 6
To Judge or Not to Judge

For more information go to: www.harveycp.com

Textual Index

Genesis

2:2	June 2
2:9	June 26
2:12	Jan. 19
4:9	Sept. 7
6:9	Apr. 4
16:13	Feb. 5
22:16-17	Aug. 14
23:19	Aug. 14
24:12	Jan. 29
24:27	May 15
26:28	Feb. 6
28:15	Feb. 25
32:24	Aug. 6
32:26	Jan. 11
39:3-4	Feb. 6
41:9	May 7
42:36	Nov. 17
50:20	June 6

Exodus

1:12	Jan. 31
3:11	Aug. 1
10:22-23	Apr. 26
13:21	July 20
15:18	Oct. 12
21: 5	May 28
23: 2	Nov. 10
32:29	June 7
33:14	Oct. 22
34:12	May 1
34:30	Mar. 15

Leviticus

19:18	Mar. 8

Numbers

9:8	July 19
14:9	June 3
23:20	Mar. 31

Deuteronomy

5:32-33	Dec. 4
8:3	Oct. 23
12:7	Sept. 14
17:19	Mar. 3
26:11	Mar. 9
28:12	July 21
32:10	July 6
32:12	Mar. 13
32:47	June 1
33:25	May 29

Joshua

1:7	Mar. 30
1:8	Feb. 20
11:15	June 14

Judges

6:14	Dec. 15
6:15	Aug. 1

Ruth

2:2	Nov. 30
2:11	Feb. 6

1 Samuel

1:27	April 11
2:19	May 20
3:10	Nov. 2
3:18	Apr. 22
9:27	Aug. 21
15:22	May 16
17:40	May 20

2 Samuel

6:20	Mar. 31
10:12	Aug. 28
22:28	Sept. 18
24:24	July 29

1 Kings		Neh. cont.	
3:9	June 17	6:9	Dec. 7
11:4	May 19	8:10	Dec. 19
17:13-15	Nov. 12	12:43	May 23
18:24	Feb. 1		
18:36-38	July 15	**Esther**	
20:4	July 13	4:16	Dec. 9

2 Kings		Job	
2:15	Sept. 27	1:8	Feb. 22
2:21	July 3	5:23	June 3
3:17-18	June 25	6:6	Oct. 14
4:9	June 5	6:25	Nov. 18
4:32-33	Feb. 7	10:12	June 1
5:13	Aug. 7	17:9	June 26
6:17	Jan. 4	22:25	Jan. 19
19:20	June 22	23:12	June 8
		29:3	Dec. 6

1 Chronicles		34:29	May 4
16:11	Sept. 29	41:25	Feb. 14
28:10	Mar. 10	42:12	Jan. 31
29:5	June 7		
29:15	Apr. 20	**Psalms**	
		1:2-3	Sept. 26
2 Chronicles		1:3	July 6
15:7	Apr. 23	4:1	May 11
15:8	Aug. 28	4:3	Feb. 16
16:9	Feb. 5	4:7	Feb. 8
18:4	Dec. 30	5:3	Feb. 23
18:13	May 27	5:8	July 20
19:2	Nov. 20	5:11	June 11
19:11	Jan. 16	16:8	June 13
30:8	Mar. 7	16:11	May 9, June 11
32:31	July 8	18:6	July 27
		19:10	Jan. 6
Ezra		19:12	Jan. 13
6:22	Aug. 10	19:14	Nov. 18
7:28	Oct. 18	25:9	Mar. 13
8:23	Apr. 11	26:2	Dec. 31
		27:4	Sept. 5
Nehemiah		27:14	Mar. 30
1:6	Nov. 22	29:2	July 17
2:20	Mar. 23	31:15	Apr. 14

Songs of Solomon

2:15	Apr. 12
4:16	Oct. 3

Isaiah

1:19	Nov. 21, Nov. 27
9:6	Apr. 17, Oct. 15
12:2	Sept. 25
12:3	Dec. 3
22:22	Jan. 25
27:3	July 6
30:15	Sept. 2
30:18	July 1
30:21	Oct. 31
32:18	June 2
33:17	Oct. 29
34:16	Apr. 7
35:10	Oct. 10
40:28	Sept. 10
40:31	Aug. 18
42:16	Oct. 31
43:10	June 18
43:22	May 8
44:3	Apr. 24
45:13	Jan. 7
48:10	Mar. 28
48:17	Jan. 7
51:7	July 18
52:1	July 25
53:5	Dec. 25
53:11	Mar. 19
54:11	Nov. 1
54:13	May 8
55: 8-9	Oct. 4
57:15	Jan. 12
58:6-7	Jan. 27
58:9	Feb. 16
62:1	Mar. 23
64:4	Feb. 26
64:7	Dec. 28
65:14	Apr. 9

Jeremiah

1:6-7	Aug. 1
1:7-8	July 12
1:9	July 12
10:23	Dec. 26
15:16	May 12, Oct. 23
17:8	Oct. 28
22:29	Aug. 30
23:4	May 10
23:22	July 16
23:28	Mar. 25
31:3	Nov. 29
32:42	Nov. 11

Lamentations

3:25	Feb. 26

Ezekiel

22:30	May 5
33:30	July 5
47:9	Nov. 8

Daniel

5:11	June 5
6:3	Nov. 16
6:10	Feb. 7
10:8	Sept. 20
12:3	Sept. 8

Hosea

2:14	Nov. 29
6:3	Dec. 26

Micah

2:7	Dec. 23
6:8	Apr. 4, Aug. 19
7:7	Jan. 2

Habakkuk

2:3	July 1
3:19	Sept. 29

Zephaniah		Matt. cont.	
3:13	Nov. 23	11:29-30	July 26
		12:30	Aug. 8
Zechariah		13:12	Feb. 10
4:10	Nov. 5	13:44	July 21
8:16	May 5	14:23	Oct. 26
14:21	Mar. 1	16:24	June 12
		17:20	Dec. 13
Malachi		20:28	Jan. 9
2:6	Nov. 23	21:2	Feb. 11
3:3	Sept. 12	21:22	May 17
		21:28	Dec. 14
Matthew		21:42	Mar. 3
1:21	Mar. 26	22:9	Feb. 11
3:11	Feb. 1	22:37	Dec. 8
4:19	Aug. 31	23:3	Jan. 21
5:5	Oct. 30	24:35	Apr. 7
5:6	May 14	24:45	Jan. 3
5:11-12	Nov. 13	25:15	May 29
5:13	Oct. 14	25:18	Apr. 6
5:14-16	Nov. 26	25:28	Apr. 6
6:6	June 13, Sept. 20	25:35-36	Apr. 13
6:10	Apr. 28	25:40	Jan. 27
6:11	Aug. 29	26:18	Feb. 11
6:14	Mar. 8	26:39	Mar. 5
6:19-21	Nov. 6	26:40	Apr. 29
6:31-32	Apr. 15	26:41	Mar. 18, Dec. 28
6:33	May 24	26:56	Aug. 13
6:34	Oct. 21	27:42	Mar. 4
7:2	Oct. 16	28:7	Apr. 3
7:7	Oct. 8	28:19	Feb. 11
7:13-14	Apr. 21		
7:16-17,20	Dec. 18	**Mark**	
7:21	Dec. 21	1:20	Jan. 14
7:24	Dec. 21	6:31	Aug. 6, Nov. 14
8:15	Dec. 7	6:46	Oct. 17
8:20	Dec. 24	7:33	Aug. 6
9:37	Nov. 30	8:38	Jan. 16
9:38	May 26	9:23	May 13
10:7	Apr. 3	10:21	Dec.11
10:8	Sept. 22	10:38	May 11
10:38	Dec. 11	11:24	Oct. 8
11:29	Aug. 19	12:14	May 27

Mark cont.		John	
12:44	Nov. 12	1:14	Oct. 29
14:9	Mar. 6	2:5	Mar. 10
16:15	Feb. 11	2:7	Apr. 1
		3:8	July 11
Luke		3:16	Nov. 9
1:53	June 25	4:11	Aug. 26
2:7	May 6, Dec. 24	5:30	Sept. 9
2:49	Feb. 24	5:39	Sept. 16
4:4	June 8	6:9	Nov. 5
5:15-16	Oct. 17	6:10	Nov. 14
6:22	Dec. 16	6:63	May 22
6:23	Nov. 7	6:66	Aug. 13
8:1	Apr. 9	7:17	Nov. 21
9:10	Nov. 14	7:24	Mar. 14
9:23	Jan. 26	7:37	Apr. 24
9:44	Jan. 24	7:38	Nov. 8
10:3	May 18	9:4	May 3
10:26	Mar. 11	10:7,10	Feb. 10
10:33	Sept. 7	11:9	Oct. 19
10:37	Dec. 14	12:32	Aug. 26
10:42	Mar. 17	12:43	Feb. 2
11:9	May 26	13:7	Nov. 25
12:24	Apr. 15	14:12-13	Sept. 11
12:37	Mar. 18	14:23	Mar. 21, Nov. 3
12:50	Mar. 19	14:27	Sept. 13
13:7	Oct. 28	15:2	Feb. 28
13:33	Aug. 29	15:3	May 22
14:21	Feb. 11	15:4	Nov. 3
14:27	Jan. 26	15:5	Dec. 1
15:18	Dec. 14	15:7	July 15, Dec. 1
16:10	Jan. 3, June 28	15:11	Dec. 19
16:12	June 28	15:13	Jan. 9
18:1	Jan. 20	15:16	Apr. 30
18:27	Jan. 23	15:20	June 20
19:17	Aug. 7	16:15	Aug. 16
21:33	Nov. 19	16:22	Aug. 10
21:34	Oct. 21	16:32	Sept. 30
22:27	Mar. 1	17:4	May 3
22:32	Feb. 7, Aug. 31	17:13	May 9
24:32	Mar. 15	17:14	May 12
24:52-53	Jan. 10	17:23	Jan. 8

John cont.			**Rom. cont.**	
17:26	Oct. 7		5:20	Oct. 6
20:4-8	July 23		6:5	Jan. 17
			6:7	Oct. 6
Acts			6:13	Mar. 7
4:13	Sept. 27		8:6	July 4
4:29	Feb. 21		8:14	May 15
4:31	June 25, Feb. 21		8:15	June 23
5:20	July 16		8:18	Aug. 20
5:32	May 16		8:31	Nov. 17
5:41	June 20		10:1	Dec. 20
6:15	Apr. 19		10:9	June 18
9:5	Nov. 27		10:17	Dec. 10
9:6	Nov. 2		12:1	July 13
9:15	Apr. 30		12:3	June 9
9:29	Mar. 30		12:11	Feb. 24
9:36	June 29		12:12	Mar. 2
10:31	Mar. 6, Nov. 22		12:16	July 14
13:47	June 21		12:21	Feb. 29
13:52	July 9		13:8	Apr. 25
16:6	Aug. 21		13:10	Dec. 8
16:7	Aug. 21		13:11	July 25
16:17	Nov. 16		14:7	Aug. 8
16:25	Apr. 2		14:8	May 30
17:11	Sept. 16		14:13	Oct. 25
17:28	Mar. 20		14:17	Oct. 10
18:9	Oct. 13		14:19	Oct. 25
19:36	Sept. 2		14:23	Dec. 10
20:27	May 10		15:2	Apr. 16
21:14	Sept. 9		15:4	Mar. 2, Mar. 29
22:14	Sept. 15		15:13	June 11
24:16	June 15			
26:7	May 18		**1 Corinthians**	
26:16	Jan. 7		1:27	Apr. 27
26:29	Mar. 22		2:2	Apr. 21
28:27	Jan. 24		2:16	July 10
			3:8	Sept. 6
			3:16	Dec. 2
Romans			4:3	Dec. 5
5:3	May 23		4:9-10	Dec. 16
5:3-4	July 8		5:6	Dec. 12
5:5	Oct. 7		6:19	Jan. 8
5:19	Aug. 22		7:16	May 19, Dec. 12

385

1 Cor. cont.

7:29	Aug. 9
10:24	Oct. 27
10:31	Feb. 15
10:33	Apr. 13
12:26	Apr. 28
12:31	Mar. 17
13:12	Nov. 25
13:13	Sept. 4
14:12	July 24
15:25	Oct. 12
15:28	Mar. 22
16:9	Aug. 11
16:13	Nov. 20

2 Corinthians

1:4	July 22
1:5	June 10
1:7	July 22
1:11	June 22
1:12	June 17
1:20	Feb. 3
3:2	Mar. 12
3:3	Mar. 12, Oct. 11
3:12	Mar. 25
3:18	Aug. 3
5:15	Mar. 4
6:10	Aug. 16, Sept. 14
6:14-16	May 6
6:16	Sept. 17, Dec. 2
7:4	Mar. 25
8:9	June 12
8:11	Mar. 10
9:2	Feb. 4, Aug. 22
9:6	Oct. 16
9:8	Jan. 1
10:4	Aug. 24
10:7	Mar. 14
11:30	Aug. 20
12:8-9	Mar. 5
12:9	Jan. 23, Apr. 1
12:10	Dec. 17
12:15	Sept. 22
13:5	Dec. 31

Galatians

1:10	Feb. 2
2:20	Feb. 18, May 30
3:6	Aug. 25
5:7	Feb. 12
5:22	Feb. 8, Sept. 4
5:25	Sept. 17
5:26	Feb. 17
6:2	Jan. 5, Apr. 8
6:3	July 14
6:4	Dec. 31
6:5	Apr. 8
6:10	Sept. 21

Ephesians

1:23	Aug. 12
2:4	Nov. 9
2:10	Sept. 28
3:9	Jan. 4
3:17	Sept. 19
3:19	Aug. 12, Nov. 9
4:1	Nov. 10
4:13	Aug. 12
5:8	June 21
5:14	July 25
5:16	Aug. 23
5:17	June 16
5:18	May 14
6:6-7	Dec. 5

Philippians

1:3-4	Apr. 2
1:21	May 30
2:3	Feb. 17
2:4	Oct. 27
2:5	July 10
2:7	Sept. 24
2:8	Sept. 24
2:12-13	Apr. 18
2:15	Jan. 22
2:16	Oct. 11
3:7-8	Jan. 30
3:8-10	May 25

Phi. cont.

3:10	Dec. 29
3:13	Dec. 4
3:14	July 24
4:4	Jan. 10
4:6	Sept. 10
4:7	Sept. 13
4:11	Apr. 5
4:11-12	Mar. 16
4:13	Dec. 13
4:18	Aug. 2

Colossians

1:11	Aug. 5
1:19	Oct. 15
1:27	July 28
2:5	July 28
3:3	Feb. 18
3:10	Jan. 17
3:15	Feb. 13
3:16	July 5
4:2	Feb. 23

1 Thessalonians

1:6-7	Aug. 3
1:6	July 9
1:8	Apr. 16
2:13	June 19
3:4	Nov. 15
3:12	Feb. 12
3:13	Jan. 22
4:9	Apr. 25
4:10	June 26
4:11	Oct. 26
5:6	Apr. 29
5:11	Oct. 9
5:15	Oct. 9
5:16-18	Apr. 2
5:23	Feb. 15

2 Thessalonians

1:7	Nov. 24
3:5	June 30
3:16	Feb. 13, Nov. 24

1 Timothy

1:18	Nov. 28
1:19	June 15
2:1	Dec. 20
2:8	June 4
4:2	June 15
4:12	July 7
4:15	Feb. 20, Mar. 24

2 Timothy

1:6	Jan. 1
1:8	July 16
1:9	Dec. 15
2:3	Nov. 28
2:21	July 2, Oct. 20
3:12	Oct. 24
4:7	June 27
4:16	Sept. 30

Titus

1:9	Jan. 18
2:7	July 7
2:14	Feb. 4
3:1	July 2, Oct. 20

Hebrews

4:1	Oct. 22
4:3	July 30
4:9	Oct. 22
4:12	Aug. 30
5:8	June 10
5:12	Aug. 27
6:1	Aug. 27
8:9	Feb. 9
8:10	Sept. 19
10:34	May 21
10:38	Mar. 27
11:1	Aug. 25
11:8	July 11
11:26	July 18, Oct. 1
11:33	Jan. 6, Feb. 3, Aug. 4
11:34	Apr. 27, Oct. 2

Heb. cont.

12:1	Aug. 5
12:2	Oct. 1
12:10	Sept. 18
12:11	Feb. 28
13:5	Feb. 25
13:6	Sept. 23
13:15	Mar. 9
13:21	Sept. 15

James

1:2	May 21
1:5-6	Dec. 6
1:22	Jan. 21
1:26	Aug. 17
2:26	Apr. 18
3:5	June 9, Aug. 17
3:6	Aug. 17
3:8-10	Aug. 17
3:17	May 4
4:3	June 4
4:6	Jan. 12
4:7-8	May 2
4:14	Apr. 20
4:17	June 14
5:16	May 7, Nov. 4
5:17	Nov. 4
5:19-20	Dec. 22
5:20	Sept. 8

1 Peter

1:6	June 24
1:7	Feb. 14
1:17	Jan. 28
1:25	Nov. 19
2:2	Sept. 26
3:13-14	Sept. 1
4:1	July 10
4:13	Nov. 7
4:15-16	Oct. 24
5:6	Sept. 3
5:8	May 2
5:10	Oct. 18, Dec. 29

2 Peter

1:3	May 24
1:4	Nov. 11
1:5-8	Dec. 27
2:9	June 24
3:14	Jan. 13

1 John

1:3	Jan. 11
2:29	June 29
3:1	June 30
3:2	July 11, Nov. 25
3:16	July 29
3:16-17	Jan. 15
3:21	June 4
3:22	May 17
4:16	June 30
4:18	Mar. 21, June 23
5:4	Feb. 29, May 13
5:14-15	Aug. 24

Revelation

1:3	Mar. 11
2:3	Jan. 5
2:10	Dec. 17
2:17	July 4
3:7	Jan. 25
7:14	June 27, Nov. 15
12:11	Dec. 9
21:7	Feb. 29

Index of Authors

Brooks, Phillips	Jan. 31, Mar. 8, Apr. 10, 18, May 30, June 15, July 7, 22, 24, Aug. 1, Sept. 7, Nov. 2, 14
Brown, H. S.	Feb. 19
Brown, P.	Oct. 26
Brown, T. E.	May 6
Browning, Elizabeth B.	May 19, 30
Browning, G. F.	Mar. 4
Browning, R.	Dec. 3
Bryan, W. J.	Apr. 13
Bunyan, John	May 27, June 27, Oct. 28, Dec. 30
Burns, James, M.A.	Mar. 21
Burton, John	Aug. 15
Bushnell, Horace	Jan. 7, Feb. 4, 6, June 6, 28, July 23, Sept. 23, Oct. 1, Nov. 26, Dec. 15, 27
Butler, Josephine	Jan. 11, Apr. 22, Sept. 2, Oct. 17
Buxton, Barclay	Apr. 24, May 14, June 22, Sept. 22, Nov. 29
Buxton, Sir. T. F.	Mar. 28
Byrom, John	Nov. 9
Caird, John	Mar. 6
Calvin, John	Mar. 22
Carlyle, T.	Oct. 25
Carter, J. C.	Dec. 27
Carmichael, Amy	Jan. 15, Nov. 28
Caughey, James	Feb. 25, June 24, Oct. 31, Nov. 22, Dec. 21
Cecil	Feb. 28, May 11
Chalmers, Thomas	Apr 11,16
Chambers, Oswald	May 26, July 11, Dec. 20
Channing, William	Oct. 13
Chesterton, G. K.	July11
Cholmondeley, Mary	Apr. 25, July 9
Chrysostom	Apr. 16, Aug. 22
Cicero	Dec. 22
Clarke, Adam	Jan. 28
Coleridge, S.	Jan. 4
Cook, Thomas	Jan. 8, 10, Feb. 13, 23, Mar. 19, Apr. 4, May 28, June 30, July 2, Aug. 3, 6, Sept. 13, Oct. 10, Nov. 8, Dec. 8.
Cowper, William	May 31, July 18, Nov. 17
Crosby, Earnest H.	Apr. 18
Crowell, Grace Noll	Sept. 16, Nov. 18

Cuyler, Theodore	Jan. 21, 29, Feb. 14, 23, Mar. 12, Mar. 18, Apr. 3, 8, 12, May 18, 20, June 8, July 25, Sept. 29, Oct. 18, 21, Nov. 1, Dec. 18
Davies, Ron	Nov. 16, 30
Denton	Feb. 28
Disraeli	Aug. 21
Divall, Edith Hickman	Dec. 13
Dixon, Dr. A. C.	Feb. 16
Doddridge, Philip	Sept. 8, Oct. 21
Dods, Marcus	Apr. 6
Doudney, Sarah	Nov. 29
Drummond, Henry	Jan. 24, Mar. 21, 22, Apr. 23, June 21, July 17, 26, Sept. 15, 27, Nov. 13, 21
Dunn, Lewis R.	Sept. 9
Dyke, Henry Van	Jan. 14, July 31
Edwards, Jonathan	Feb. 22, Mar. 13, July 22
Emerson, R. W.	Sept. 21, Dec. 5
Enc. of Poetical Illus., p. 65	May 12
Eva, Sister, of Friedenshort	Feb. 12, Mar. 11, June 13, July 10, Aug. 16, 24, Sept. 11, Oct. 3
Evans, J. H.	Oct. 31
Faber, F.	Jan. 1, May 28, July 19, 26, Sept. 9, 22, Oct. 24, Nov. 10, 24,
Farrar, Dean	Jan. 22, Apr. 13, June 28
Fénelon	Mar. 16, Aug. 14, 20
Finch	Nov. 10
Finney, Charles G.	Feb. 2, 29, June 14, July 4, Aug. 22, Aug. 31, Oct. 9, Nov. 8, Dec. 5
Flavel	Jan. 29
Fletcher, John	Apr. 2, Sept. 9, Oct. 15
Flint, Annie Johnson	Mar. 27, Apr. 8, May 21, Aug. 3, 12, Oct. 9, Dec. 2
Follette, John Wright	June 18, Nov. 23
Foster, Bishop	Sept. 12, Oct. 6
Fowler, Bishop	May 22
Fox, Charles	Jan. 23
Fox, George	Jan. 13, Apr. 16
Francis, St., of Assisi	Aug. 5
Fry, Caroline	Oct. 30

Gainder, Doris	Oct. 20
Garfield, James A.	Mar. 30
Garrett, Charles	Jan. 18
Gerhardt, Paul	Apr. 28
Gibbons, Thomas	July 21
Gilfillan	June 26
Giovanni, Fra	Mar. 14
Gladstone, William	Apr. 7
Goethe, Johann Wolfgang Von	Apr. 20
Gordon, General	Mar. 30
Gordon, S. D.	Feb. 7, 20, June 16, July 5, 19, Sept. 20, Dec. 3, 7
Grenfell, Sir Wilfred	Feb. 16, May 13
Grimes, E. May	Sept. 4
Groves, A. N.	Dec. 4
Grubb, Norman	June 12
Guthrie	Feb. 15
Guyon, Madame	Apr. 5, May 6, Oct. 12
Hall, Bishop	Apr. 19, Nov. 6
Hall, Joseph	Oct. 5
Hamilton, Anna E.	Dec. 9
Hamilton, E. H.	Sept. 25
Hamilton, James	July 31
Harris, Reader	Jan. 3, Mar. 25, Apr. 18, May 7, May 10, 13, 14, Oct. 8, 24, Nov. 17, Dec. 14
Harris, Thoro	Jan. 17
Harrison, John	Jan. 5, Mar. 16, Apr. 9, 15, June 3, Aug. 12, 23, Nov. 30
Havergal, Frances Ridley	Feb. 25, Apr. 1, 4, May 14, 24, June 10, Aug. 2, 16, Sept. 13, 28, Dec. 23
Hay, John	Sept. 22
Hellier, Benjamin	Feb. 15, Oct. 14
Henry, Matthew	Sept. 8
Heschel, Abraham	Mar. 10
Hewitson	Sept. 10
Hinton	Oct. 9
Hitchcock	Apr. 3
Hogg, Henry	Mar. 25
Holland, J. G.	July 8, Nov. 20
Hopkins, C. B.	July 28

Horne, Bishop	May 31
Houghton	Jan. 31, Sept. 8
Huckel, Dr. Oliver	Mar. 5
Hunt, John	Mar. 7, Apr. 13, June 15
Huntingdon, Countess of	Sept. 12
Ingram, George	Feb. 10, Oct. 12
Inwood, Charles	June 3
Irons	Feb. 16
James, William	June 1
John, Griffith	Mar. 4
Johnson, Dr. Samuel	June 3
Jones, S.	Mar. 30, Oct. 19
Jowett, J. H.	Jan. 3, Mar. 1, 24, June 3, Aug. 11, Oct. 16, Nov. 1, Dec. 9, 29
Judson, Adoniram	Jan. 15, Oct. 5, Nov. 17
Keble, John	Apr. 16, Sept. 17
Kingsley, Charles	Jan. 1, Apr. 23, Dec. 5, 16, 23
Knight, G. H.	June 17
Knox, John	July 27
Krum, Nathaniel	Sept. 12
Latimer	Apr. 13
Lecky, W. E. H.	Apr. 20
Lee, Kate	Mar. 18, Sept. 29
Lehman, F. M.	June 2
Lemmel, Helen H.	Feb. 29
Lincoln, Abraham	Mar. 30, Aug. 13, Sept. 6
Livingstone, David	Jan. 30, Apr. 30, June 14, Oct. 1
Livingstone, John	Oct. 6
Longfellow, H. W.	Feb. 26, May 19, June 6, July 19
Lowell, James R.	Mar. 14, May 5
Luff, William	July 30
Luther, Martin	Jan. 8, Aug. 28, Sept. 23, Oct.13, Nov. 13
Lynch, T. T.	Feb. 4
Lyon, Mary	Aug. 8
Lyte, Henry Francis	Sept. 18
Macgregor, Duncan	Dec. 14
Mackay, Charles	Jan. 22

Maclaren, Alexander	Jan. 18, Apr. 21, May 1, June 23, Aug. 13, Sept. 5, 26, Dec. 20
Mahan, Asa	Sept. 18
Mandel, Morris	Jan. 14
Mann, Horace	Aug. 9
Mant, Bishop	Apr. 7
Martineau, James	May 19, July 24
Martyn, Henry	Jan. 15, Feb. 2, Aug. 9
Mason, Mary A.	Dec. 12
Matheson, Duncan	July 29
Matheson, George	Mar. 20, Apr. 17, 29, May 4, Aug. 5, Aug. 26, Dec. 17
Maxwell, Gordon	Jan 4
McCheyne, Robert Murray	Feb. 6, May 3, Sept. 14, Oct. 15, 28
Menge, Pansy B.	May 26
M., E. S.	Feb. 8
Merritt, Stephen	Nov. 5
Miller, Hugh	Sept. 29
Miller, J. R.	Mar. 3, Apr. 16, May 3, June 13, Sept. 21
Milton, John	Dec. 17
Mitchell, L. F.	July 6
Moffat, Robert	Sept. 11
Monod, A.	Sept. 2
Montgomery, James	Mar. 29
Moody, D. L.	Feb. 17, Mar. 26, Apr. 7, May 6, 17, May 18, June 21, Aug. 13, 29
Moore, Esther Pritchard	June 16
Morgan, Angela	Apr. 27, Oct. 2
Morris, J.	July 14
Morrison, G. H.	Aug. 18
Muller, George	Feb. 18, Mar. 13, Apr. 15, May 24, June 5, July 8, Aug. 18, 21, Oct. 23, Nov. 6, Dec. 6, 10, 28
Munger, T. T.	Sept. 23
Murray, Andrew	Jan. 23, Mar. 3, 22, Apr. 1, May 17, June 1, July 13, 30, Sept. 4, Oct. 7, Nov. 3
Nelson, John	May 17
Newman, J. H.	Dec. 11
Newton, John	Aug. 24, Dec. 19
Nicholson, Martha Snell	July 15
Nicoll, W. Robertson	Apr. 11
Nightingale, Florence	Feb. 11, May 16

Seneca	Aug. 9
Sherwood, Alice E.	Apr. 9
Simpson, A. B.	Jan. 2, 24, Mar. 17, May 9, 21, June 25, Sept. 17, Oct. 11
Simpson, Clara	Jan. 25, Nov. 11
Smiley, Maurice	Jan. 13
Smith, Hannah W.	Oct. 2
Smith, Mrs. M. R.	Apr. 22
Sparks, F. H.	Oct. 28
Spence, Rev. F. H.	May 31
Spurgeon, C. H.	Feb. 3, 4, Mar. 28, May 12, 16, 22, July 1, 6, Aug. 15, Sept. 8, 30, Nov. 4, 11, 19, 28
Stanger, Frank Bateman	Feb. 1
Steele, Daniel	Jan. 15, Apr. 2, May 28, June 11, Sept. 19, Oct. 10, Nov. 2, 24, Dec. 8, 16
Stennet, Samuel	Dec. 25
Sterling, Julia	Nov. 19
Stetson, Charlotte Perkins	Feb. 19
Stowe, Harriet B.	Mar. 16, Apr. 11, Nov. 3
Stowell, Hugh	Apr. 2
Studd, C. T.	Jan. 9, Mar. 23, Apr. 15, 27, Oct. 1
Studd, Mrs. C. T.	Dec. 26
Stumpf, J. H.	Jan. 29
Suffield, Mrs. F. W.	Dec. 26
Talmage, De Witt	Jan. 29, Apr. 26, May 19, June 20, June 27, July 25, Dec. 1, 19
Tauler, J.	Mar. 20
Taylor, James Hudson	Feb. 23, Mar. 2, May 16, 22, July 15, Aug. 4, 10, 13, Sept. 3, Nov. 27
Taylor, Mrs. Howard	Mar. 19
Taylor, I	June 18
Taylor, Jeremy	Apr. 20, Nov. 4
Taylor, W. M.	Dec. 30
Temple, Bishop, William	May 4, Dec. 5
Tennyson, Alfred Lord	Jan. 10
Tersteegen, Gerhardt	Oct. 10, 16, Nov. 14
Theresa, Saint	Feb. 16, May 7
Tholuck	Oct. 18
Thomson, Prosser	Apr. 19
Thoreau	July 7
Toplady, A.	May 25

Torrey, R. A.	Feb. 1
Traherne, Thomas	Feb. 4
Trench, Richard Chenevix	May 31, June 12, Sept. 2, Nov. 15, Dec. 1, 15
Trotter, I. Lilias	Jan. 23, Apr. 1, June 3, 20, Aug. 31
Upham, Thomas	Feb. 28, May 13, Aug. 20, Nov. 1, 9, 13
Ussher, Howard T. N.	Mar. 31
Vaughan, Dean	Aug. 5, Sept. 25
Wagner, Charles	July 12
Walford, William	May 8
Warner, Anna	Dec. 6
Watkinson, W. L.	May 29
Watson, G. D.	Feb. 21, May 10
Watson, Jean H.	Jan. 16, May 15
Watson, Dr. John	Sept. 30
Watson, T.	Oct. 8
Wells, Amos R.	Feb. 2, Mar. 11
Wesley, Charles	Feb. 20, Mar. 3, Apr. 23, July 20, Nov. 15, Dec. 8, 11
Wesley, John	Mar. 17, 25, 29, Apr. 18, May 7, June 9, 24, July 13, Aug. 11, Aug. 25, Sept. 1, Oct. 2, 4, 24, 27, 30 Nov. 29, Dec. 14, 16, 23
Westcott, Canon	Apr. 25, Aug. 1
Whittier, J. G.	Feb. 13, Aug. 25, 29, Sept. 26, Oct. 3, 12, Nov. 16
Wilberforce, William	Jan. 20
Wilcox, Ella Wheeler	Jan. 5, Mar. 2, Apr. 25, May 25, Dec. 8
Wilkes, Paget	June 4, Nov. 20, 23
Winkworth/Dessler	Jan. 11
Wood, J. A.	June 26